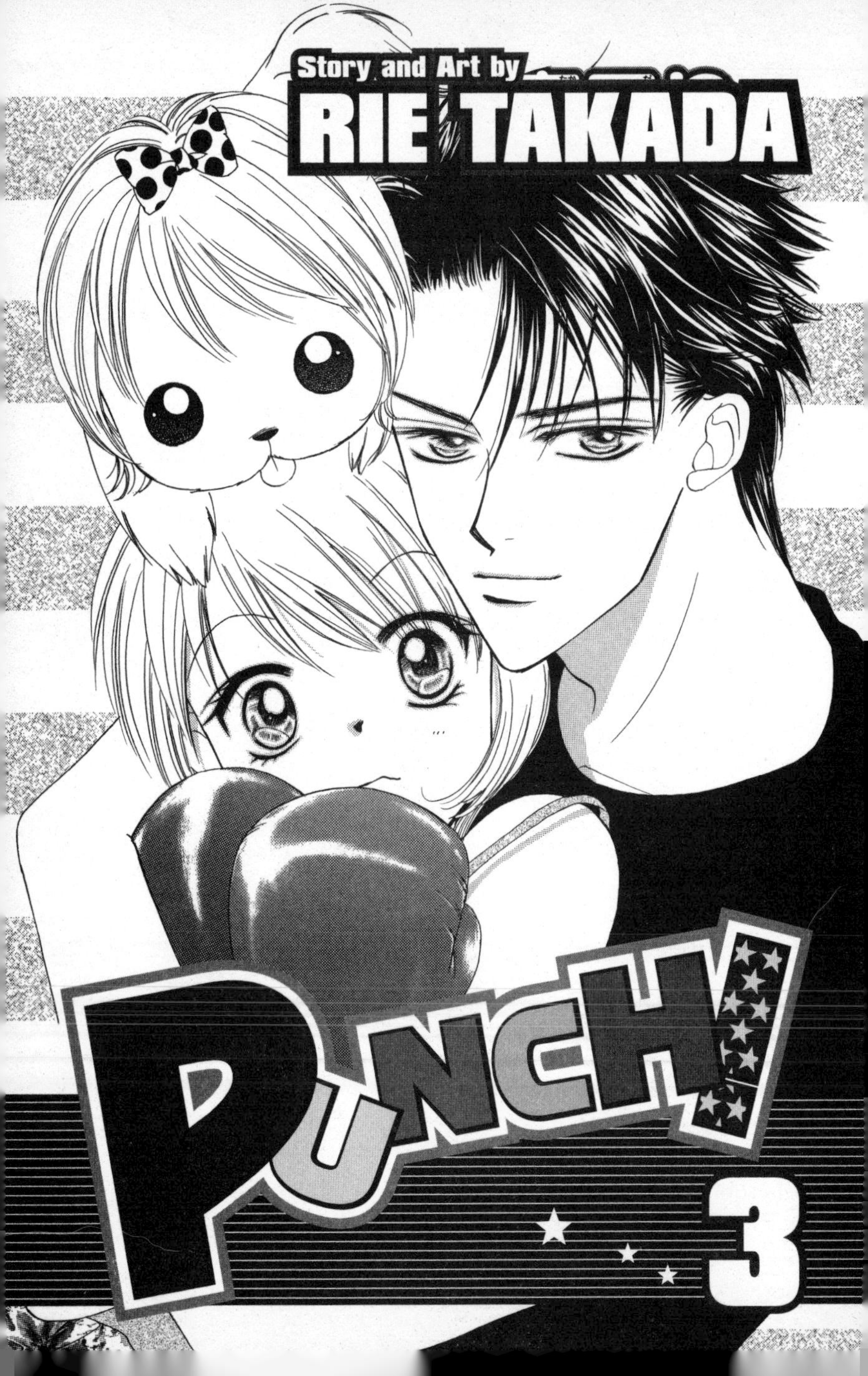
Story and Art by
RIE TAKADA
PUNCH!
3

3

STORY ★

Elle truly hates living in a martial arts gym. She's also stuck in an arranged engagement to Ruo, the grandson of her grandpa's dearest friend.

Then one day Elle meets Kazuki Shindo—and her world turns upside down! At first, Kazuki just poses as her boyfriend to trick Ruo. Before long, he has moved into the gym and enrolled at Elle's school.

Against all odds, Elle and Kazuki become a real couple! But Kazuki has training on the brain, to Elle's everlasting frustration. Soon Kazuki enters his first match, pretending to be another fighter. Elle is upset at first, but winds up cheering him on.

When Kazuki wins, they get even closer. But now some promoters want him for a major fight. Will Kazuki come out swinging—or will he throw in the towel?

CHARACTERS ★

GIGI NAGAHARA

Elle's grandpa. Former kickboxing champion and present owner of Nagahara Martial Arts Gym.

Elle Nagahara

A peace-loving girl from a family of fighters. All she wants is a normal life and a normal boyfriend.

Ruo M. Eschuck

A stubborn kickboxing champion. He's been engaged to Elle since childhood and refuses to let her go.

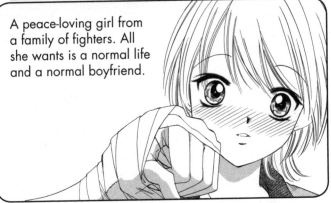

Kazuki Shindo

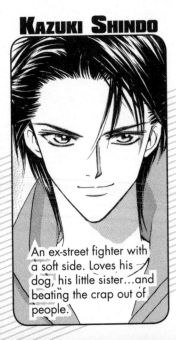

An ex-street fighter with a soft side. Loves his dog, his little sister...and beating the crap out of people.

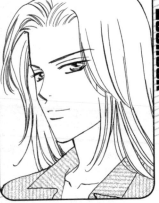

PUNCH! 3

TABLE OF CONTENTS

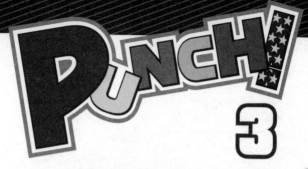

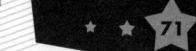

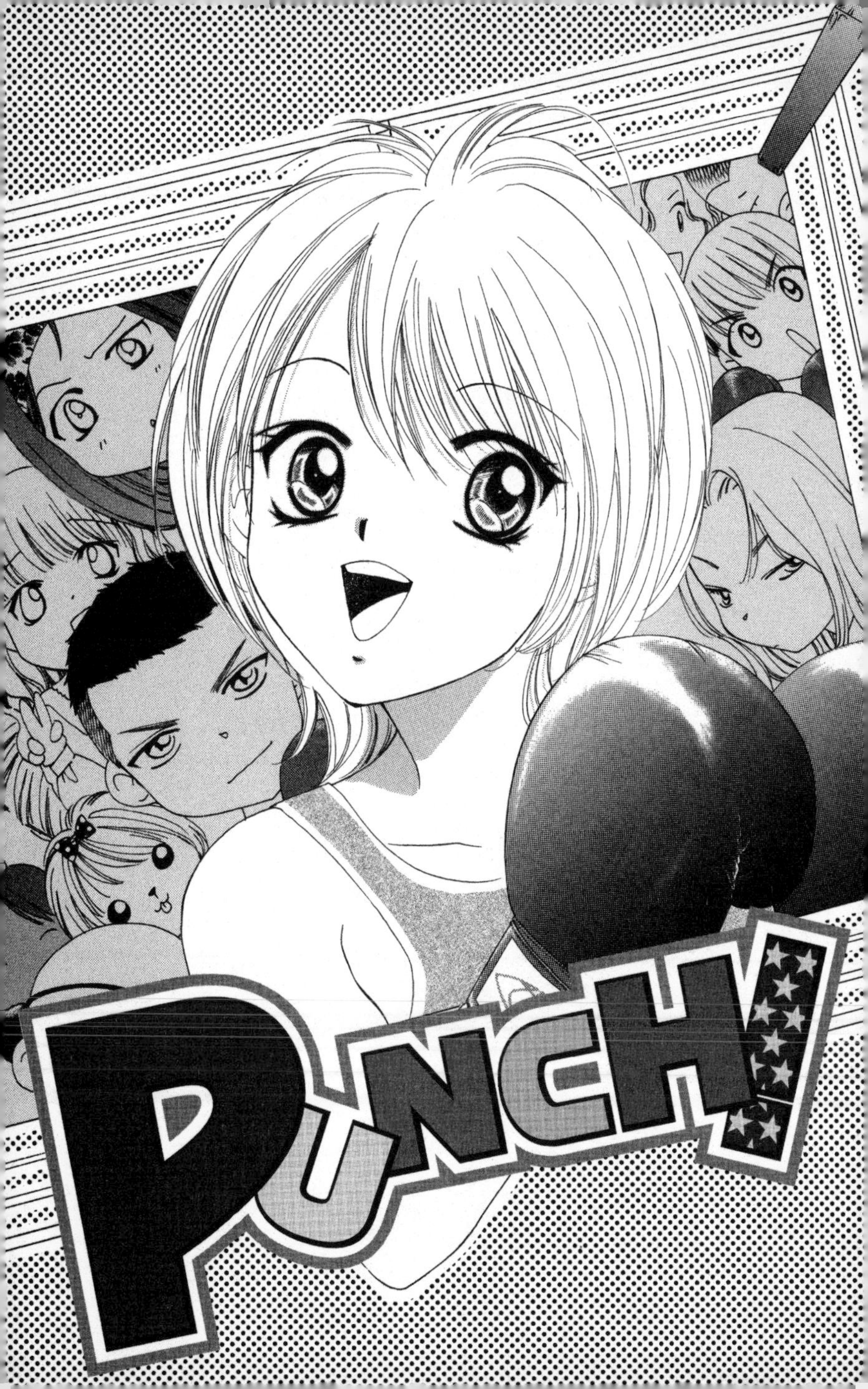
PUNCH!

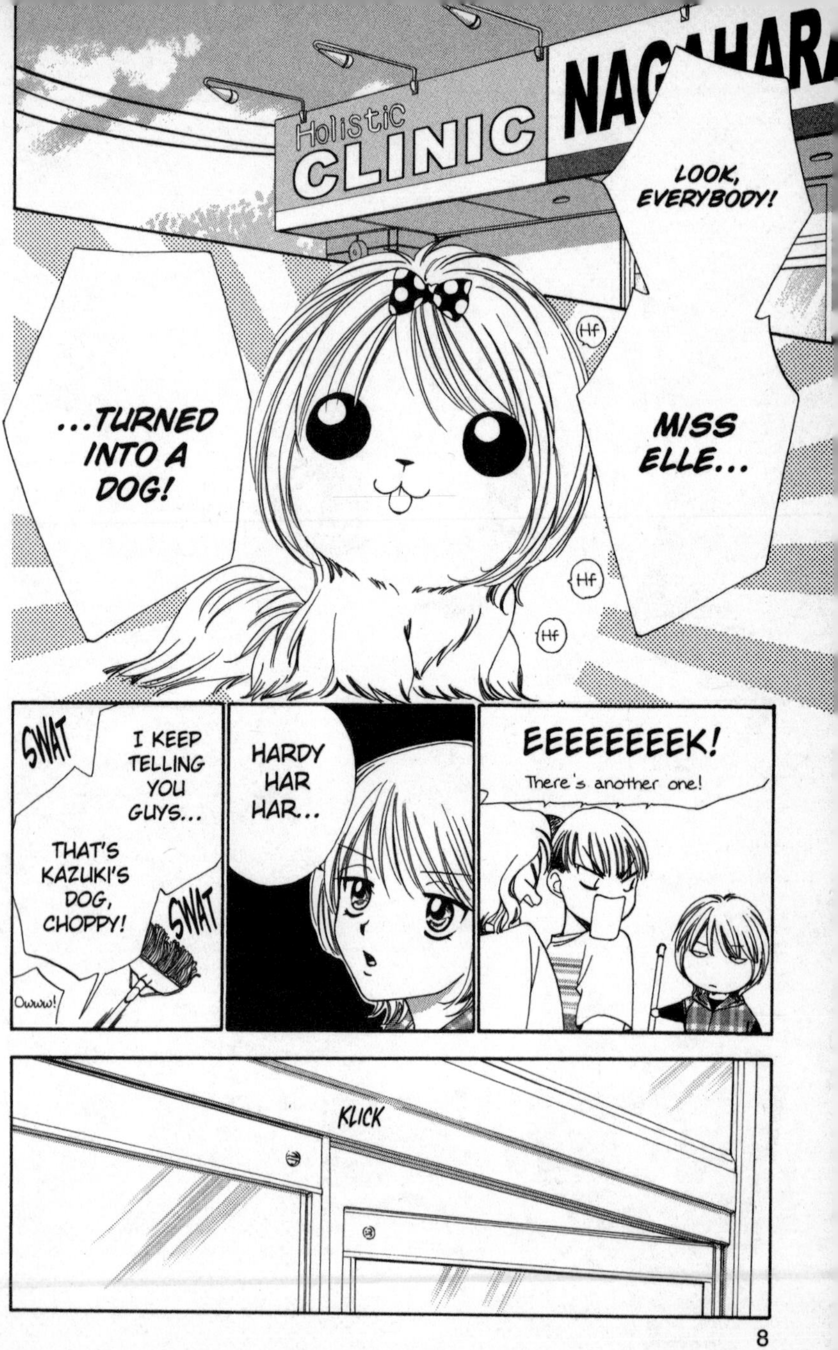
Holistic CLINIC
NAGAHAR
LOOK, EVERYBODY!
MISS ELLE...
...TURNED INTO A DOG!
Hf
Hf
Hf
EEEEEEEEK!
There's another one!
HARDY HAR HAR...
I KEEP TELLING YOU GUYS...
THAT'S KAZUKI'S DOG, CHOPPY!
SWAT
SWAT
Owww!
KLICK

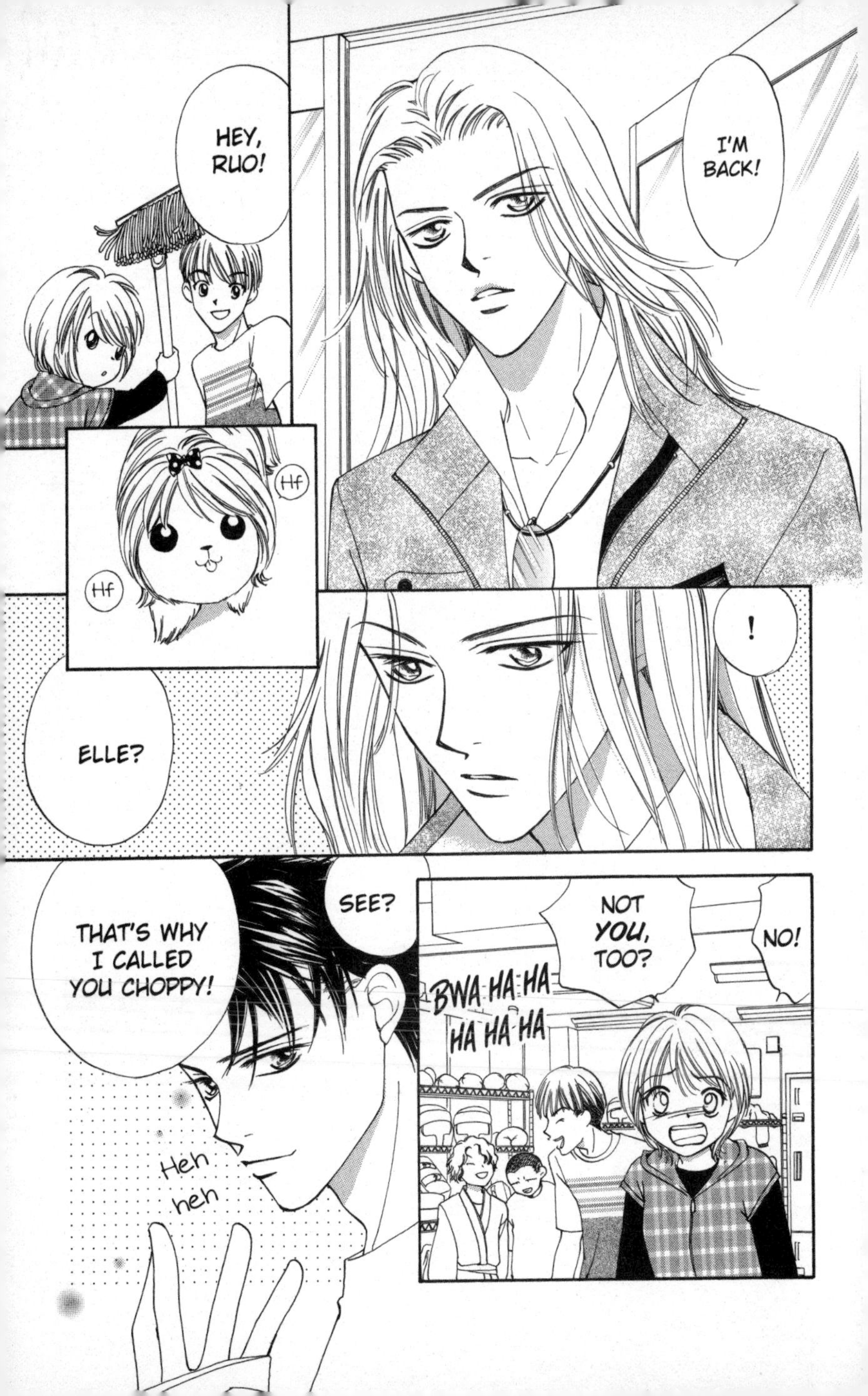
I'M BACK!
HEY, RUO!
Hf
Hf
!
ELLE?
NO!
NOT YOU, TOO?
BWA HA HA HA HA HA
SEE?
THAT'S WHY I CALLED YOU CHOPPY!
Heh heh

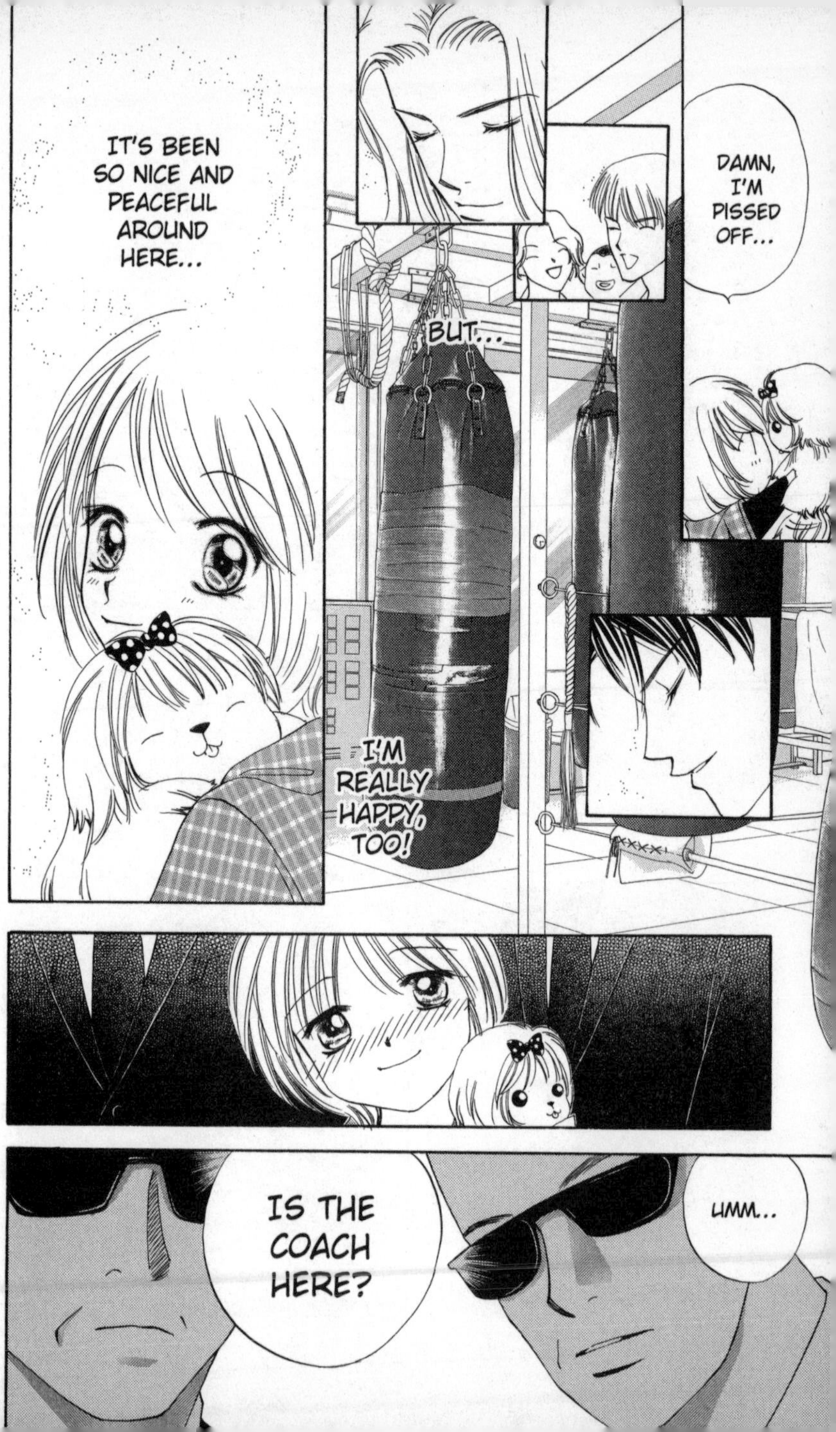
DAMN, I'M PISSED OFF...
BUT...
IT'S BEEN SO NICE AND PEACEFUL AROUND HERE...
I'M REALLY HAPPY, TOO!
UMM...
IS THE COACH HERE?

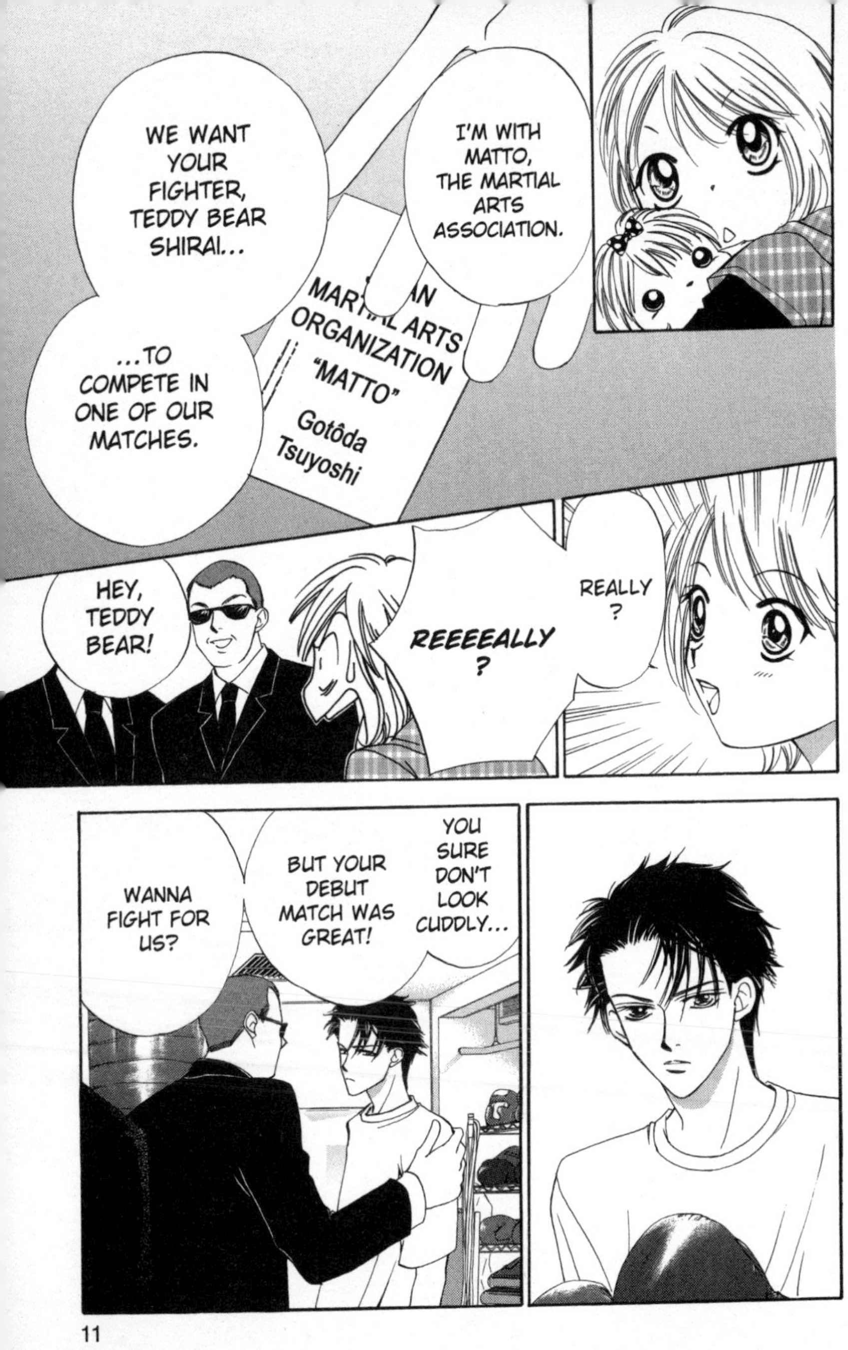
I'M WITH MATTO, THE MARTIAL ARTS ASSOCIATION.
WE WANT YOUR FIGHTER, TEDDY BEAR SHIRAI...
MARTIAL ARTS ORGANIZATION
“MATTO”
Gotôda Tsuyoshi
...TO COMPETE IN ONE OF OUR MATCHES.
REALLY?
REEEEALLY?
HEY, TEDDY BEAR!
YOU SURE DON'T LOOK CUDDLY...
BUT YOUR DEBUT MATCH WAS GREAT!
WANNA FIGHT FOR US?

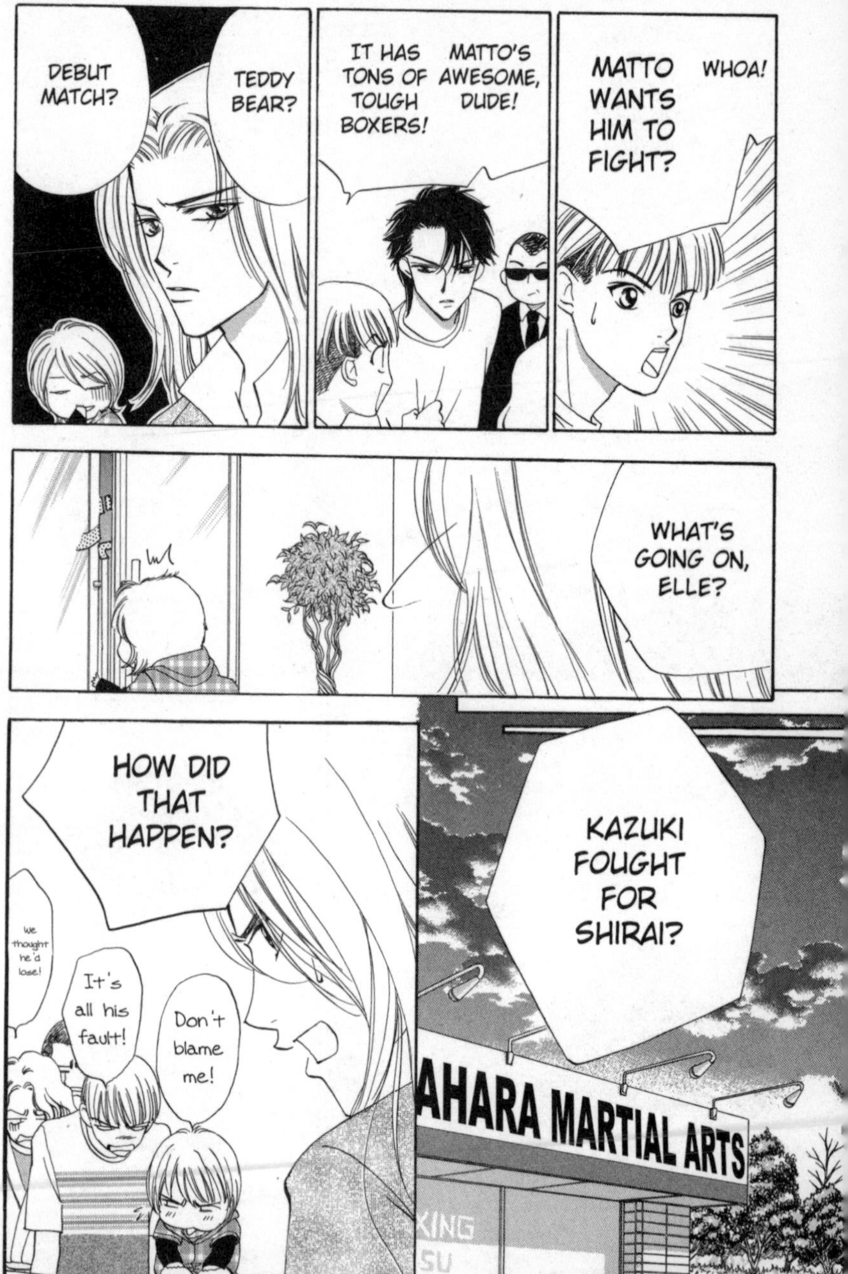
WHOA!
MATTO WANTS HIM TO FIGHT?
MATTO'S AWESOME, DUDE!
IT HAS TONS OF TOUGH BOXERS!
TEDDY BEAR?
DEBUT MATCH?
WHAT'S GOING ON, ELLE?
KAZUKI FOUGHT FOR SHIRAI?
AHARA MARTIAL ARTS
HOW DID THAT HAPPEN?
Don't blame me!
It's all his fault!
We thought he'd lose!

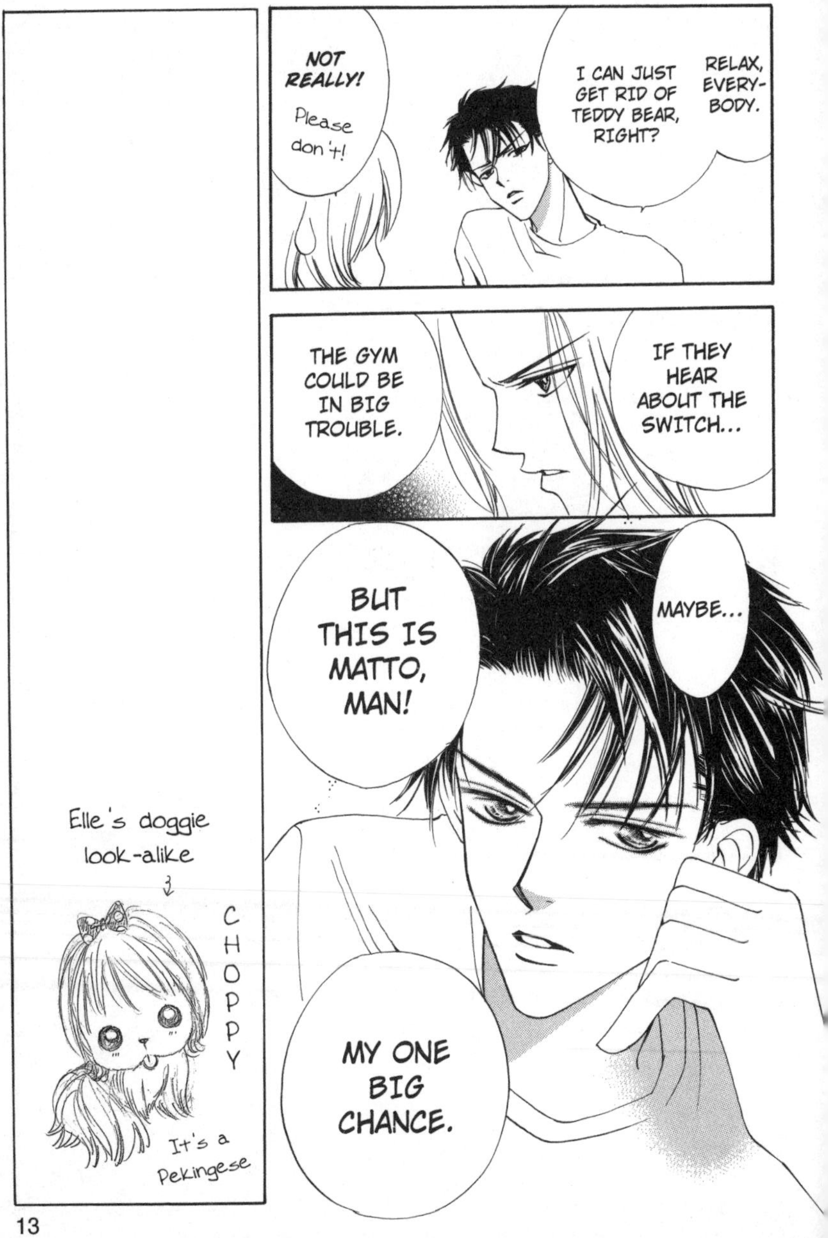
RELAX, EVERYBODY.
I CAN JUST GET RID OF TEDDY BEAR, RIGHT?
NOT REALLY!
Please don't!
IF THEY HEAR ABOUT THE SWITCH...
THE GYM COULD BE IN BIG TROUBLE.
MAYBE...
BUT THIS IS MATTO, MAN!
MY ONE BIG CHANCE.
Elle's doggie look-alike
CHOPPY
It's a Pekingese

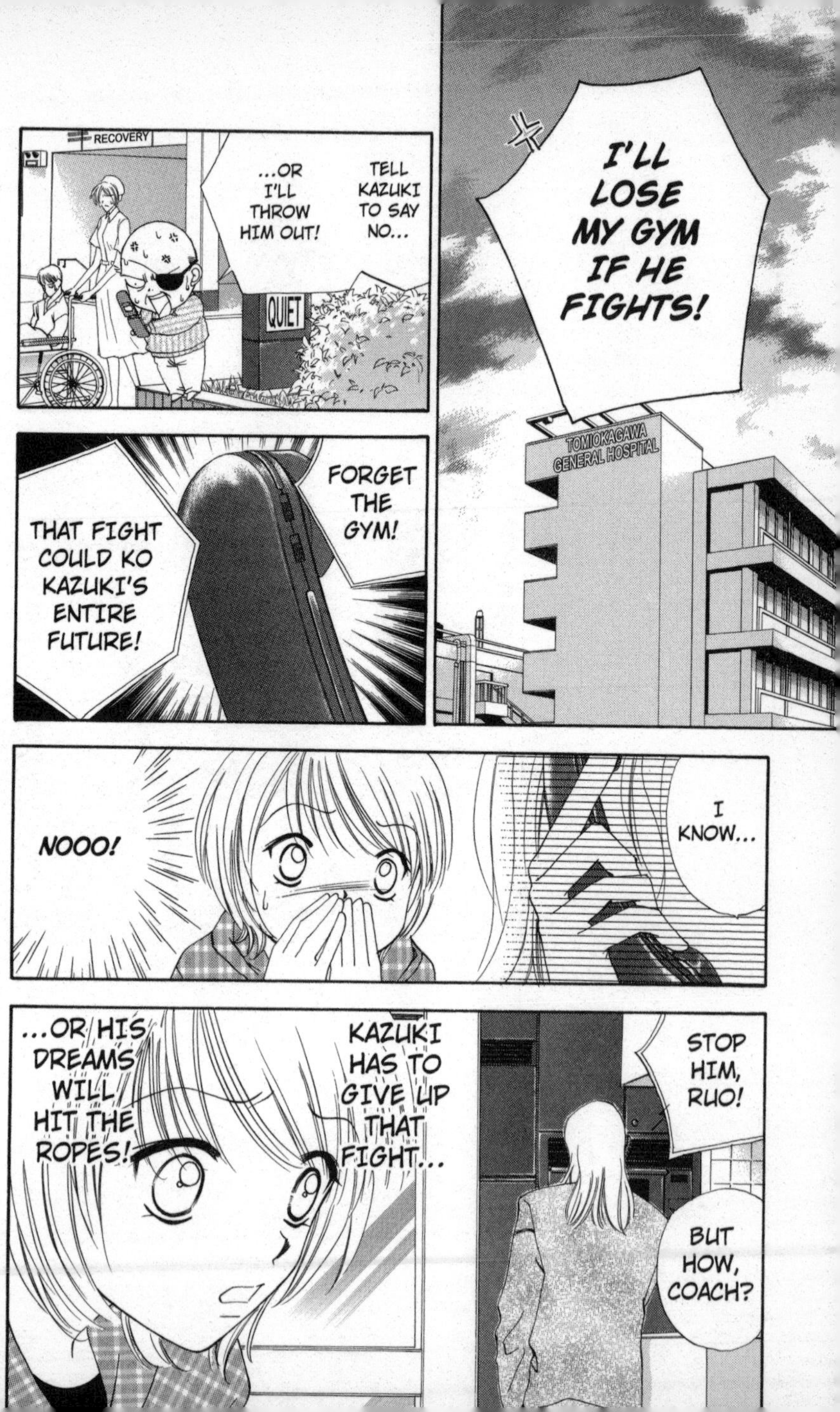
I'LL LOSE MY GYM IF HE FIGHTS!
TOMIOKAGAWA GENERAL HOSPITAL
RECOVERY
TELL KAZUKI TO SAY NO...
...OR I'LL THROW HIM OUT!
QUIET
FORGET THE GYM!
THAT FIGHT COULD KO KAZUKI'S ENTIRE FUTURE!
I KNOW...
NOOO!
STOP HIM, RUO!
BUT HOW, COACH?
KAZUKI HAS TO GIVE UP THAT FIGHT...
...OR HIS DREAMS WILL HIT THE ROPES!

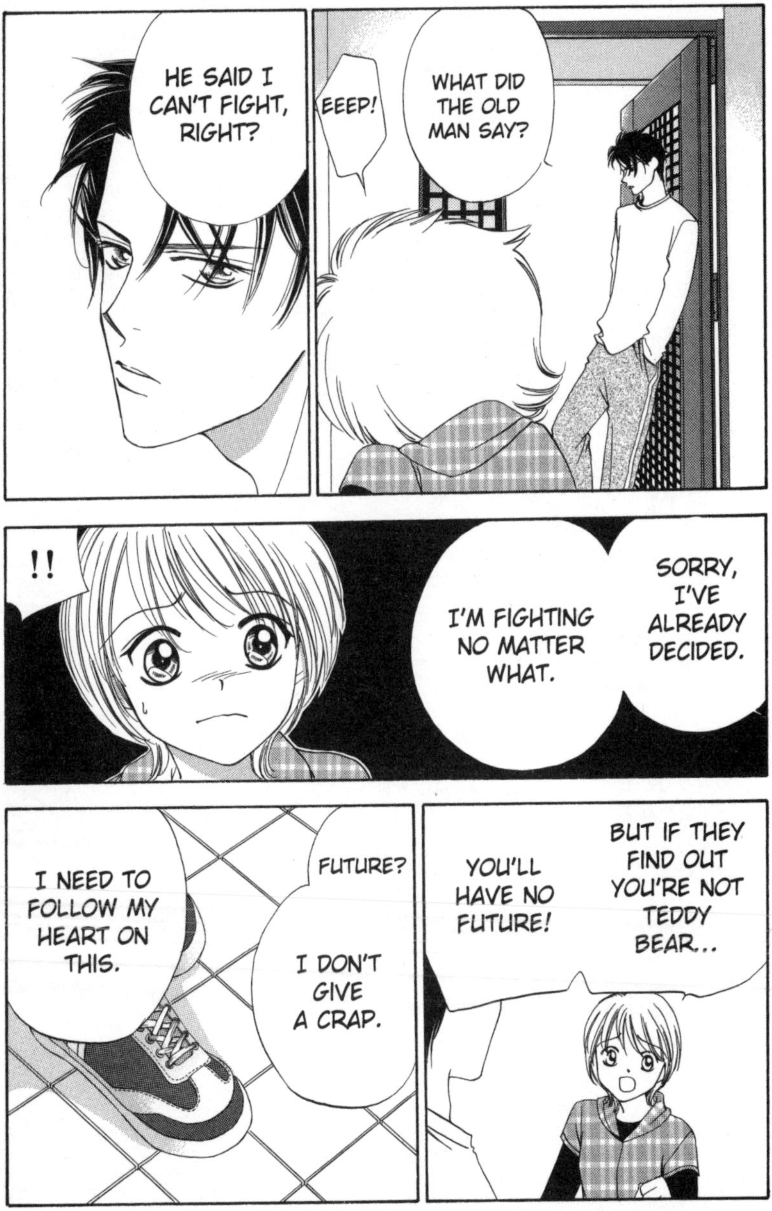
WHAT DID THE OLD MAN SAY?
EEEP!
HE SAID I CAN'T FIGHT, RIGHT?
SORRY, I'VE ALREADY DECIDED.
I'M FIGHTING NO MATTER WHAT.
!!
BUT IF THEY FIND OUT YOU'RE NOT TEDDY BEAR...
YOU'LL HAVE NO FUTURE!
FUTURE?
I DON'T GIVE A CRAP.
I NEED TO FOLLOW MY HEART ON THIS.

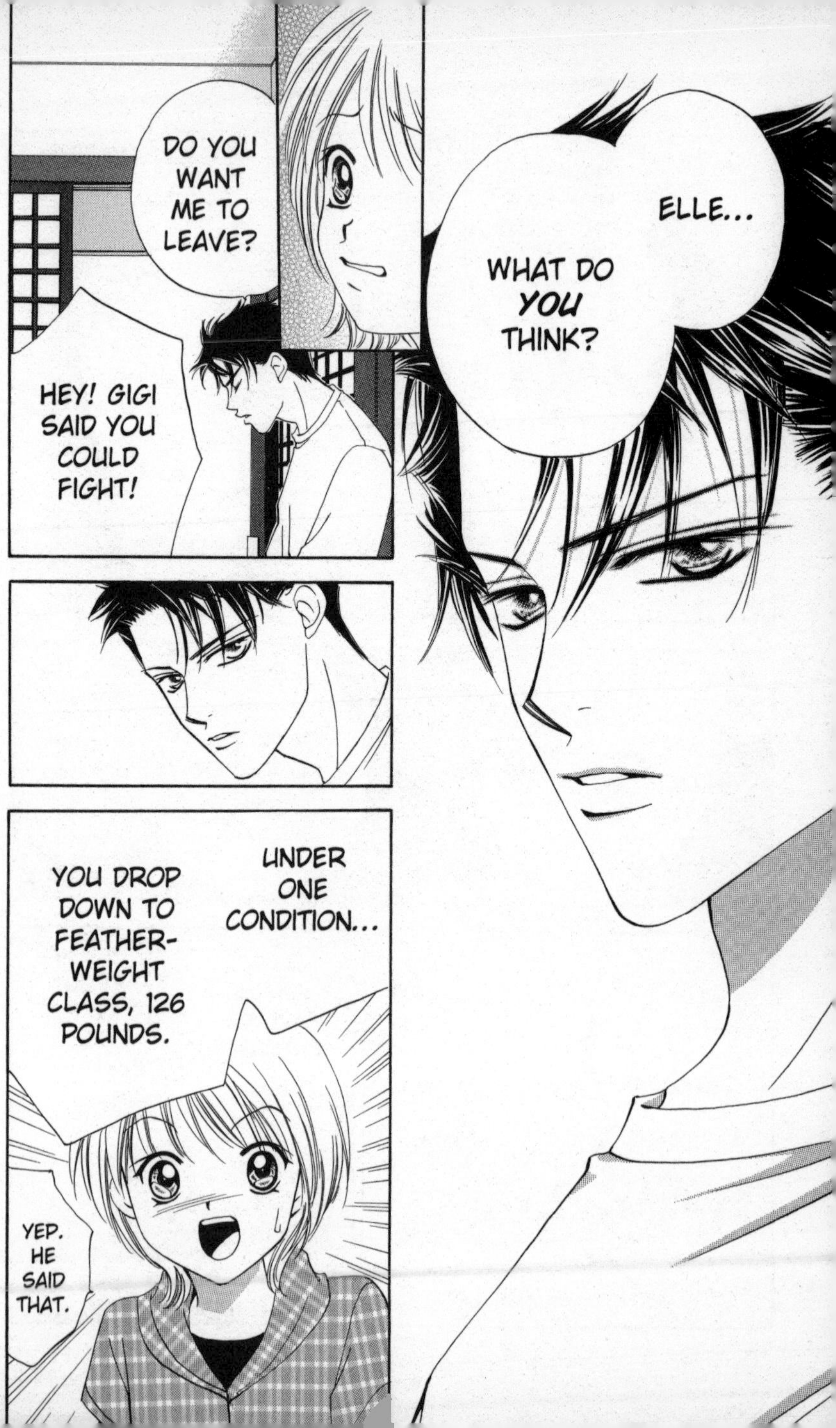
ELLE...
WHAT DO *YOU* THINK?
DO YOU WANT ME TO LEAVE?
HEY! GIGI SAID YOU COULD FIGHT!
UNDER ONE CONDITION...
YOU DROP DOWN TO FEATHER-WEIGHT CLASS, 126 POUNDS.
YEP. HE SAID THAT.

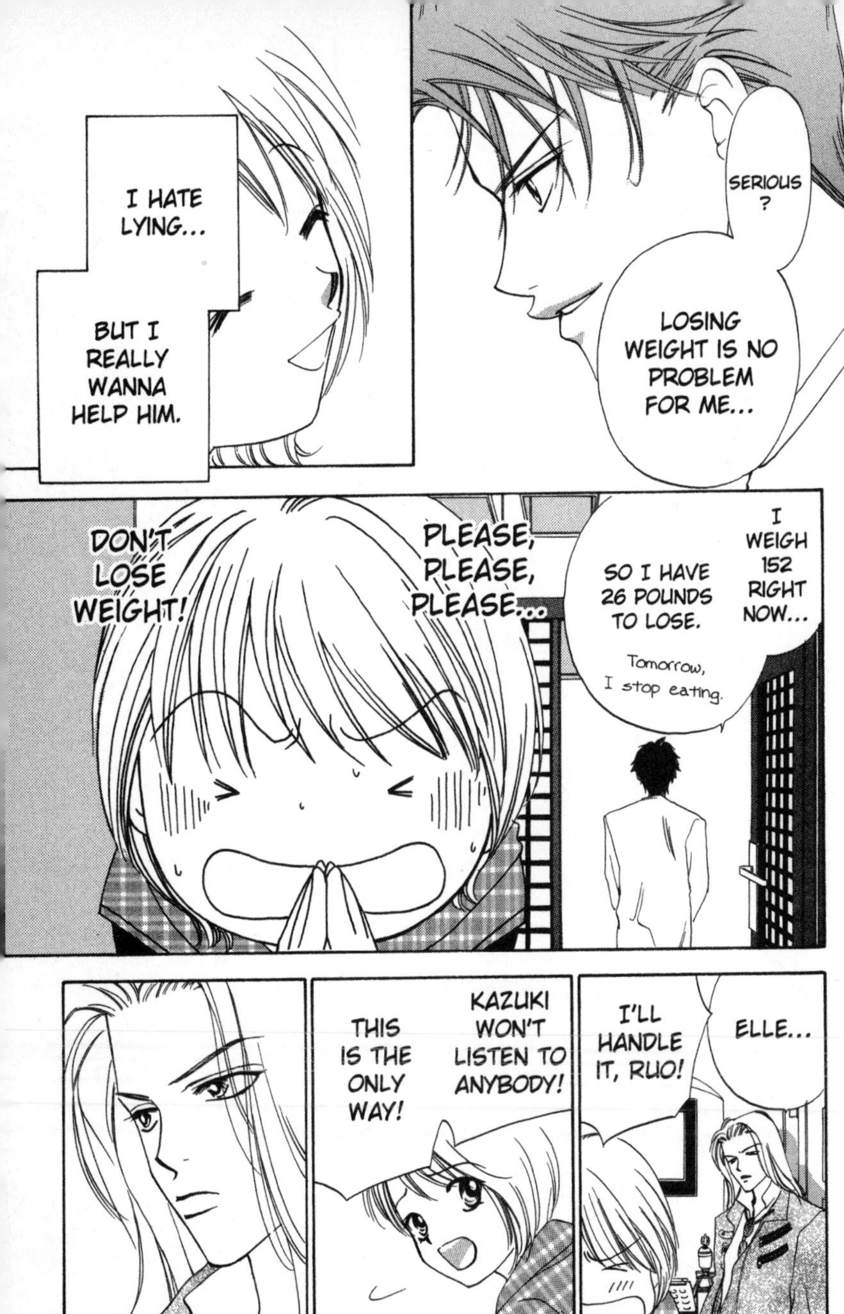
SERIOUS?
LOSING WEIGHT IS NO PROBLEM FOR ME...
I HATE LYING...
BUT I REALLY WANNA HELP HIM.
I WEIGH 152 RIGHT NOW...
SO I HAVE 26 POUNDS TO LOSE.
Tomorrow, I stop eating.
PLEASE, PLEASE, PLEASE...
DON'T LOSE WEIGHT!
ELLE...
I'LL HANDLE IT, RUO!
KAZUKI WON'T LISTEN TO ANYBODY!
THIS IS THE ONLY WAY!

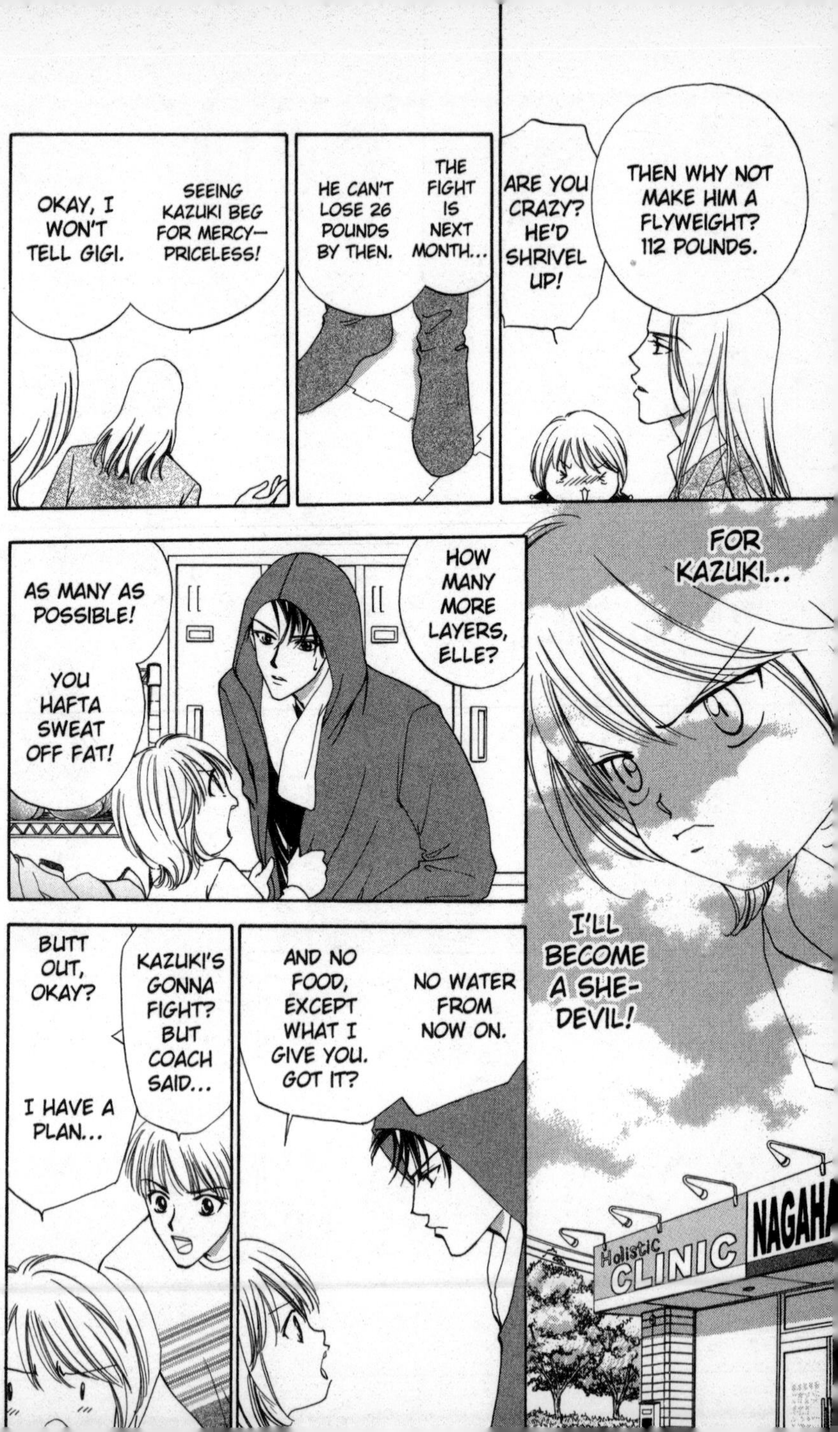
THEN WHY NOT MAKE HIM A FLYWEIGHT? 112 POUNDS.
ARE YOU CRAZY? HE'D SHRIVEL UP!
THE FIGHT IS NEXT MONTH...
HE CAN'T LOSE 26 POUNDS BY THEN.
SEEING KAZUKI BEG FOR MERCY—PRICELESS!
OKAY, I WON'T TELL GIGI.
FOR KAZUKI...
I'LL BECOME A SHE-DEVIL!
NAGAHA
Holistic CLINIC
HOW MANY MORE LAYERS, ELLE?
AS MANY AS POSSIBLE!
YOU HAFTA SWEAT OFF FAT!
NO WATER FROM NOW ON.
AND NO FOOD, EXCEPT WHAT I GIVE YOU. GOT IT?
KAZUKI'S GONNA FIGHT? BUT COACH SAID...
BUTT OUT, OKAY?
I HAVE A PLAN...

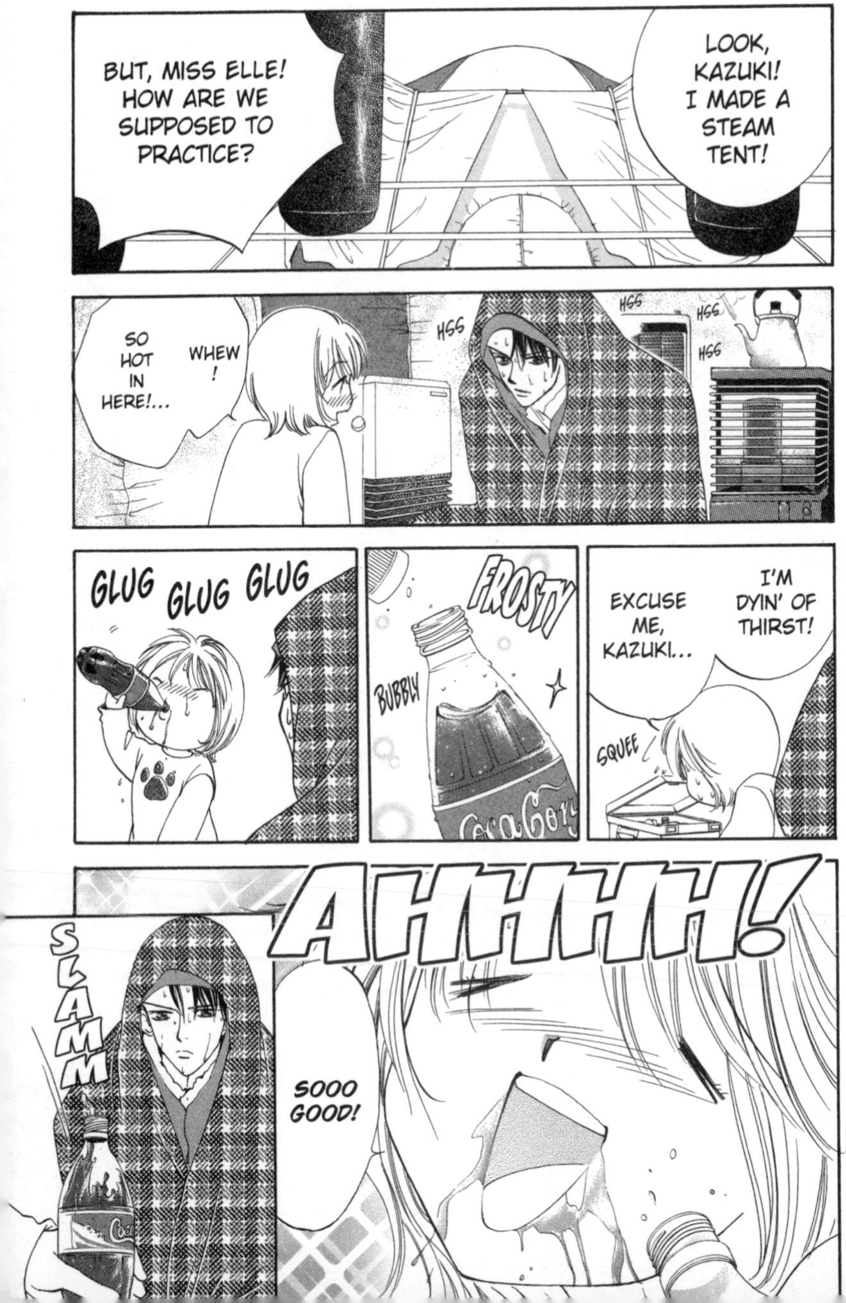
LOOK, KAZUKI! I MADE A STEAM TENT!
BUT, MISS ELLE! HOW ARE WE SUPPOSED TO PRACTICE?
HSS
HSS
HSS
HSS
WHEW!
SO HOT IN HERE!...
I'M DYIN' OF THIRST!
EXCUSE ME, KAZUKI...
SQUEE
FROSTY
BUBBLY
GLUG
GLUG GLUG
AHHHHH!
SOOO GOOD!
SLAMM

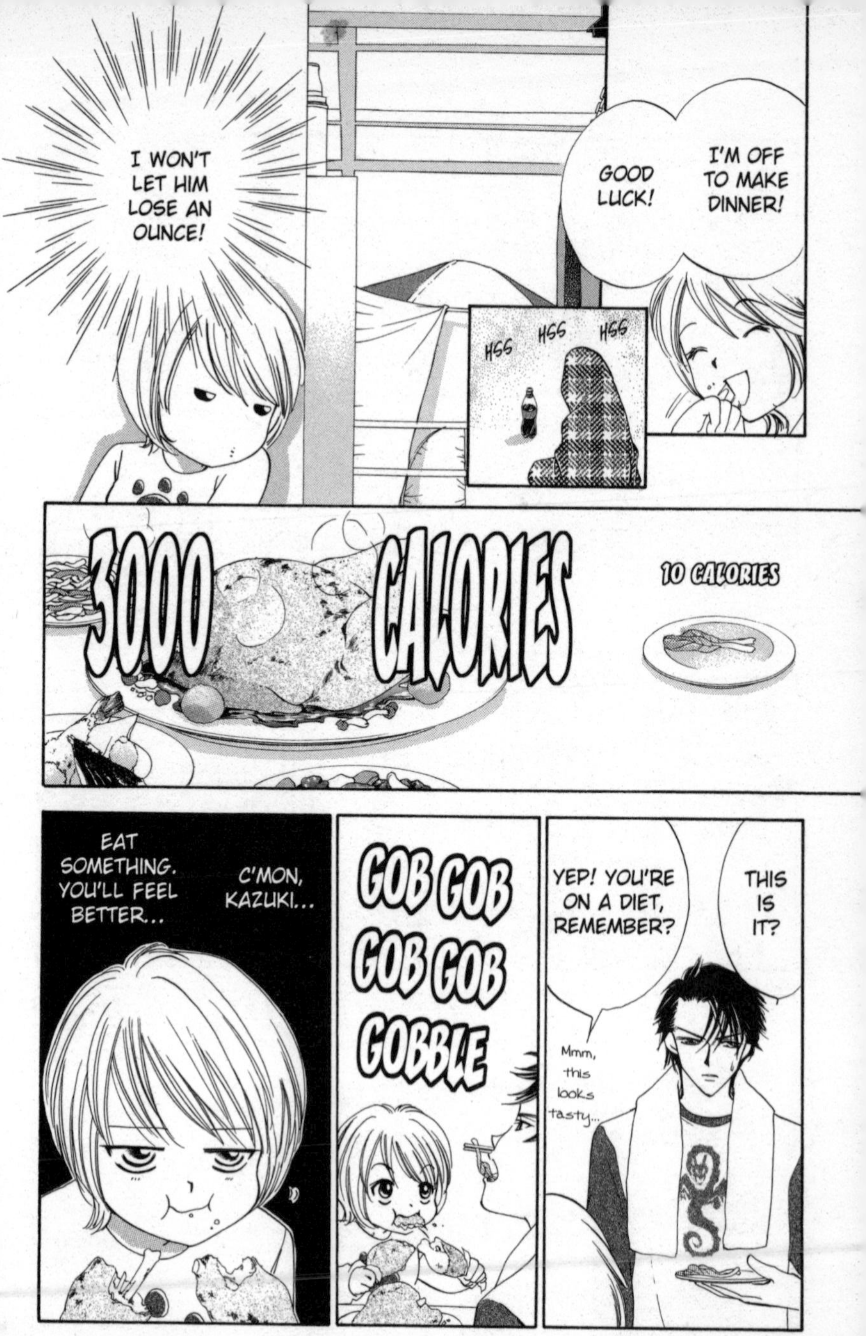
I'M OFF TO MAKE DINNER!
GOOD LUCK!
HSS HSS HSS
I WON'T LET HIM LOSE AN OUNCE!
10 CALORIES
3000 CALORIES
THIS IS IT?
YEP! YOU'RE ON A DIET, REMEMBER?
Mmm, this looks tasty...
GOB GOB GOB GOB GOBBLE
C'MON, KAZUKI...
EAT SOMETHING. YOU'LL FEEL BETTER...

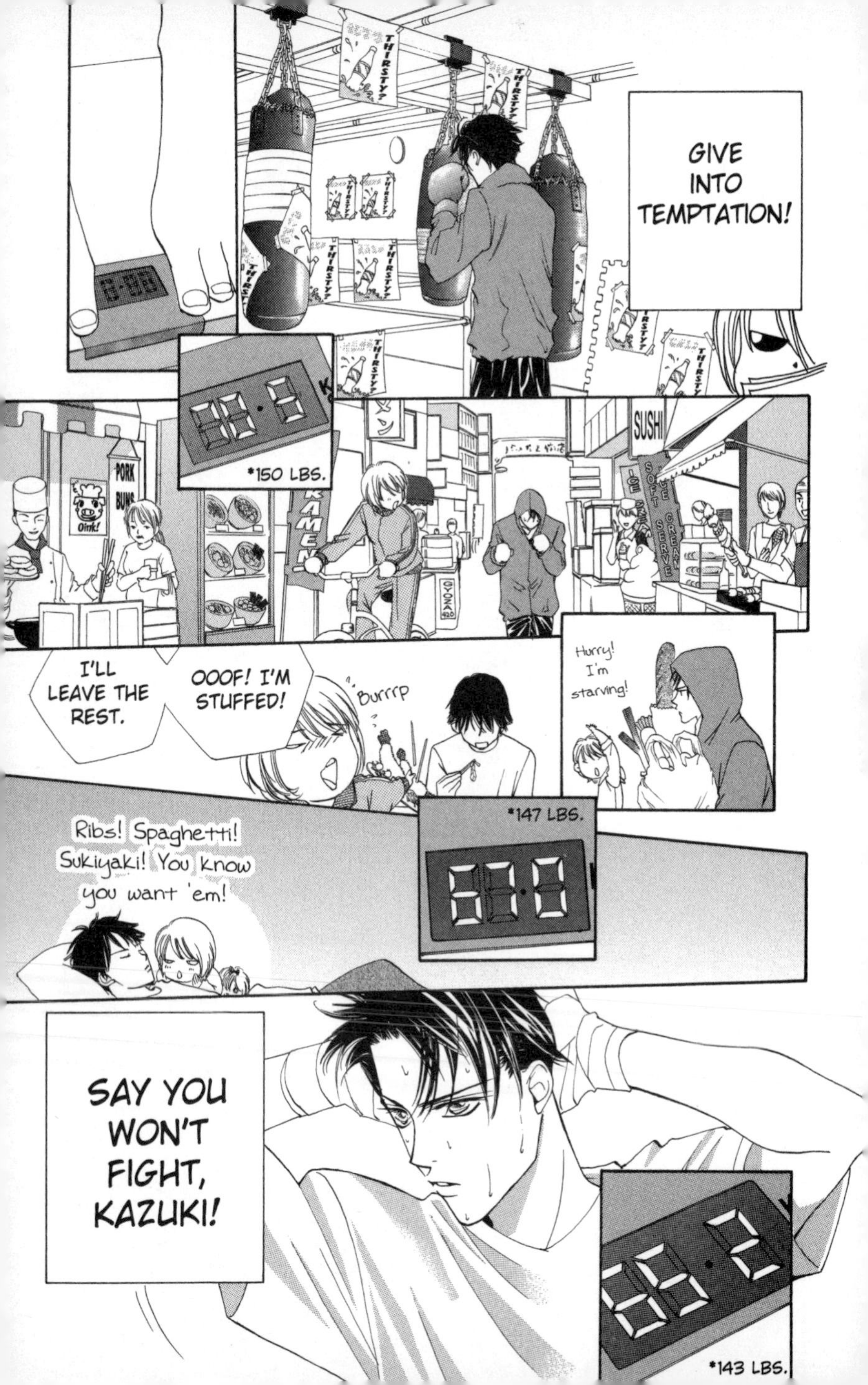
GIVE INTO TEMPTATION!
THIRSTY?
*150 LBS.
SUSHI
SOFT SERVE
ICE CREAM
RAMEN
GYOZA
PORK BUNS
Oink!
Hurry! I'm starving!
Burrrp
OOOF! I'M STUFFED!
I'LL LEAVE THE REST.
*147 LBS.
Ribs! Spaghetti! Sukiyaki! You know you want 'em!
*143 LBS.
SAY YOU WON'T FIGHT, KAZUKI!

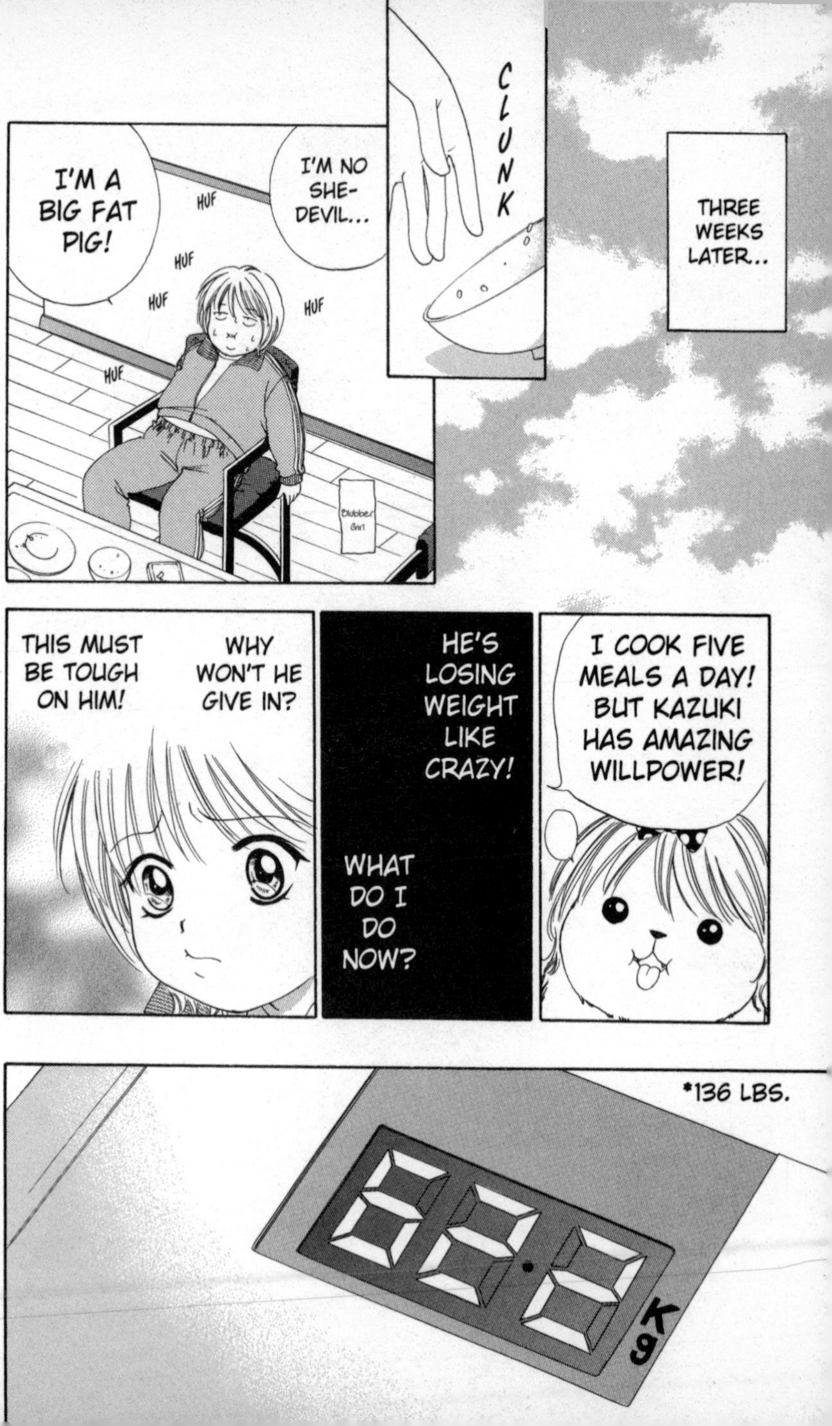
THREE WEEKS LATER...
CLUNK
I'M NO SHE-DEVIL...
I'M A BIG FAT PIG!
HUF
HUF
HUF
HUF
HUF
Blubber Girl
I COOK FIVE MEALS A DAY! BUT KAZUKI HAS AMAZING WILLPOWER!
HE'S LOSING WEIGHT LIKE CRAZY!
WHAT DO I DO NOW?
WHY WON'T HE GIVE IN?
THIS MUST BE TOUGH ON HIM!
*136 LBS.
Kg

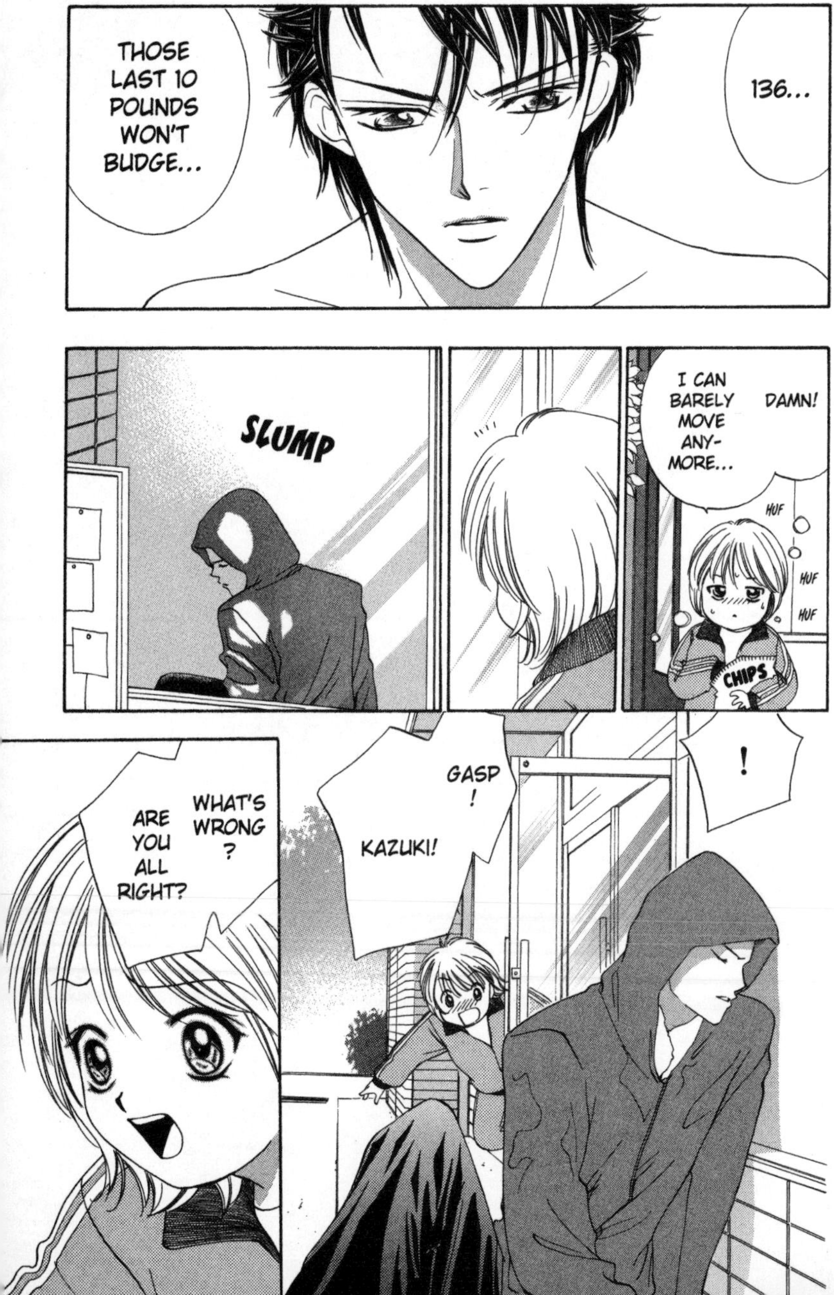
136...
THOSE LAST 10 POUNDS WON'T BUDGE...
DAMN!
I CAN BARELY MOVE ANYMORE...
HUF
HUF
HUF
CHIPS
SLUMP
!
GASP!
KAZUKI!
WHAT'S WRONG?
ARE YOU ALL RIGHT?

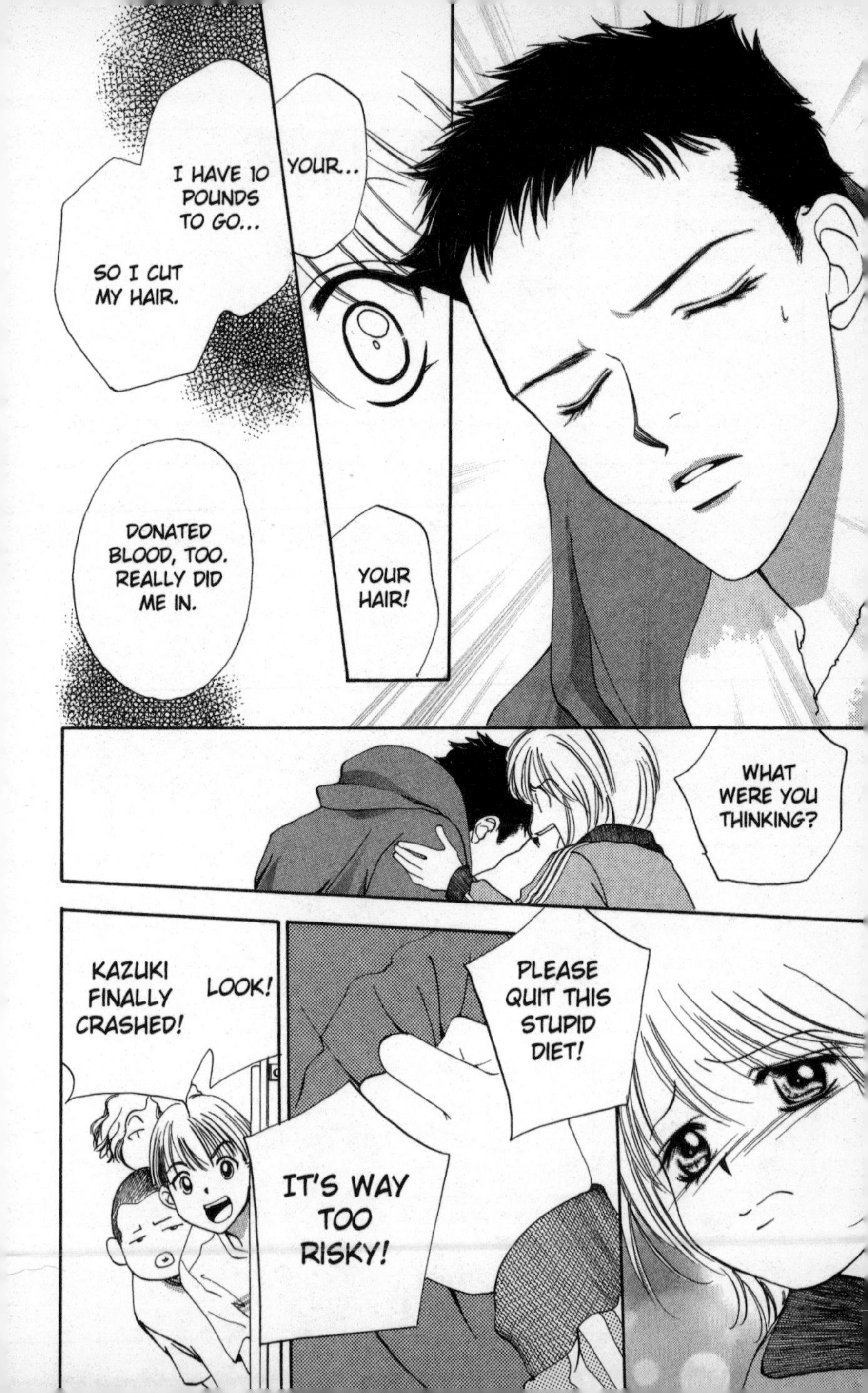
YOUR...
YOUR HAIR!
I HAVE 10 POUNDS TO GO...
SO I CUT MY HAIR.
DONATED BLOOD, TOO. REALLY DID ME IN.
WHAT WERE YOU THINKING?
PLEASE QUIT THIS STUPID DIET!
IT'S WAY TOO RISKY!
LOOK!
KAZUKI FINALLY CRASHED!

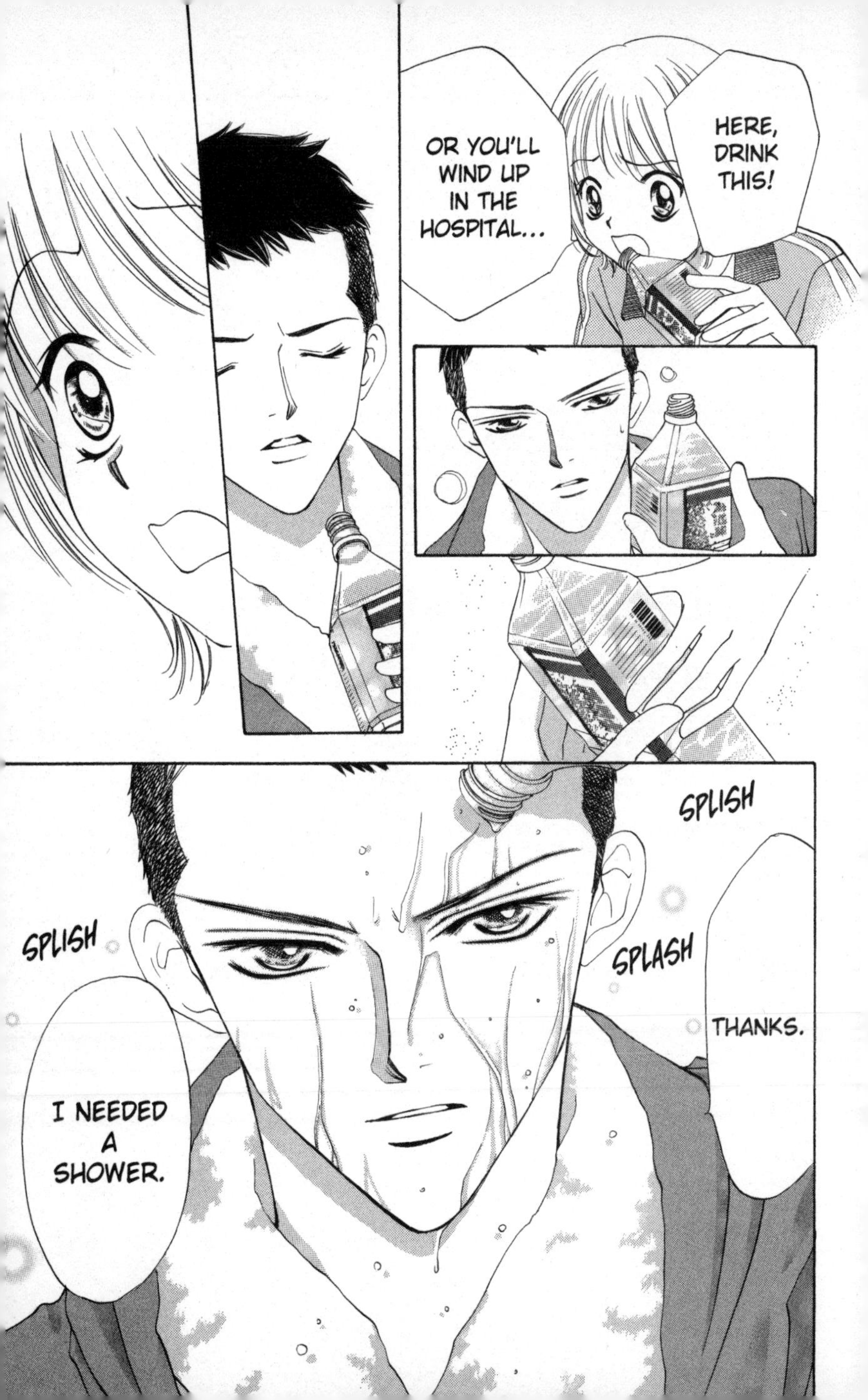
HERE, DRINK THIS!
OR YOU'LL WIND UP IN THE HOSPITAL...
SPLISH
THANKS.
SPLASH
SPLISH
I NEEDED A SHOWER.

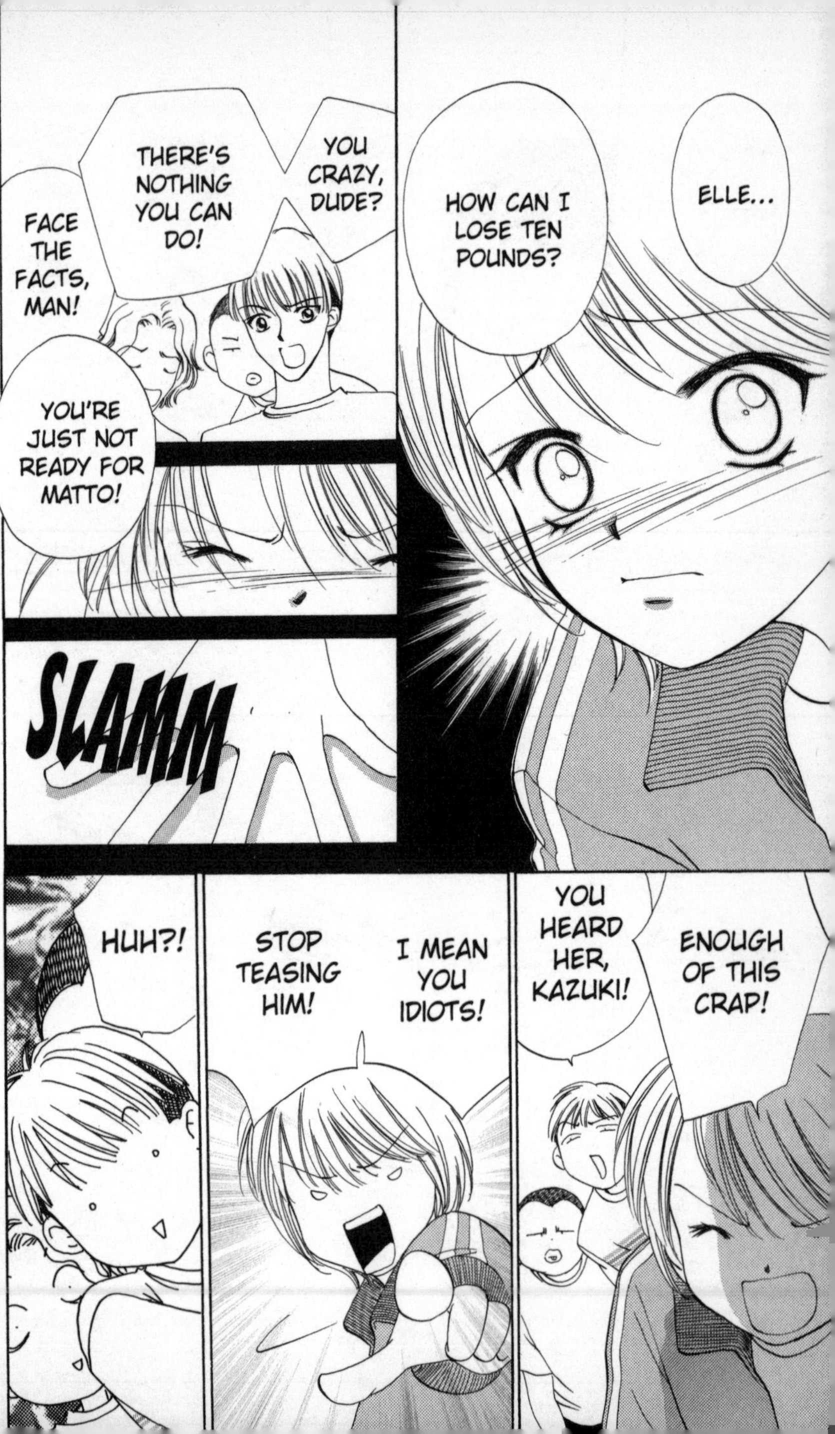
ELLE...
HOW CAN I LOSE TEN POUNDS?
YOU CRAZY, DUDE?
THERE'S NOTHING YOU CAN DO!
FACE THE FACTS, MAN!
YOU'RE JUST NOT READY FOR MATTO!
SLAMM
ENOUGH OF THIS CRAP!
YOU HEARD HER, KAZUKI!
I MEAN YOU IDIOTS!
STOP TEASING HIM!
HUH?!

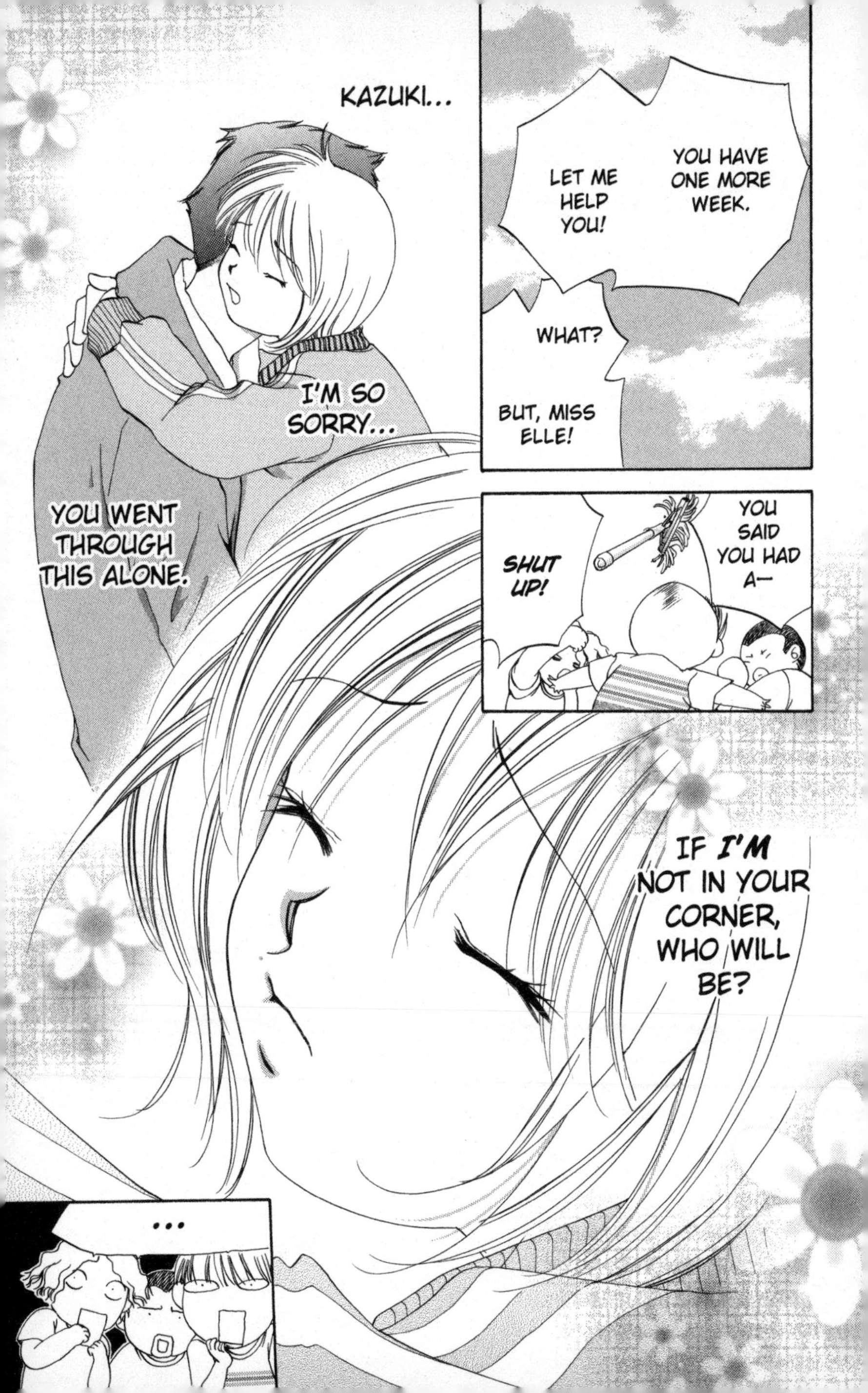
YOU HAVE ONE MORE WEEK.
LET ME HELP YOU!
WHAT?
BUT, MISS ELLE!
YOU SAID YOU HAD A—
SHUT UP!
KAZUKI...
I'M SO SORRY...
YOU WENT THROUGH THIS ALONE.
IF *I'M* NOT IN YOUR CORNER, WHO WILL BE?
...

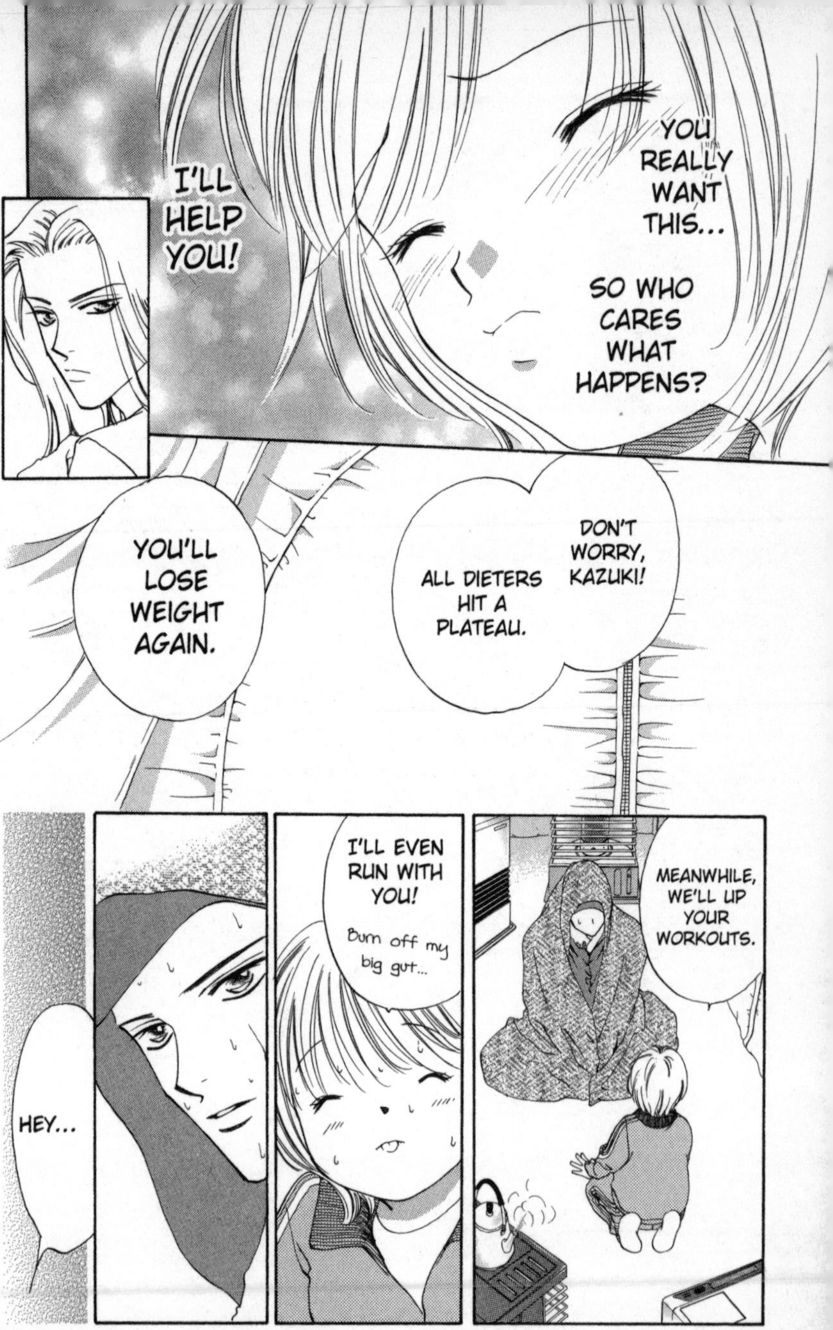
YOU REALLY WANT THIS...
SO WHO CARES WHAT HAPPENS?
I'LL HELP YOU!
DON'T WORRY, KAZUKI!
ALL DIETERS HIT A PLATEAU.
YOU'LL LOSE WEIGHT AGAIN.
MEANWHILE, WE'LL UP YOUR WORKOUTS.
I'LL EVEN RUN WITH YOU!
Burn off my big gut...
HEY...

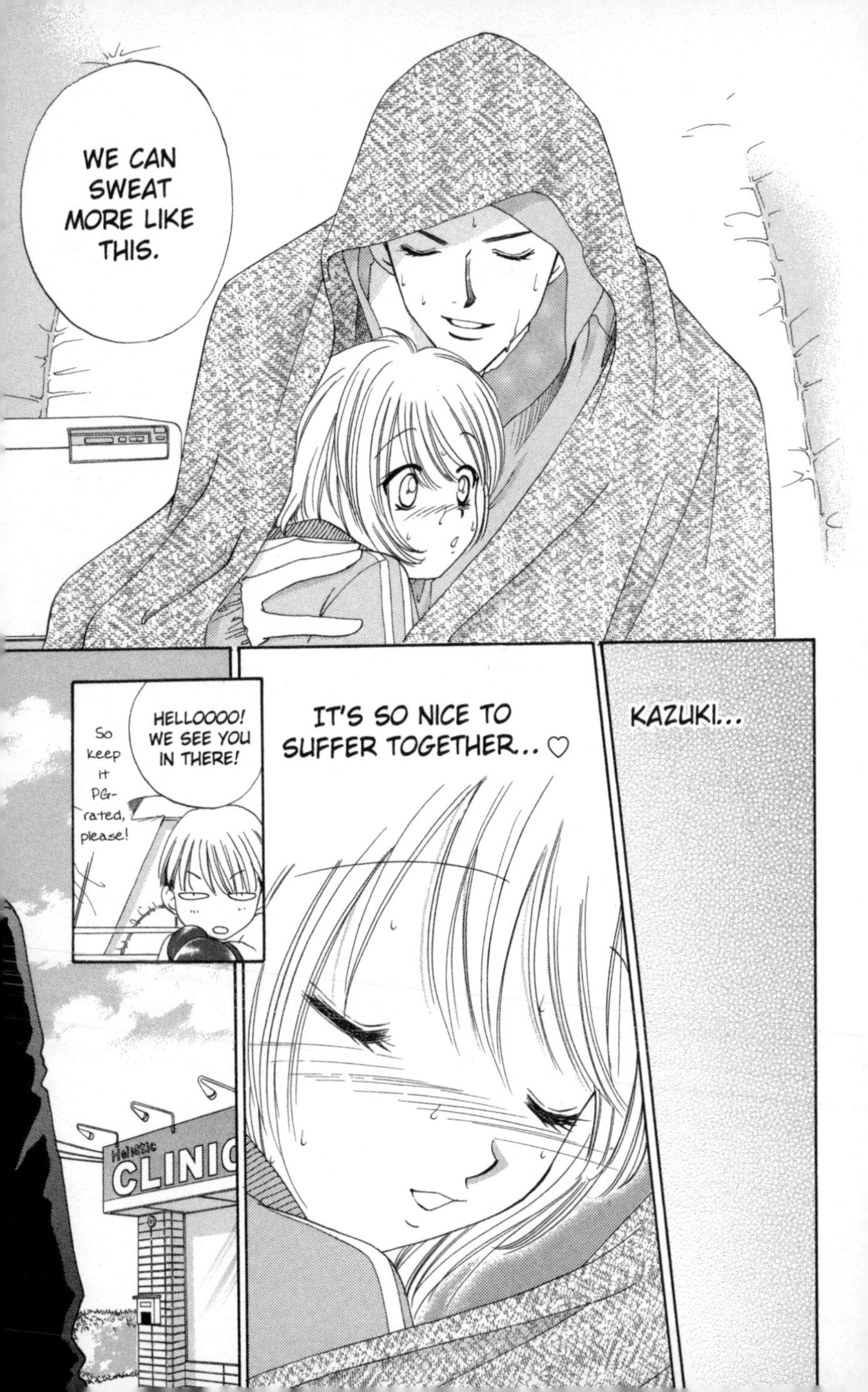
WE CAN SWEAT MORE LIKE THIS.
KAZUKI...
IT'S SO NICE TO SUFFER TOGETHER... ♡
HELLOOOO! WE SEE YOU IN THERE!
So keep it PG-rated, please!

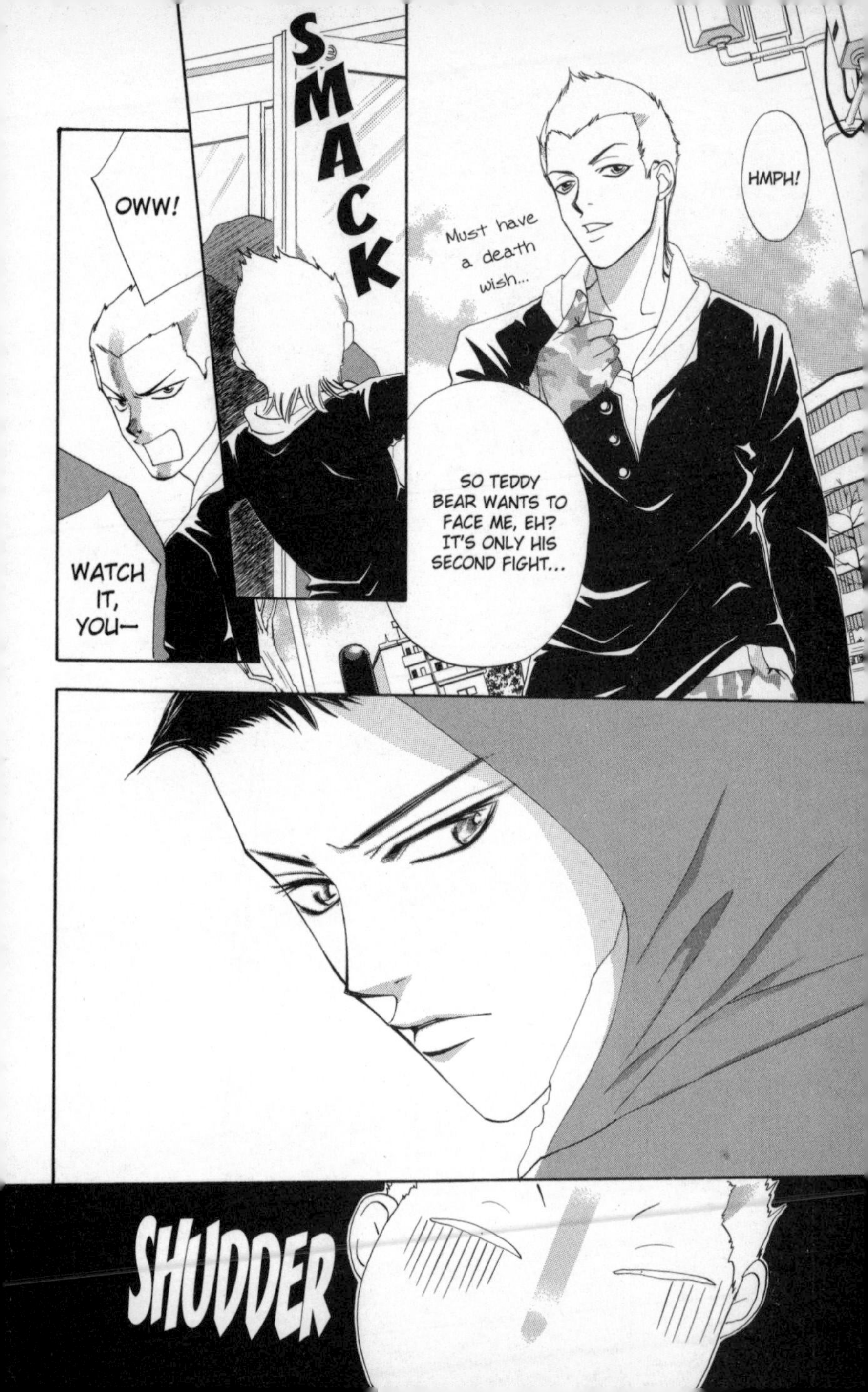
HMPH!
Must have a death wish...
SO TEDDY BEAR WANTS TO FACE ME, EH? IT'S ONLY HIS SECOND FIGHT...
SMACK
OWW!
WATCH IT, YOU—
SHUDDER

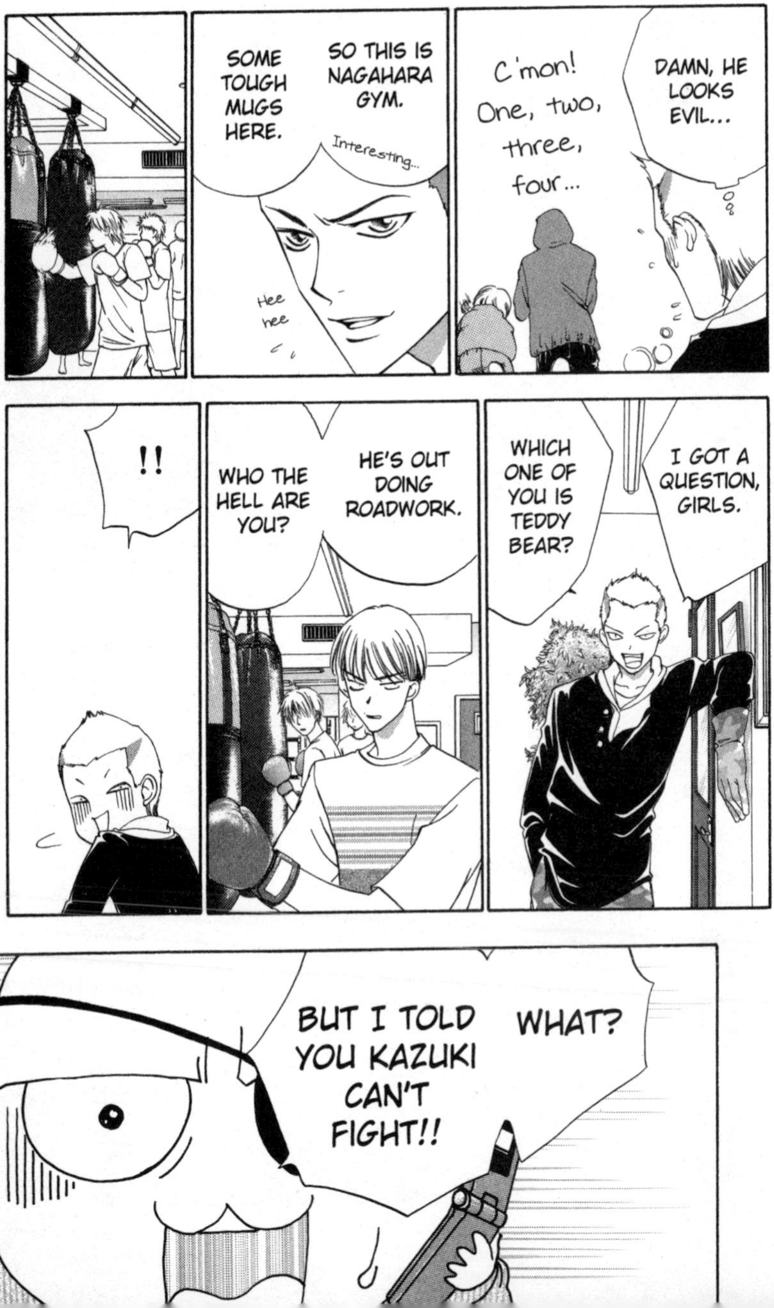
DAMN, HE LOOKS EVIL...
C'mon! One, two, three, four...
SO THIS IS NAGAHARA GYM.
SOME TOUGH MUGS HERE.
Interesting...
Hee hee
I GOT A QUESTION, GIRLS.
WHICH ONE OF YOU IS TEDDY BEAR?
HE'S OUT DOING ROADWORK.
WHO THE HELL ARE YOU?
!!
WHAT?
BUT I TOLD YOU KAZUKI CAN'T FIGHT!!

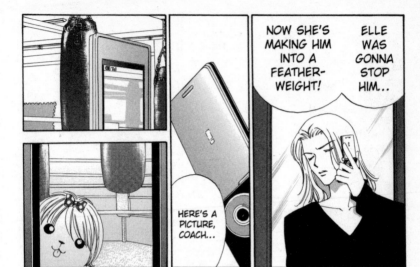

ELLE WAS GONNA STOP HIM...
NOW SHE'S MAKING HIM INTO A FEATHER-WEIGHT!
HERE'S A PICTURE, COACH...
ELLE?
STOP SMILING! GIGI IS VERY ANGRY!
UH, THAT'S A DOG...
SHOULD I BUST HIS LEG IN A SPARRING MATCH?

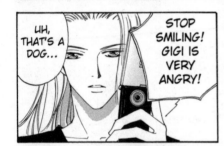

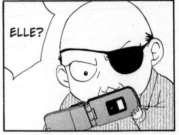

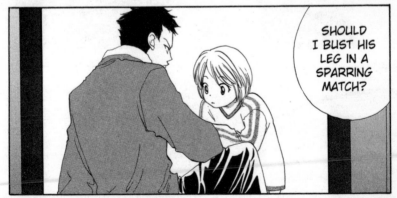

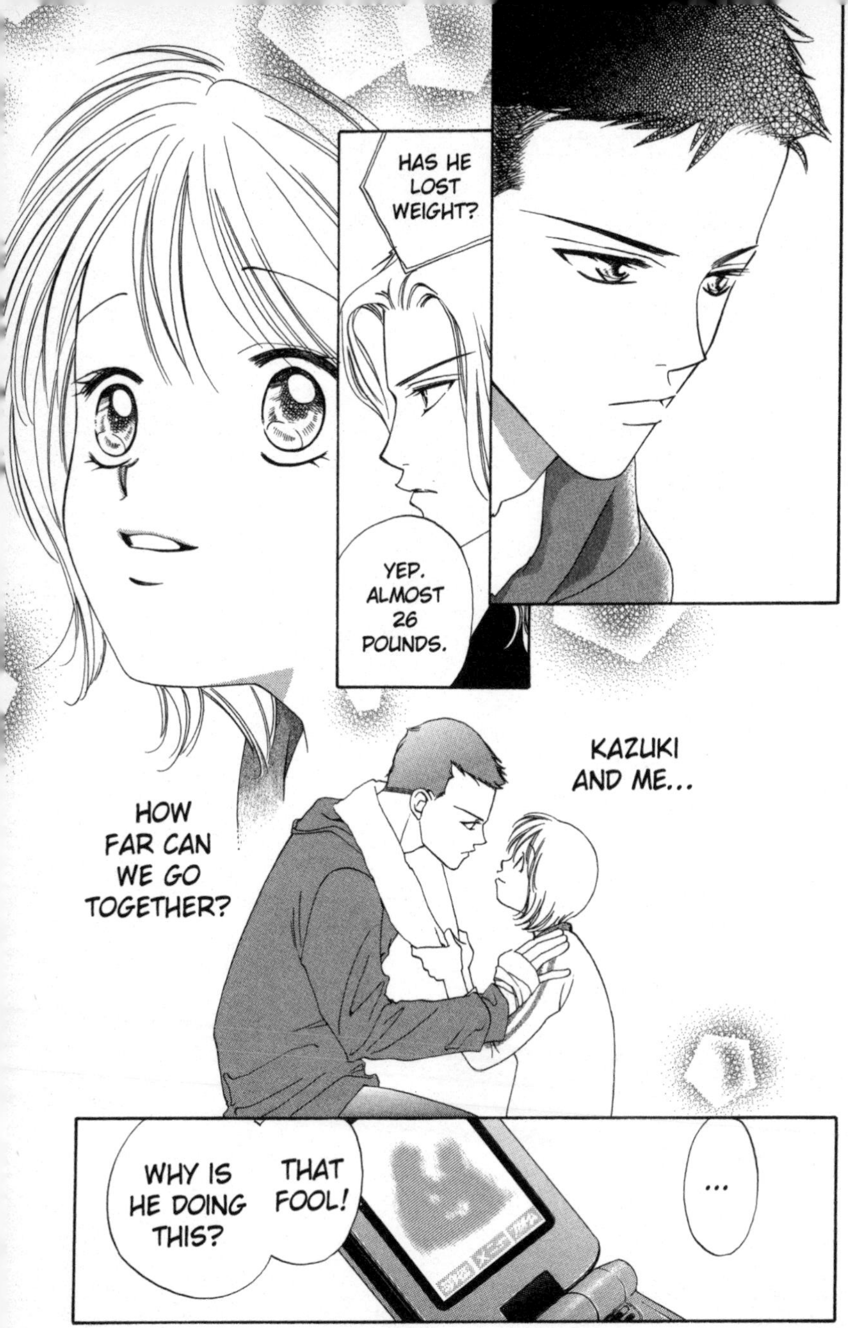
HAS HE LOST WEIGHT?
YEP. ALMOST 26 POUNDS.
KAZUKI AND ME...
HOW FAR CAN WE GO TOGETHER?
...
THAT FOOL!
WHY IS HE DOING THIS?

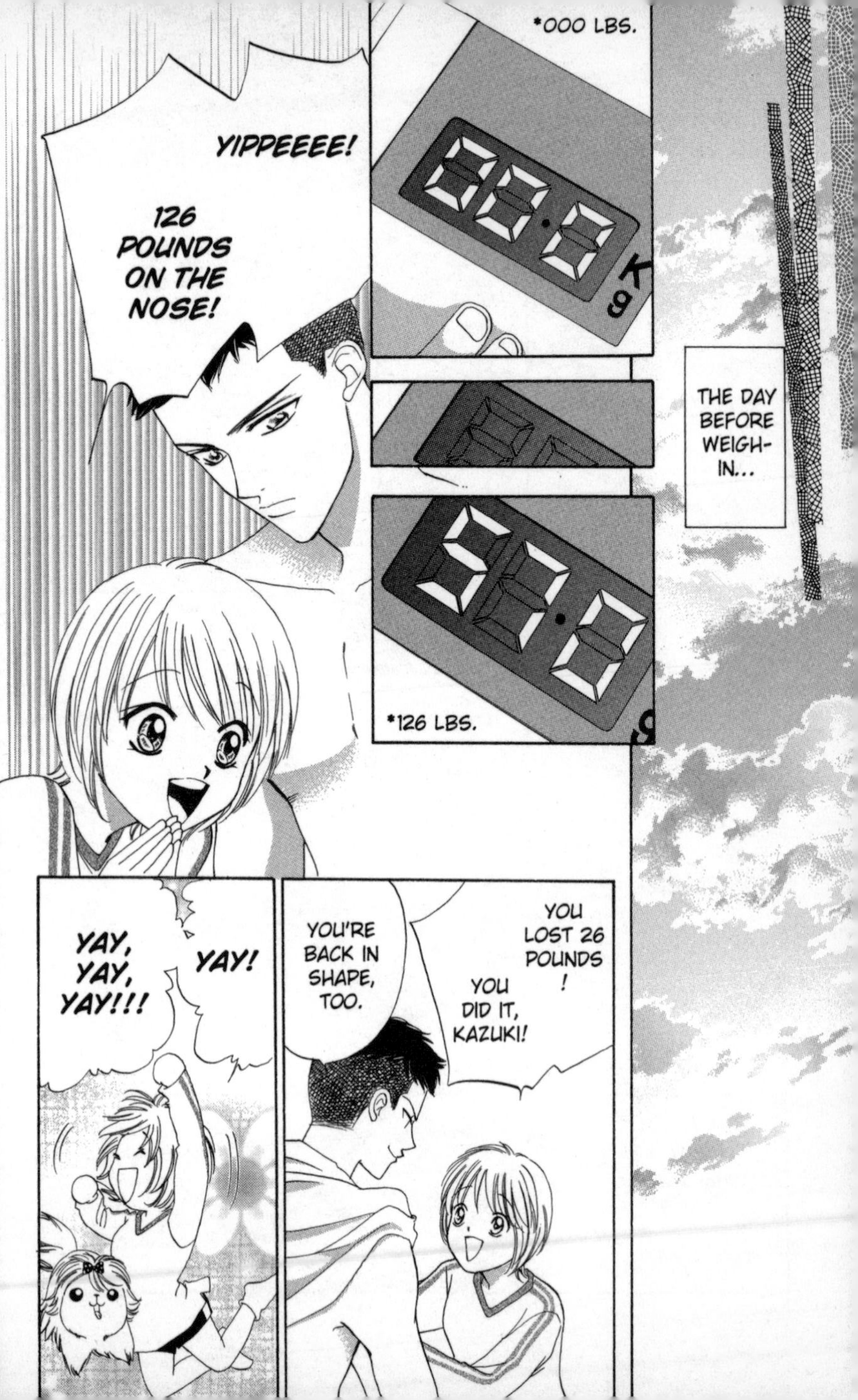
THE DAY BEFORE WEIGH-IN...
*000 LBS.
*126 LBS.
YIPPEEEE!
126 POUNDS ON THE NOSE!
YOU LOST 26 POUNDS!
YOU DID IT, KAZUKI!
YOU'RE BACK IN SHAPE, TOO.
YAY!
YAY, YAY, YAY!!!

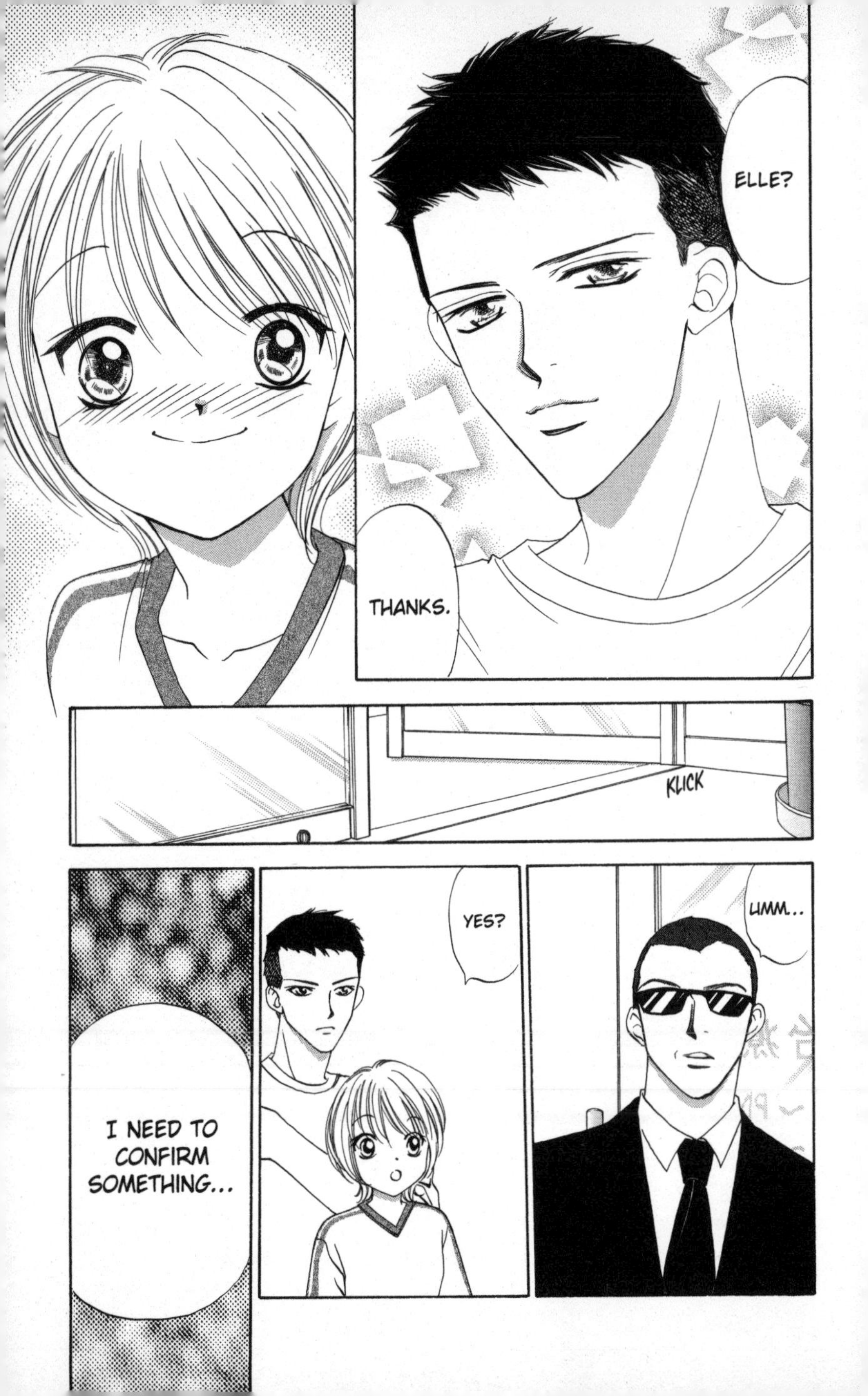
ELLE?
THANKS.
KLICK
UMM...
YES?
I NEED TO CONFIRM SOMETHING...

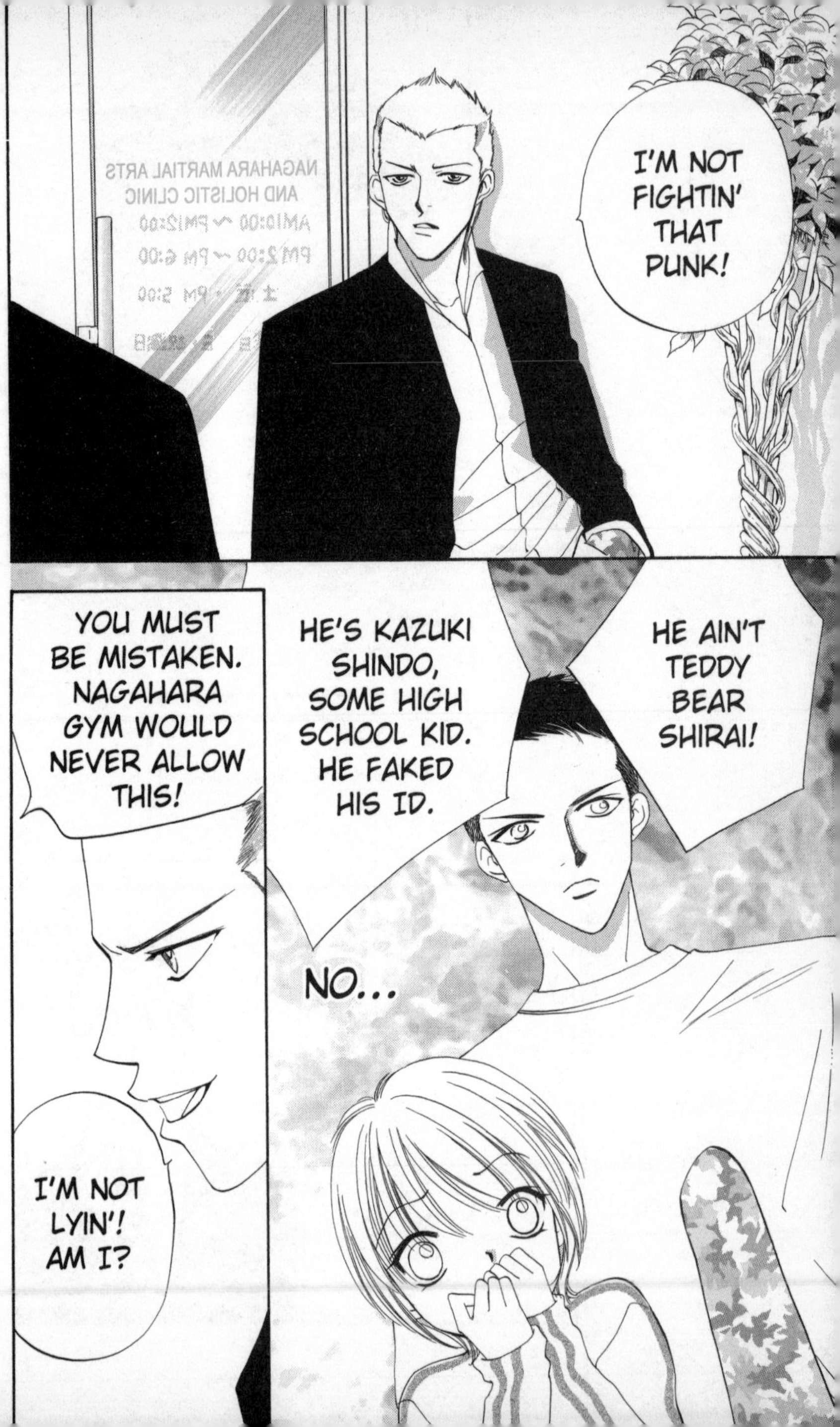
I'M NOT FIGHTIN' THAT PUNK!
NAGAHARA MARTIAL ARTS
AND HOLISTIC CLINIC
HE AIN'T TEDDY BEAR SHIRAI!
HE'S KAZUKI SHINDO, SOME HIGH SCHOOL KID. HE FAKED HIS ID.
YOU MUST BE MISTAKEN. NAGAHARA GYM WOULD NEVER ALLOW THIS!
NO...
I'M NOT LYIN'! AM I?

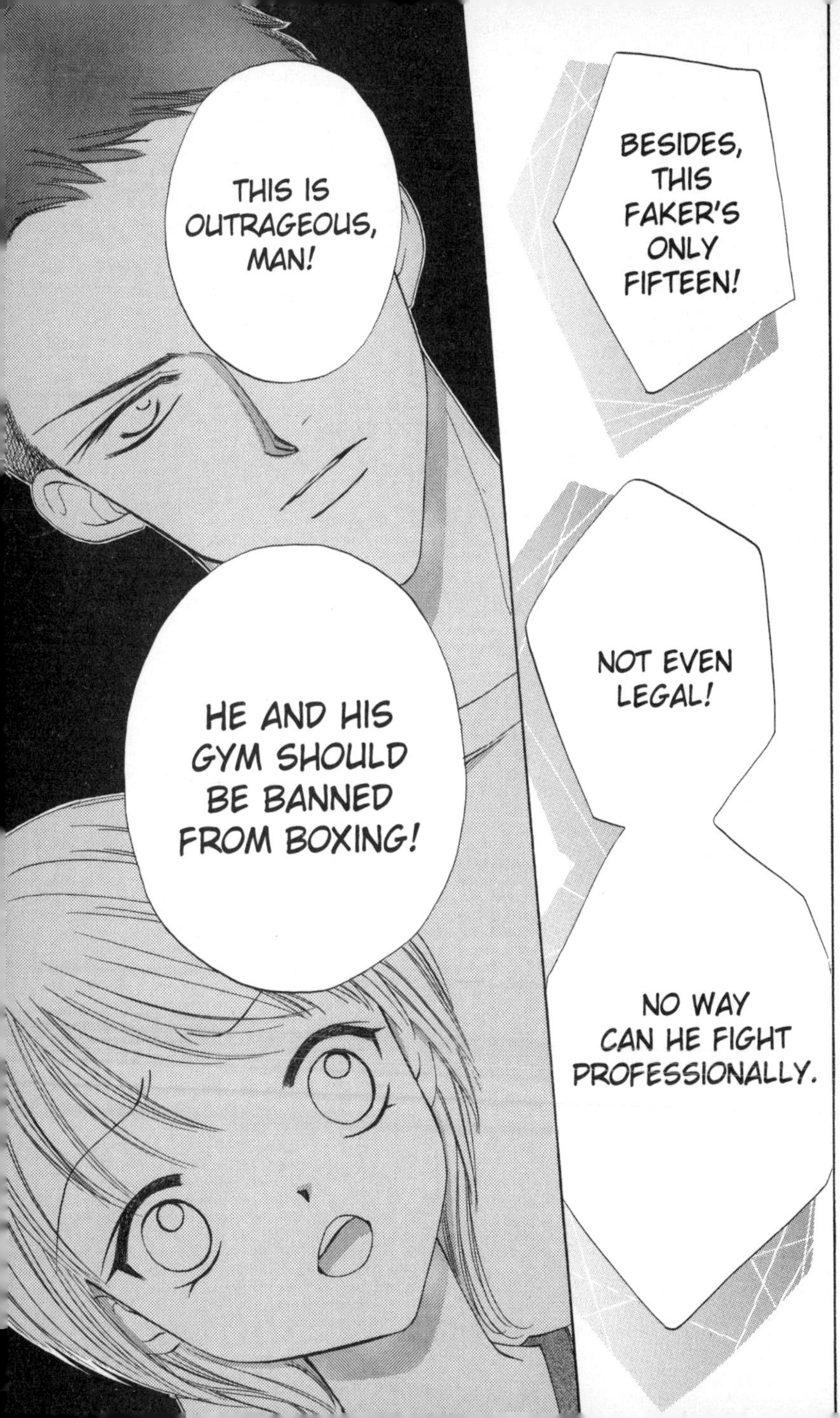
BESIDES, THIS FAKER'S ONLY FIFTEEN!
NOT EVEN LEGAL!
NO WAY CAN HE FIGHT PROFESSIONALLY.
THIS IS OUTRAGEOUS, MAN!
HE AND HIS GYM SHOULD BE BANNED FROM BOXING!

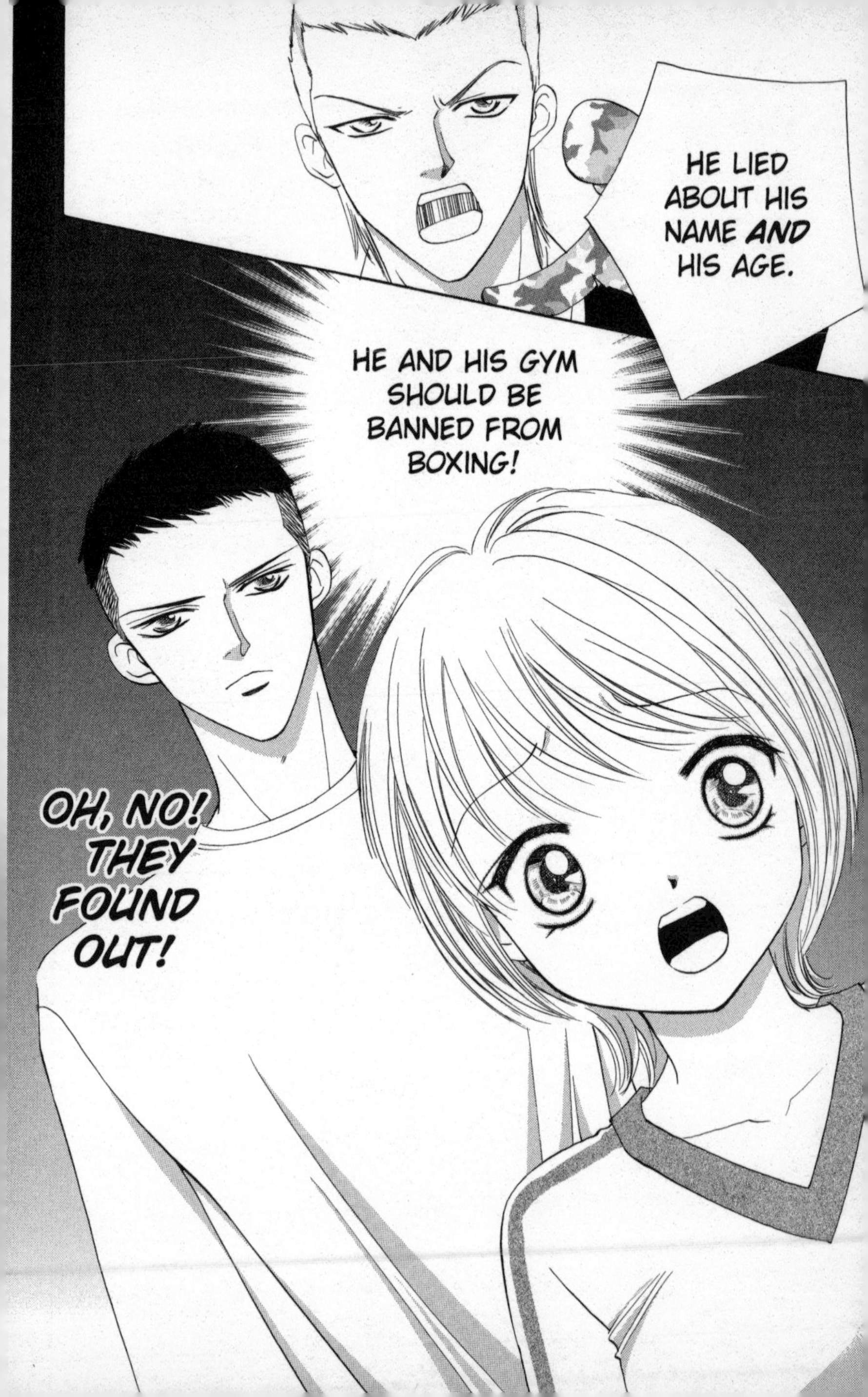
HE LIED ABOUT HIS NAME AND HIS AGE.
HE AND HIS GYM SHOULD BE BANNED FROM BOXING!
OH, NO! THEY FOUND OUT!

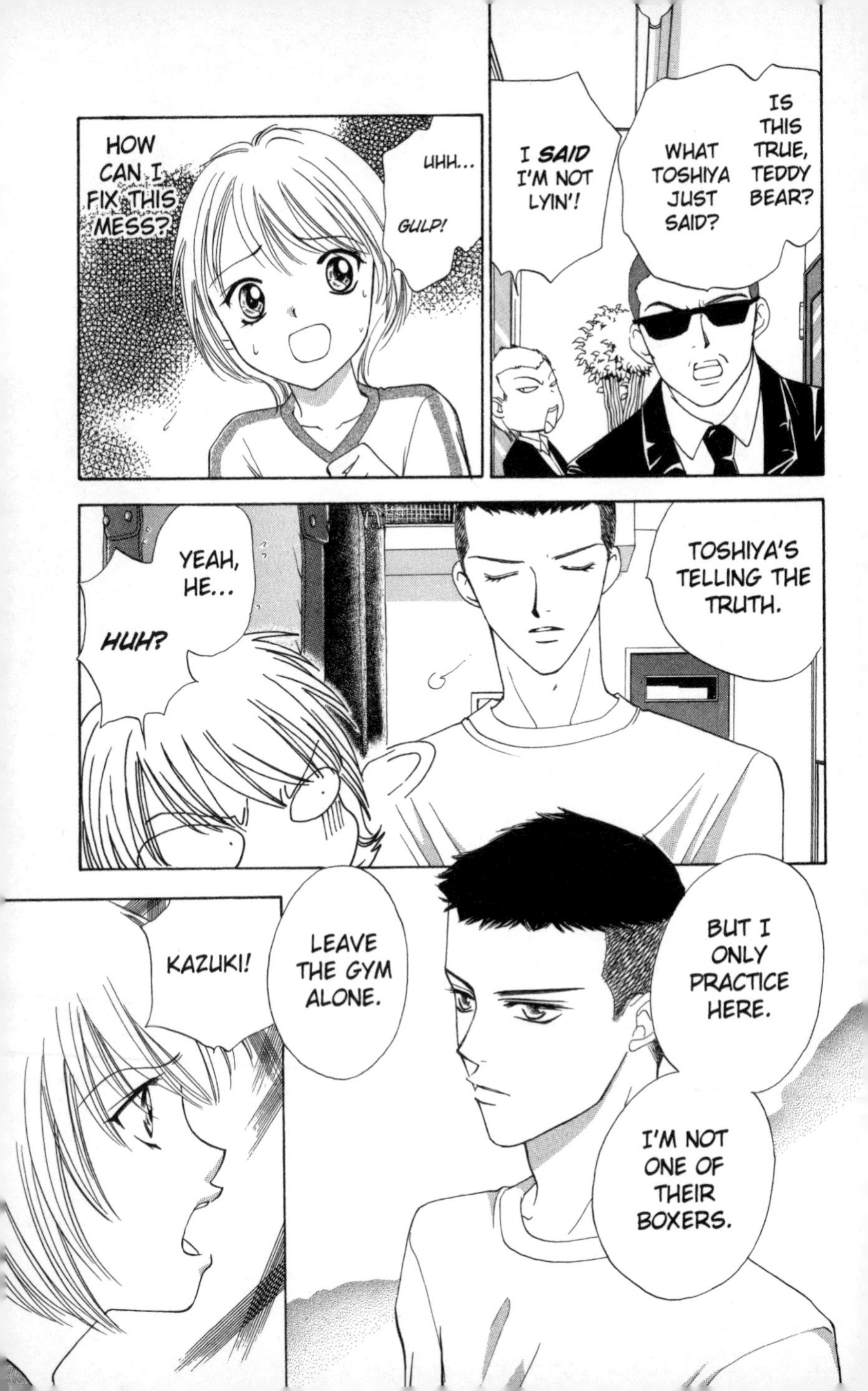
IS THIS TRUE, TEDDY BEAR? WHAT TOSHIYA JUST SAID?
I *SAID* I'M NOT LYIN'!
UHH...
GULP!
HOW CAN I FIX THIS MESS?
TOSHIYA'S TELLING THE TRUTH.
YEAH, HE...
HUH?
BUT I ONLY PRACTICE HERE.
I'M NOT ONE OF THEIR BOXERS.
LEAVE THE GYM ALONE.
KAZUKI!

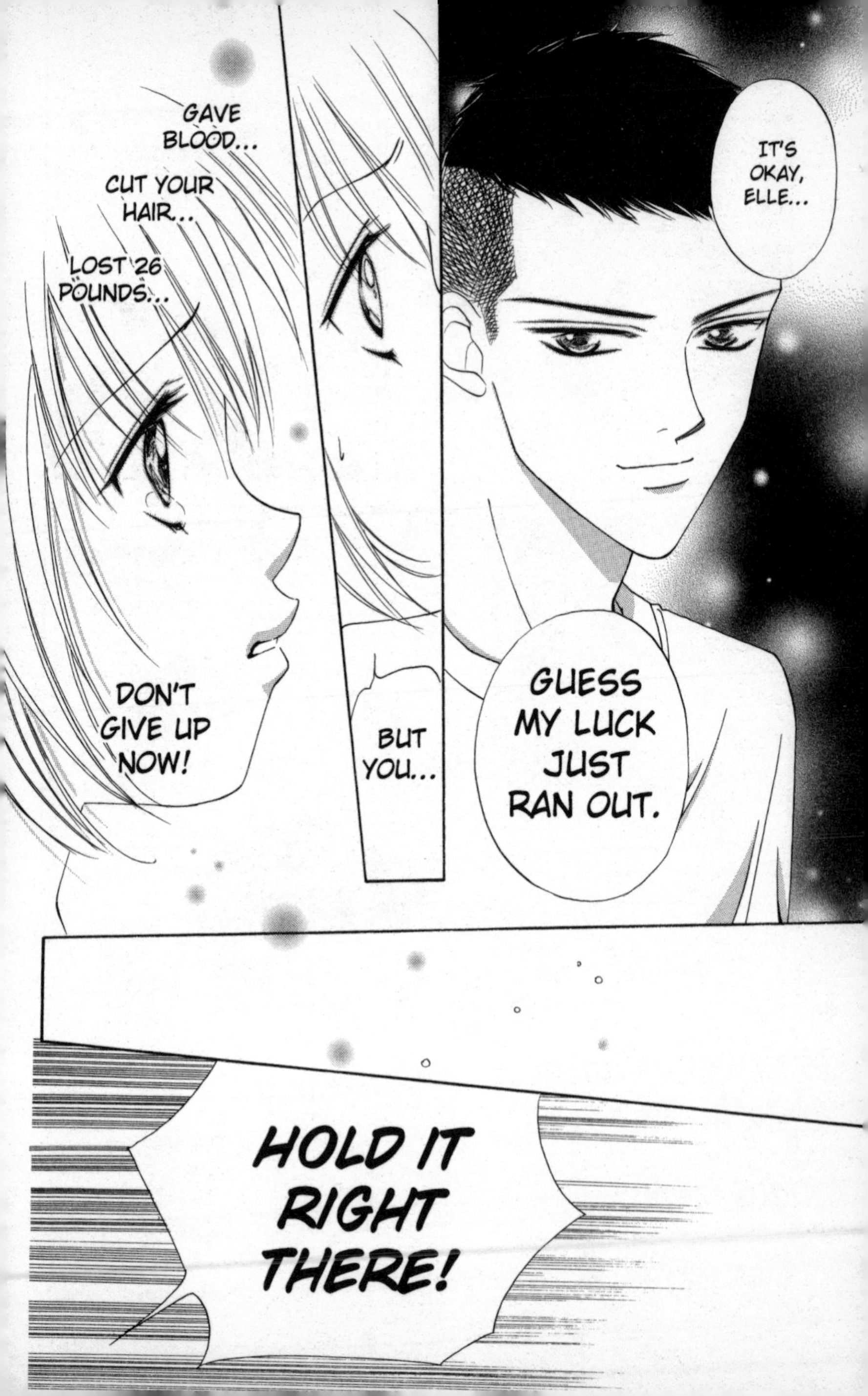
IT'S OKAY, ELLE...
GUESS MY LUCK JUST RAN OUT.
BUT YOU...
GAVE BLOOD...
CUT YOUR HAIR...
LOST 26 POUNDS...
DON'T GIVE UP NOW!
HOLD IT RIGHT THERE!

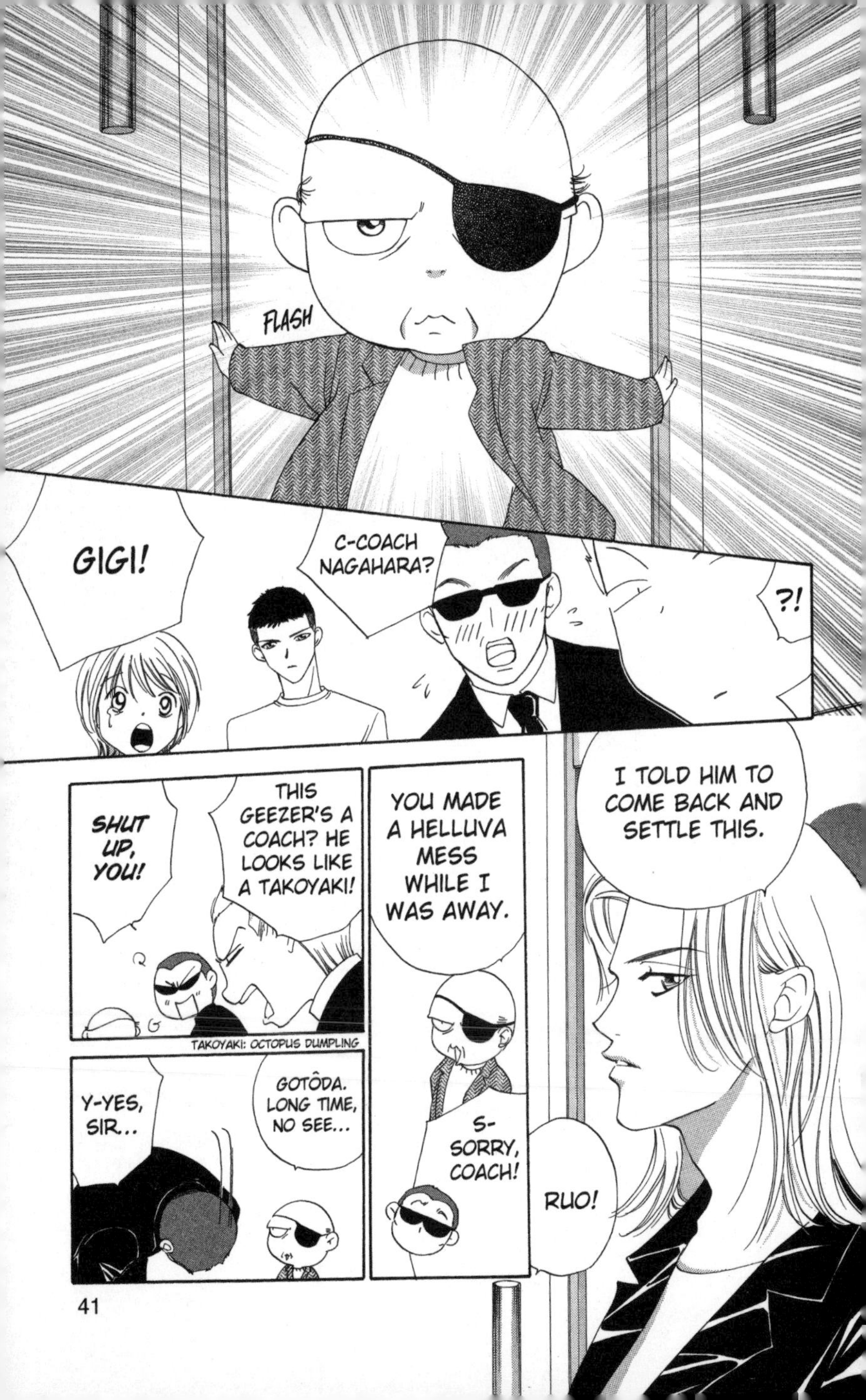
FLASH
?!
C-COACH NAGAHARA?
GIGI!
I TOLD HIM TO COME BACK AND SETTLE THIS.
RUO!
YOU MADE A HELLUVA MESS WHILE I WAS AWAY.
S-SORRY, COACH!
THIS GEEZER'S A COACH? HE LOOKS LIKE A TAKOYAKI!
SHUT UP, YOU!
TAKOYAKI: OCTOPUS DUMPLING
GOTÔDA. LONG TIME, NO SEE...
Y-YES, SIR...

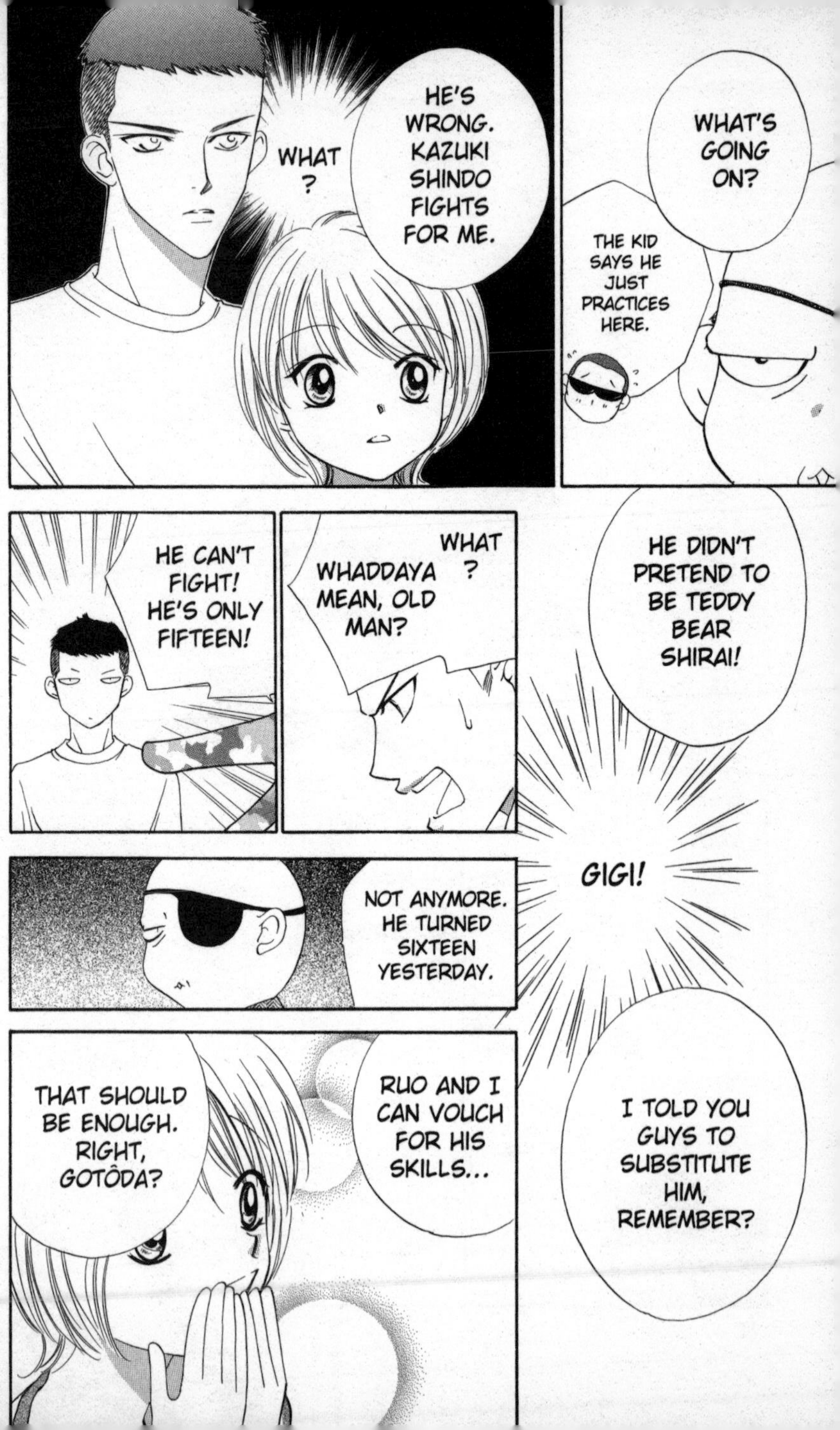
WHAT'S GOING ON?
THE KID SAYS HE JUST PRACTICES HERE.
HE'S WRONG. KAZUKI SHINDO FIGHTS FOR ME.
WHAT ?
HE DIDN'T PRETEND TO BE TEDDY BEAR SHIRAI!
GIGI!
I TOLD YOU GUYS TO SUBSTITUTE HIM, REMEMBER?
WHAT ?
WHADDAYA MEAN, OLD MAN?
HE CAN'T FIGHT! HE'S ONLY FIFTEEN!
NOT ANYMORE. HE TURNED SIXTEEN YESTERDAY.
RUO AND I CAN VOUCH FOR HIS SKILLS...
THAT SHOULD BE ENOUGH. RIGHT, GOTÔDA?

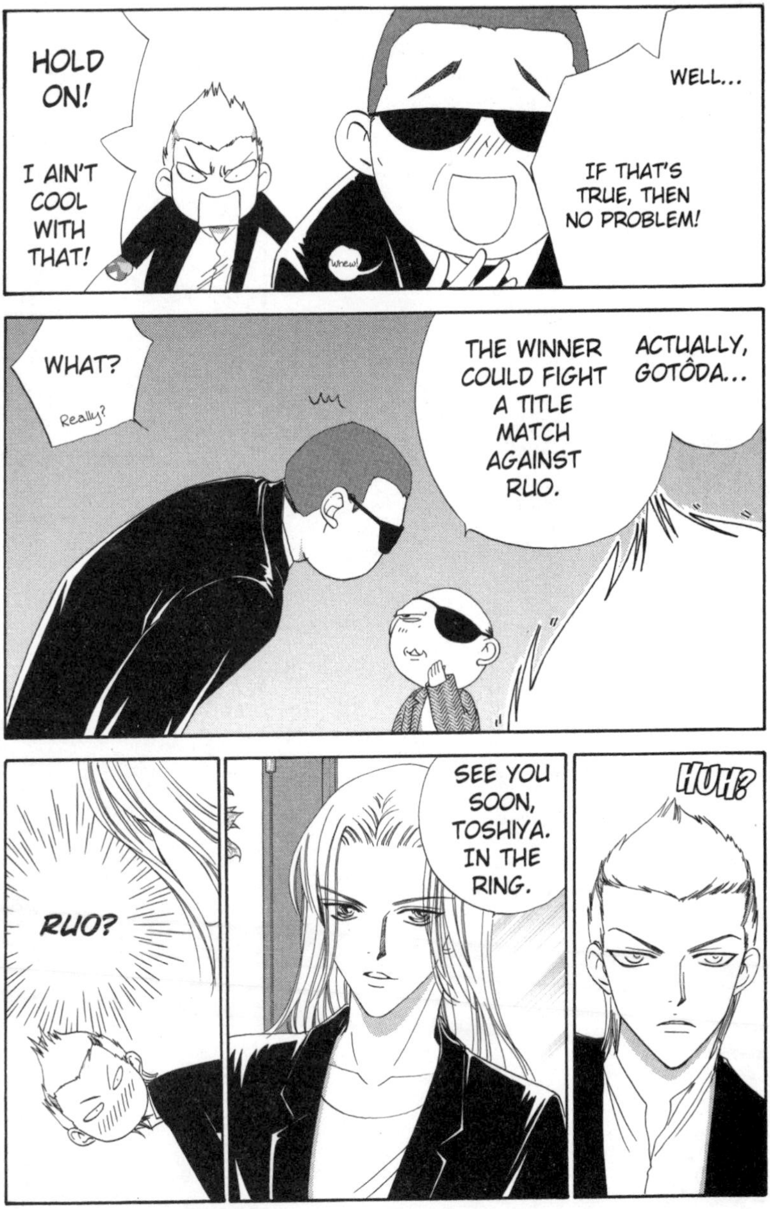
WELL...
IF THAT'S TRUE, THEN NO PROBLEM!
Whew!
HOLD ON!
I AIN'T COOL WITH THAT!
ACTUALLY, GOTÔDA...
THE WINNER COULD FIGHT A TITLE MATCH AGAINST RUO.
WHAT?
Really?
HUH?
SEE YOU SOON, TOSHIYA. IN THE RING.
RUO?

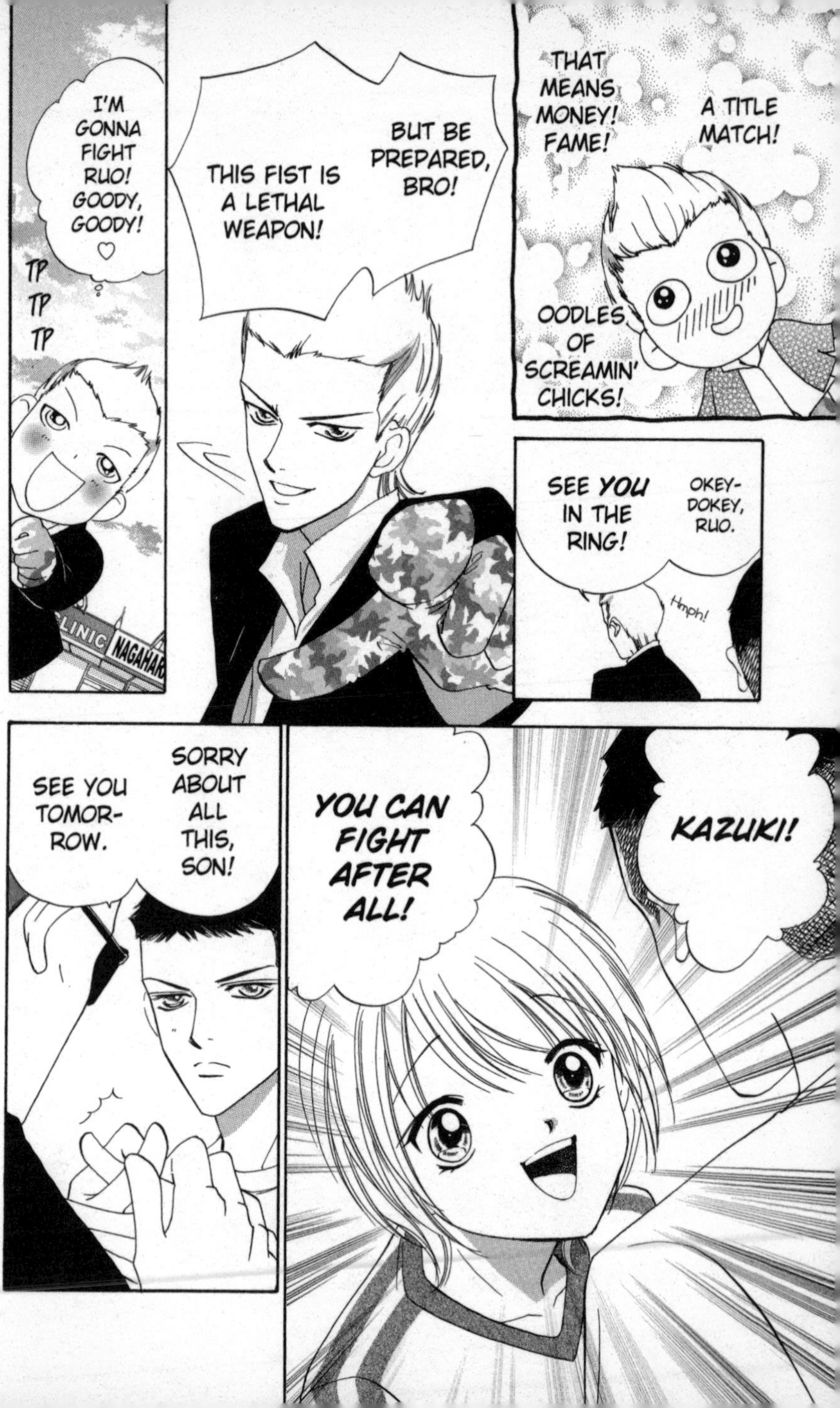

A TITLE MATCH!
THAT MEANS MONEY! FAME!
OODLES OF SCREAMIN' CHICKS!
OKEY-DOKEY, RUO.
SEE *YOU* IN THE RING!
Hmph!
BUT BE PREPARED, BRO!
THIS FIST IS A LETHAL WEAPON!
I'M GONNA FIGHT RUO! GOODY, GOODY! ♡
TP TP TP
LINIC NAGAHAR
KAZUKI!
YOU CAN FIGHT AFTER ALL!
SORRY ABOUT ALL THIS, SON!
SEE YOU TOMOR-ROW.

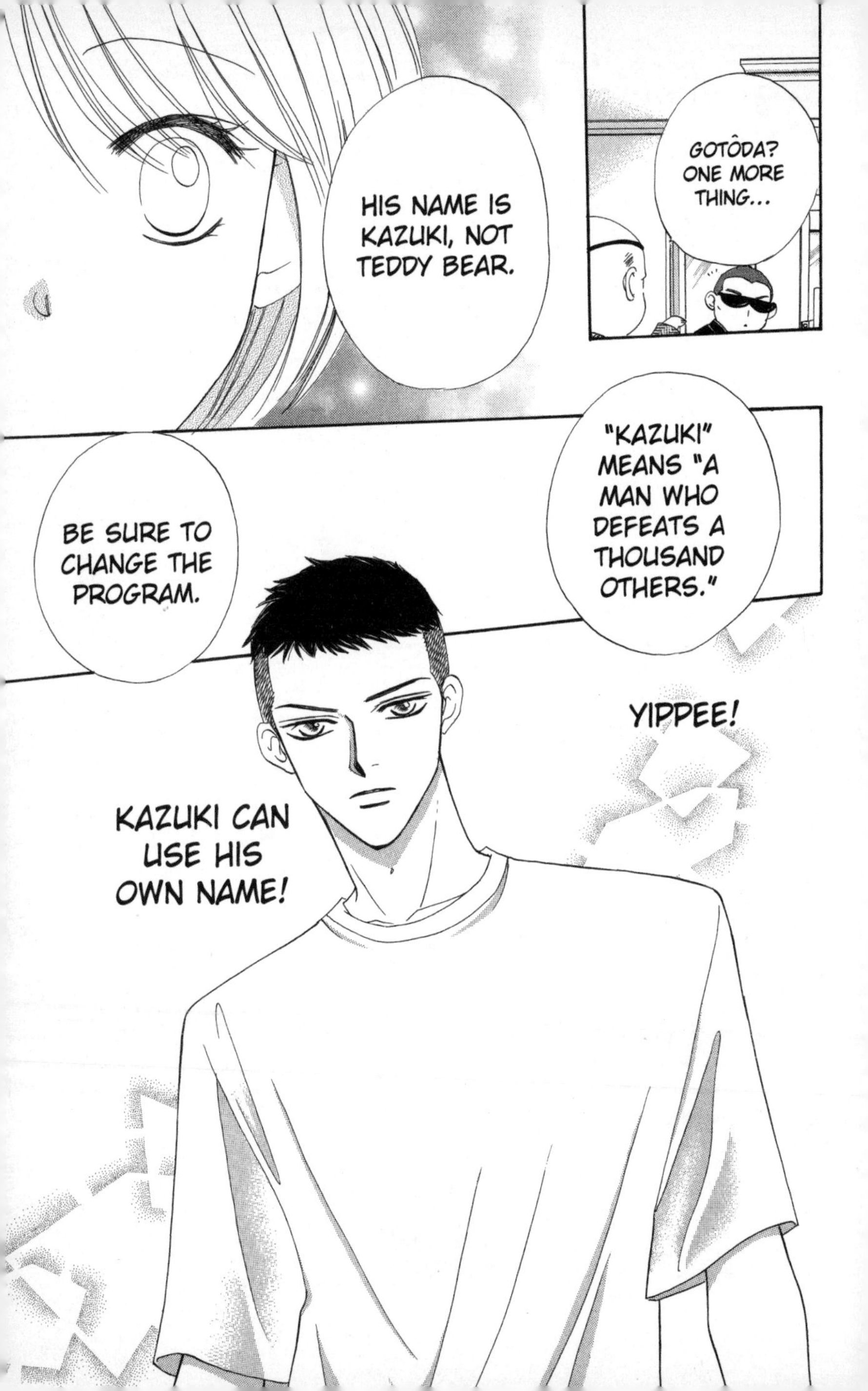
GOTÔDA? ONE MORE THING...
HIS NAME IS KAZUKI, NOT TEDDY BEAR.
"KAZUKI" MEANS "A MAN WHO DEFEATS A THOUSAND OTHERS."
BE SURE TO CHANGE THE PROGRAM.
YIPPEE!
KAZUKI CAN USE HIS OWN NAME!

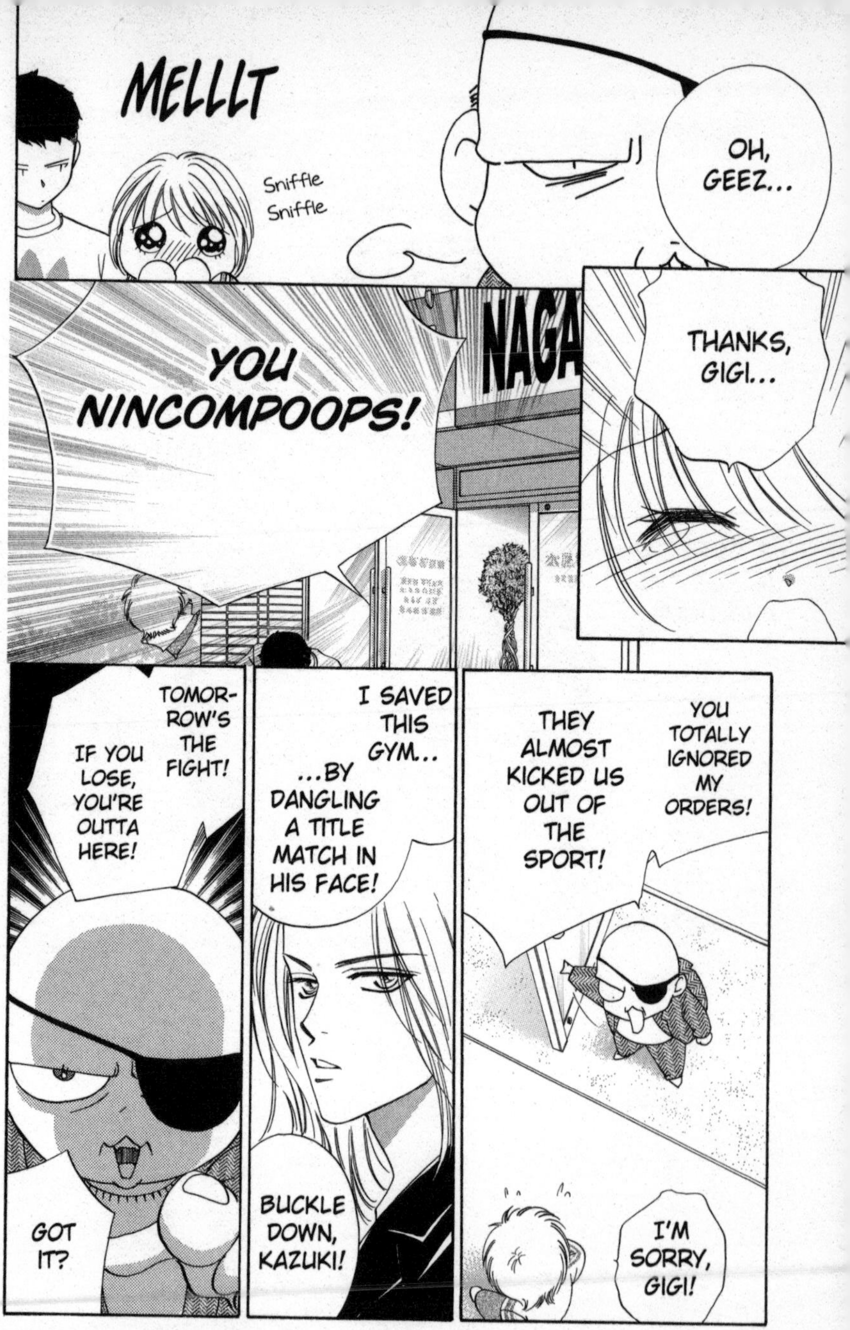
OH, GEEZ...
MELLLT
Sniffle
Sniffle
THANKS, GIGI...
YOU NINCOMPOOPS!
NAGA
YOU TOTALLY IGNORED MY ORDERS!
THEY ALMOST KICKED US OUT OF THE SPORT!
I'M SORRY, GIGI!
I SAVED THIS GYM...
...BY DANGLING A TITLE MATCH IN HIS FACE!
BUCKLE DOWN, KAZUKI!
TOMOR-ROW'S THE FIGHT!
IF YOU LOSE, YOU'RE OUTTA HERE!
GOT IT?

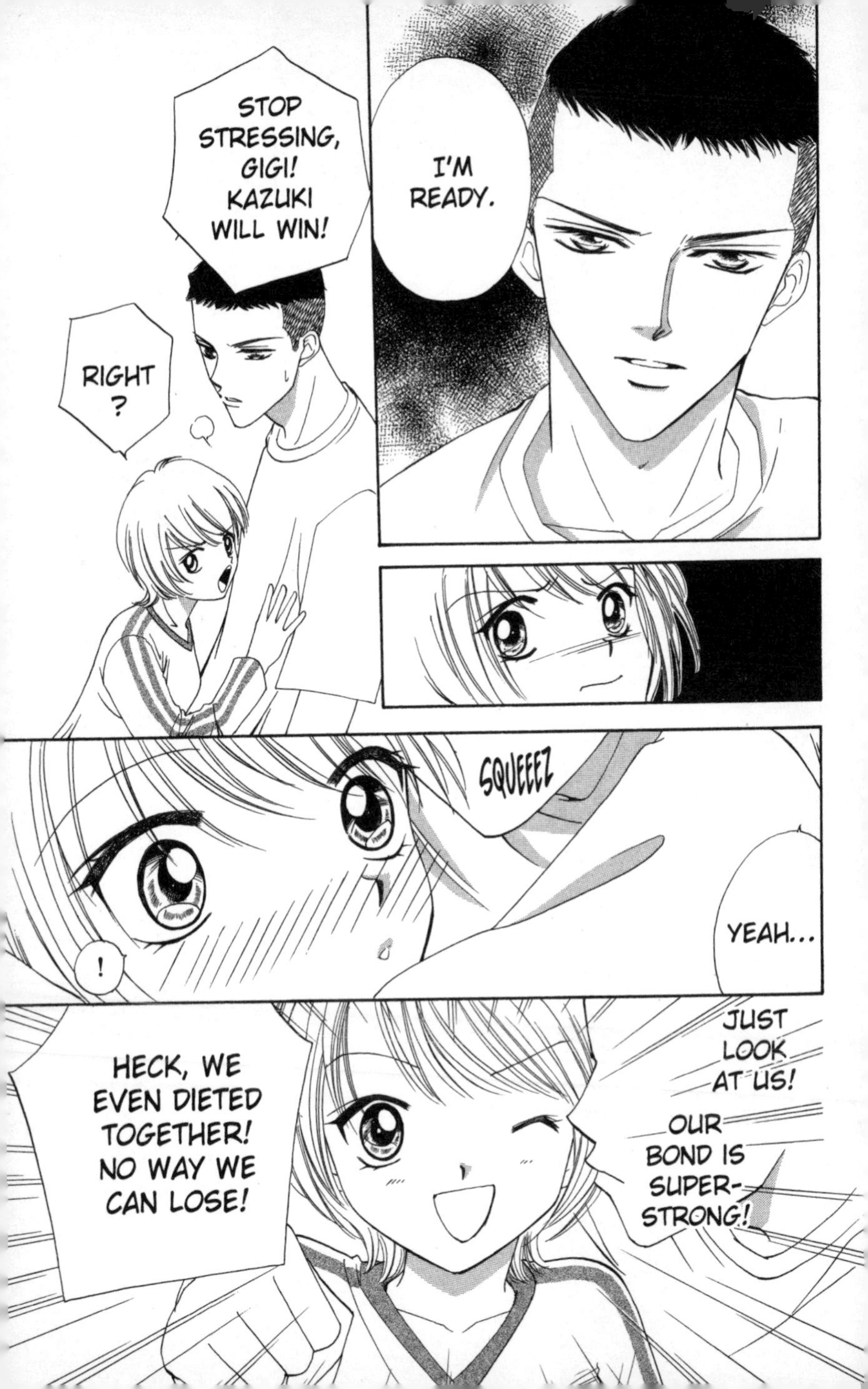
I'M READY.
STOP STRESSING, GIGI! KAZUKI WILL WIN!
RIGHT ?
SQUEEEZ
YEAH...
!
JUST LOOK AT US!
OUR BOND IS SUPER-STRONG!
HECK, WE EVEN DIETED TOGETHER! NO WAY WE CAN LOSE!

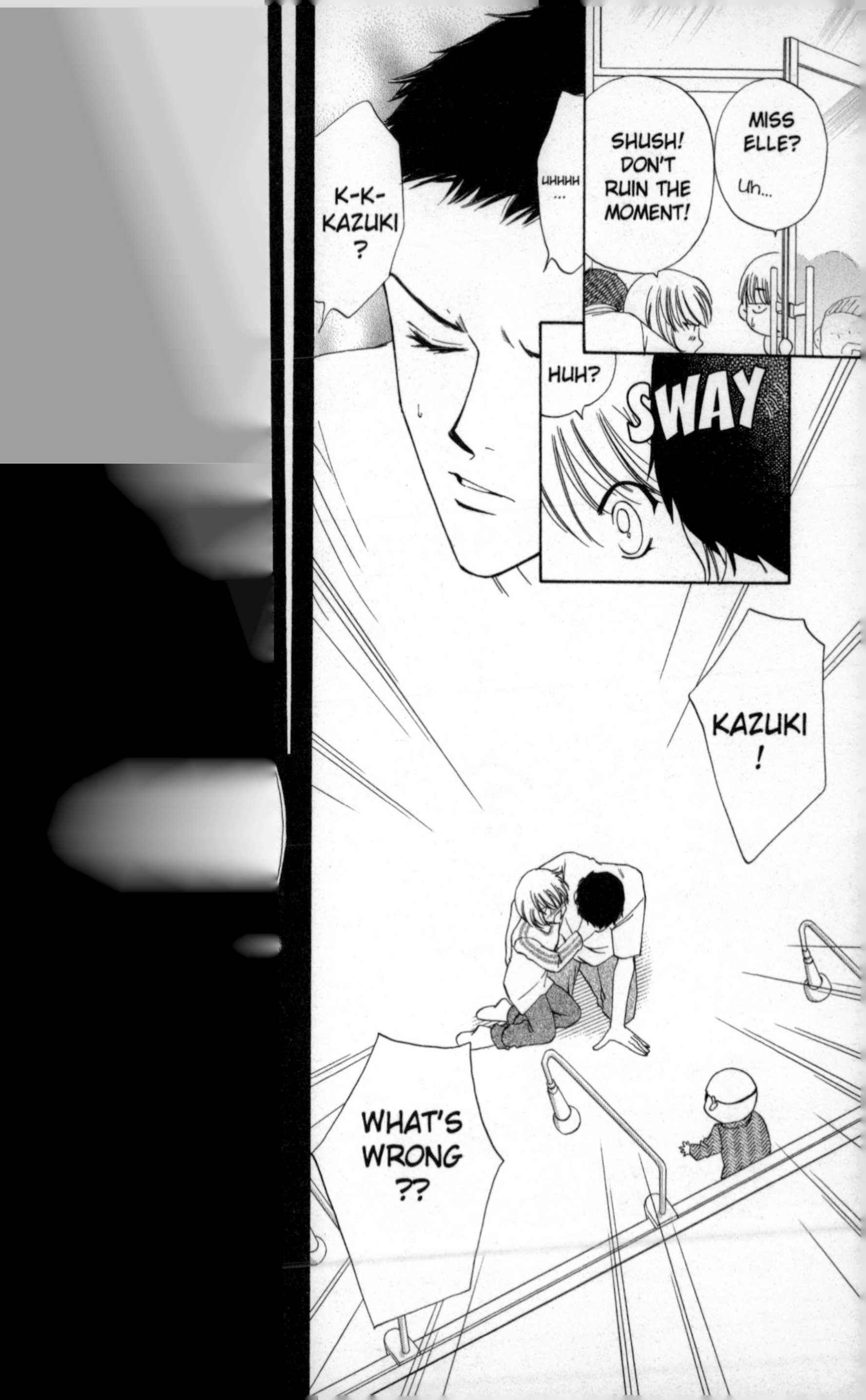
MISS ELLE?
Uh...
SHUSH! DON'T RUIN THE MOMENT!
HUH?
SWAY
UHHHH...
K-K-KAZUKI?
KAZUKI!
WHAT'S WRONG??

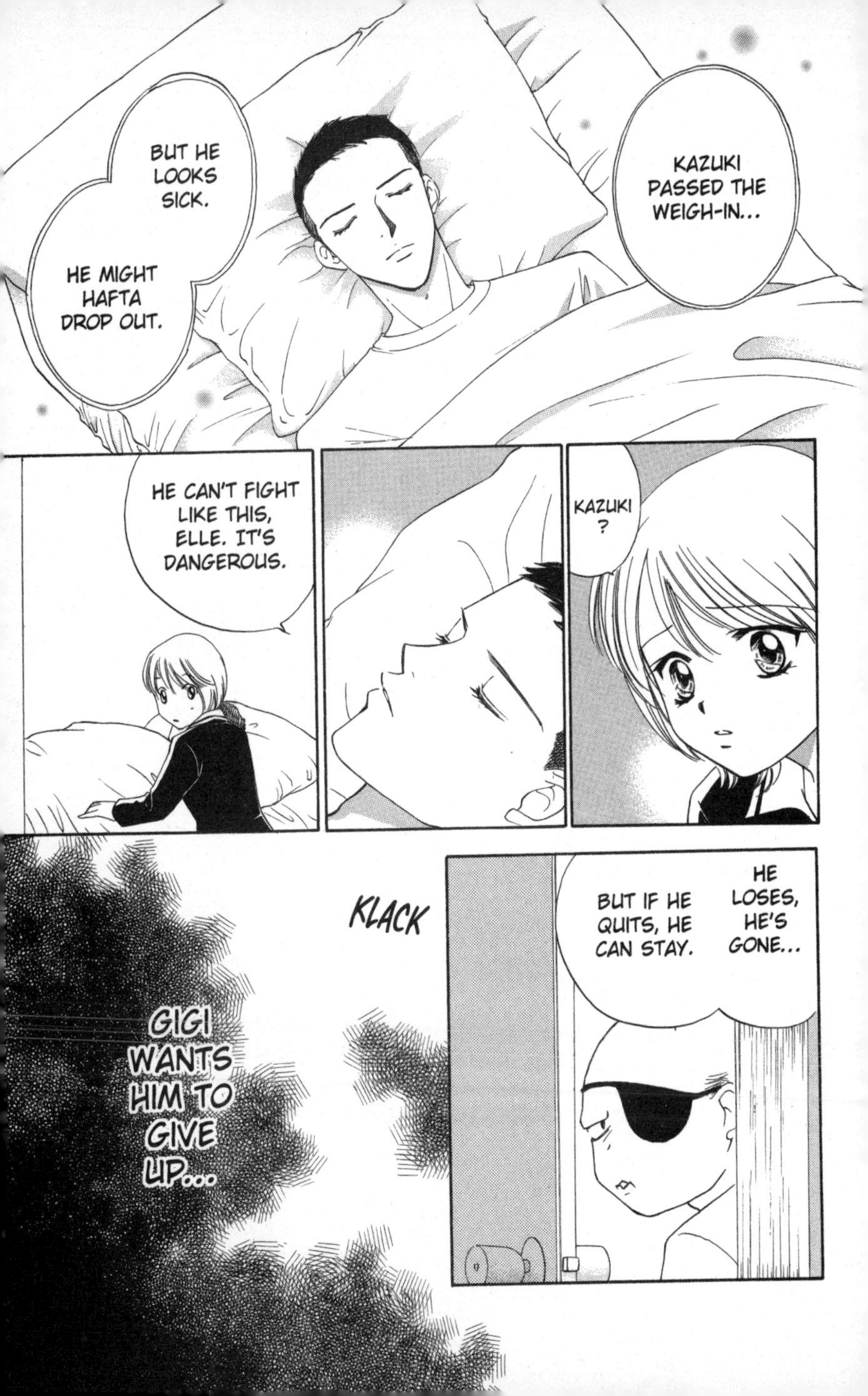
KAZUKI PASSED THE WEIGH-IN...
BUT HE LOOKS SICK.
HE MIGHT HAFTA DROP OUT.
KAZUKI ?
HE CAN'T FIGHT LIKE THIS, ELLE. IT'S DANGEROUS.
HE LOSES, HE'S GONE...
BUT IF HE QUITS, HE CAN STAY.
KLACK
GIGI WANTS HIM TO GIVE UP...

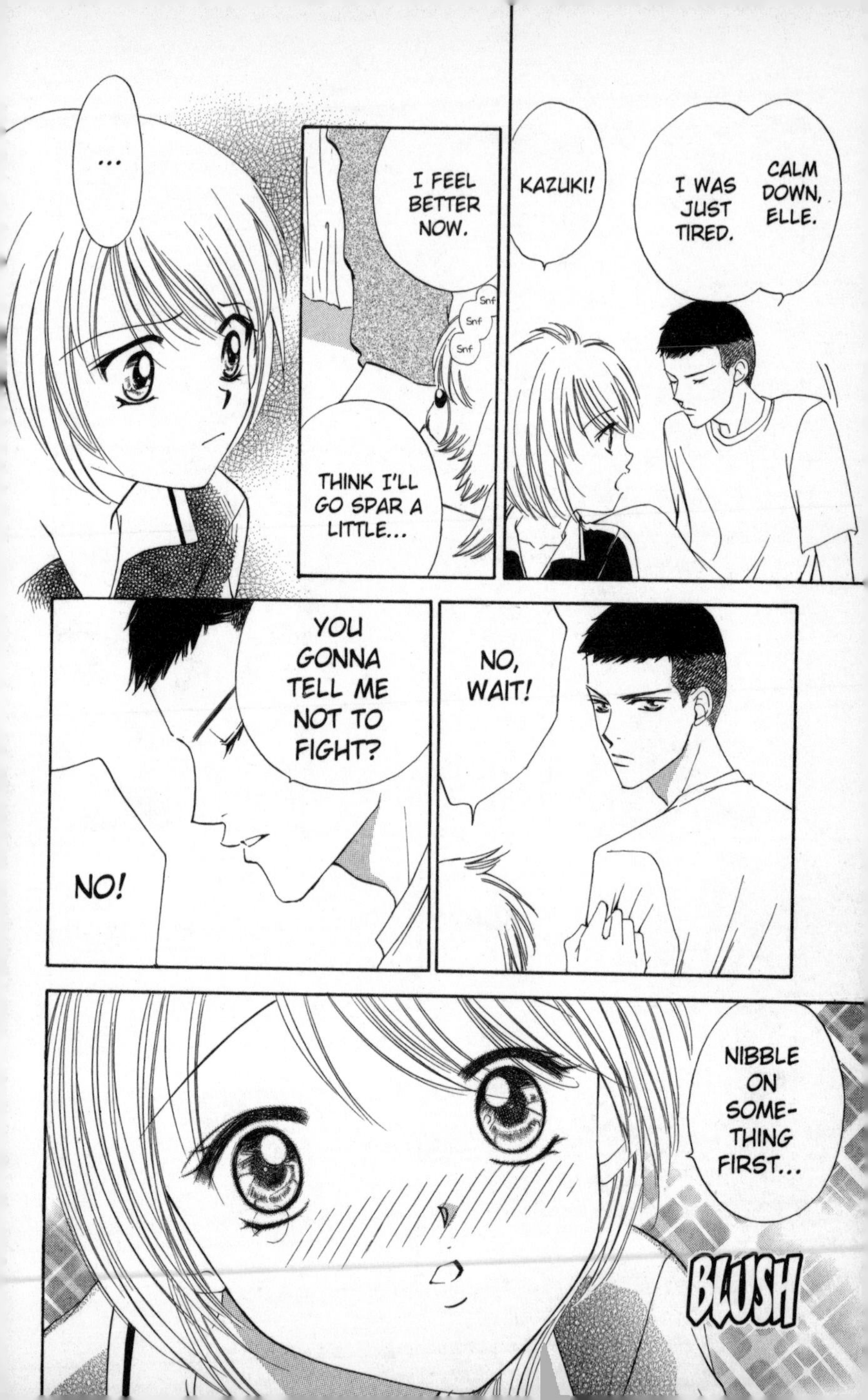
CALM DOWN, ELLE.
I WAS JUST TIRED.
KAZUKI!
I FEEL BETTER NOW.
Snf
Snf
Snf
THINK I'LL GO SPAR A LITTLE...
...
NO, WAIT!
YOU GONNA TELL ME NOT TO FIGHT?
NO!
NIBBLE ON SOMETHING FIRST...
BLUSH

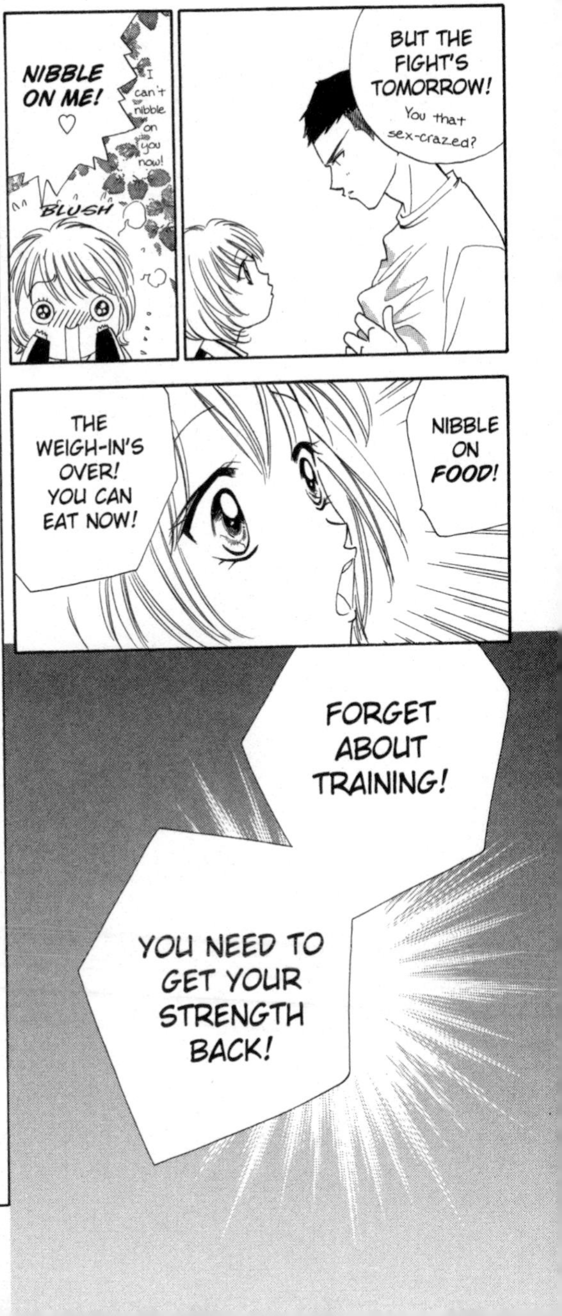
BUT THE FIGHT'S TOMORROW!
You that sex-crazed?
NIBBLE ON ME! ♡
I can't nibble on you now!
BLUSH
NIBBLE ON FOOD!
THE WEIGH-IN'S OVER! YOU CAN EAT NOW!
FORGET ABOUT TRAINING!
YOU NEED TO GET YOUR STRENGTH BACK!

When I was little, I had a strange dog...

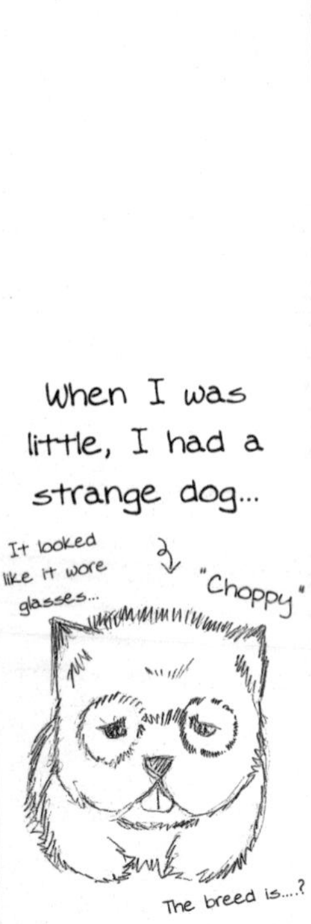
It looked like it wore glasses...
"Choppy"
The breed is....?

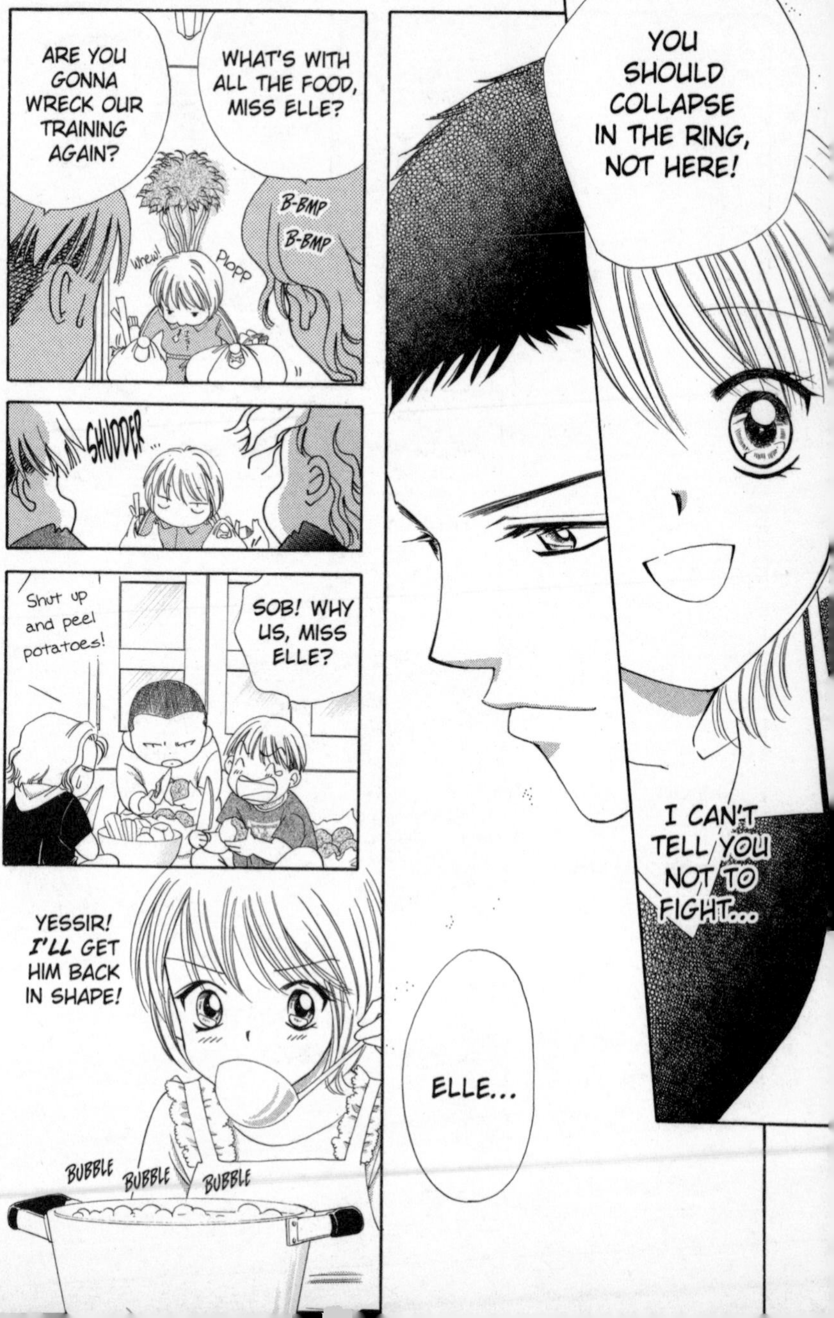
YOU SHOULD COLLAPSE IN THE RING, NOT HERE!
I CAN'T TELL YOU NOT TO FIGHT...
ELLE...
WHAT'S WITH ALL THE FOOD, MISS ELLE?
ARE YOU GONNA WRECK OUR TRAINING AGAIN?
B-BMP
B-BMP
Plopp
Whew!
SHUDDER
SOB! WHY US, MISS ELLE?
Shut up and peel potatoes!
YESSIR! *I'LL* GET HIM BACK IN SHAPE!
BUBBLE
BUBBLE
BUBBLE

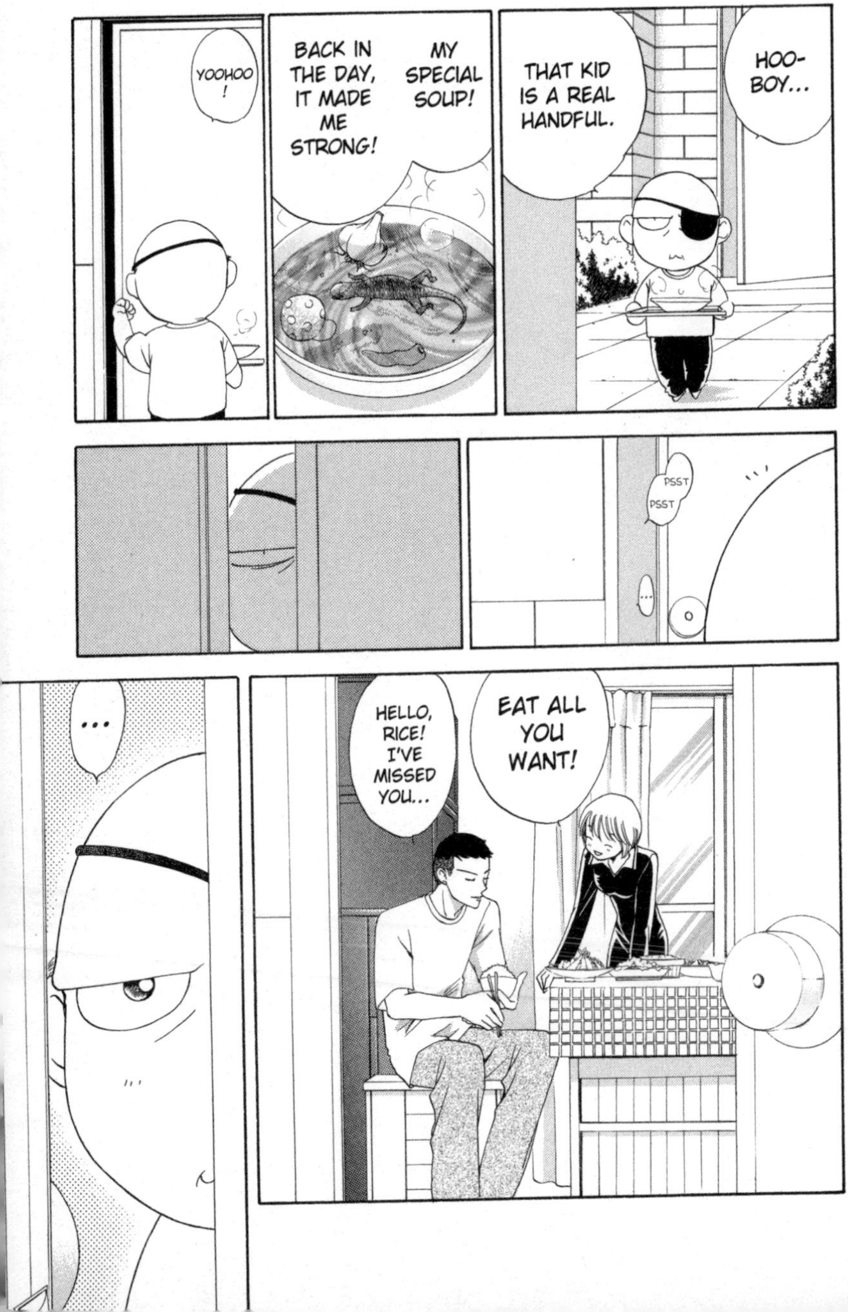
HOO-BOY...
THAT KID IS A REAL HANDFUL.
MY SPECIAL SOUP!
BACK IN THE DAY, IT MADE ME STRONG!
YOOHOO!
PSST PSST
...
EAT ALL YOU WANT!
HELLO, RICE! I'VE MISSED YOU...
...

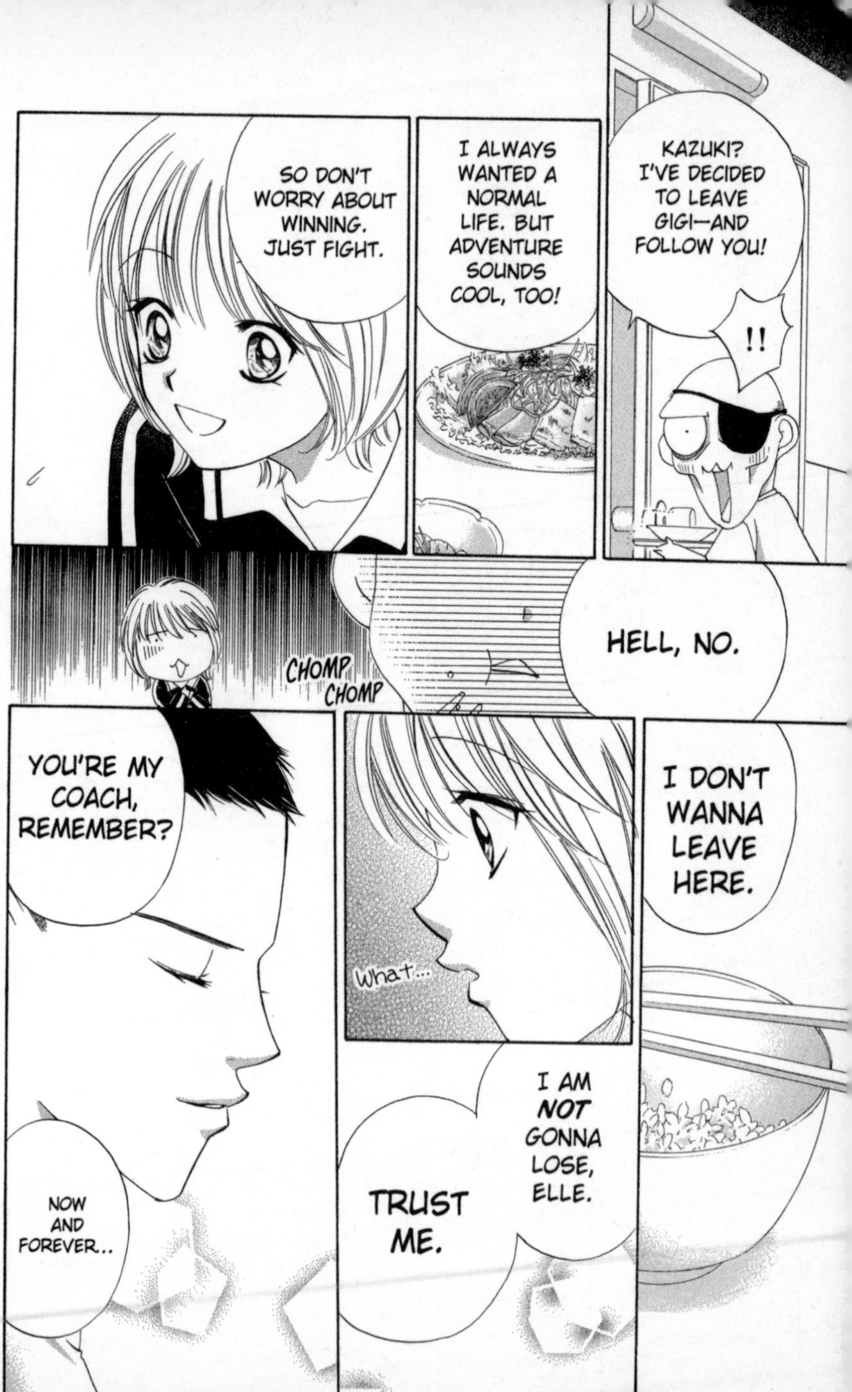
KAZUKI? I'VE DECIDED TO LEAVE GIGI—AND FOLLOW YOU!
!!
I ALWAYS WANTED A NORMAL LIFE. BUT ADVENTURE SOUNDS COOL, TOO!
SO DON'T WORRY ABOUT WINNING. JUST FIGHT.
HELL, NO.
CHOMP CHOMP
I DON'T WANNA LEAVE HERE.
What...
I AM NOT GONNA LOSE, ELLE.
TRUST ME.
YOU'RE MY COACH, REMEMBER?
NOW AND FOREVER...

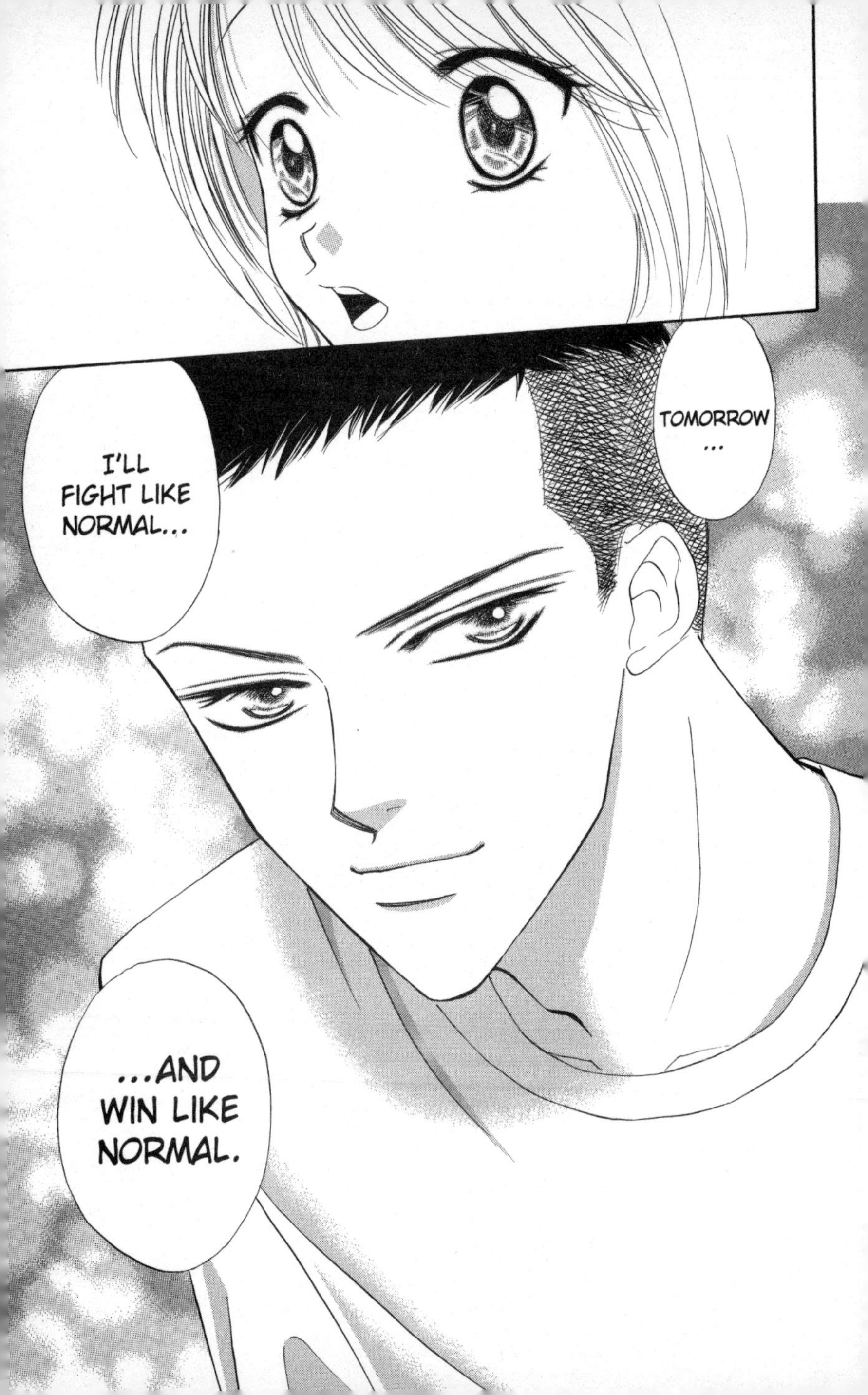
TOMORROW ...
I'LL FIGHT LIKE NORMAL...
...AND WIN LIKE NORMAL.

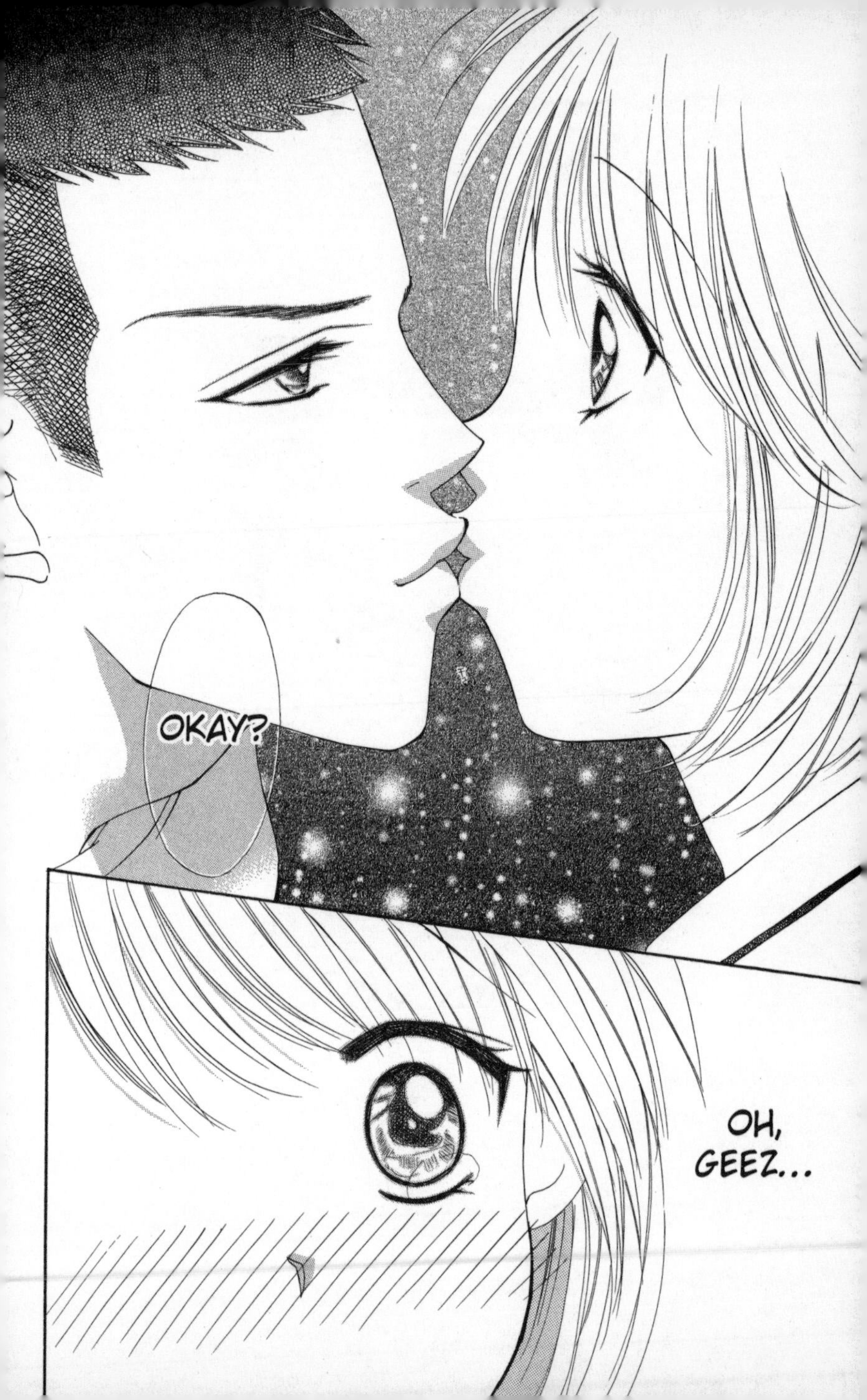
OKAY?
OH, GEEZ...

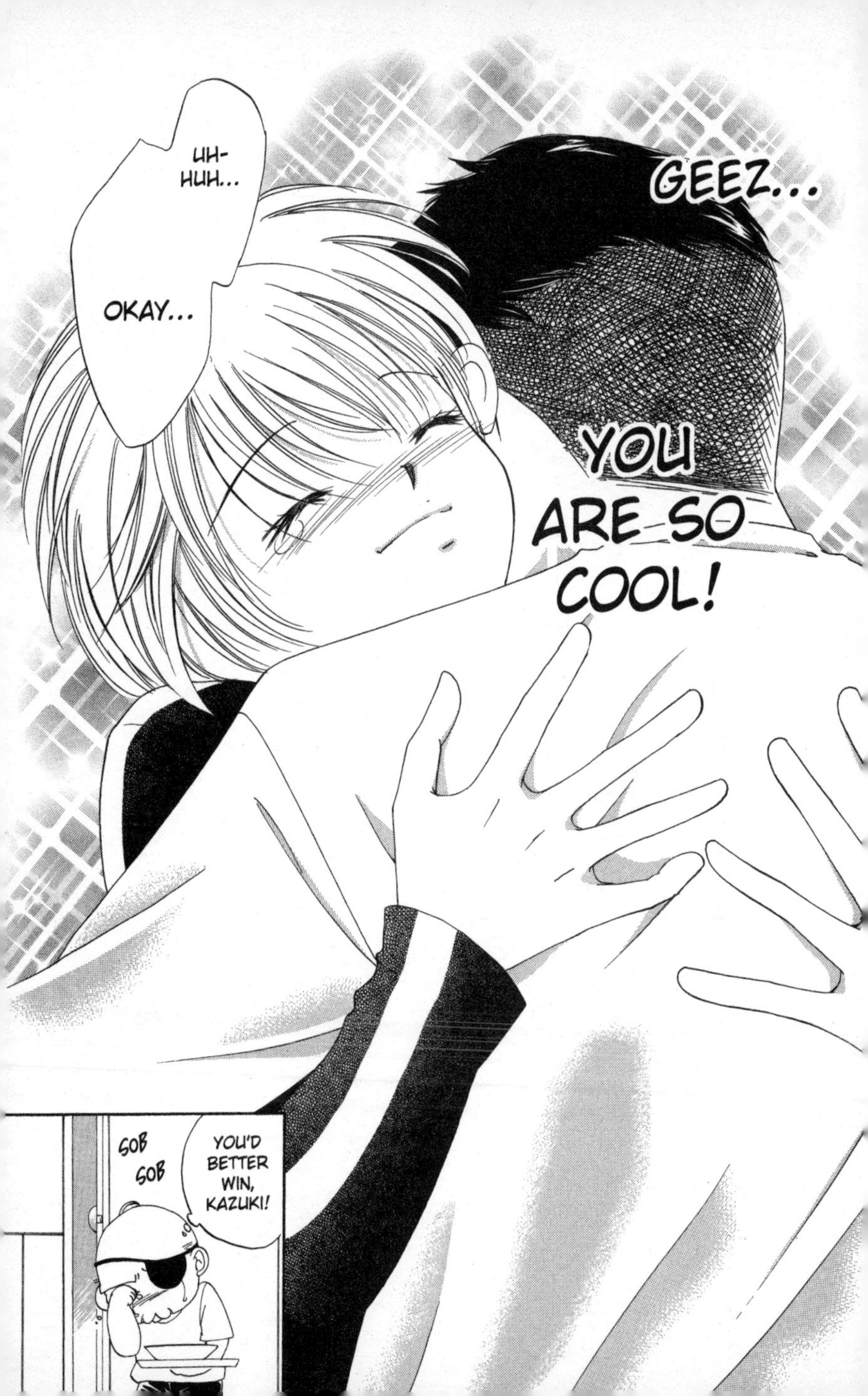
GEEZ... YOU ARE SO COOL!
UH-HUH... OKAY...
YOU'D BETTER WIN, KAZUKI!
SOB SOB

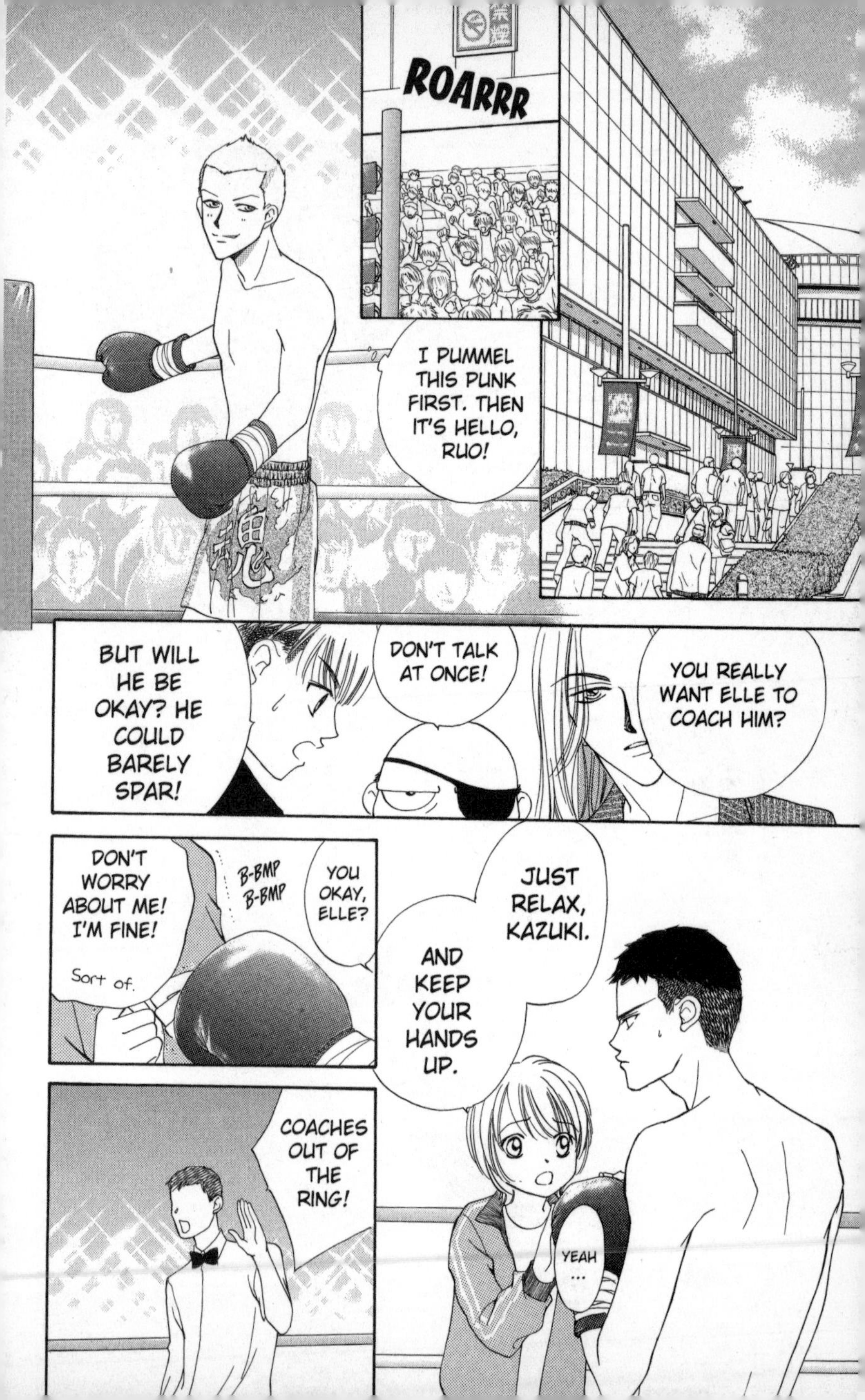
ROARRR
I PUMMEL THIS PUNK FIRST. THEN IT'S HELLO, RUO!
YOU REALLY WANT ELLE TO COACH HIM?
DON'T TALK AT ONCE!
BUT WILL HE BE OKAY? HE COULD BARELY SPAR!
JUST RELAX, KAZUKI.
AND KEEP YOUR HANDS UP.
YEAH ...
YOU OKAY, ELLE?
B-BMP B-BMP
DON'T WORRY ABOUT ME! I'M FINE!
Sort of.
COACHES OUT OF THE RING!

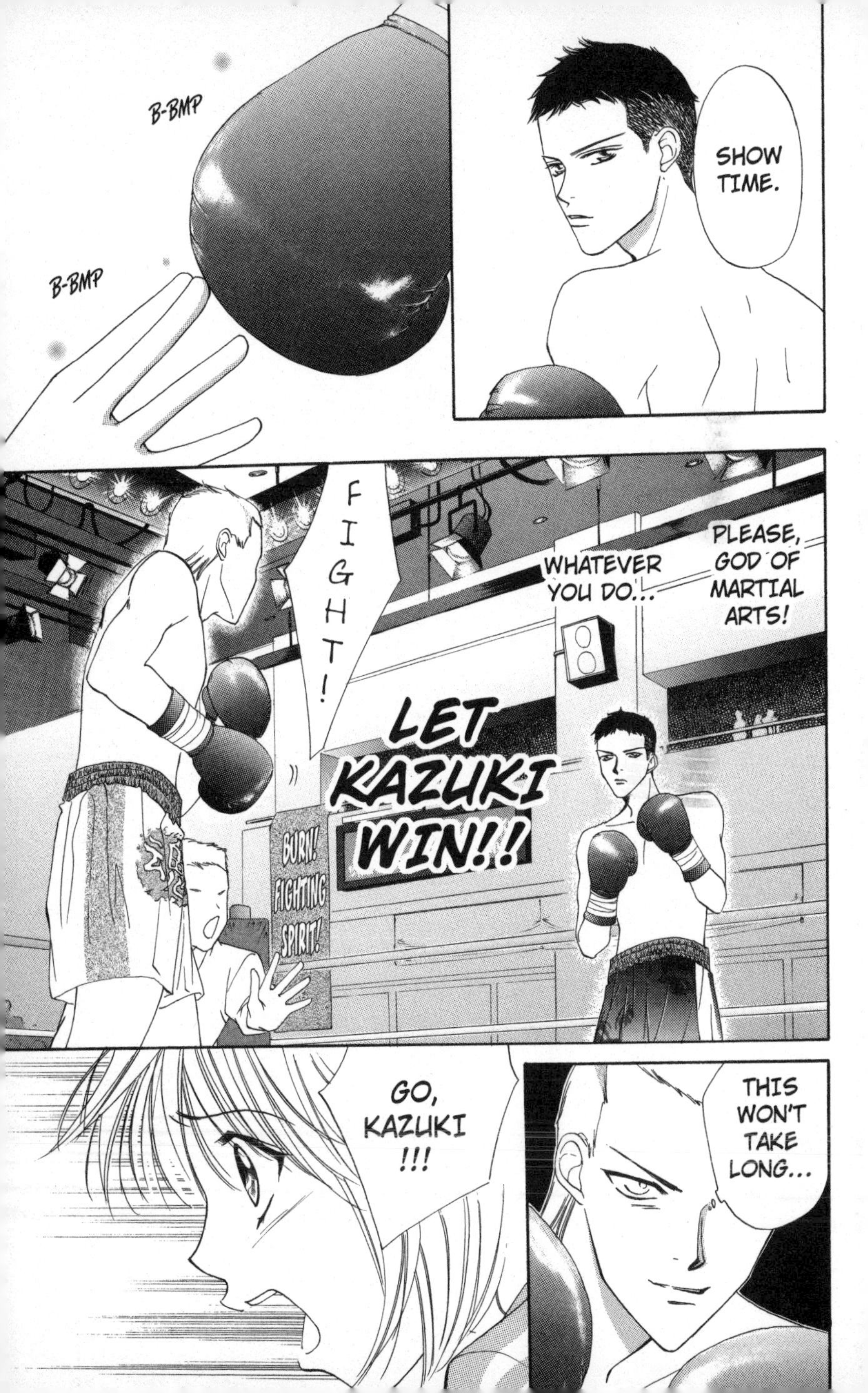
SHOW TIME.
B-BMP
B-BMP
PLEASE, GOD OF MARTIAL ARTS!
WHATEVER YOU DO...
LET KAZUKI WIN!!
FIGHT!
BURN! FIGHTING SPIRIT!
THIS WON'T TAKE LONG...
GO, KAZUKI!!!

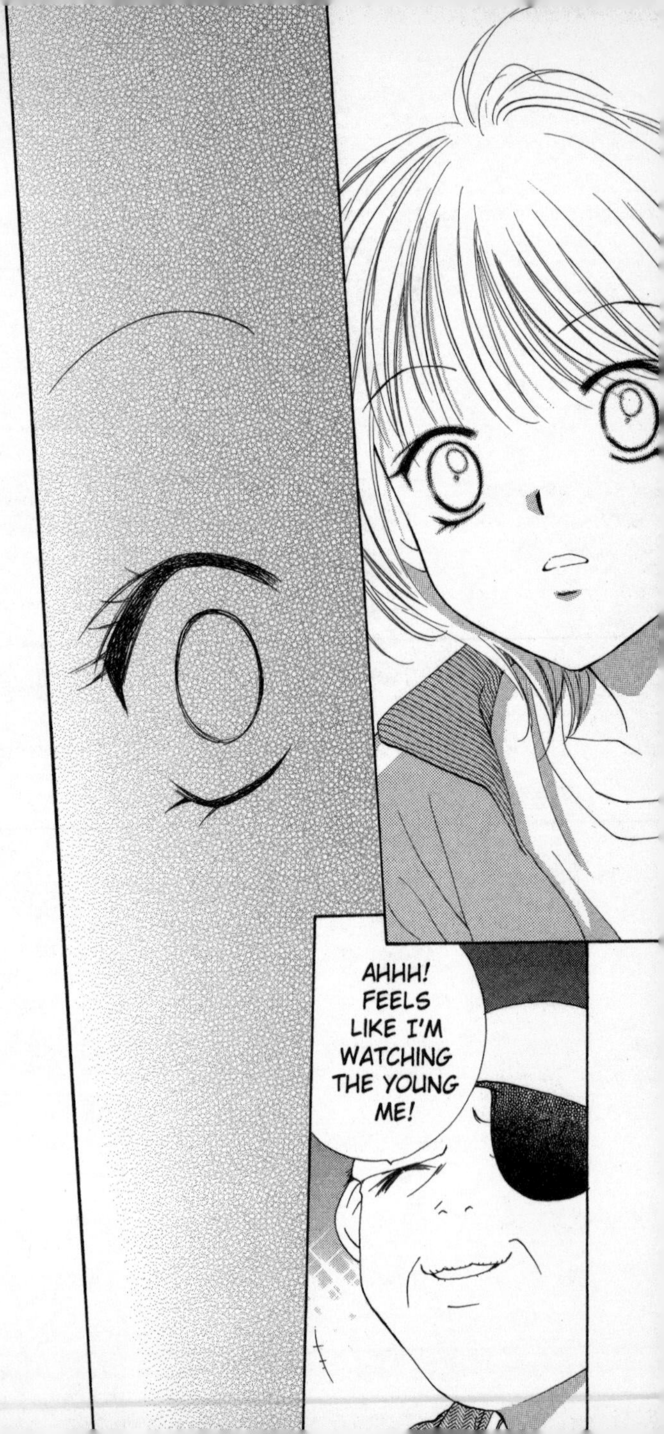
AHHH! FEELS LIKE I'M WATCHING THE YOUNG ME!

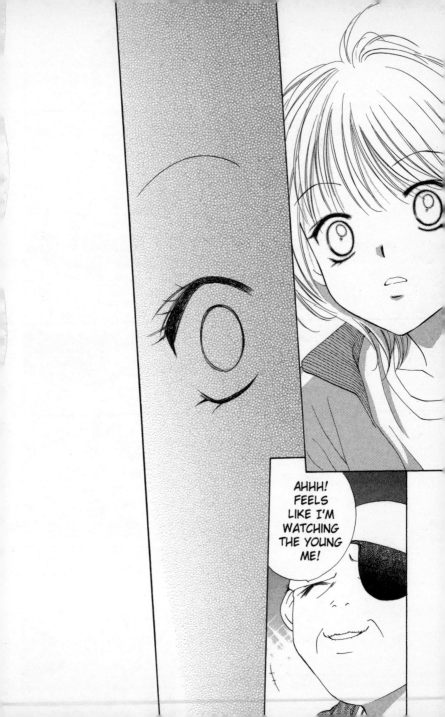

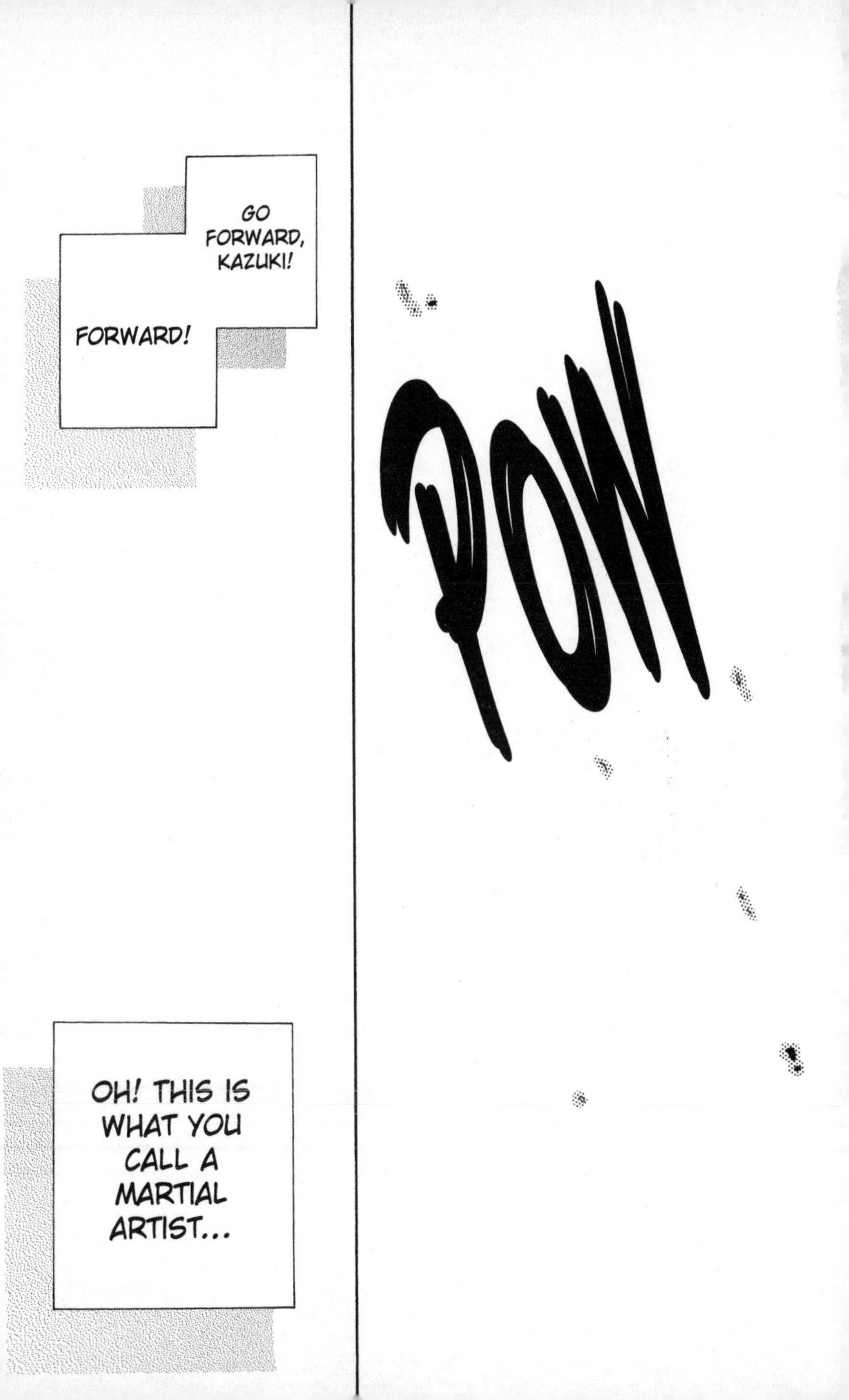
POW
GO FORWARD, KAZUKI!
FORWARD!
OH! THIS IS WHAT YOU CALL A MARTIAL ARTIST...

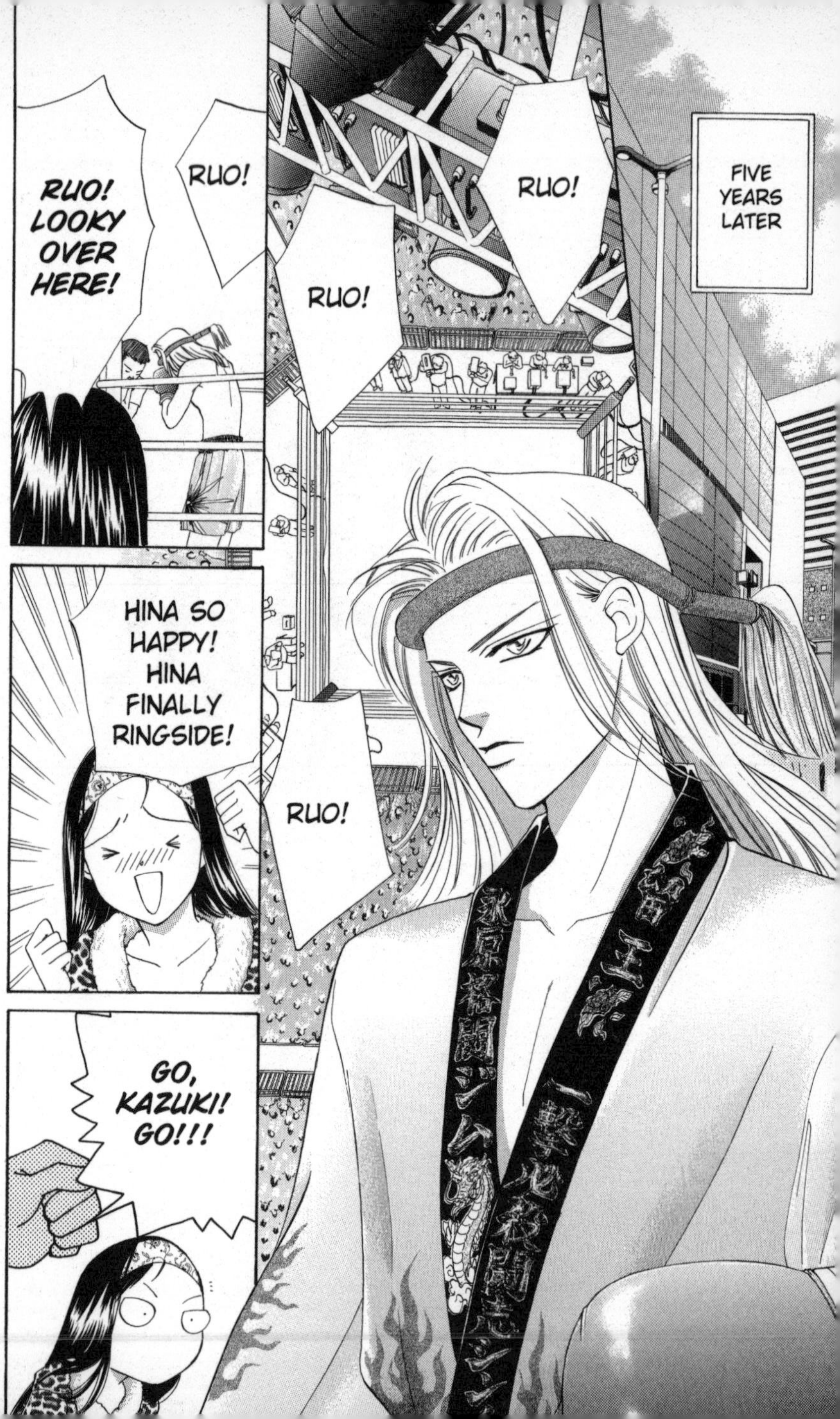
FIVE YEARS LATER
RUO!
RUO!
RUO!
RUO!
RUO! LOOKY OVER HERE!
HINA SO HAPPY! HINA FINALLY RINGSIDE!
GO, KAZUKI! GO!!!

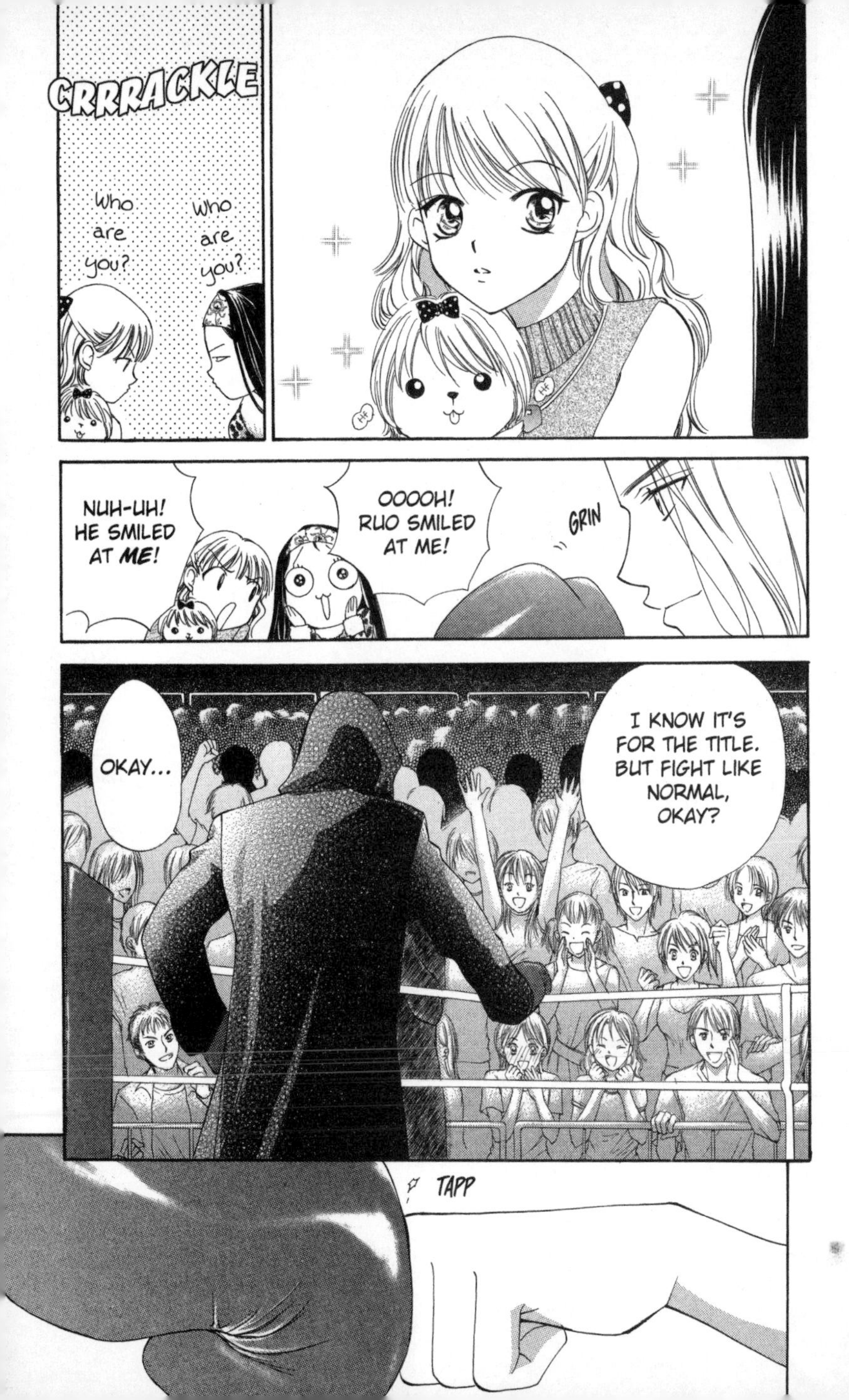
CRRRACKLE
Who are you?
Who are you?
GRIN
OOOOH! RUO SMILED AT ME!
NUH-UH! HE SMILED AT ME!
I KNOW IT'S FOR THE TITLE. BUT FIGHT LIKE NORMAL, OKAY?
OKAY...
TAPP

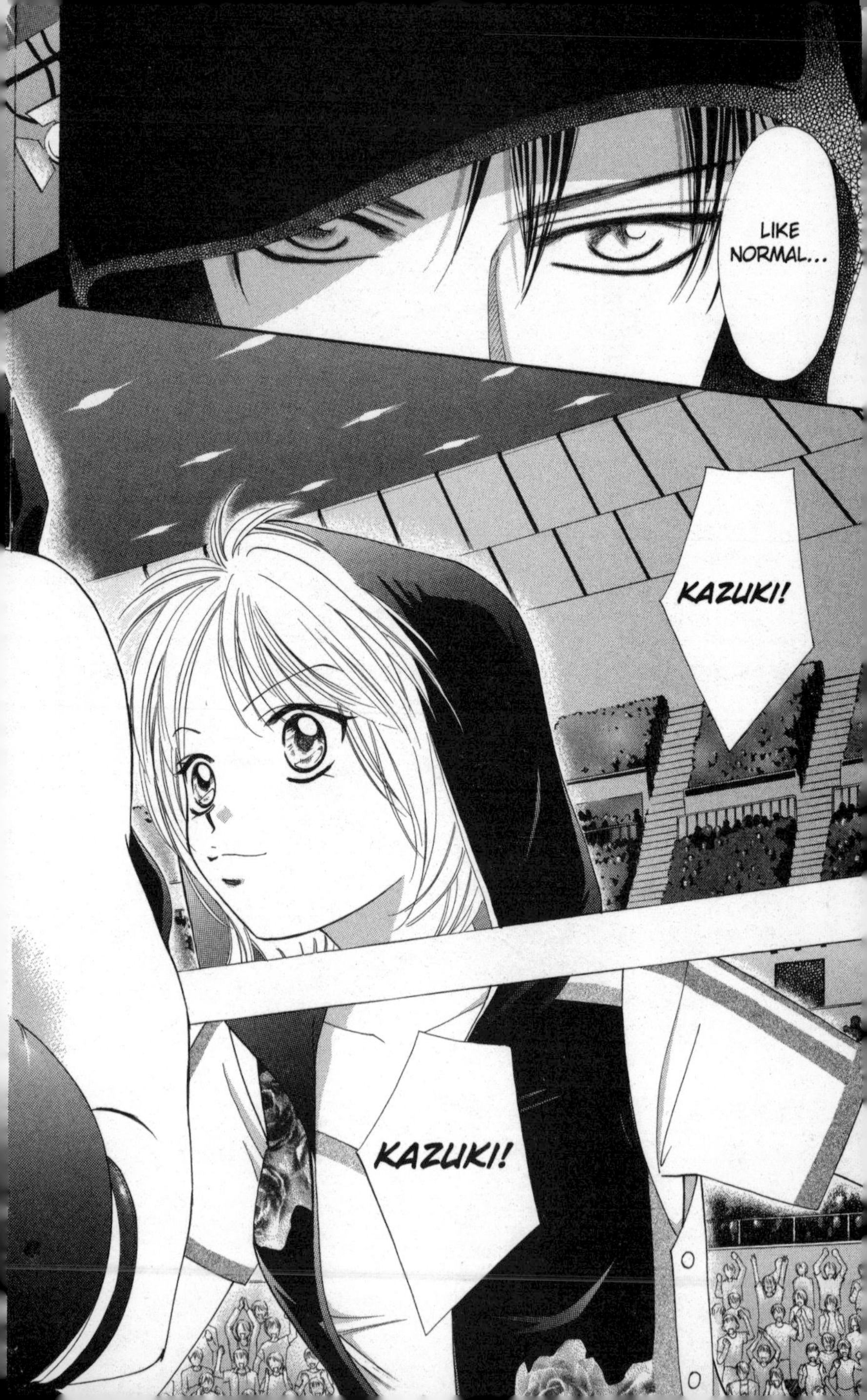
LIKE NORMAL...
KAZUKI!
KAZUKI!

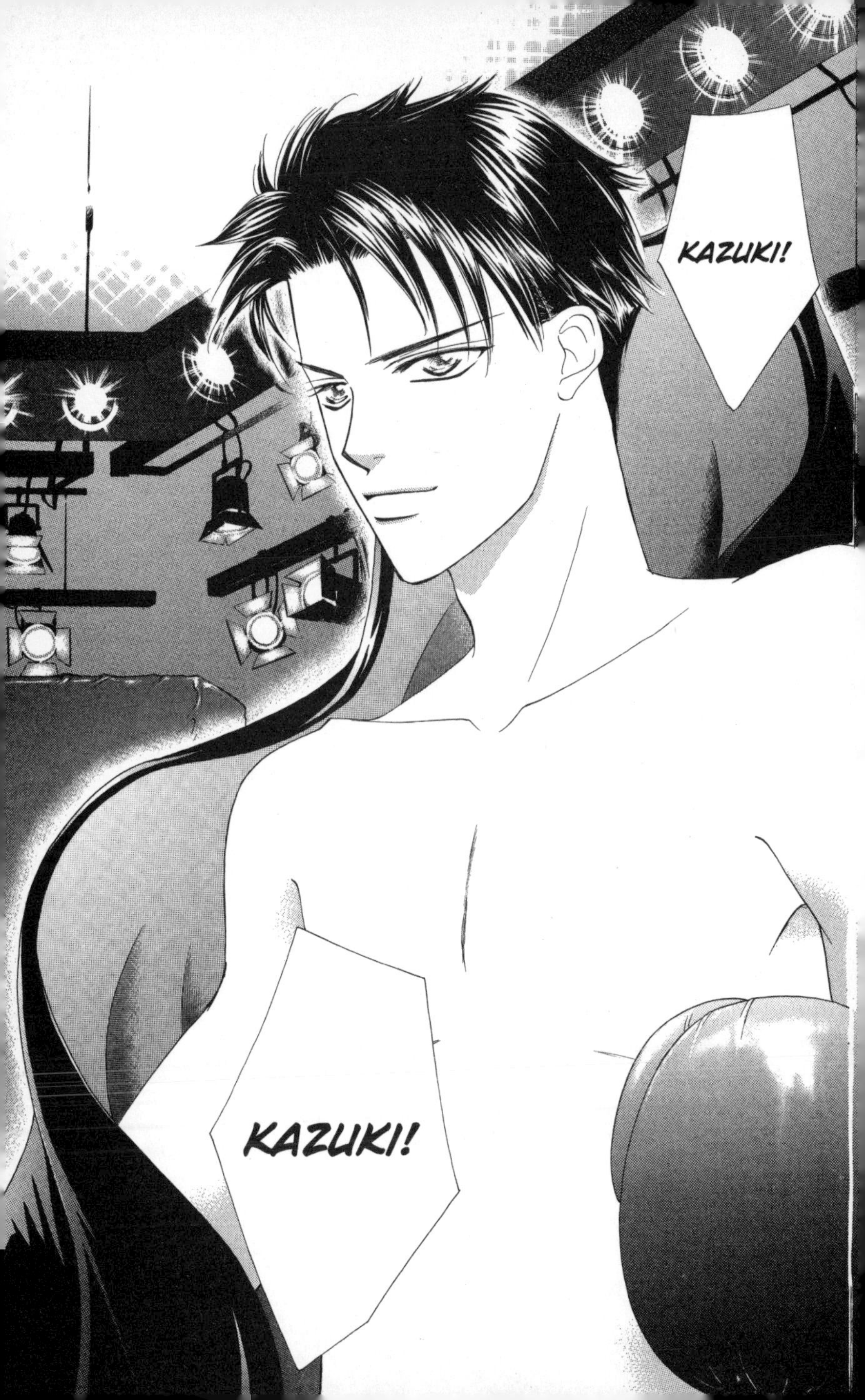
KAZUKI!
KAZUKI!

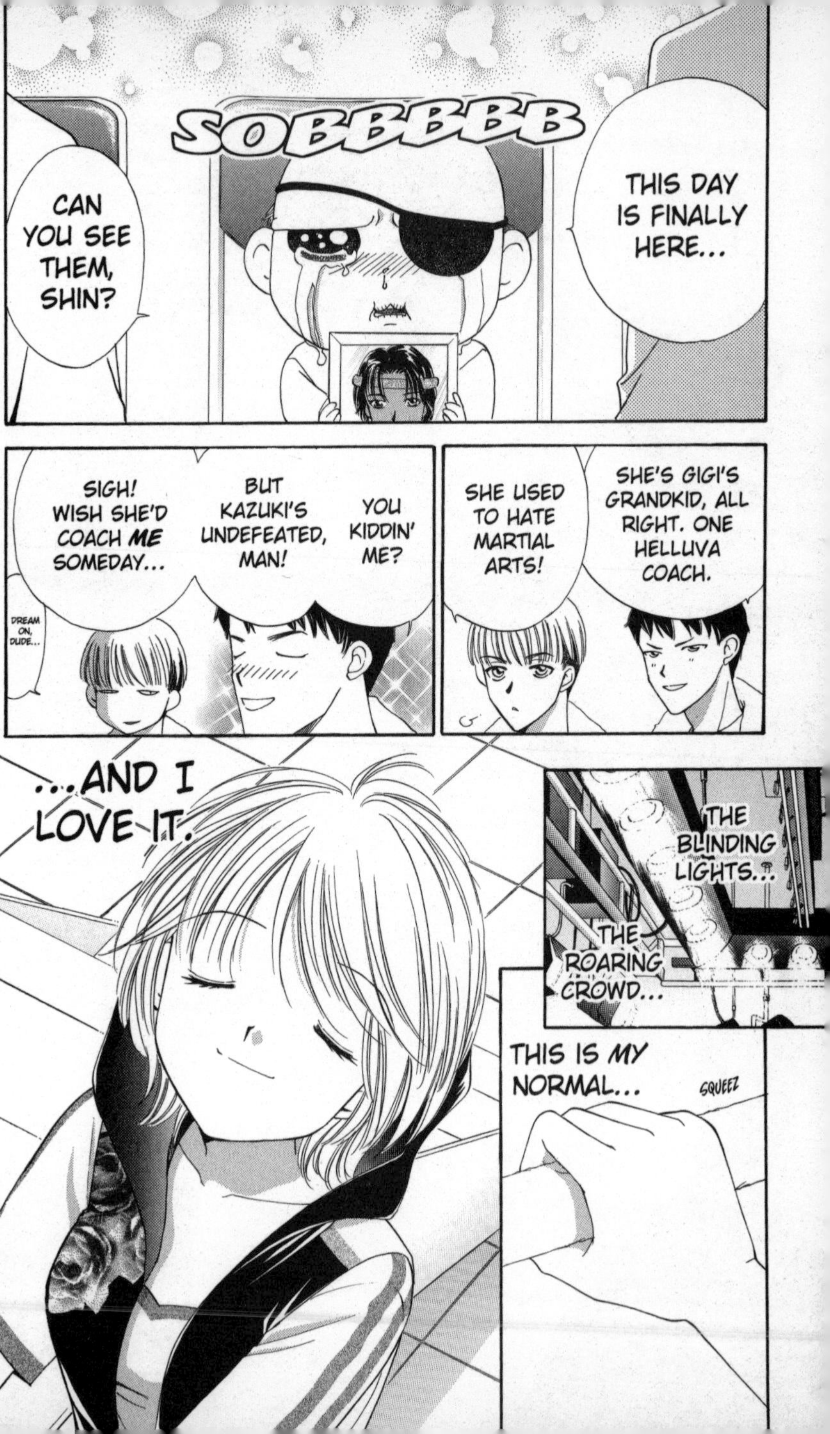
THIS DAY IS FINALLY HERE...
SOBBBBB
CAN YOU SEE THEM, SHIN?
SHE'S GIGI'S GRANDKID, ALL RIGHT. ONE HELLUVA COACH.
SHE USED TO HATE MARTIAL ARTS!
YOU KIDDIN' ME?
BUT KAZUKI'S UNDEFEATED, MAN!
SIGH! WISH SHE'D COACH *ME* SOMEDAY...
DREAM ON, DUDE...
THE BLINDING LIGHTS...
THE ROARING CROWD...
THIS IS *MY* NORMAL...
SQUEEZ
...AND I LOVE IT.

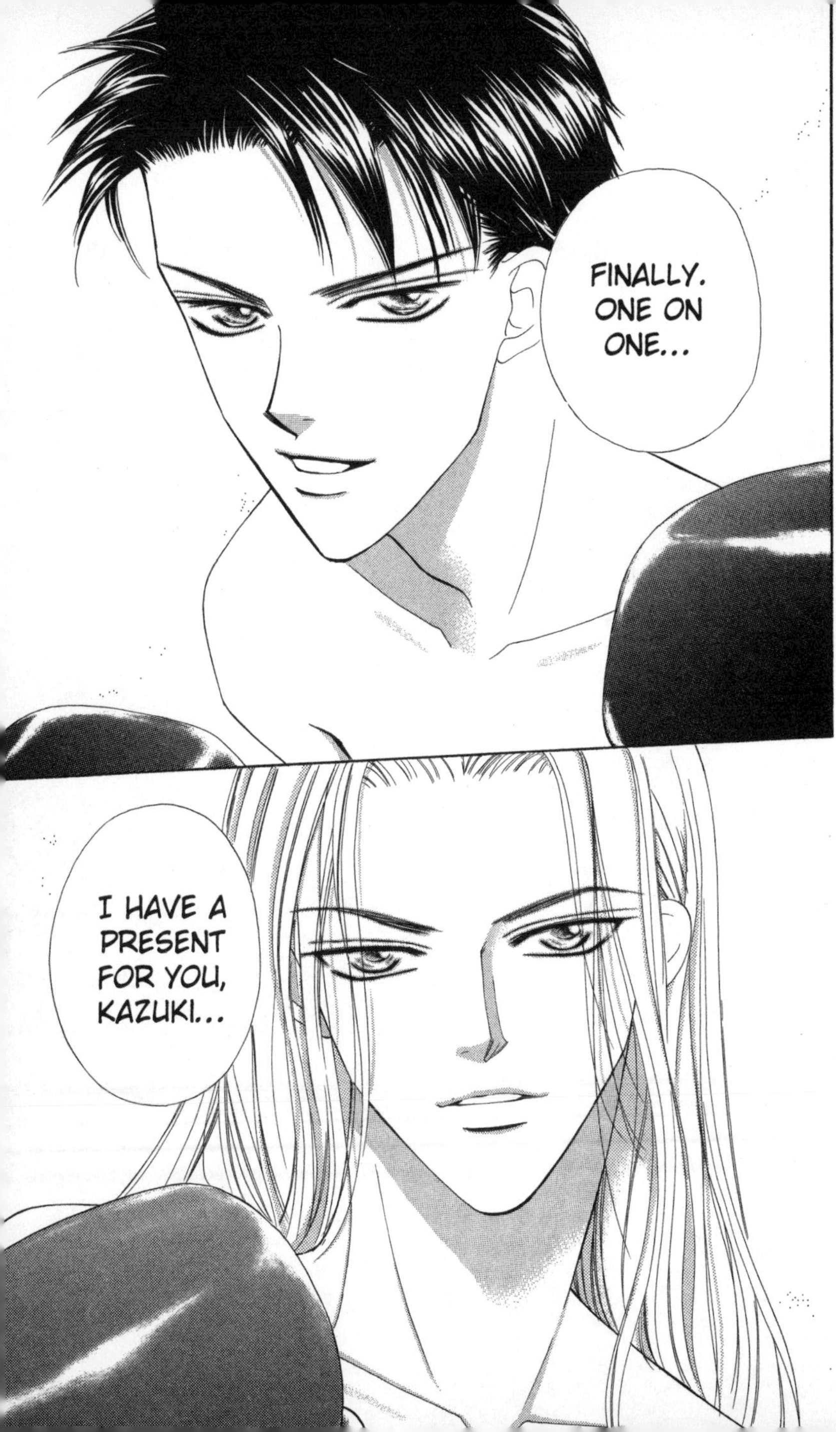
FINALLY. ONE ON ONE...
I HAVE A PRESENT FOR YOU, KAZUKI...

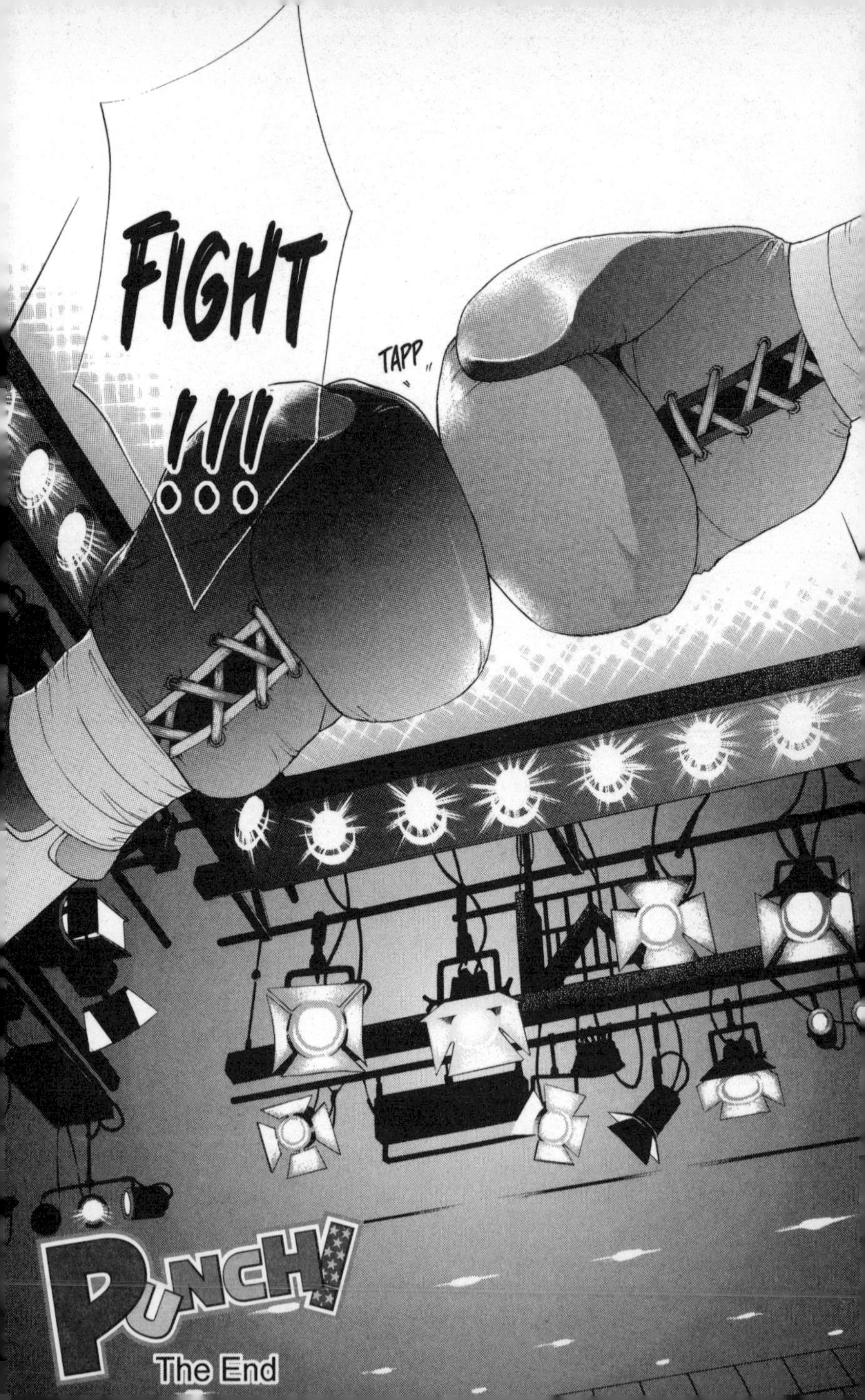
FIGHT!!!
TAPP
PUNCH!
The End

Whenever we
went for a walk...
People asked,
"Is that a fox?"
For sixteen years,
it only listened
to me.

↓

"Fuki"
was a
mutt.

We
ate
pork
buns
together.

PUNCH!

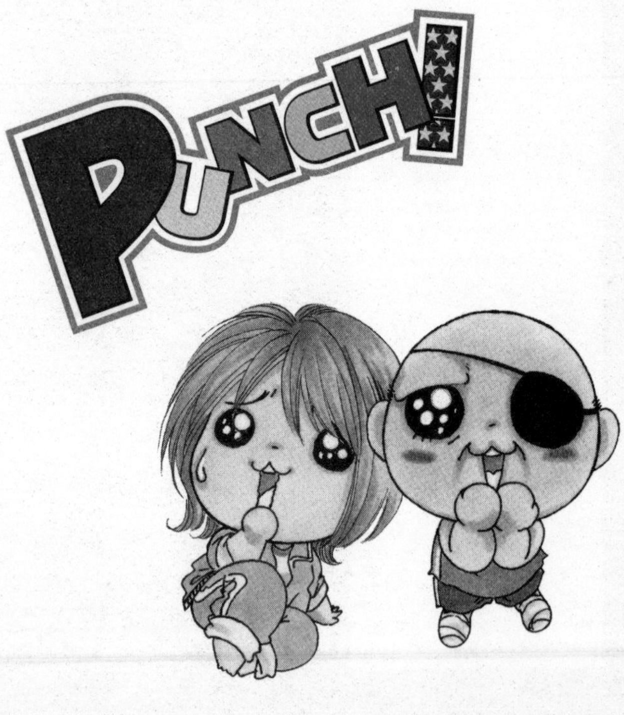

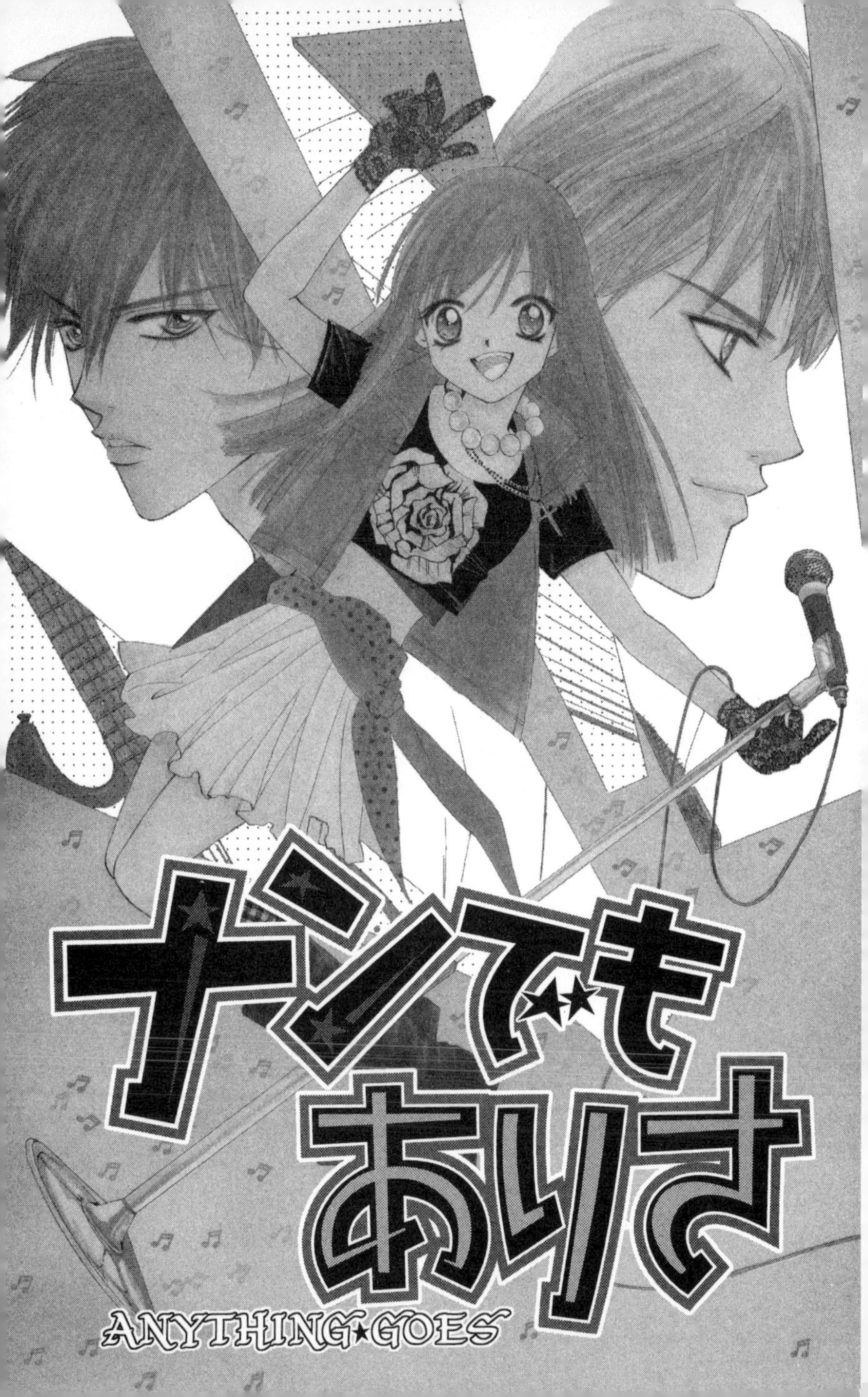
ナンでもあり☆さ
ANYTHING★GOES

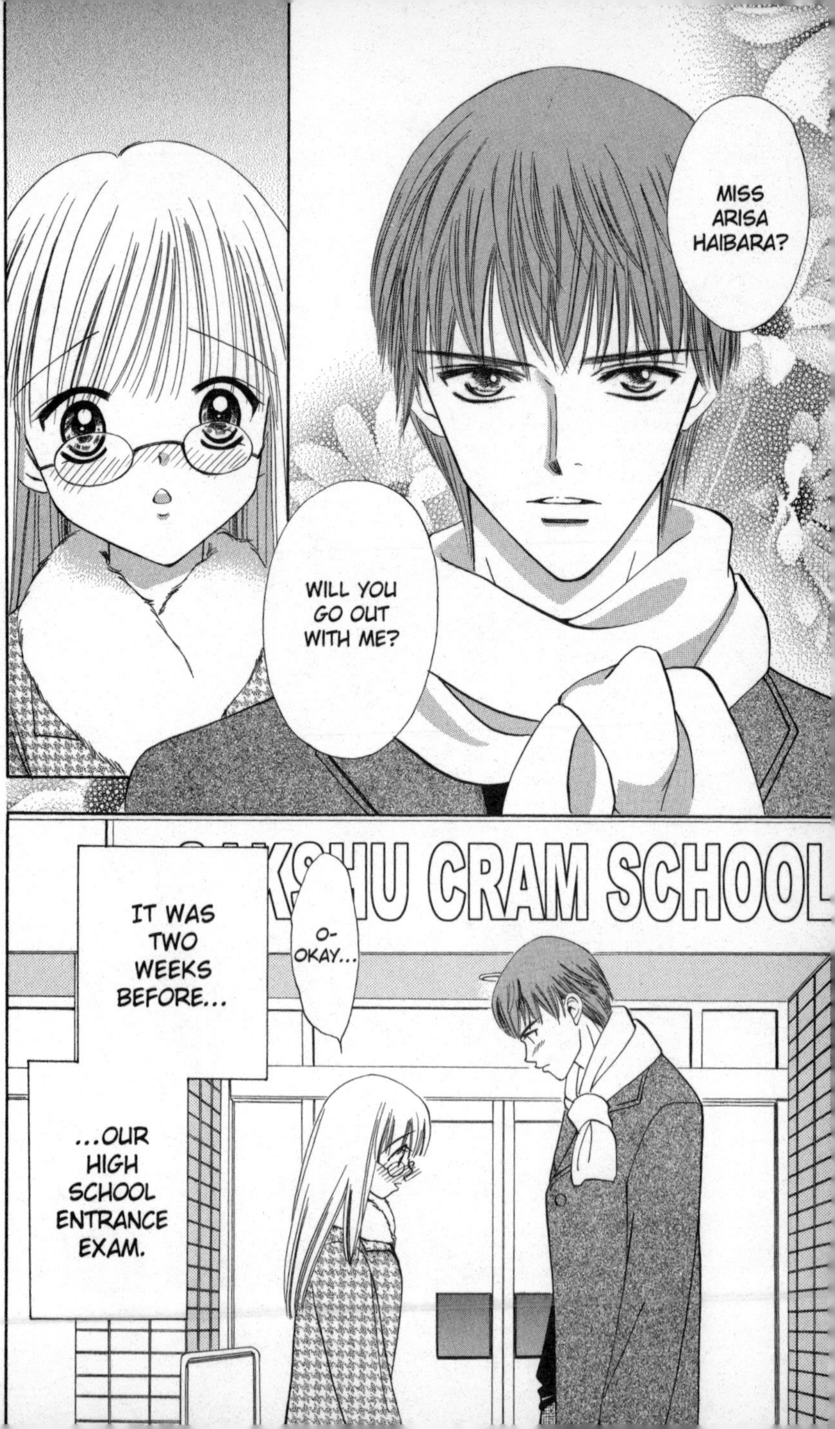
MISS ARISA HAIBARA?
WILL YOU GO OUT WITH ME?
KSHU CRAM SCHOOL
O-OKAY...
IT WAS TWO WEEKS BEFORE...
...OUR HIGH SCHOOL ENTRANCE EXAM.

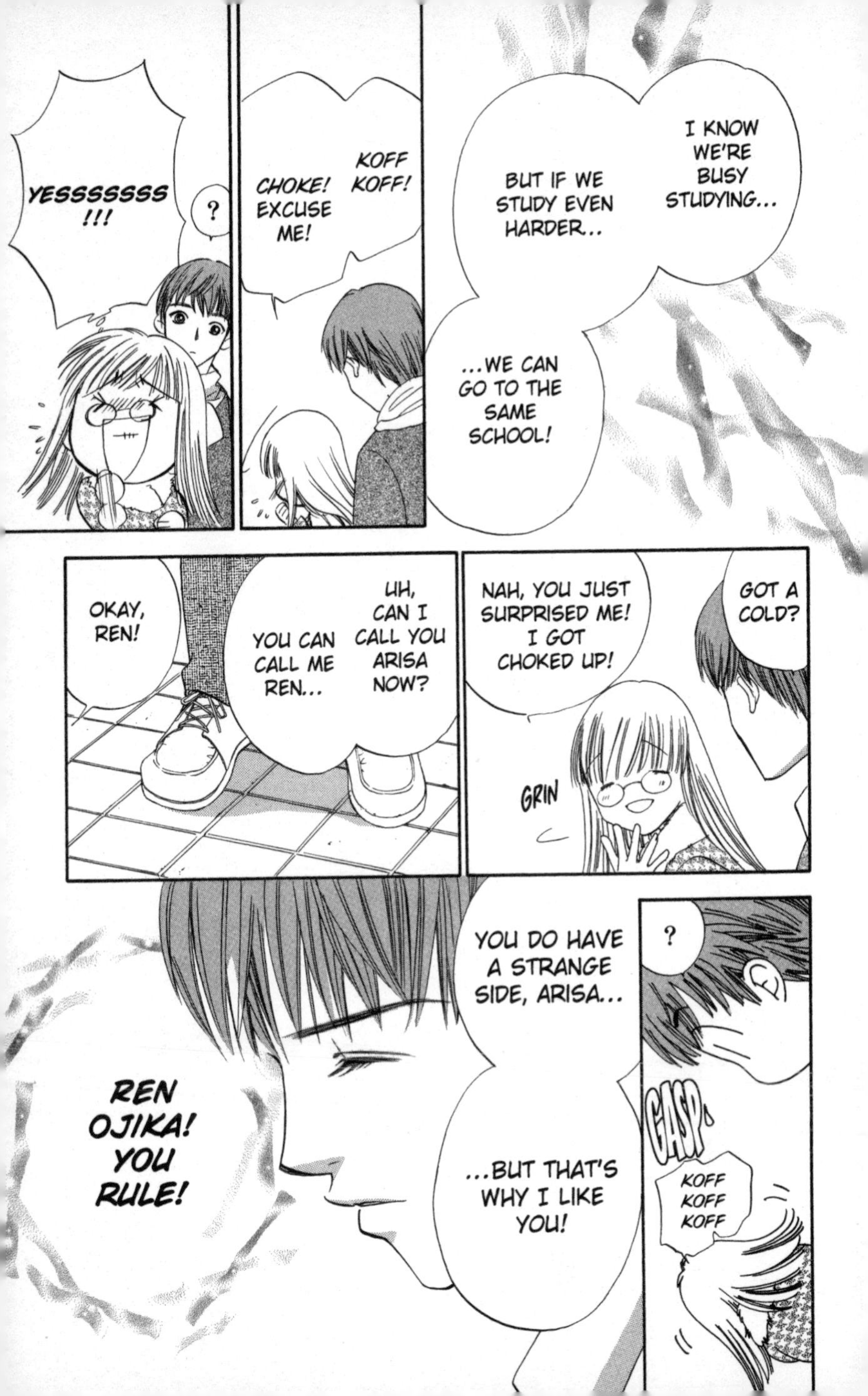
I KNOW WE'RE BUSY STUDYING...
BUT IF WE STUDY EVEN HARDER...
...WE CAN GO TO THE SAME SCHOOL!
KOFF KOFF!
CHOKE! EXCUSE ME!
YESSSSSSS !!!
?
GOT A COLD?
NAH, YOU JUST SURPRISED ME! I GOT CHOKED UP!
GRIN
UH, CAN I CALL YOU ARISA NOW?
YOU CAN CALL ME REN...
OKAY, REN!
?
GASP
KOFF KOFF KOFF
YOU DO HAVE A STRANGE SIDE, ARISA...
...BUT THAT'S WHY I LIKE YOU!
REN OJIKA! YOU RULE!

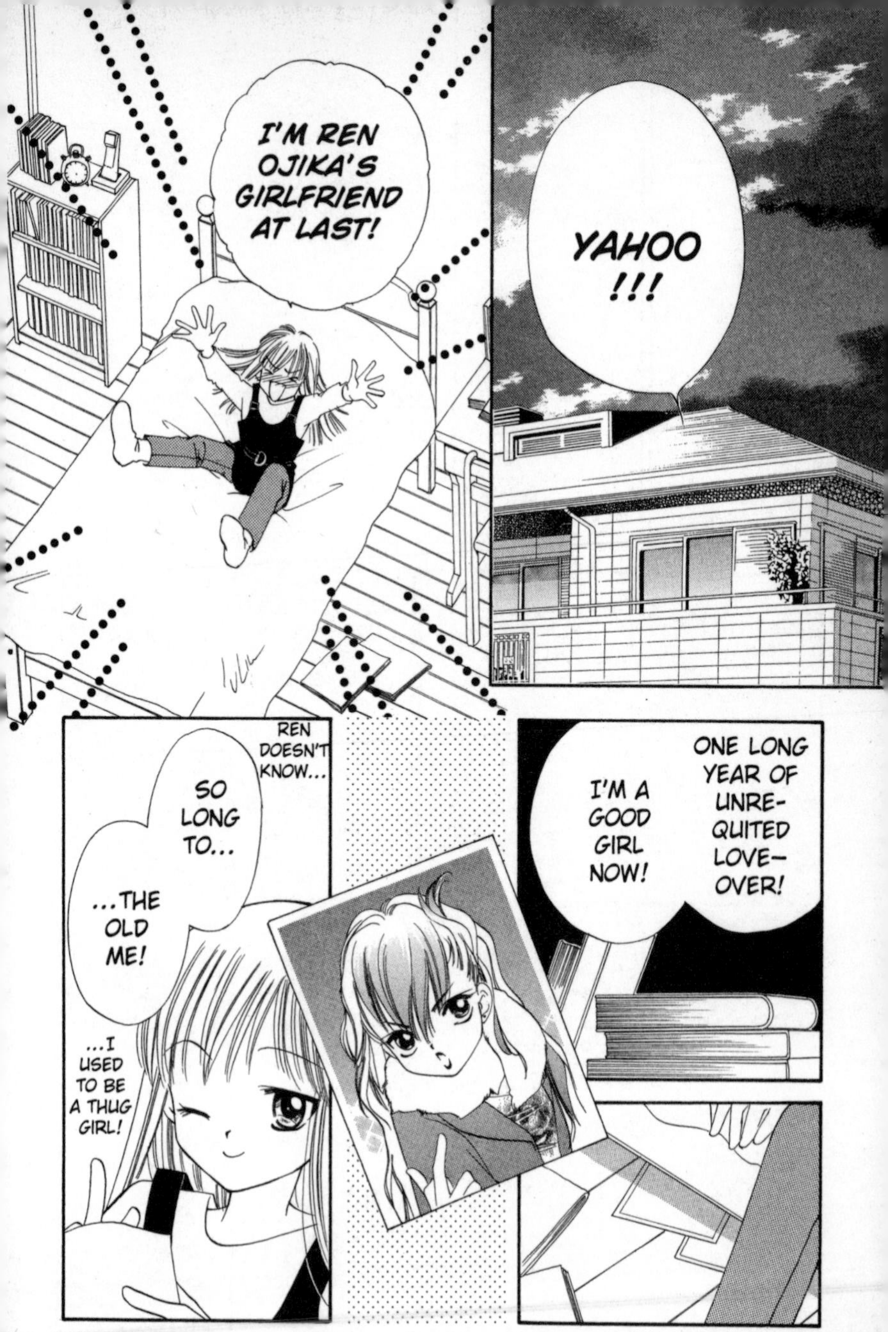
YAHOO !!!
I'M REN OJIKA'S GIRLFRIEND AT LAST!
ONE LONG YEAR OF UNRE-QUITED LOVE—OVER!
I'M A GOOD GIRL NOW!
REN DOESN'T KNOW...
SO LONG TO...
...THE OLD ME!
...I USED TO BE A THUG GIRL!

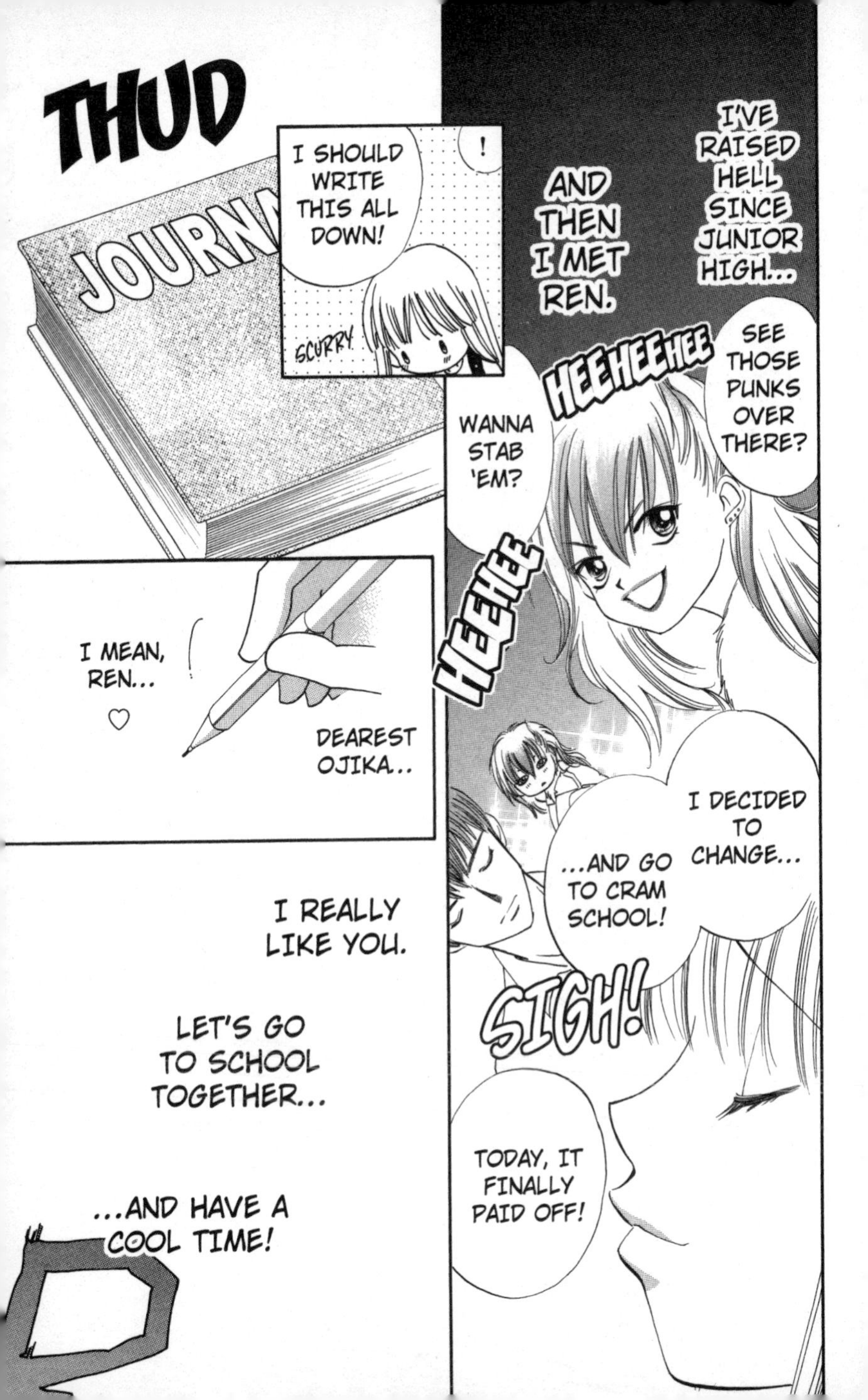

I'VE RAISED HELL SINCE JUNIOR HIGH...
AND THEN I MET REN.
SEE THOSE PUNKS OVER THERE?
HEEHEEHEE
WANNA STAB 'EM?
HEEHEE
I DECIDED TO CHANGE...
...AND GO TO CRAM SCHOOL!
SIGH!
TODAY, IT FINALLY PAID OFF!
!
I SHOULD WRITE THIS ALL DOWN!
SCURRY
THUD
JOURN
DEAREST OJIKA...
I MEAN, REN... ♡
I REALLY LIKE YOU.
LET'S GO TO SCHOOL TOGETHER...
...AND HAVE A COOL TIME!

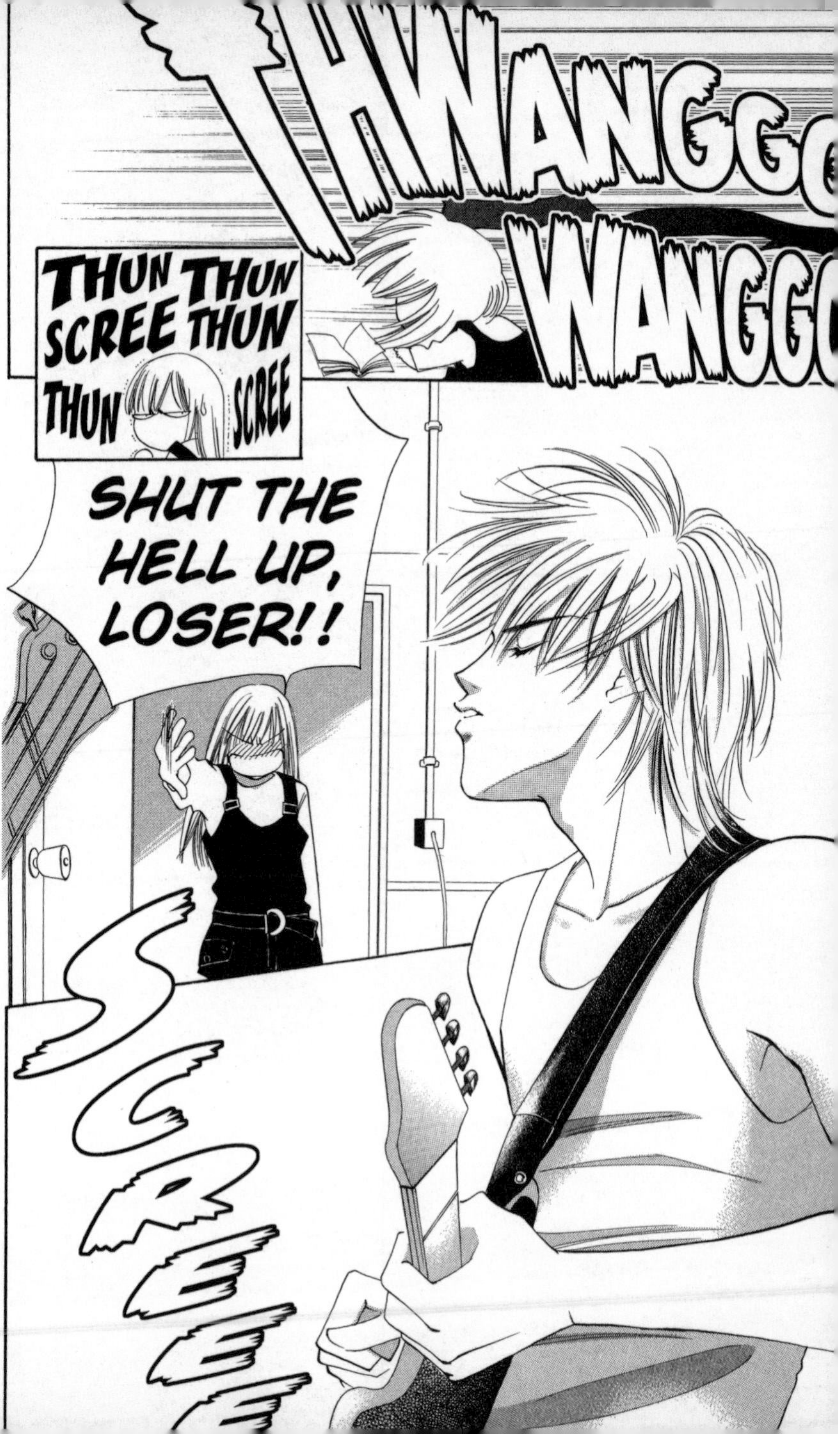
THWANGG
WANGG
THUN THUN
SCREE THUN
THUN SCREE
SHUT THE HELL UP, LOSER!!
SCREEE

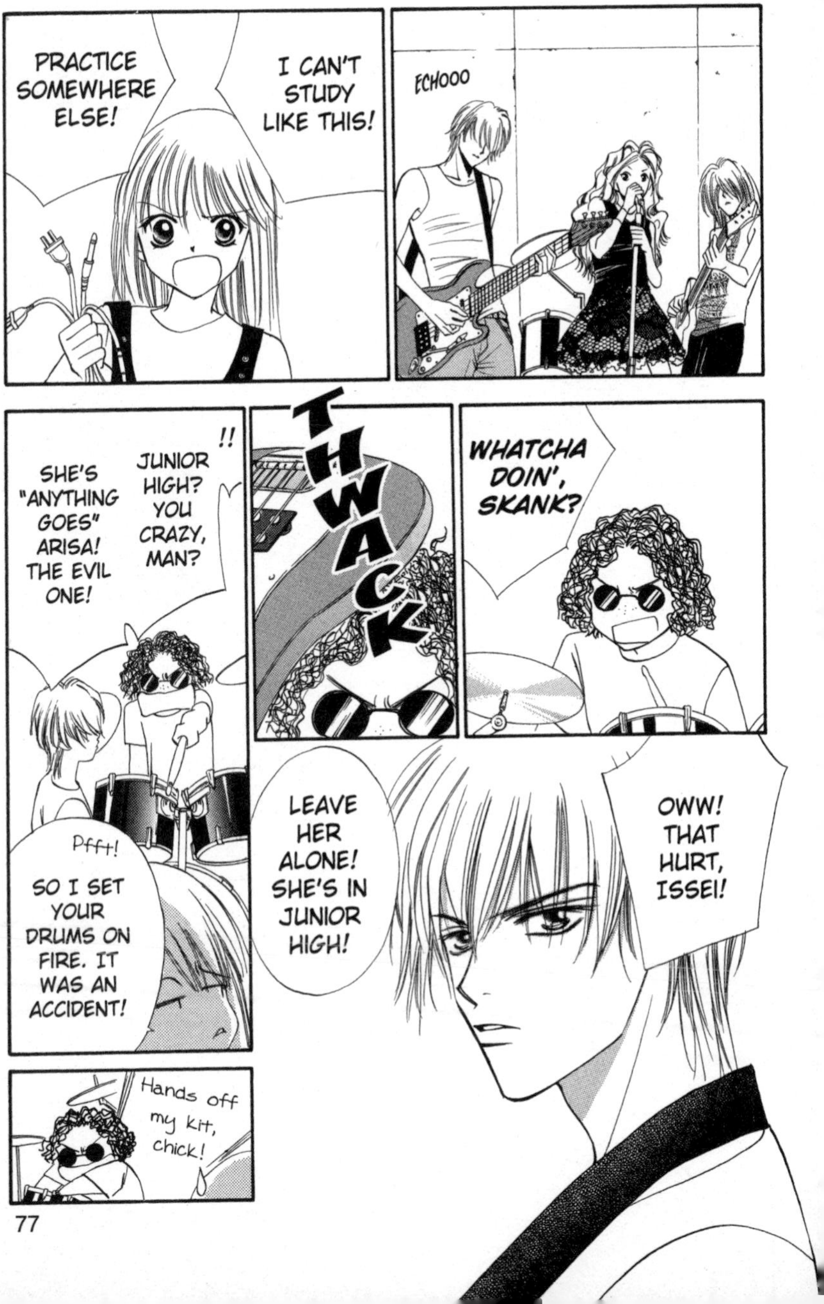
ECHOOO
I CAN'T STUDY LIKE THIS!
PRACTICE SOMEWHERE ELSE!
WHATCHA DOIN', SKANK?
THWACK
OWW! THAT HURT, ISSEI!
LEAVE HER ALONE! SHE'S IN JUNIOR HIGH!
!!
JUNIOR HIGH? YOU CRAZY, MAN?
SHE'S "ANYTHING GOES" ARISA! THE EVIL ONE!
Pfft!
SO I SET YOUR DRUMS ON FIRE. IT WAS AN ACCIDENT!
Hands off my kit, chick!

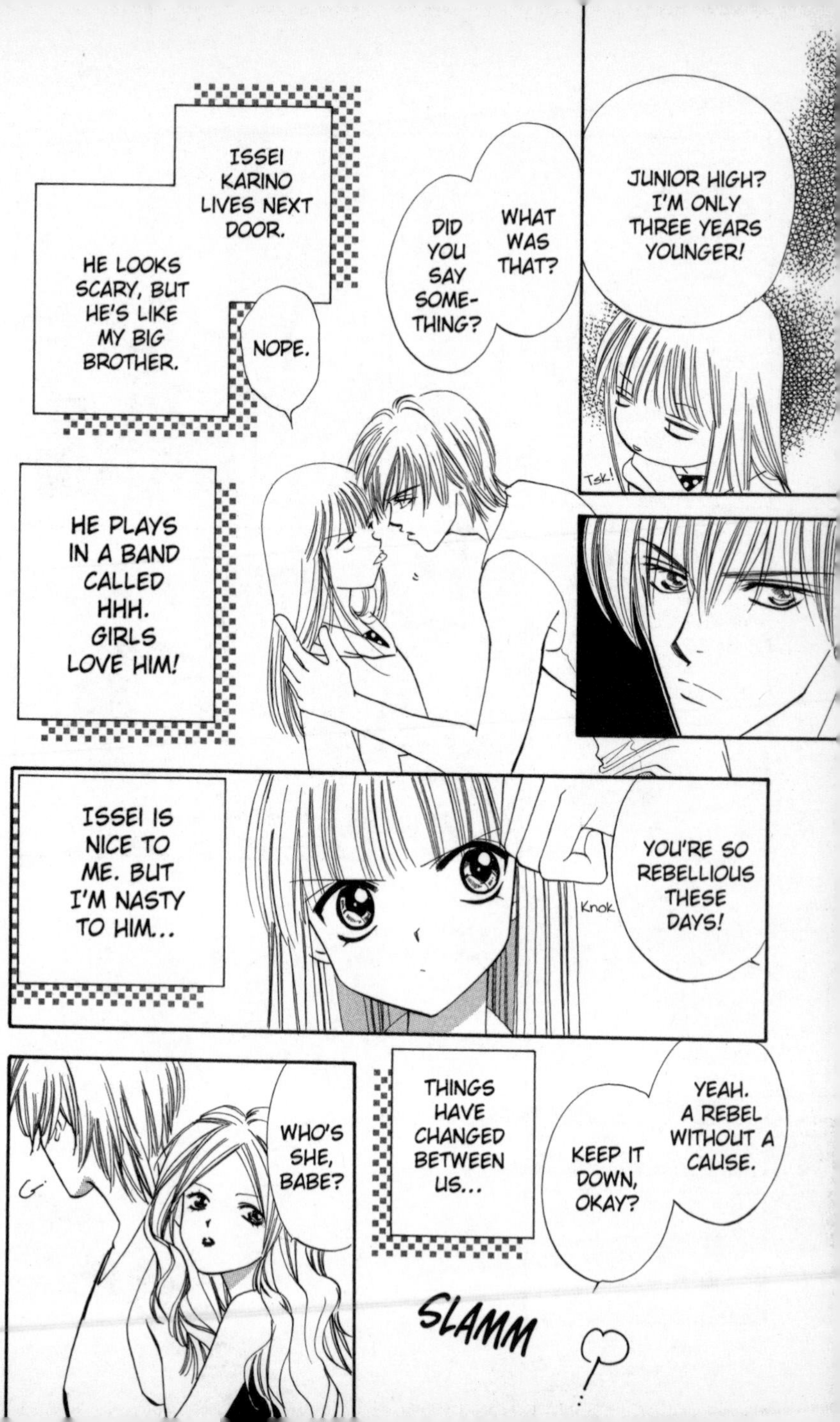
JUNIOR HIGH? I'M ONLY THREE YEARS YOUNGER!
Tsk!
WHAT WAS THAT?
DID YOU SAY SOMETHING?
NOPE.
ISSEI KARINO LIVES NEXT DOOR.
HE LOOKS SCARY, BUT HE'S LIKE MY BIG BROTHER.
HE PLAYS IN A BAND CALLED HHH. GIRLS LOVE HIM!
YOU'RE SO REBELLIOUS THESE DAYS!
Knok
ISSEI IS NICE TO ME. BUT I'M NASTY TO HIM...
YEAH. A REBEL WITHOUT A CAUSE.
KEEP IT DOWN, OKAY?
THINGS HAVE CHANGED BETWEEN US...
SLAMM
WHO'S SHE, BABE?

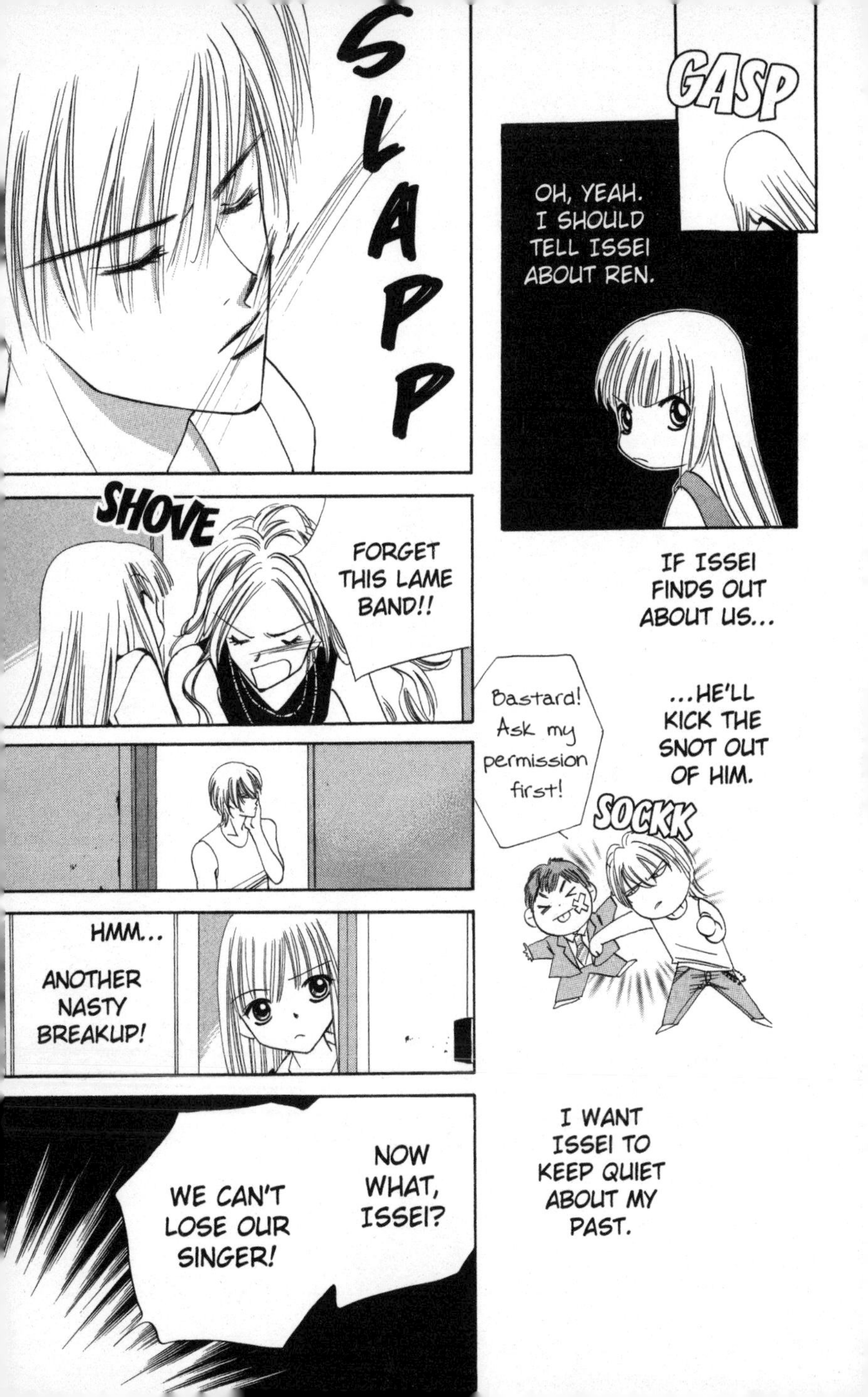

GASP
OH, YEAH. I SHOULD TELL ISSEI ABOUT REN.
SLAPP
SHOVE
FORGET THIS LAME BAND!!
IF ISSEI FINDS OUT ABOUT US...
...HE'LL KICK THE SNOT OUT OF HIM.
Bastard! Ask my permission first!
SOCKK
HMM...
ANOTHER NASTY BREAKUP!
I WANT ISSEI TO KEEP QUIET ABOUT MY PAST.
NOW WHAT, ISSEI?
WE CAN'T LOSE OUR SINGER!

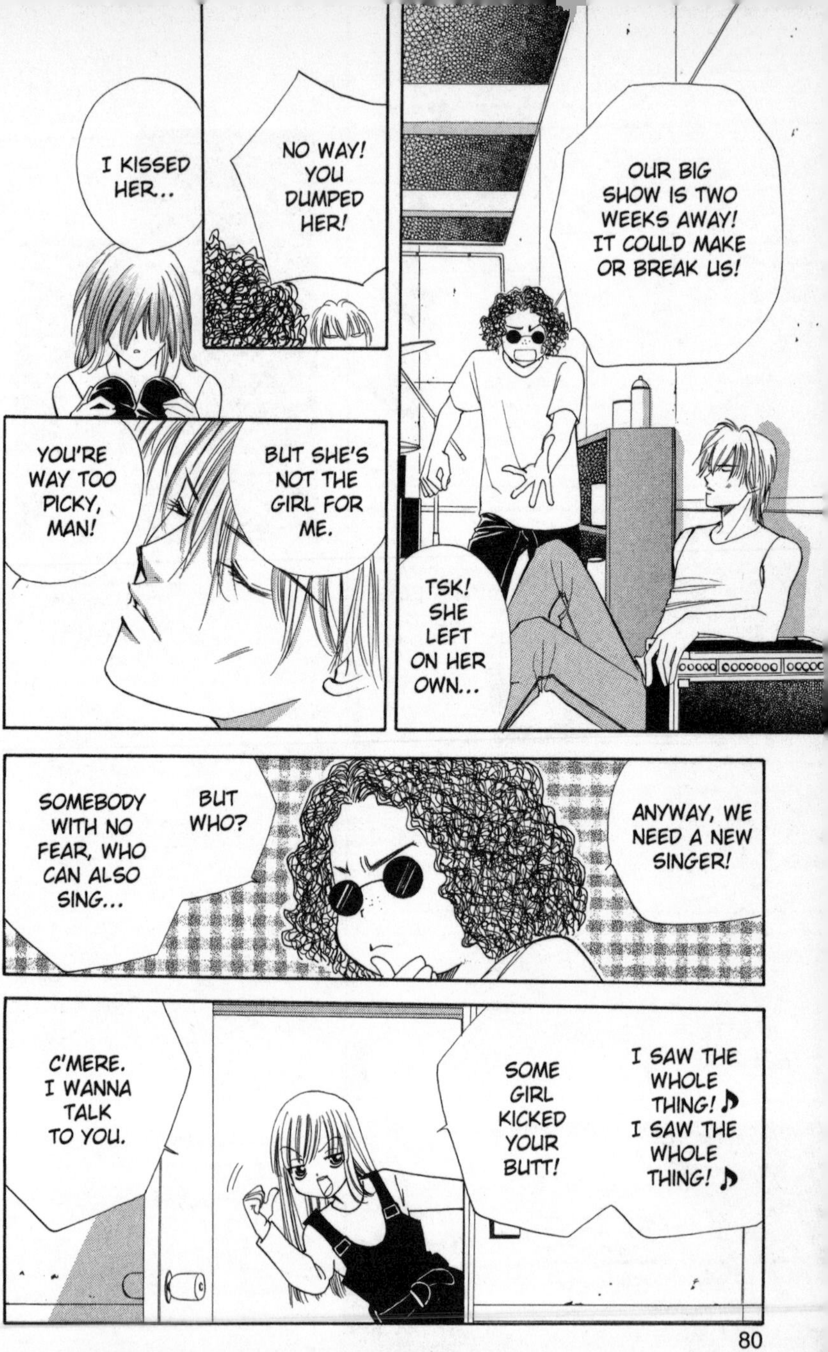
OUR BIG SHOW IS TWO WEEKS AWAY! IT COULD MAKE OR BREAK US!
TSK! SHE LEFT ON HER OWN...
NO WAY! YOU DUMPED HER!
I KISSED HER...
BUT SHE'S NOT THE GIRL FOR ME.
YOU'RE WAY TOO PICKY, MAN!
ANYWAY, WE NEED A NEW SINGER!
BUT WHO?
SOMEBODY WITH NO FEAR, WHO CAN ALSO SING...
I SAW THE WHOLE THING! ♪ I SAW THE WHOLE THING! ♪
SOME GIRL KICKED YOUR BUTT!
C'MERE. I WANNA TALK TO YOU.

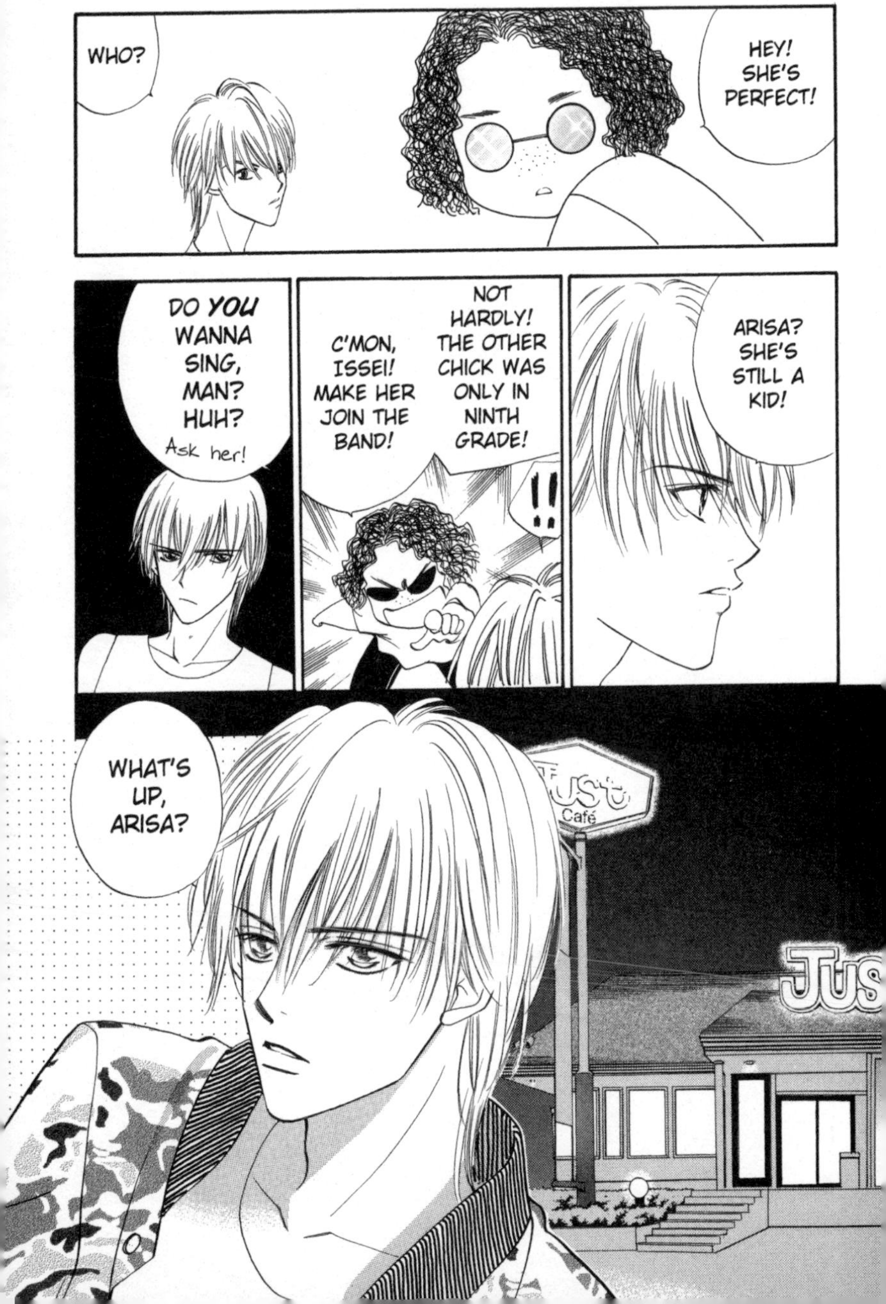
HEY! SHE'S PERFECT!
WHO?
ARISA? SHE'S STILL A KID!
NOT HARDLY! THE OTHER CHICK WAS ONLY IN NINTH GRADE!
C'MON, ISSEI! MAKE HER JOIN THE BAND!
!!
DO YOU WANNA SING, MAN? HUH?
Ask her!
WHAT'S UP, ARISA?
Café

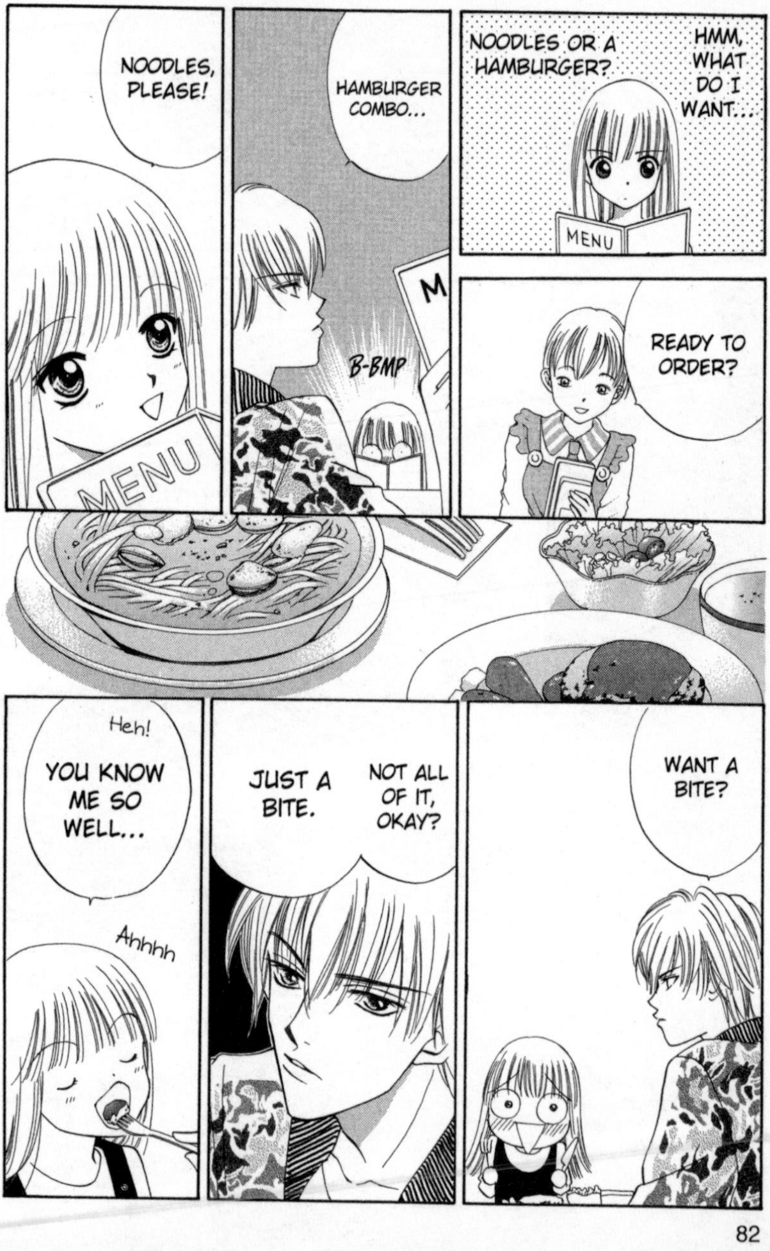
HMM, WHAT DO I WANT...
NOODLES OR A HAMBURGER?
MENU
READY TO ORDER?
HAMBURGER COMBO...
B-BMP
M
NOODLES, PLEASE!
MENU
WANT A BITE?
NOT ALL OF IT, OKAY?
JUST A BITE.
Heh!
YOU KNOW ME SO WELL...
Ahhhh

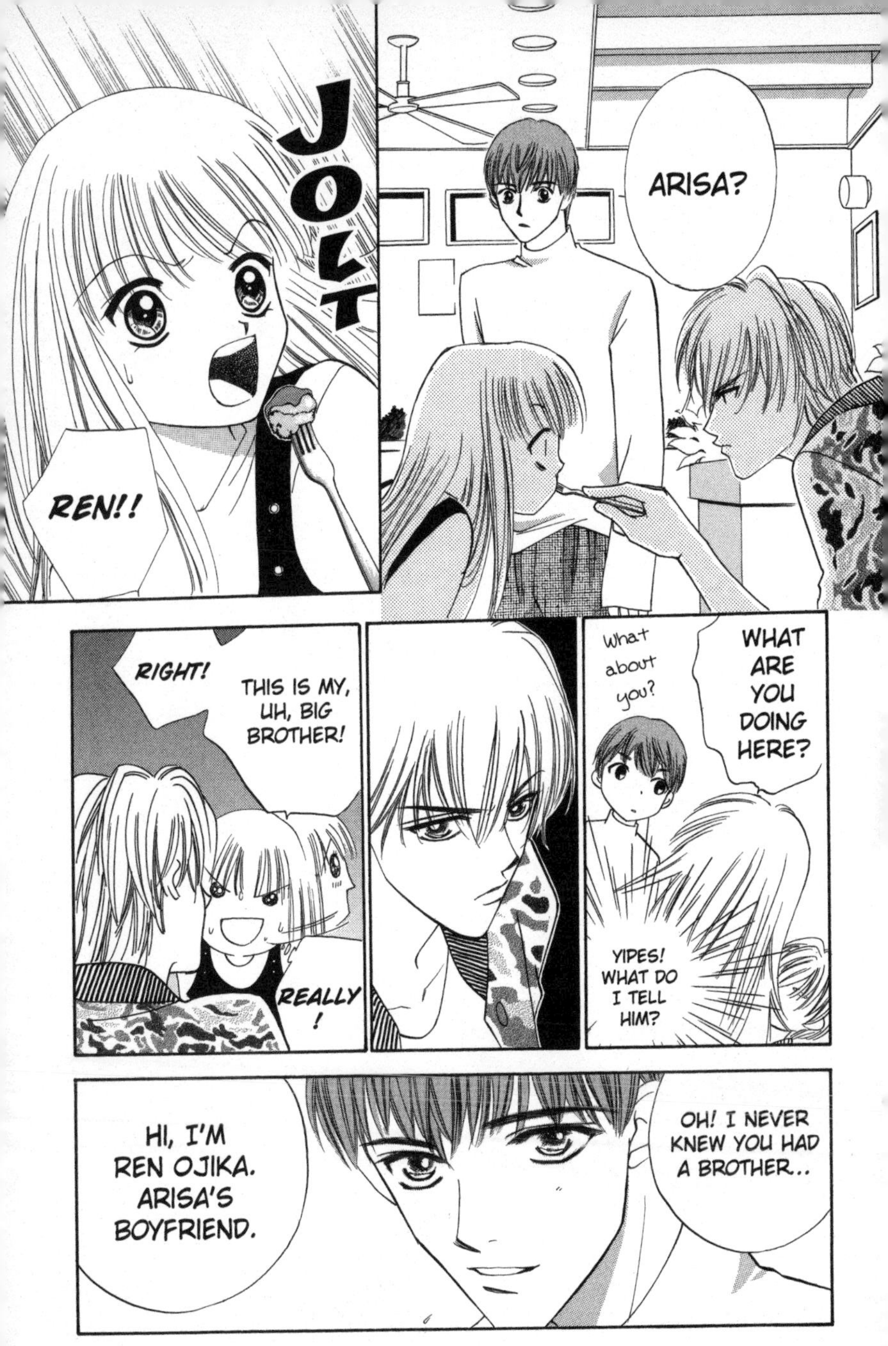
ARISA?
JOLT
REN!!
WHAT ARE YOU DOING HERE?
What about you?
YIPES! WHAT DO I TELL HIM?
RIGHT!
THIS IS MY, UH, BIG BROTHER!
REALLY!
OH! I NEVER KNEW YOU HAD A BROTHER...
HI, I'M REN OJIKA. ARISA'S BOYFRIEND.

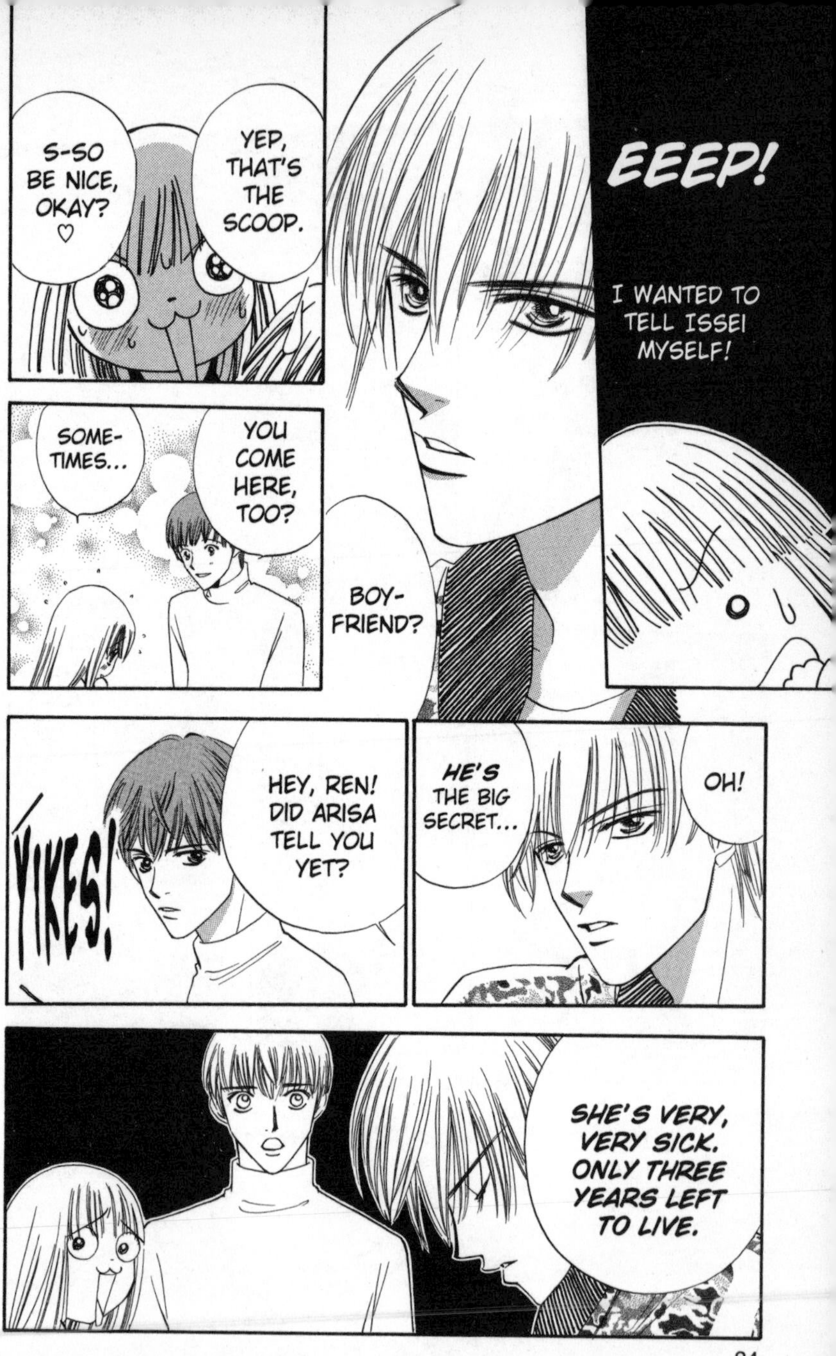
EEEP!
I WANTED TO TELL ISSEI MYSELF!
BOY-FRIEND?
YEP, THAT'S THE SCOOP.
S-SO BE NICE, OKAY? ♡
YOU COME HERE, TOO?
SOME-TIMES...
OH!
HE'S THE BIG SECRET...
HEY, REN! DID ARISA TELL YOU YET?
YIKES!
SHE'S VERY, VERY SICK. ONLY THREE YEARS LEFT TO LIVE.

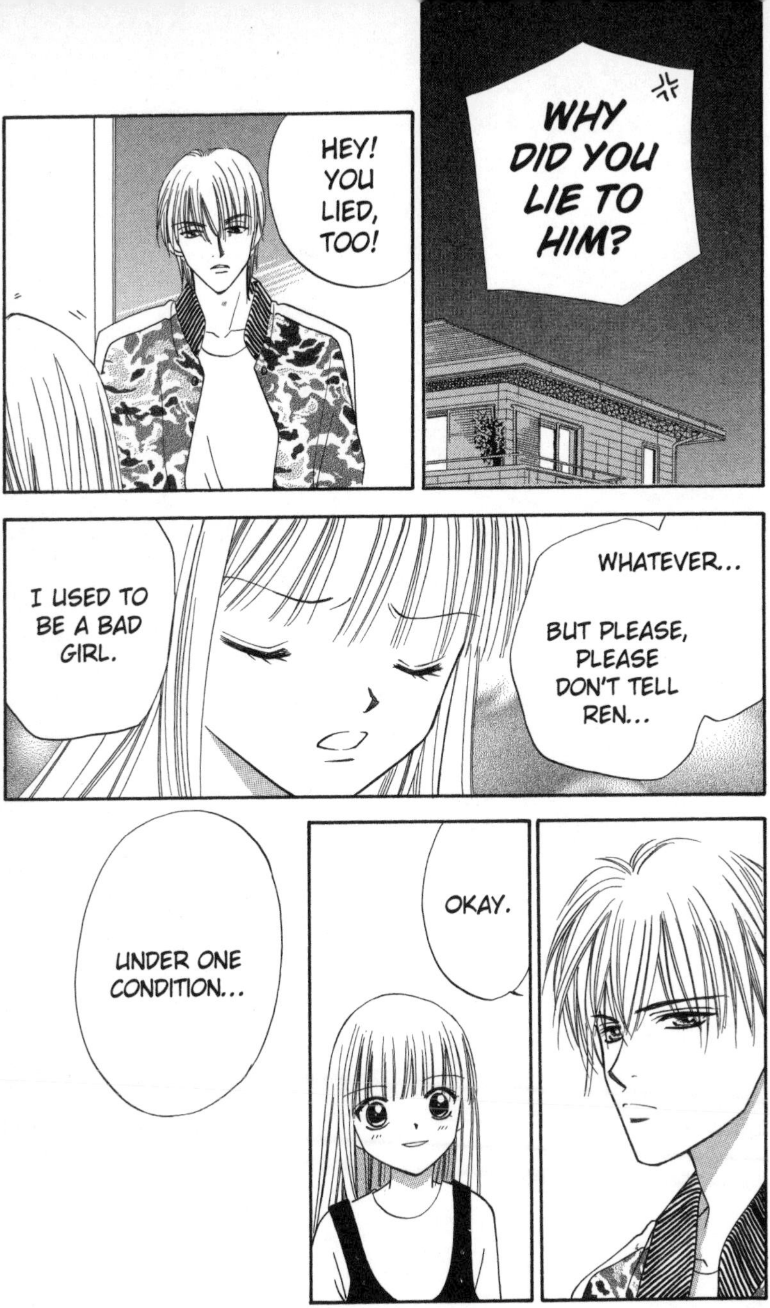
WHY DID YOU LIE TO HIM?
HEY! YOU LIED, TOO!
WHATEVER...
BUT PLEASE, PLEASE DON'T TELL REN...
I USED TO BE A BAD GIRL.
OKAY.
UNDER ONE CONDITION...

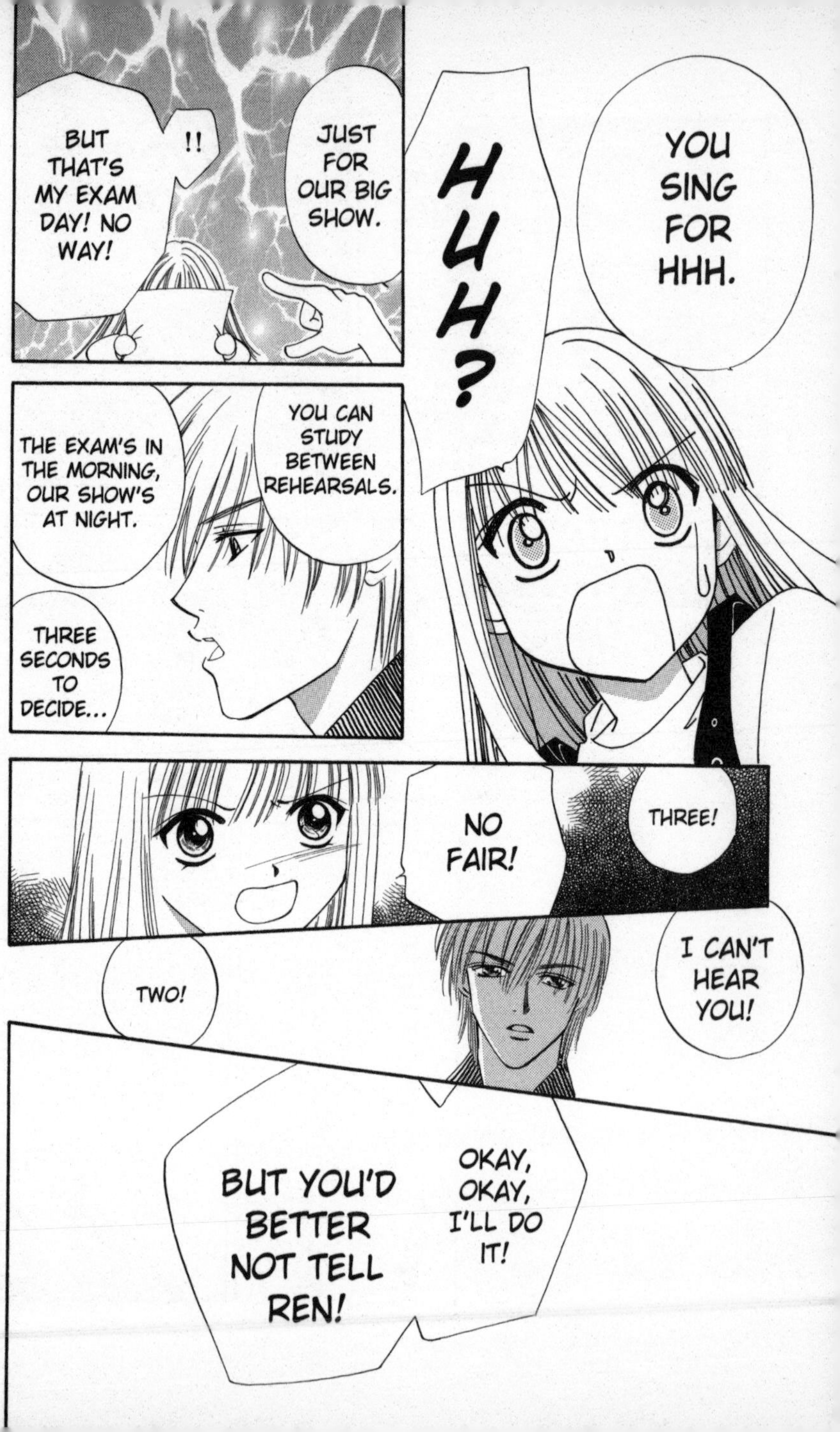
YOU SING FOR HHH.
HUH?
JUST FOR OUR BIG SHOW.
!!
BUT THAT'S MY EXAM DAY! NO WAY!
YOU CAN STUDY BETWEEN REHEARSALS.
THE EXAM'S IN THE MORNING, OUR SHOW'S AT NIGHT.
THREE SECONDS TO DECIDE...
THREE!
NO FAIR!
I CAN'T HEAR YOU!
TWO!
OKAY, OKAY, I'LL DO IT!
BUT YOU'D BETTER NOT TELL REN!

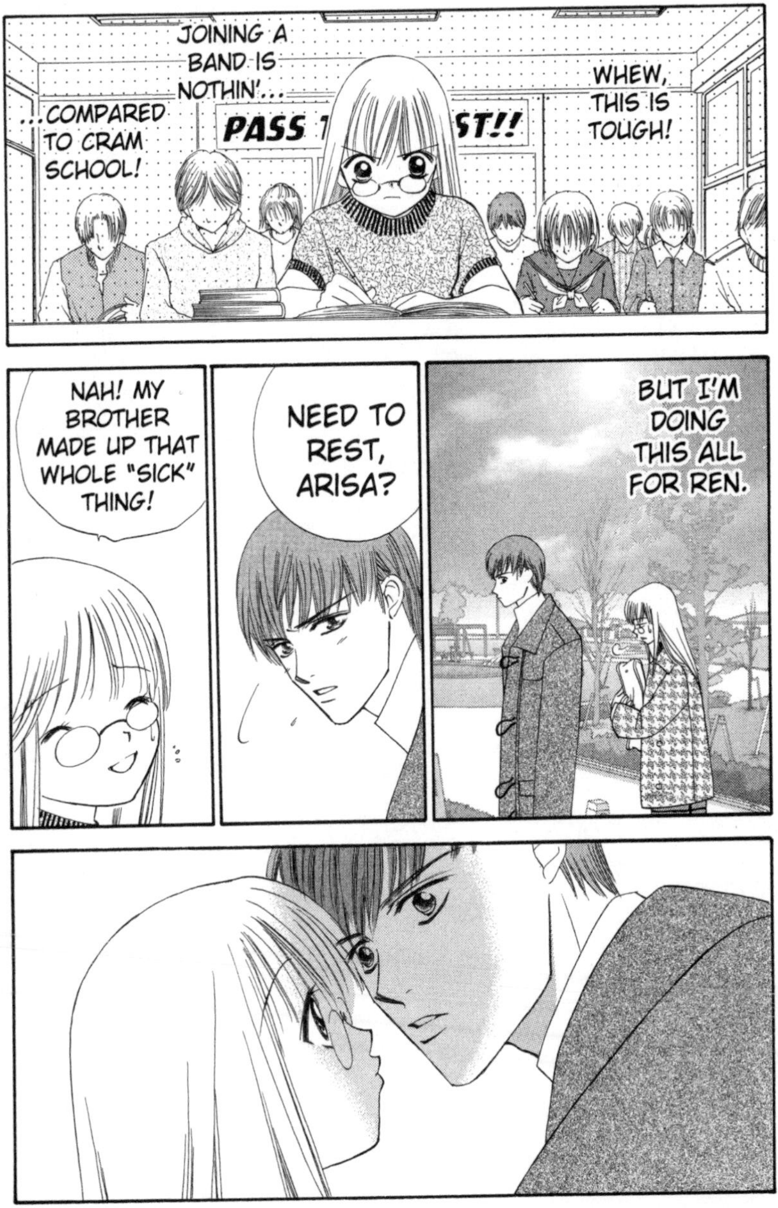
WHEW, THIS IS TOUGH!
JOINING A BAND IS NOTHIN'...
PASS
...COMPARED TO CRAM SCHOOL!
BUT I'M DOING THIS ALL FOR REN.
NEED TO REST, ARISA?
NAH! MY BROTHER MADE UP THAT WHOLE "SICK" THING!

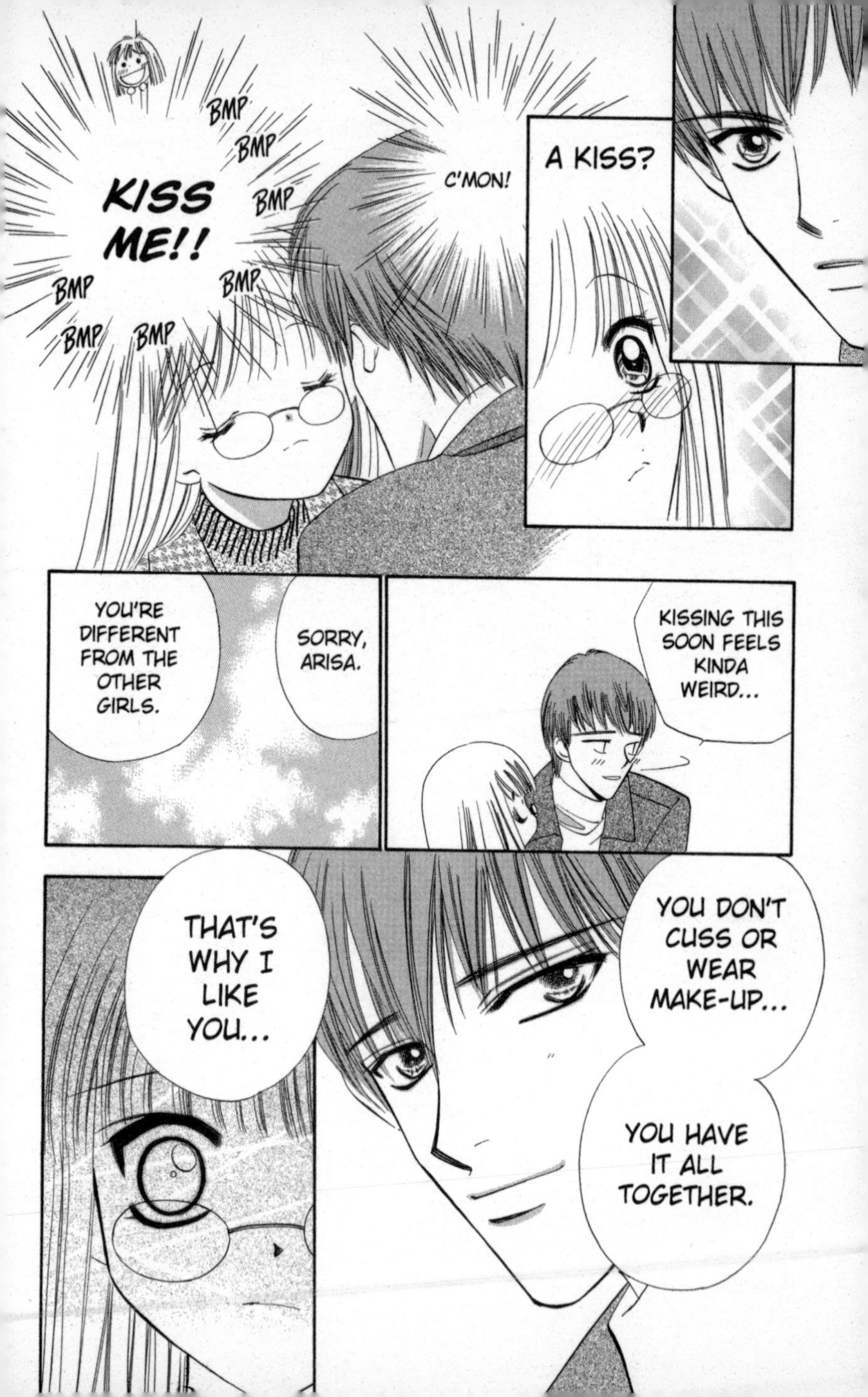
A KISS?
C'MON!
BMP
BMP
BMP
KISS ME!!
BMP
BMP
BMP
BMP
KISSING THIS SOON FEELS KINDA WEIRD...
SORRY, ARISA.
YOU'RE DIFFERENT FROM THE OTHER GIRLS.
YOU DON'T CUSS OR WEAR MAKE-UP...
YOU HAVE IT ALL TOGETHER.
THAT'S WHY I LIKE YOU...

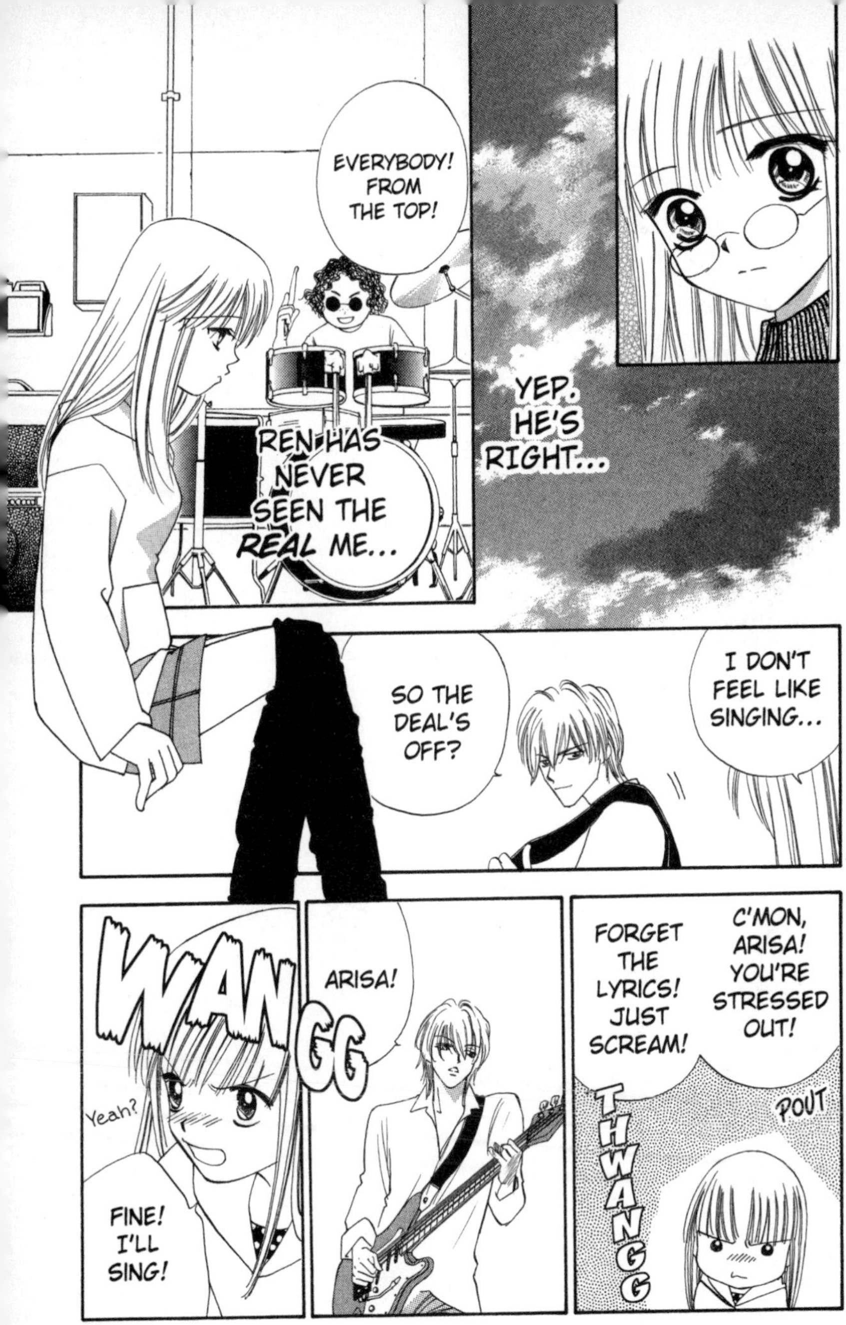
YEP. HE'S RIGHT...
EVERYBODY! FROM THE TOP!
REN HAS NEVER SEEN THE *REAL* ME...
I DON'T FEEL LIKE SINGING...
SO THE DEAL'S OFF?
C'MON, ARISA! YOU'RE STRESSED OUT!
FORGET THE LYRICS! JUST SCREAM!
POUT
THWANGG
ARISA!
WANGG
Yeah?
FINE! I'LL SING!

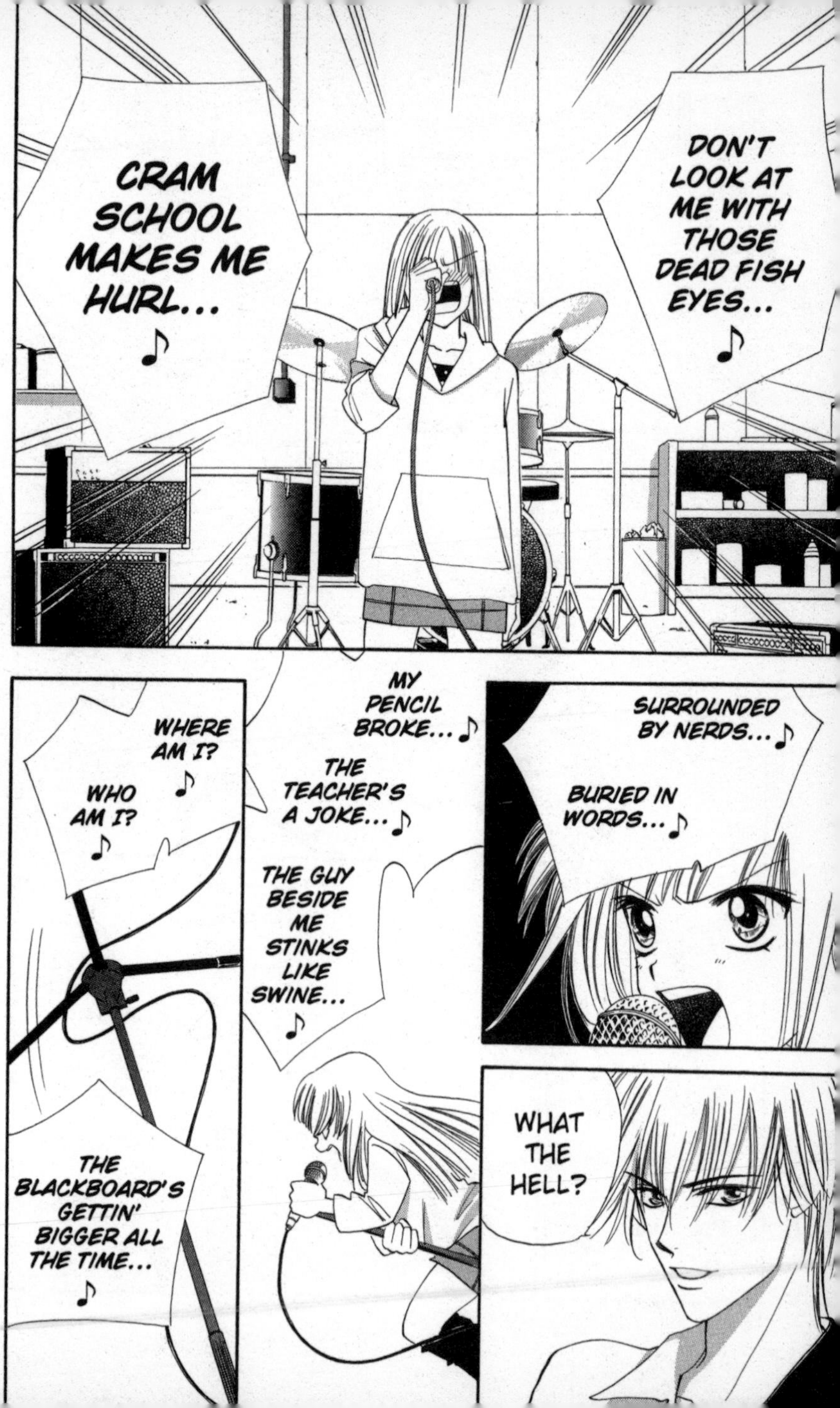
DON'T LOOK AT ME WITH THOSE DEAD FISH EYES... ♪
CRAM SCHOOL MAKES ME HURL... ♪
SURROUNDED BY NERDS... ♪
BURIED IN WORDS... ♪
WHAT THE HELL?
MY PENCIL BROKE... ♪
THE TEACHER'S A JOKE... ♪
THE GUY BESIDE ME STINKS LIKE SWINE... ♪
WHERE AM I? ♪
WHO AM I? ♪
THE BLACKBOARD'S GETTIN' BIGGER ALL THE TIME... ♪

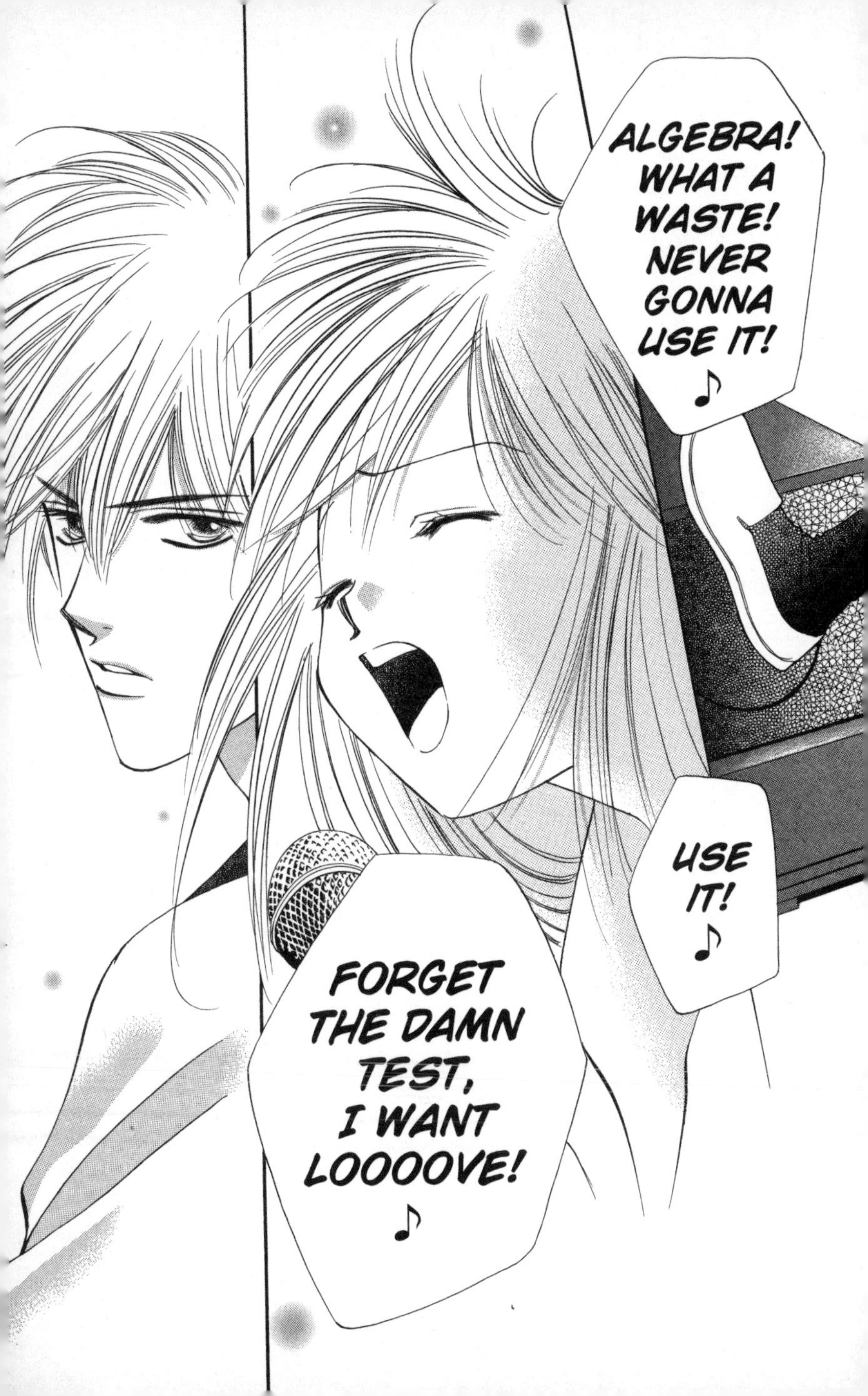
ALGEBRA! WHAT A WASTE! NEVER GONNA USE IT! ♪
USE IT! ♪
FORGET THE DAMN TEST, I WANT LOOOOVE! ♪

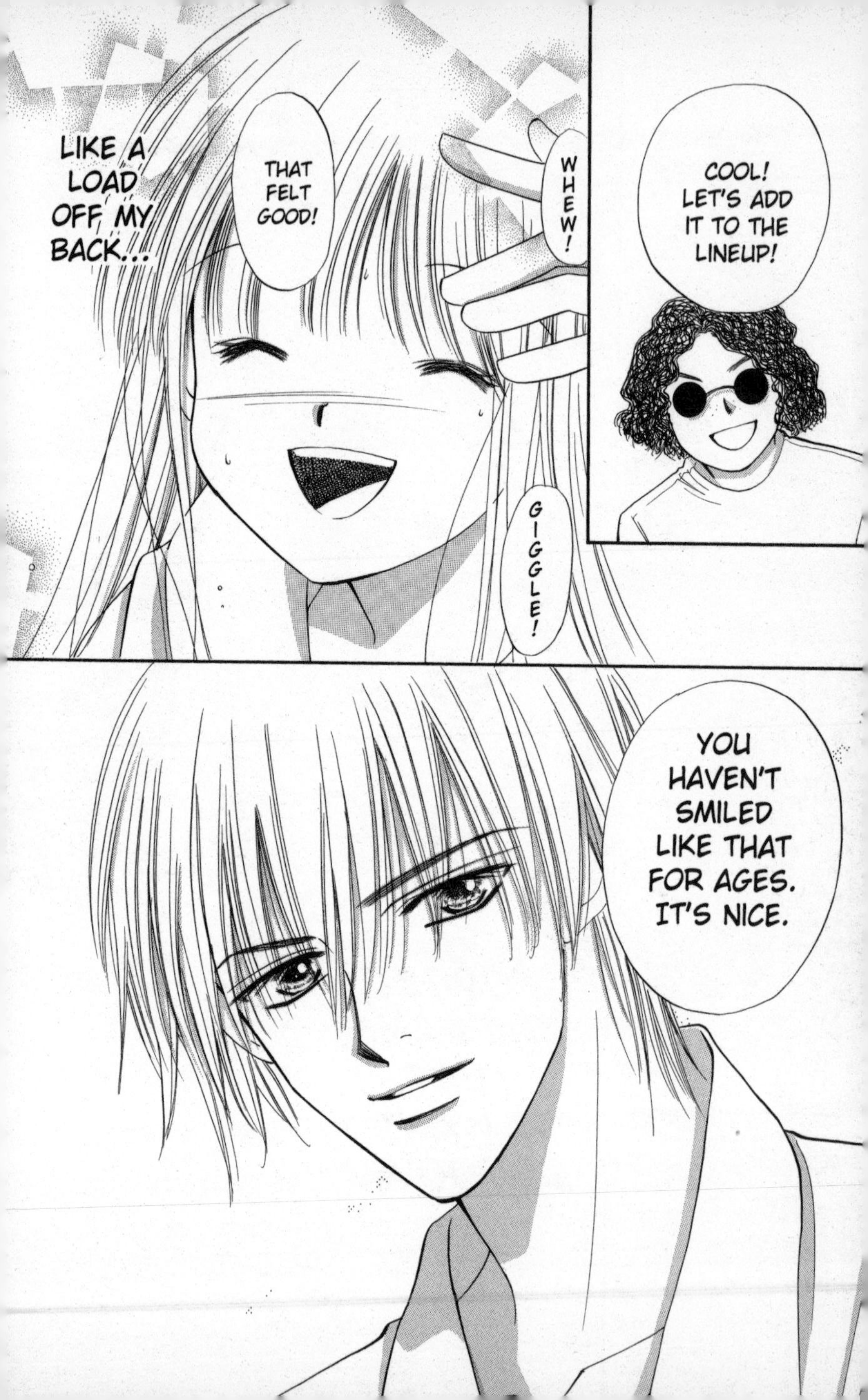
COOL! LET'S ADD IT TO THE LINEUP!
WHEW!
THAT FELT GOOD!
LIKE A LOAD OFF MY BACK...
GIGGLE!
YOU HAVEN'T SMILED LIKE THAT FOR AGES. IT'S NICE.

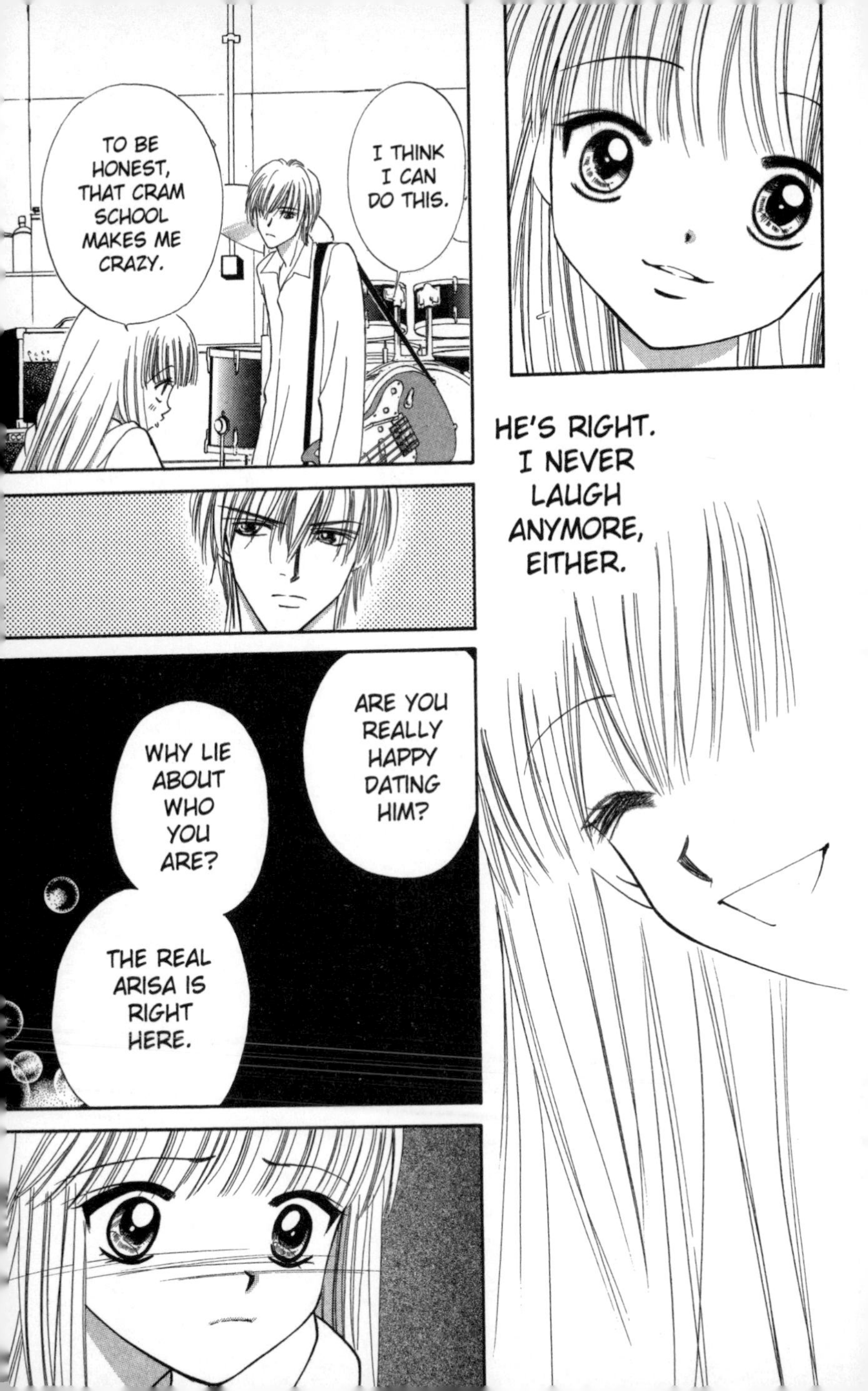
I THINK I CAN DO THIS.
TO BE HONEST, THAT CRAM SCHOOL MAKES ME CRAZY.
HE'S RIGHT. I NEVER LAUGH ANYMORE, EITHER.
ARE YOU REALLY HAPPY DATING HIM?
WHY LIE ABOUT WHO YOU ARE?
THE REAL ARISA IS RIGHT HERE.

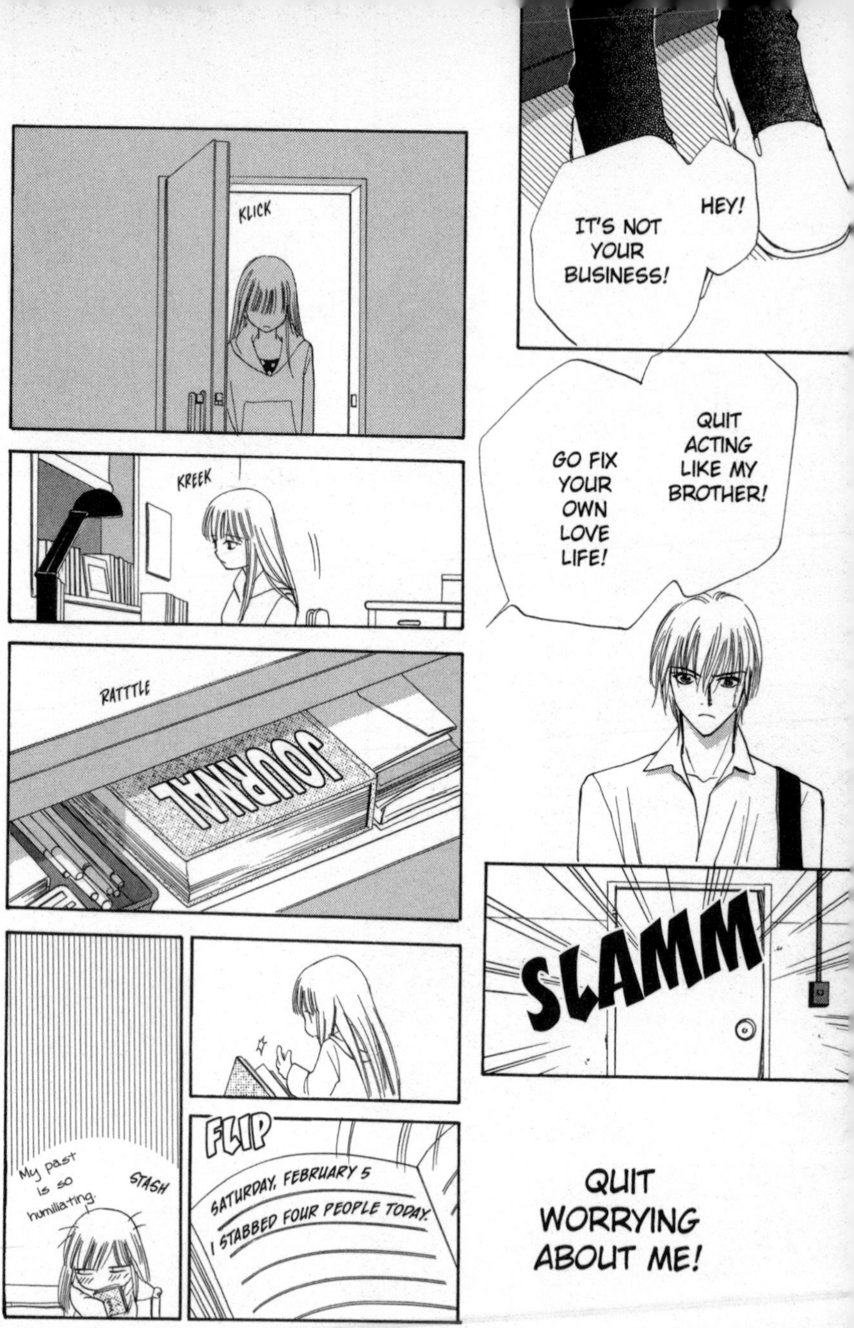
HEY!
IT'S NOT YOUR BUSINESS!
QUIT ACTING LIKE MY BROTHER!
GO FIX YOUR OWN LOVE LIFE!
SLAMM
QUIT WORRYING ABOUT ME!
KLICK
KREEK
RATTTLE
JOURNAL
FLIP
SATURDAY, FEBRUARY 5
I STABBED FOUR PEOPLE TODAY.
STASH
My past is so humiliating.

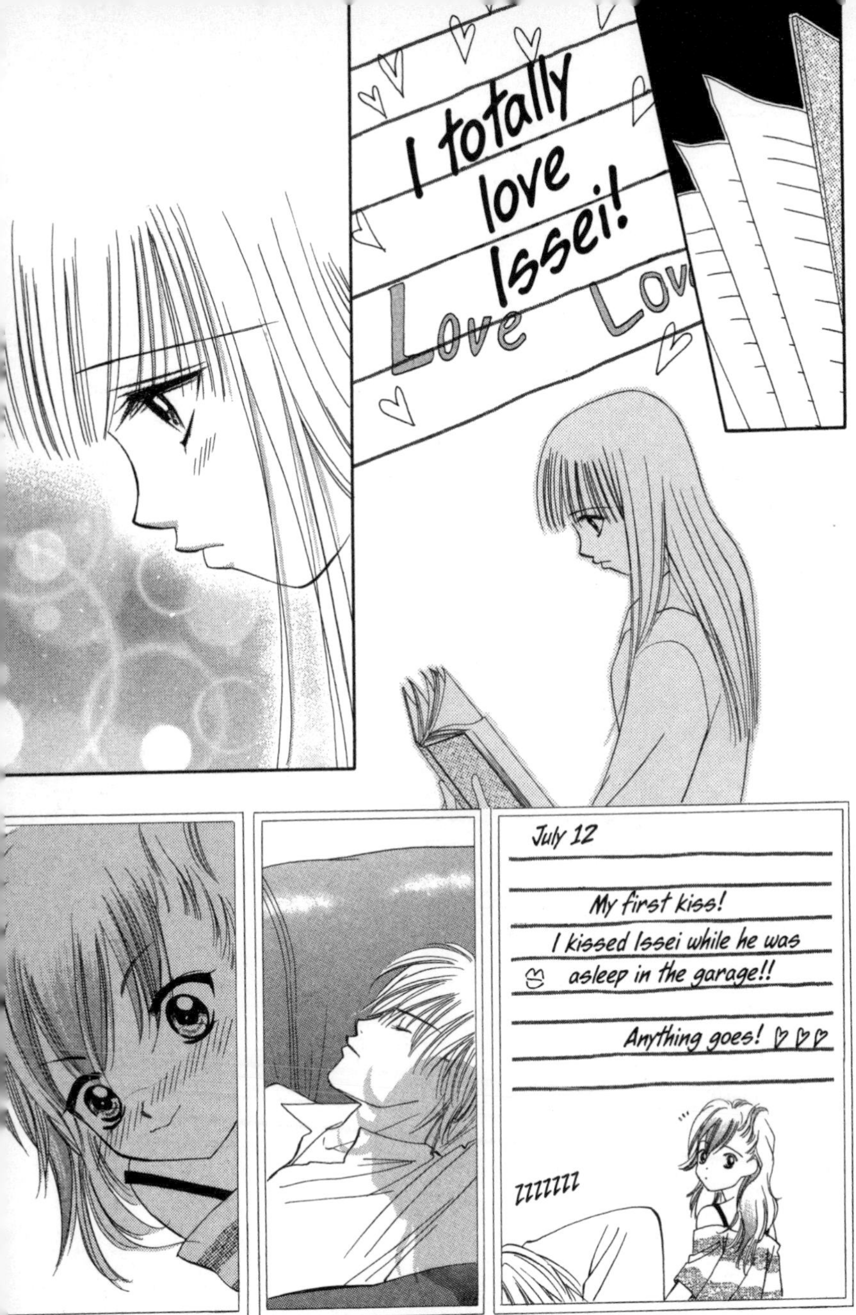
I totally love Issei!
Love Love
July 12
My first kiss!
I kissed Issei while he was asleep in the garage!!
Anything goes!
ZZZZZZZ

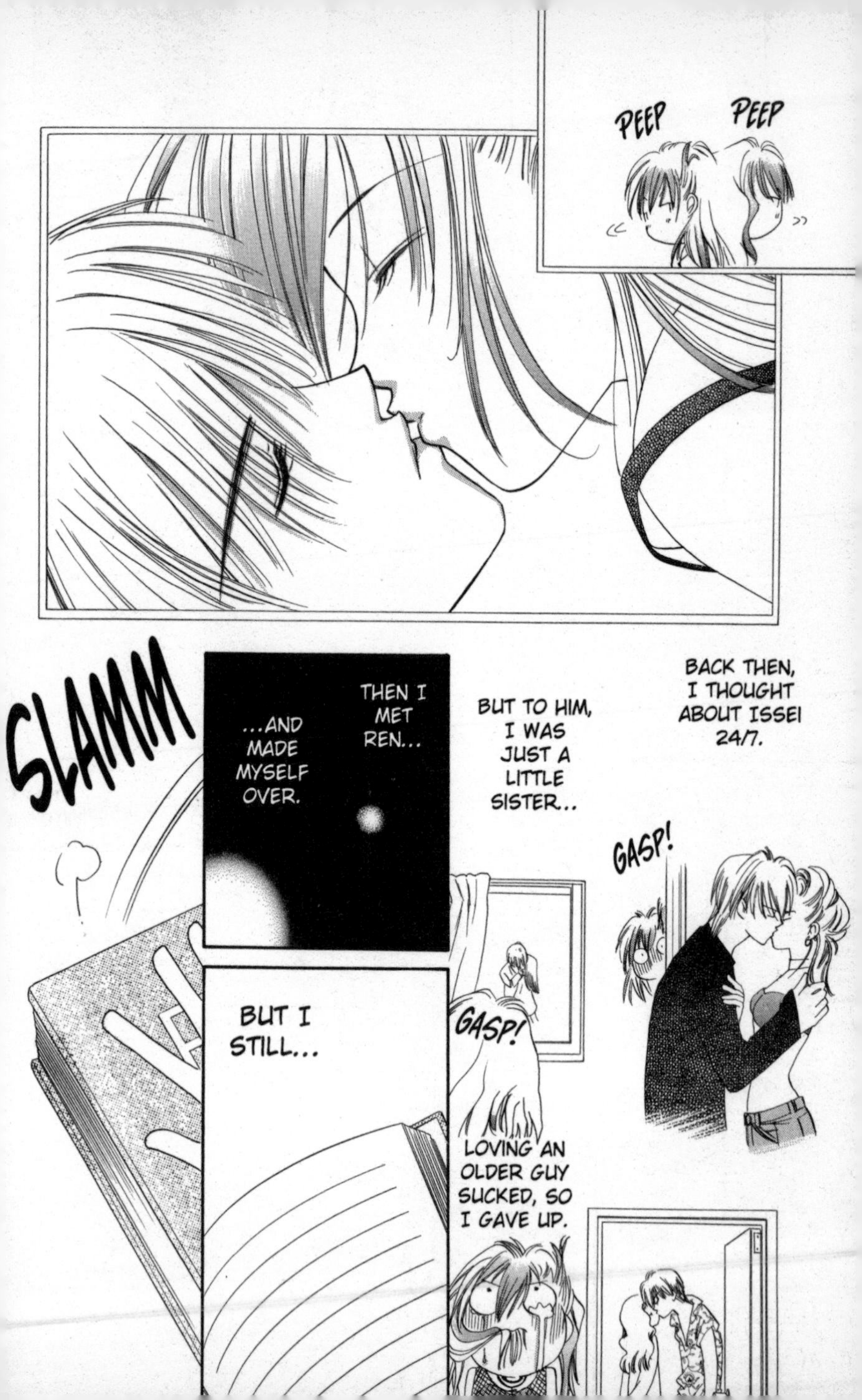
PEEP PEEP
BACK THEN, I THOUGHT ABOUT ISSEI 24/7.
GASP!
BUT TO HIM, I WAS JUST A LITTLE SISTER...
GASP!
LOVING AN OLDER GUY SUCKED, SO I GAVE UP.
THEN I MET REN...
...AND MADE MYSELF OVER.
BUT I STILL...
SLAMM

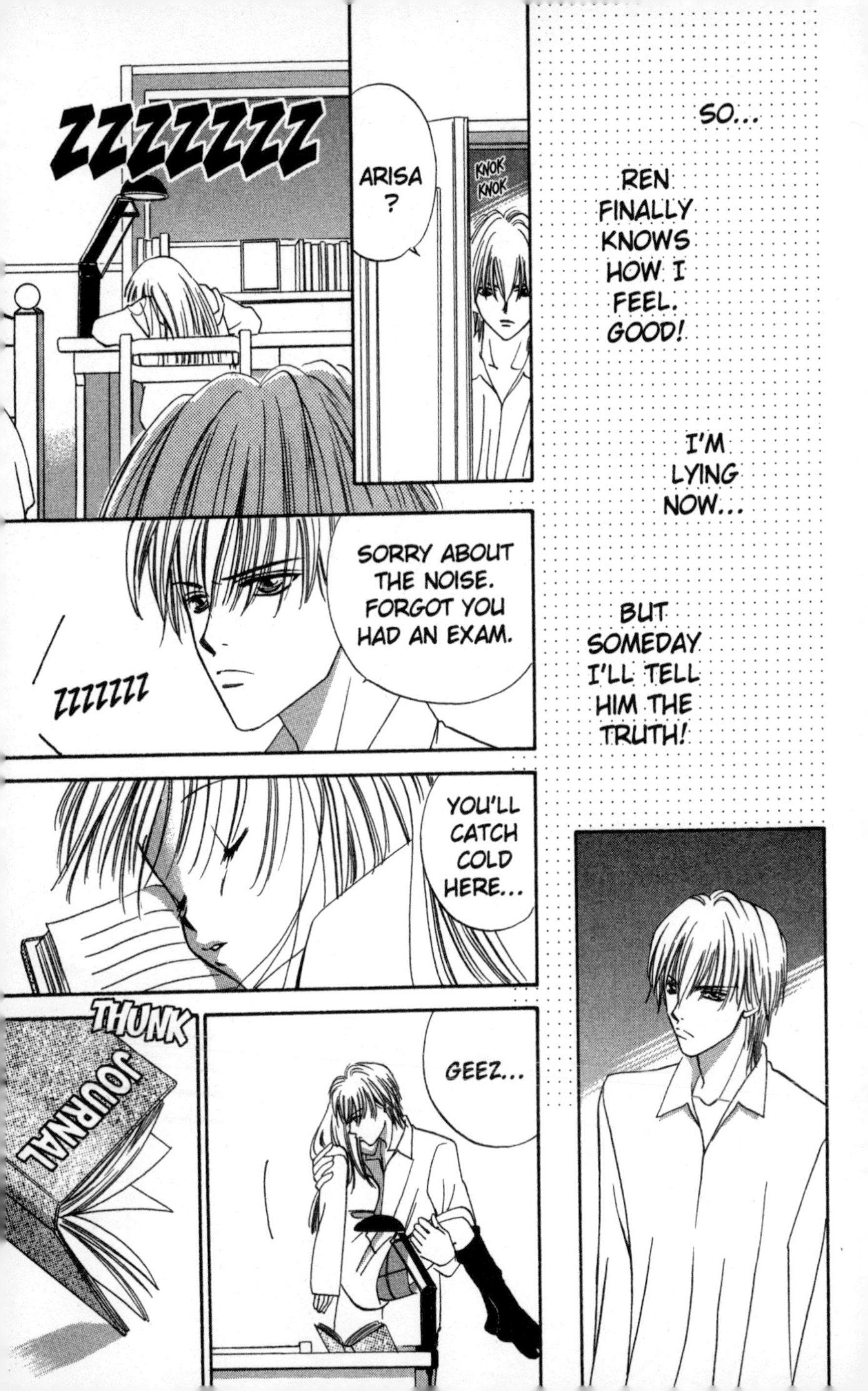
SO...
REN FINALLY KNOWS HOW I FEEL. GOOD!
I'M LYING NOW...
BUT SOMEDAY I'LL TELL HIM THE TRUTH!
KNOK KNOK
ARISA?
ZZZZZZZZ
SORRY ABOUT THE NOISE. FORGOT YOU HAD AN EXAM.
ZZZZZZZ
YOU'LL CATCH COLD HERE...
GEEZ...
THUNK
JOURNAL

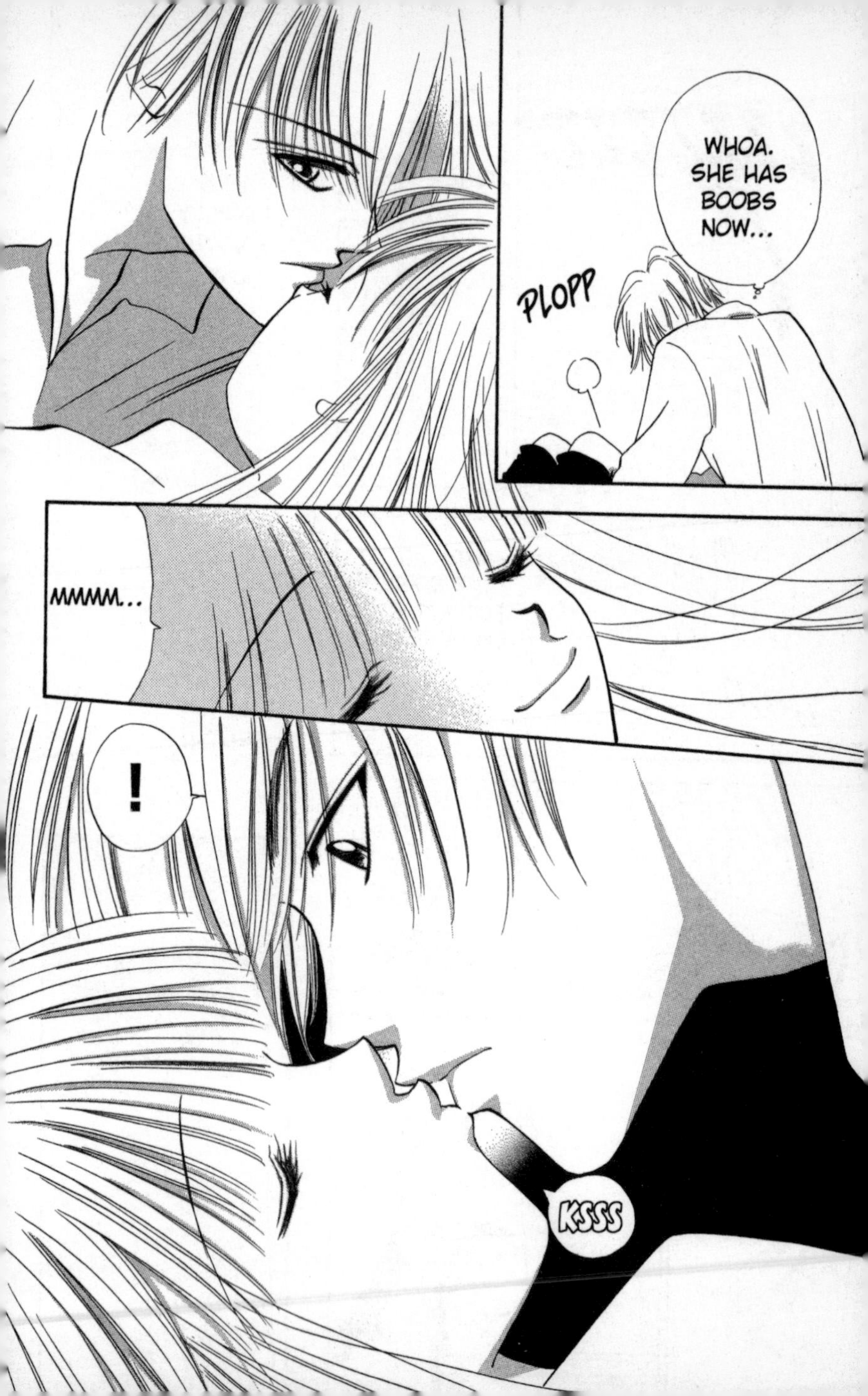
WHOA. SHE HAS BOOBS NOW...
PLOPP
MMMM...
!
KSSS

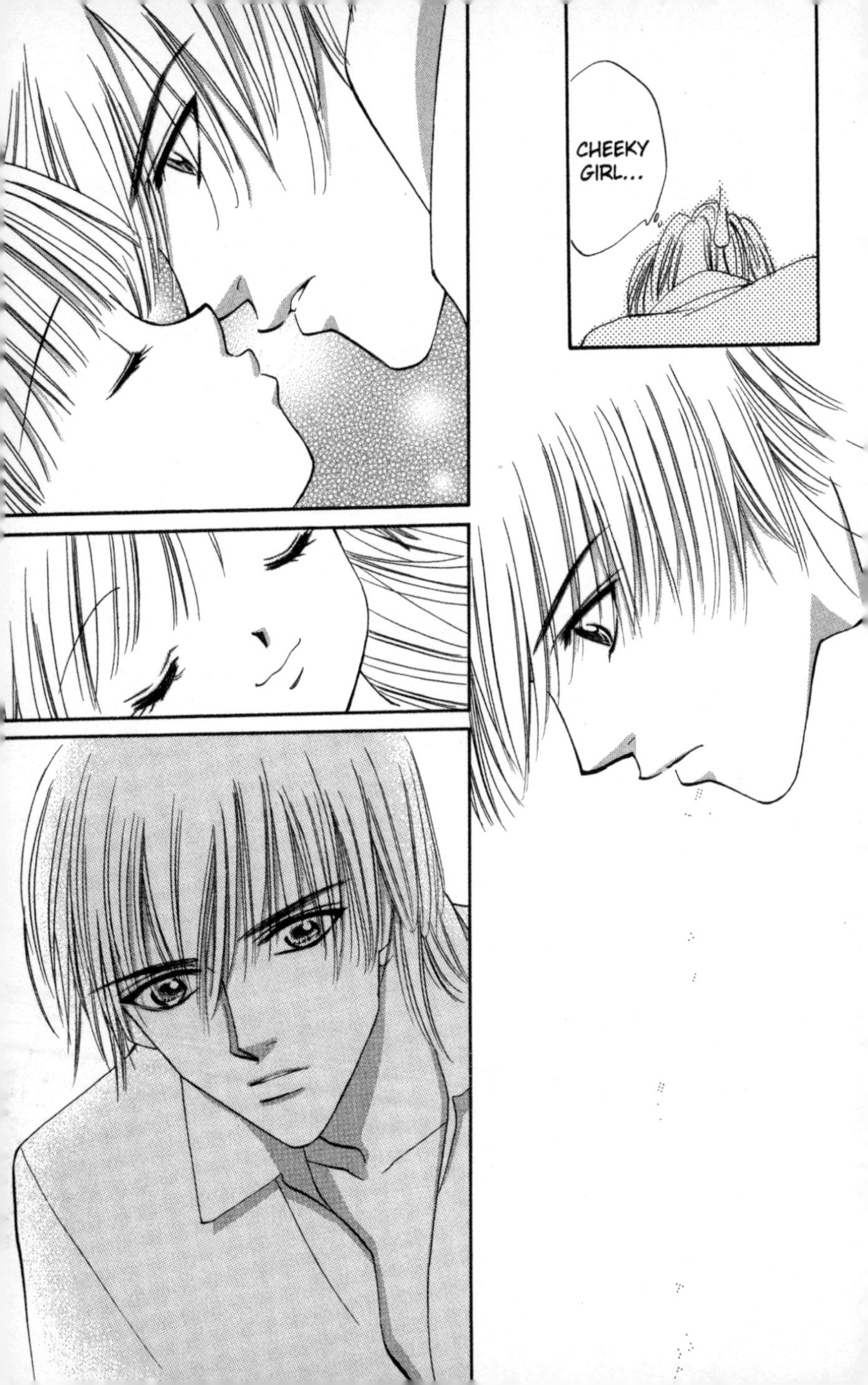
CHEEKY GIRL...

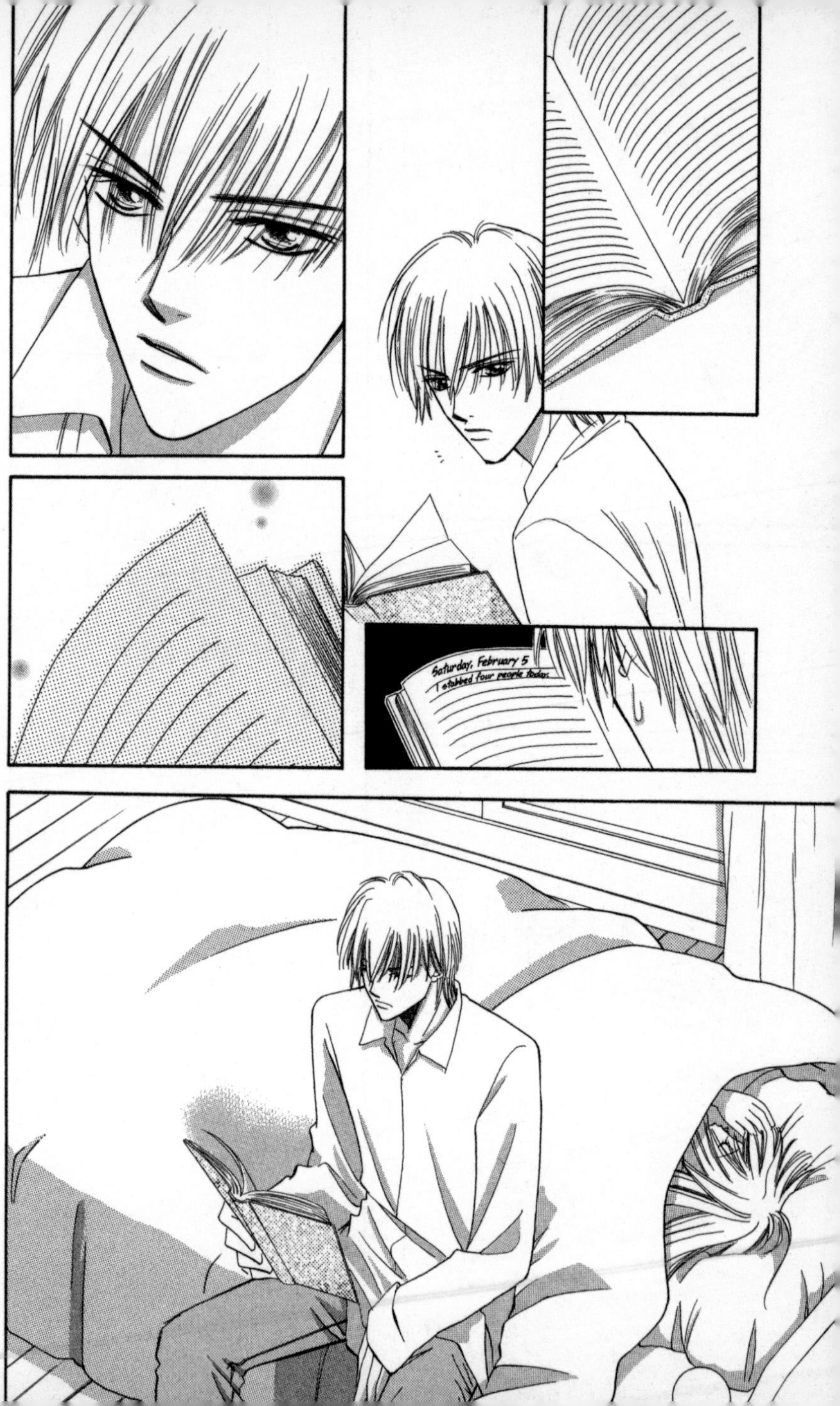
Saturday, February 5
I stabbed four people today.

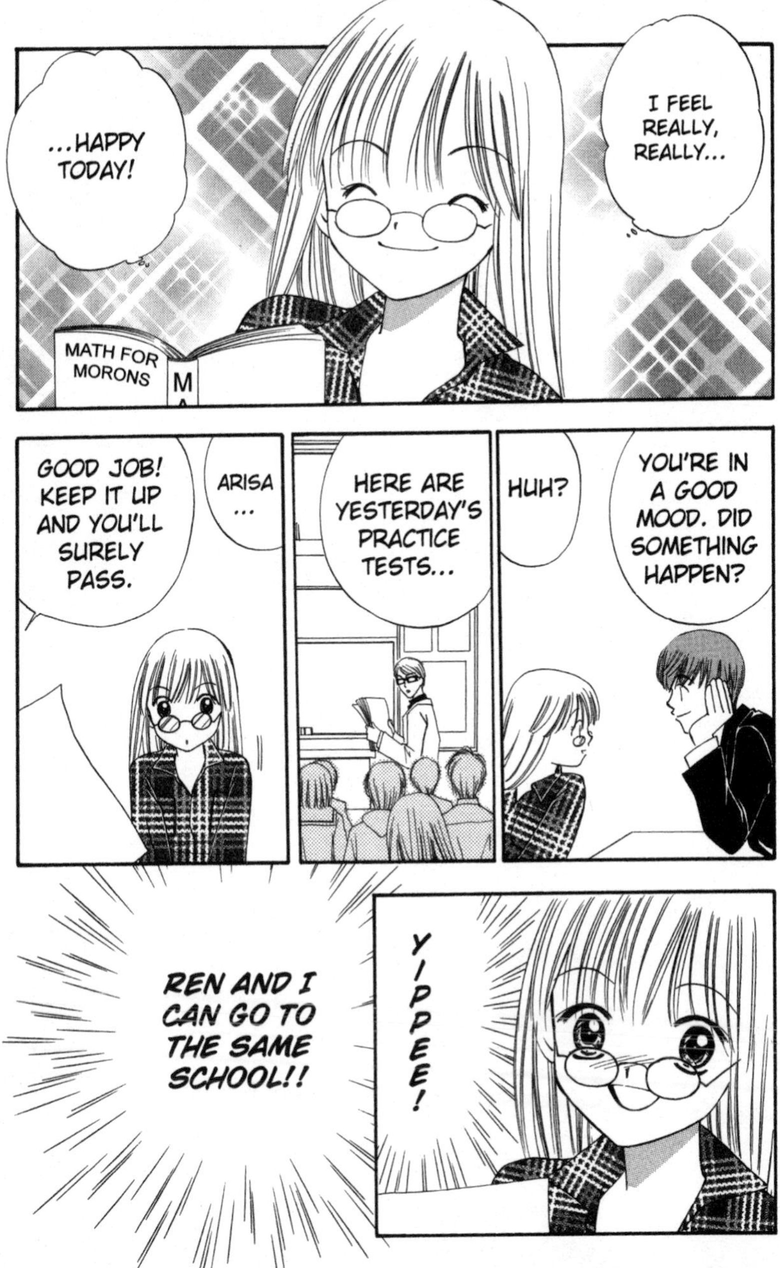
I FEEL REALLY, REALLY...
...HAPPY TODAY!
MATH FOR MORONS
M
YOU'RE IN A GOOD MOOD. DID SOMETHING HAPPEN?
HUH?
HERE ARE YESTERDAY'S PRACTICE TESTS...
ARISA ...
GOOD JOB! KEEP IT UP AND YOU'LL SURELY PASS.
YIPPEE!
REN AND I CAN GO TO THE SAME SCHOOL!!

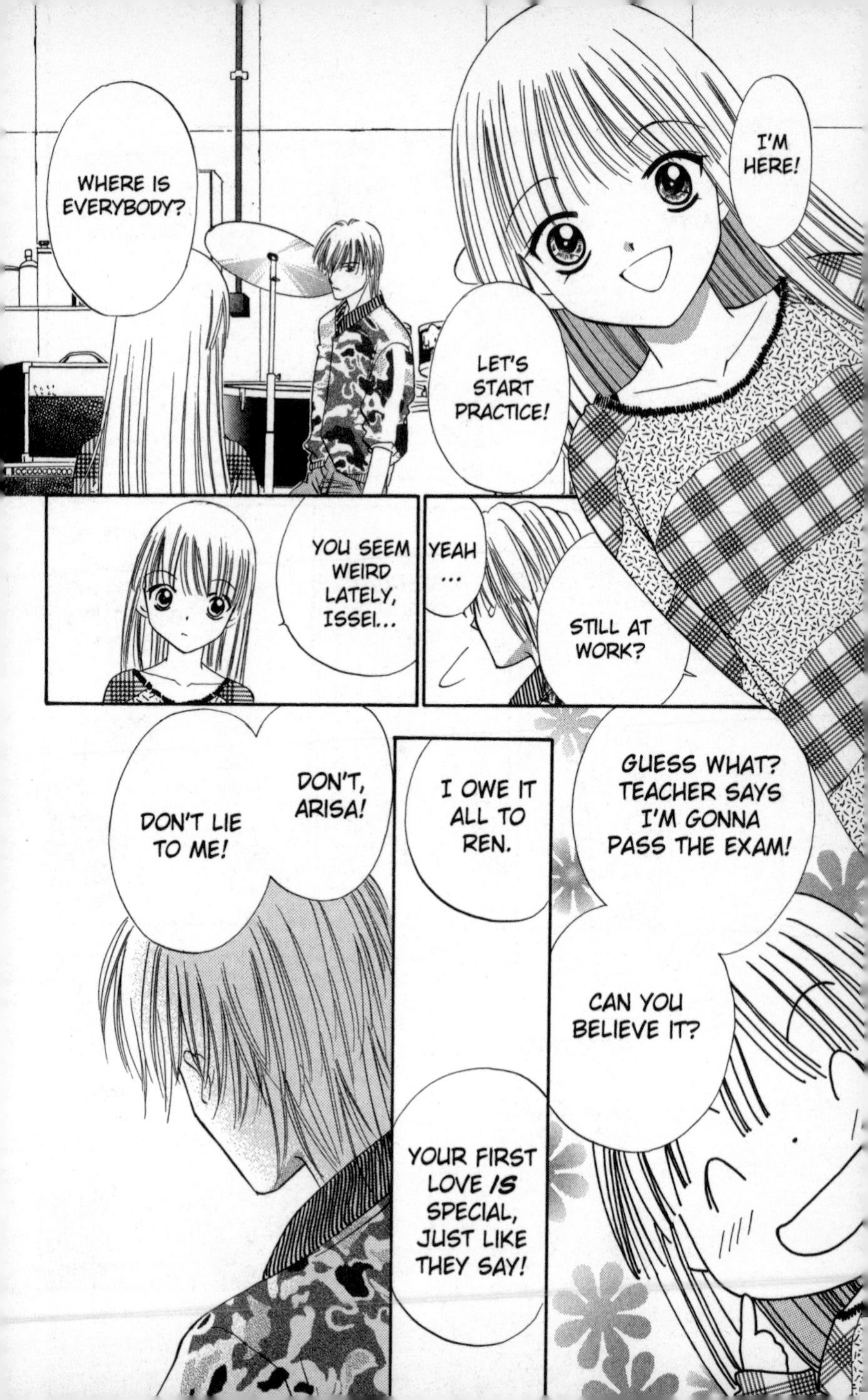
I'M HERE!
LET'S START PRACTICE!
WHERE IS EVERYBODY?
STILL AT WORK?
YEAH ...
YOU SEEM WEIRD LATELY, ISSEI...
GUESS WHAT? TEACHER SAYS I'M GONNA PASS THE EXAM!
CAN YOU BELIEVE IT?
I OWE IT ALL TO REN.
YOUR FIRST LOVE *IS* SPECIAL, JUST LIKE THEY SAY!
DON'T, ARISA!
DON'T LIE TO ME!

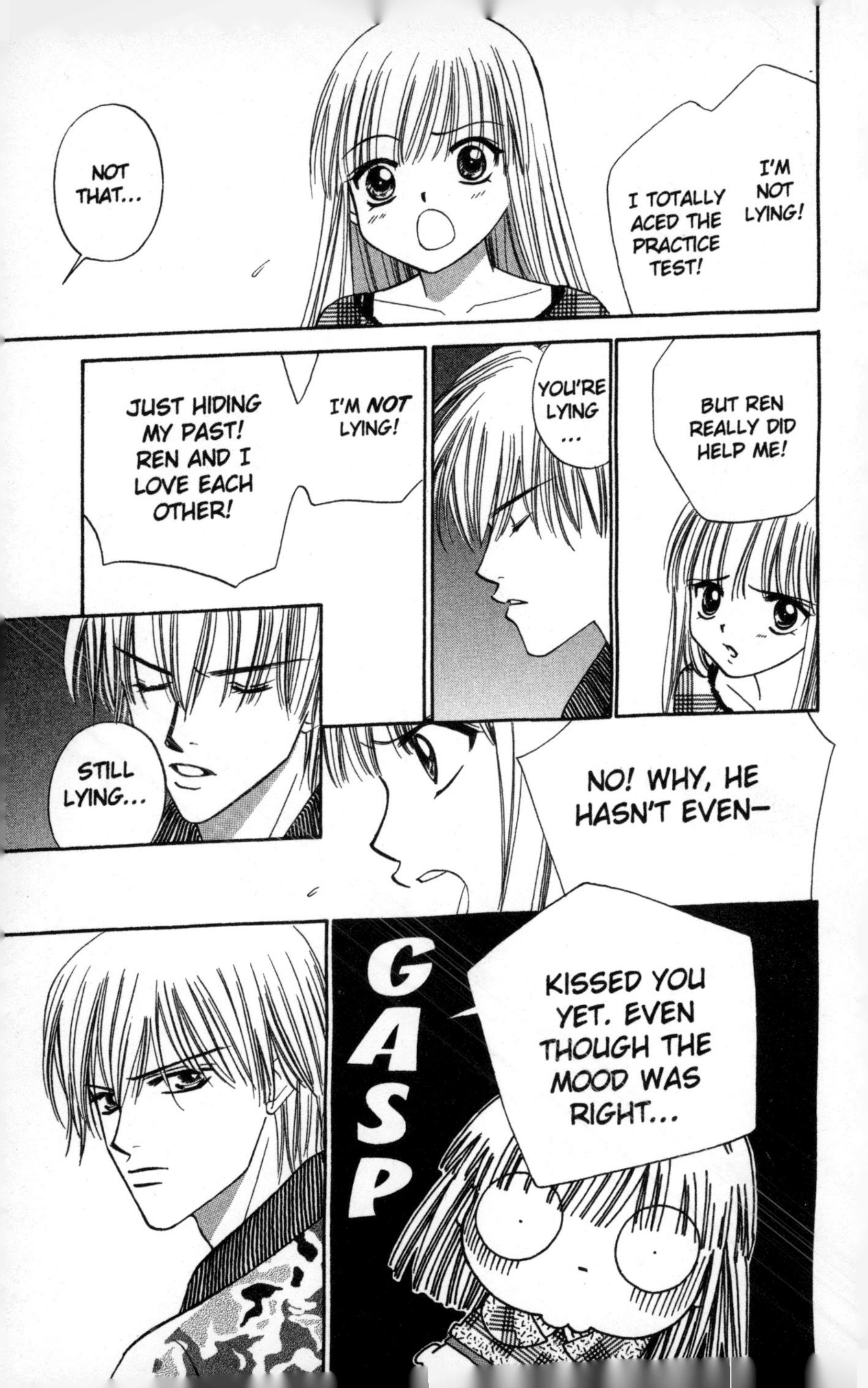
I'M NOT LYING!
I TOTALLY ACED THE PRACTICE TEST!
NOT THAT...
BUT REN REALLY DID HELP ME!
YOU'RE LYING ...
I'M *NOT* LYING!
JUST HIDING MY PAST! REN AND I LOVE EACH OTHER!
NO! WHY, HE HASN'T EVEN—
STILL LYING...
KISSED YOU YET. EVEN THOUGH THE MOOD WAS RIGHT...
GASP

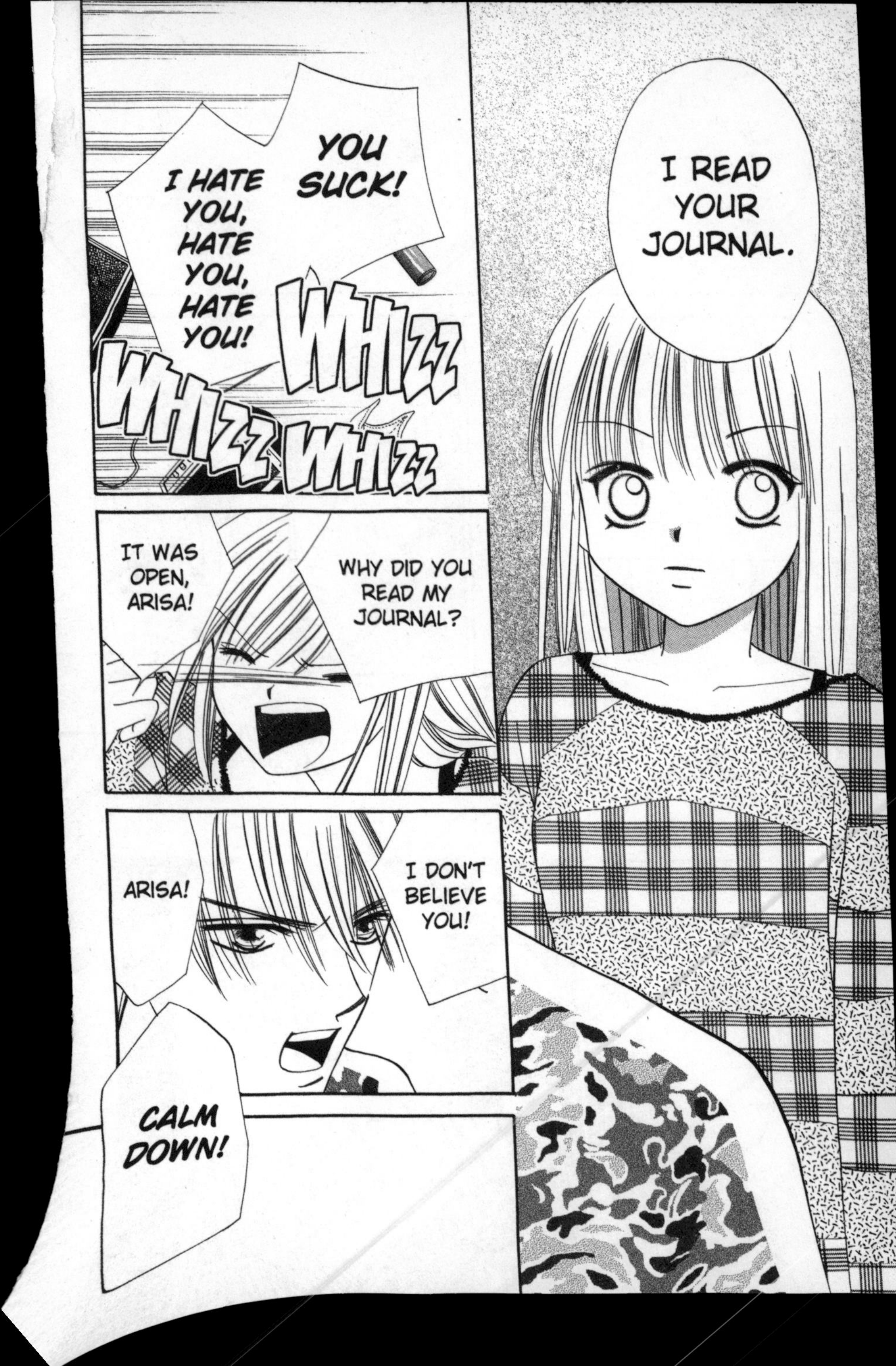
I READ YOUR JOURNAL.
YOU SUCK!
I HATE YOU, HATE YOU, HATE YOU!
WHIZZ
WHIZZ
WHIZZ
WHY DID YOU READ MY JOURNAL?
IT WAS OPEN, ARISA!
I DON'T BELIEVE YOU!
ARISA!
CALM DOWN!

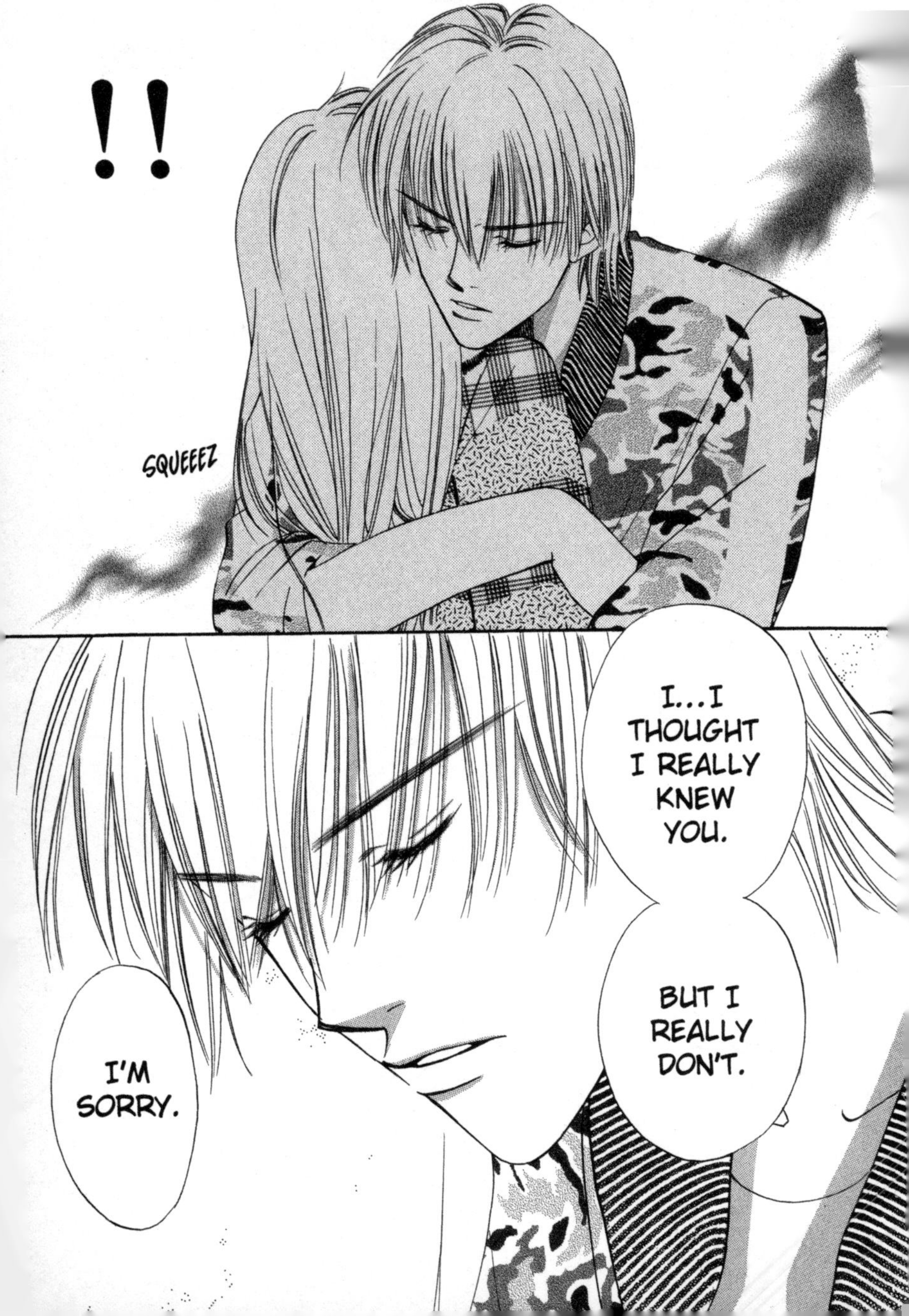
!!
SQUEEEZ
I...I THOUGHT I REALLY KNEW YOU.
BUT I REALLY DON'T.
I'M SORRY.

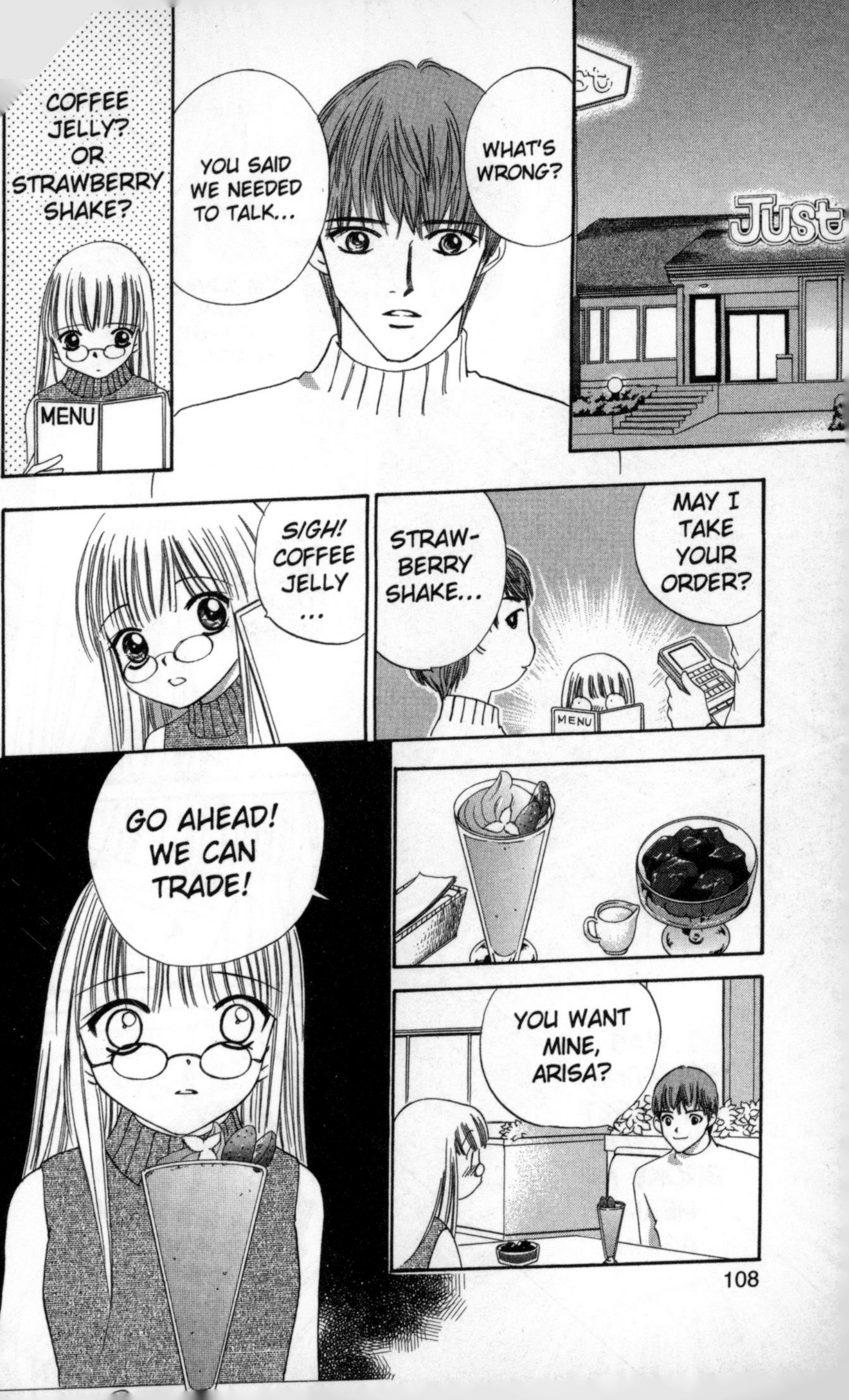
Just
WHAT'S WRONG?
YOU SAID WE NEEDED TO TALK...
COFFEE JELLY? OR STRAWBERRY SHAKE?
MENU
MAY I TAKE YOUR ORDER?
STRAW-BERRY SHAKE...
MENU
SIGH! COFFEE JELLY ...
YOU WANT MINE, ARISA?
GO AHEAD! WE CAN TRADE!

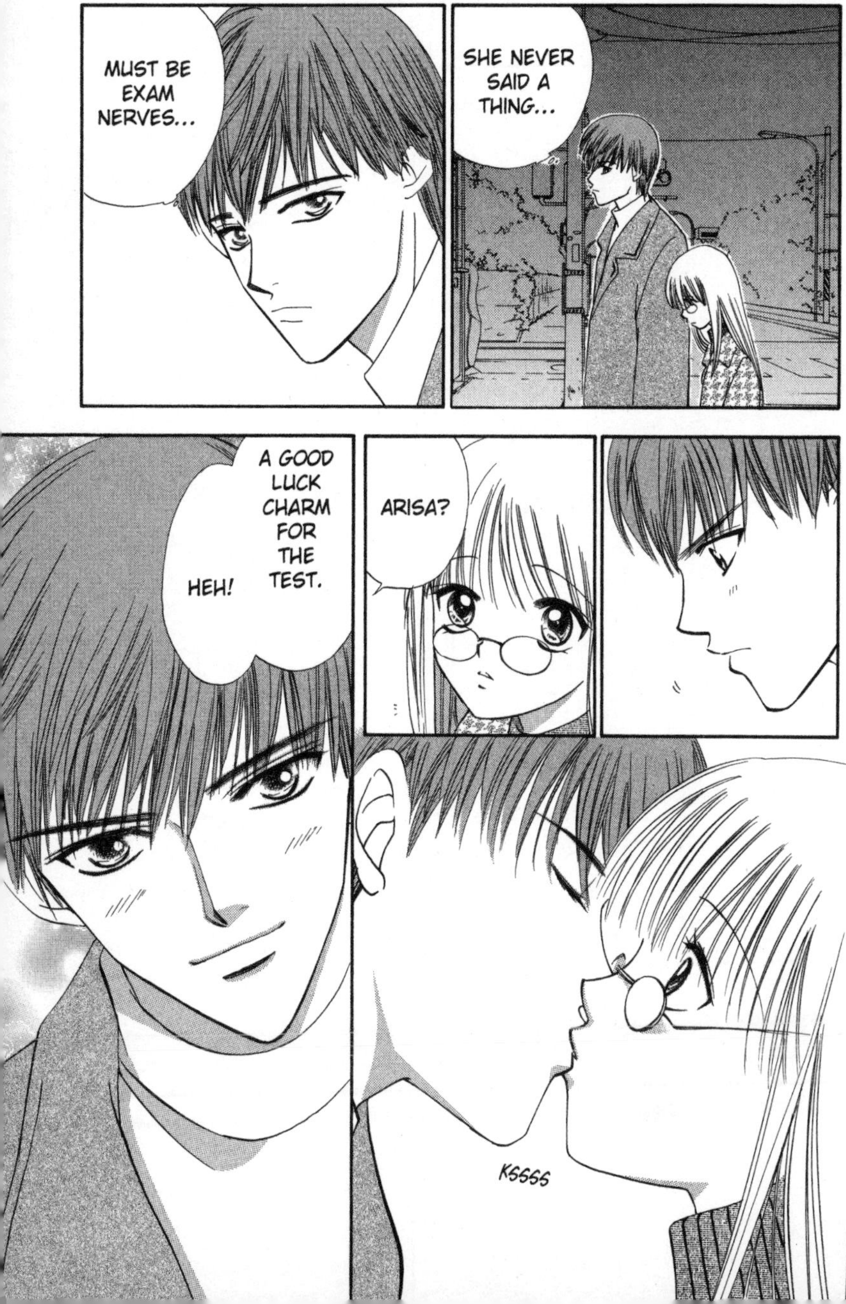
SHE NEVER SAID A THING...
MUST BE EXAM NERVES...
ARISA?
KSSSS
A GOOD LUCK CHARM FOR THE TEST.
HEH!

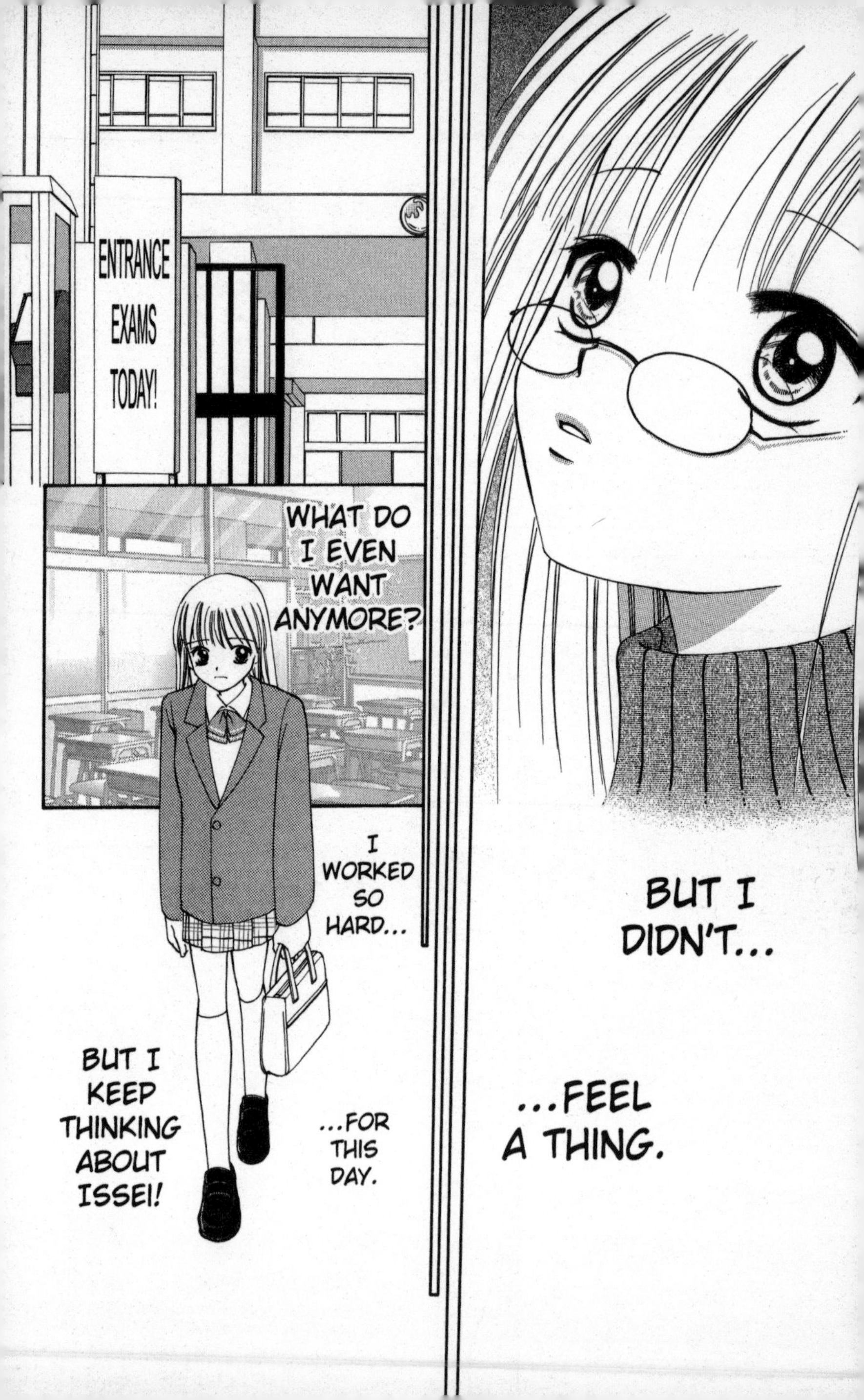
BUT I DIDN'T...
...FEEL A THING.
ENTRANCE EXAMS TODAY!
WHAT DO I EVEN WANT ANYMORE?
I WORKED SO HARD...
...FOR THIS DAY.
BUT I KEEP THINKING ABOUT ISSEI!

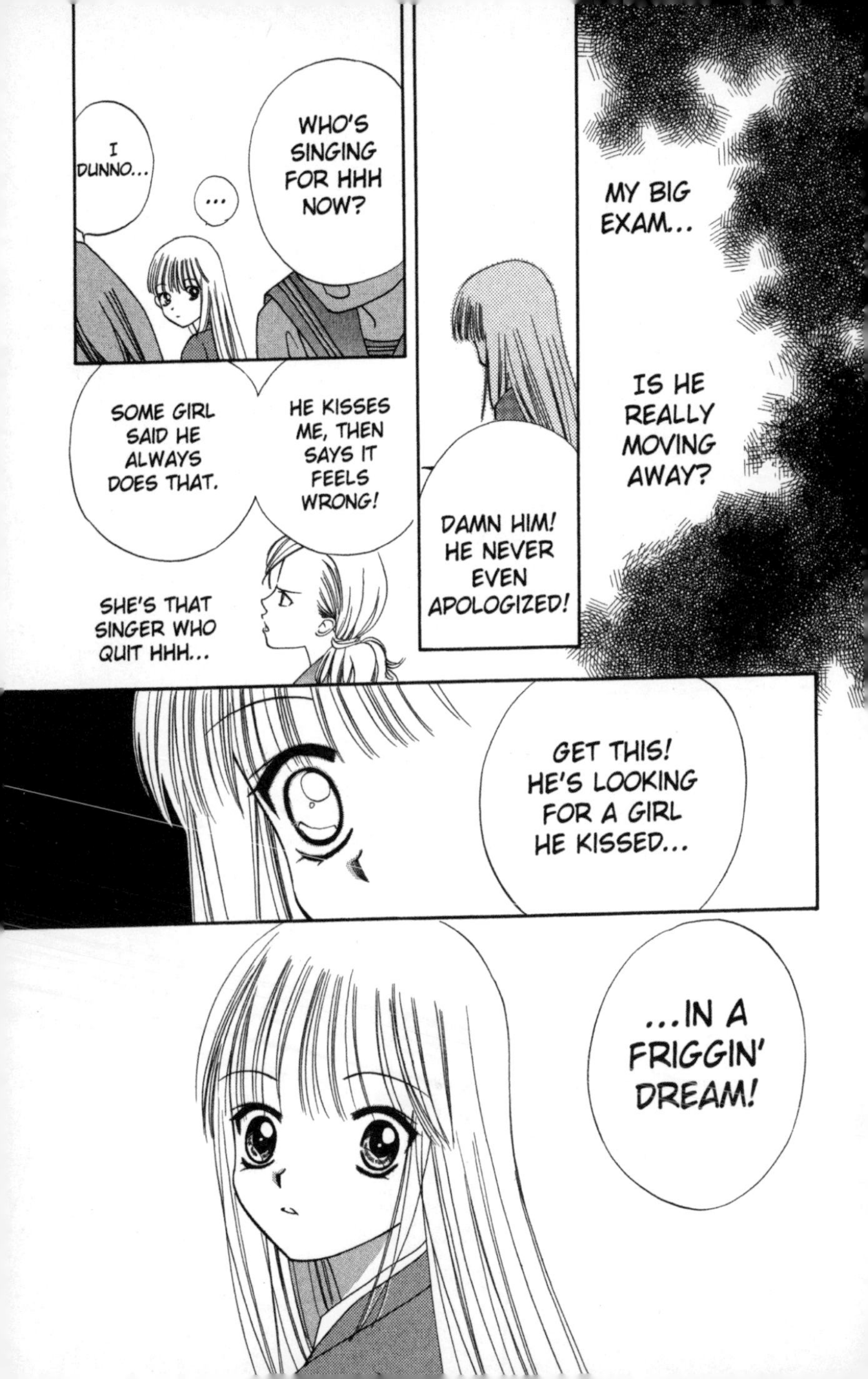
MY BIG EXAM...
IS HE REALLY MOVING AWAY?
DAMN HIM! HE NEVER EVEN APOLOGIZED!
WHO'S SINGING FOR HHH NOW?
...
I DUNNO...
HE KISSES ME, THEN SAYS IT FEELS WRONG!
SOME GIRL SAID HE ALWAYS DOES THAT.
SHE'S THAT SINGER WHO QUIT HHH...
GET THIS! HE'S LOOKING FOR A GIRL HE KISSED...
...IN A FRIGGIN' DREAM!

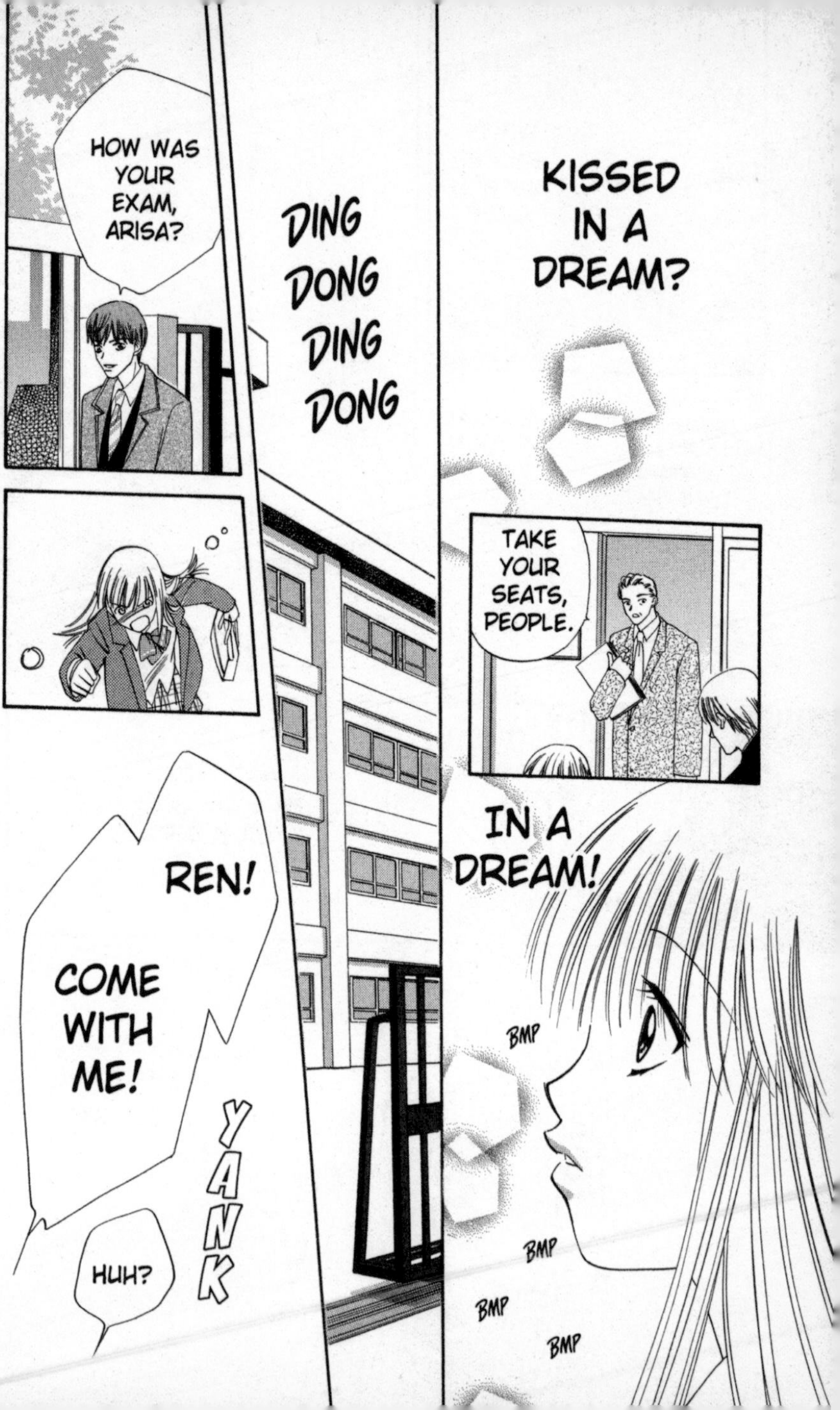
KISSED IN A DREAM?
TAKE YOUR SEATS, PEOPLE.
IN A DREAM!
BMP
BMP
BMP
BMP
DING DONG DING DONG
HOW WAS YOUR EXAM, ARISA?
REN!
COME WITH ME!
YANK
HUH?

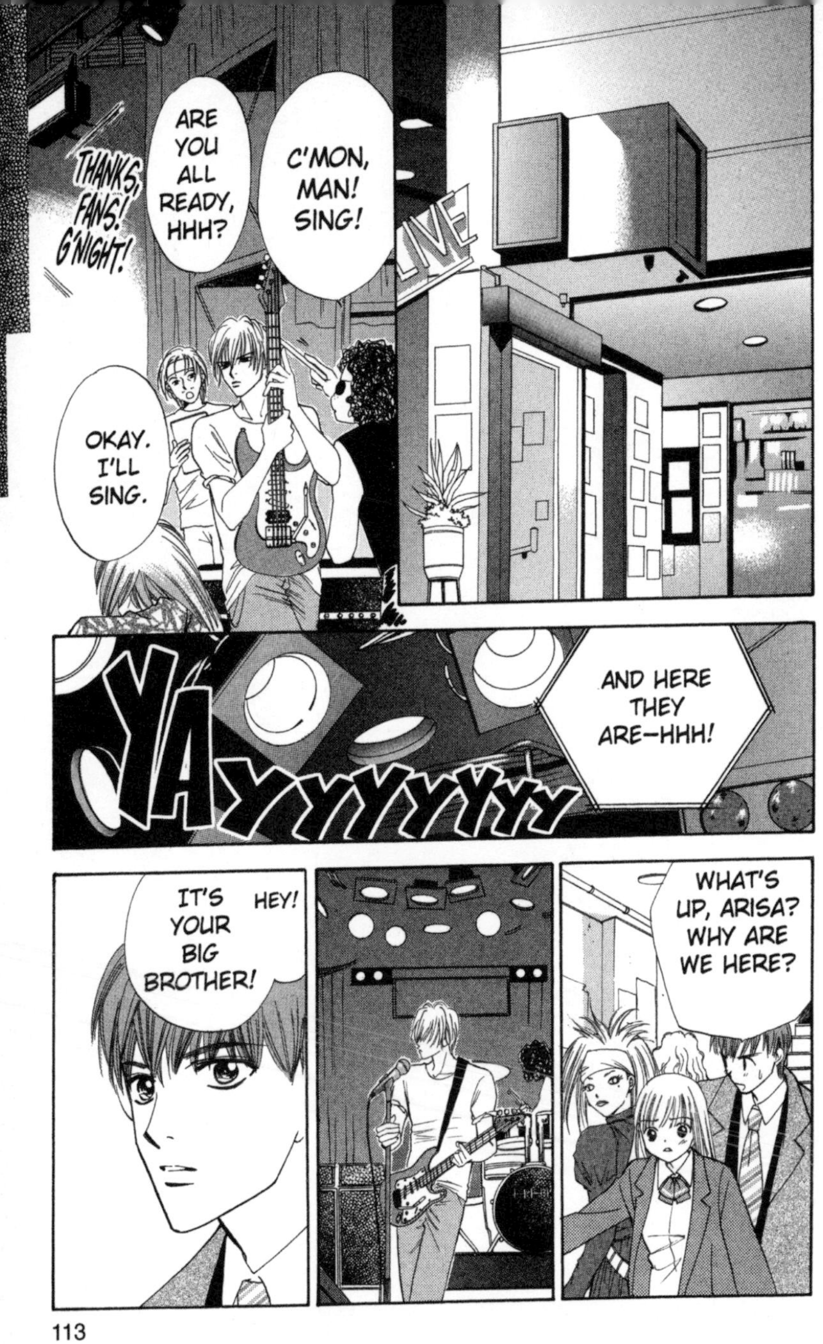
LIVE
C'MON, MAN! SING!
ARE YOU ALL READY, HHH?
THANKS, FANS! G'NIGHT!
OKAY. I'LL SING.
AND HERE THEY ARE—HHH!
YAYYYYYYYY
WHAT'S UP, ARISA? WHY ARE WE HERE?
HEY!
IT'S YOUR BIG BROTHER!

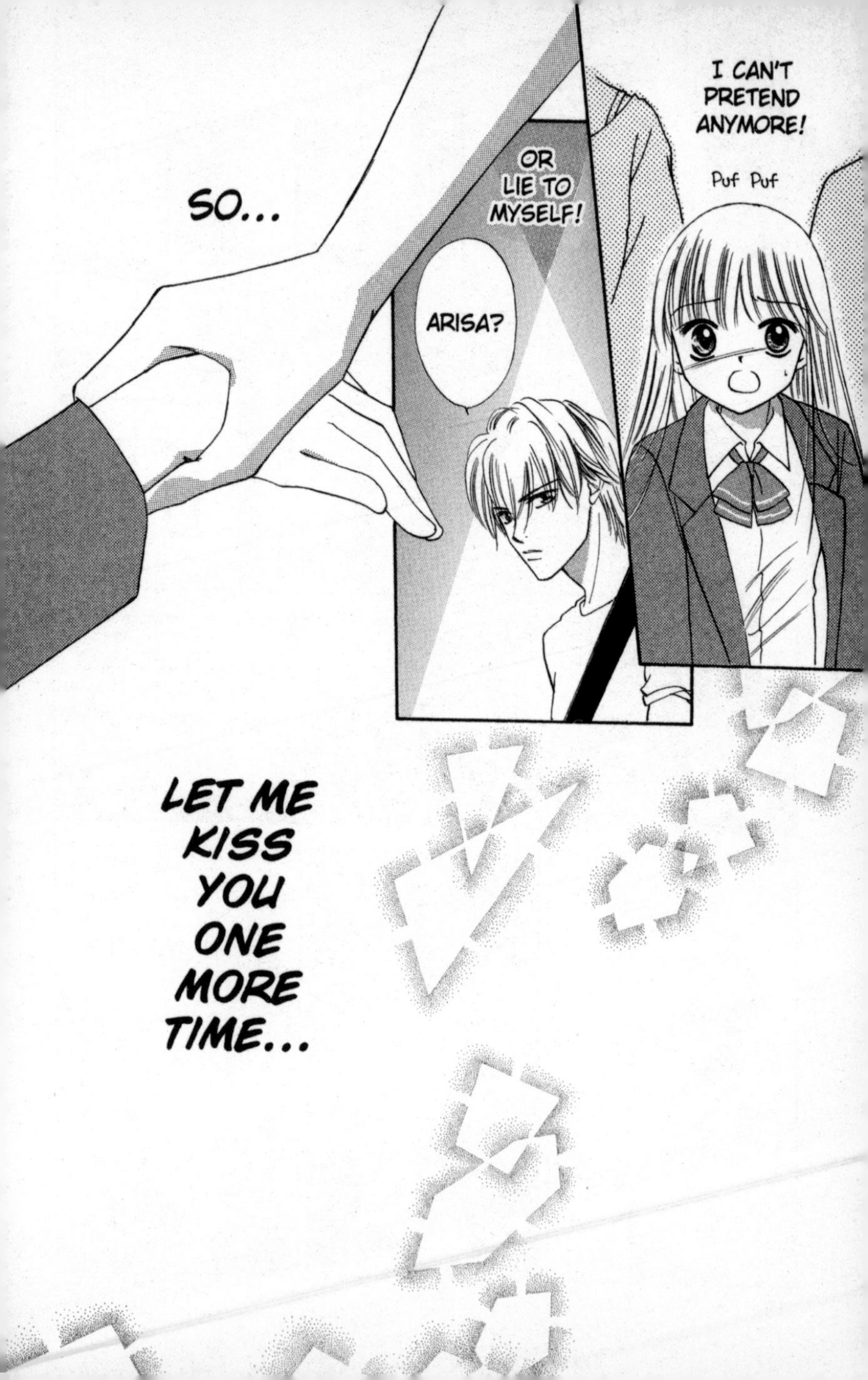
I CAN'T PRETEND ANYMORE!
Puf Puf
OR LIE TO MYSELF!
ARISA?
SO...
LET ME KISS YOU ONE MORE TIME...

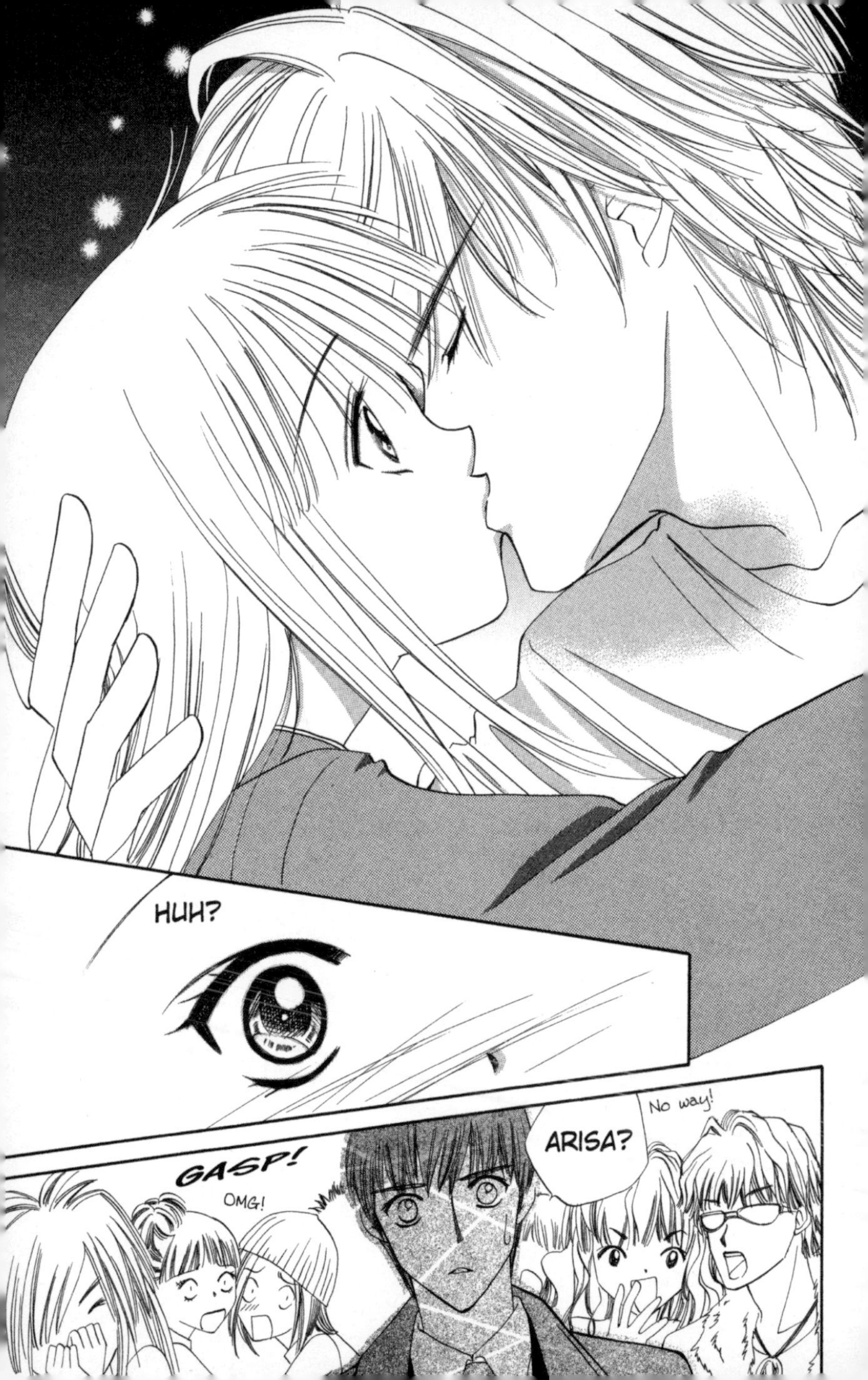
HUH?
No way!
ARISA?
GASP!
OMG!

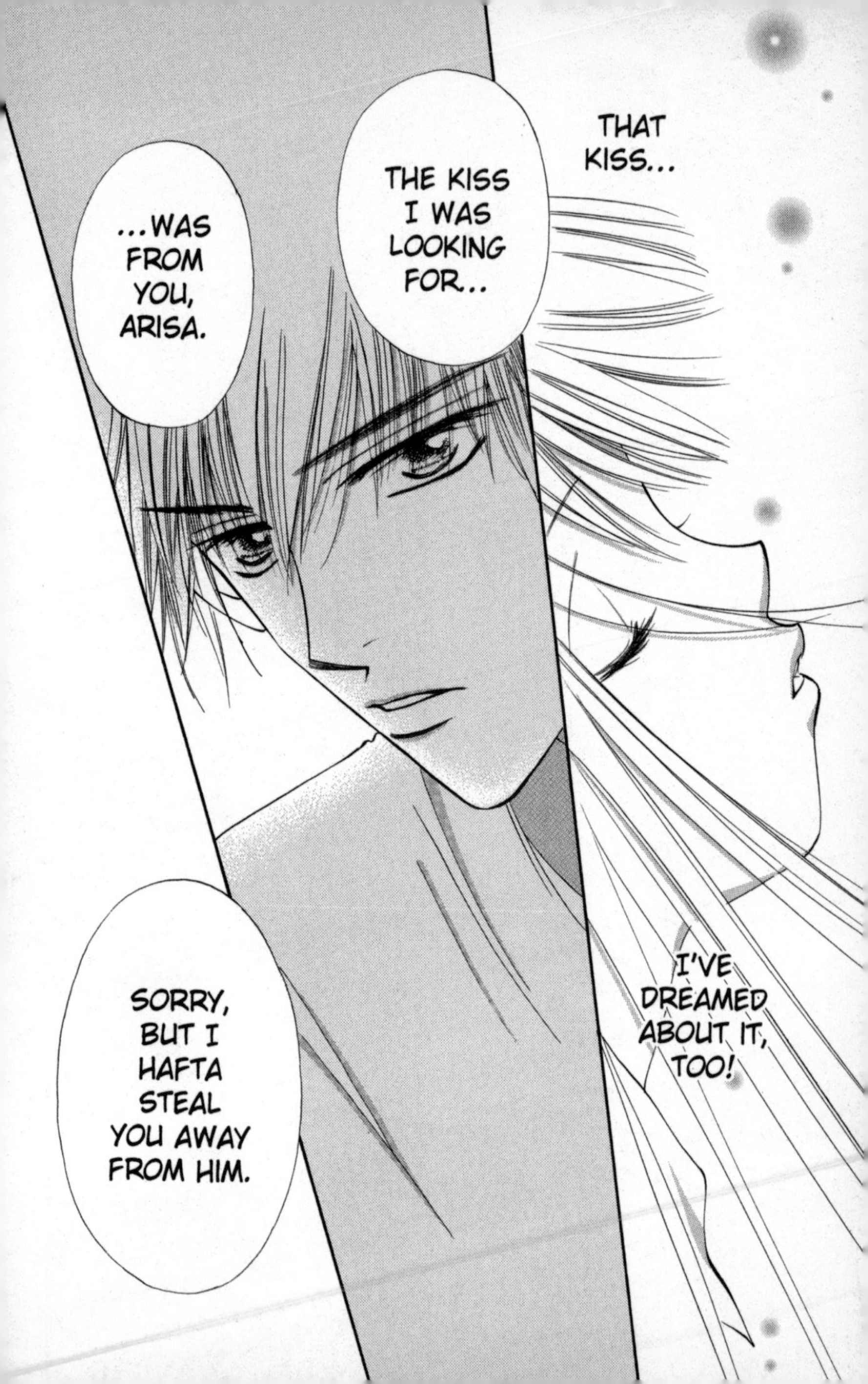
THAT KISS...
THE KISS I WAS LOOKING FOR...
...WAS FROM YOU, ARISA.
I'VE DREAMED ABOUT IT, TOO!
SORRY, BUT I HAFTA STEAL YOU AWAY FROM HIM.

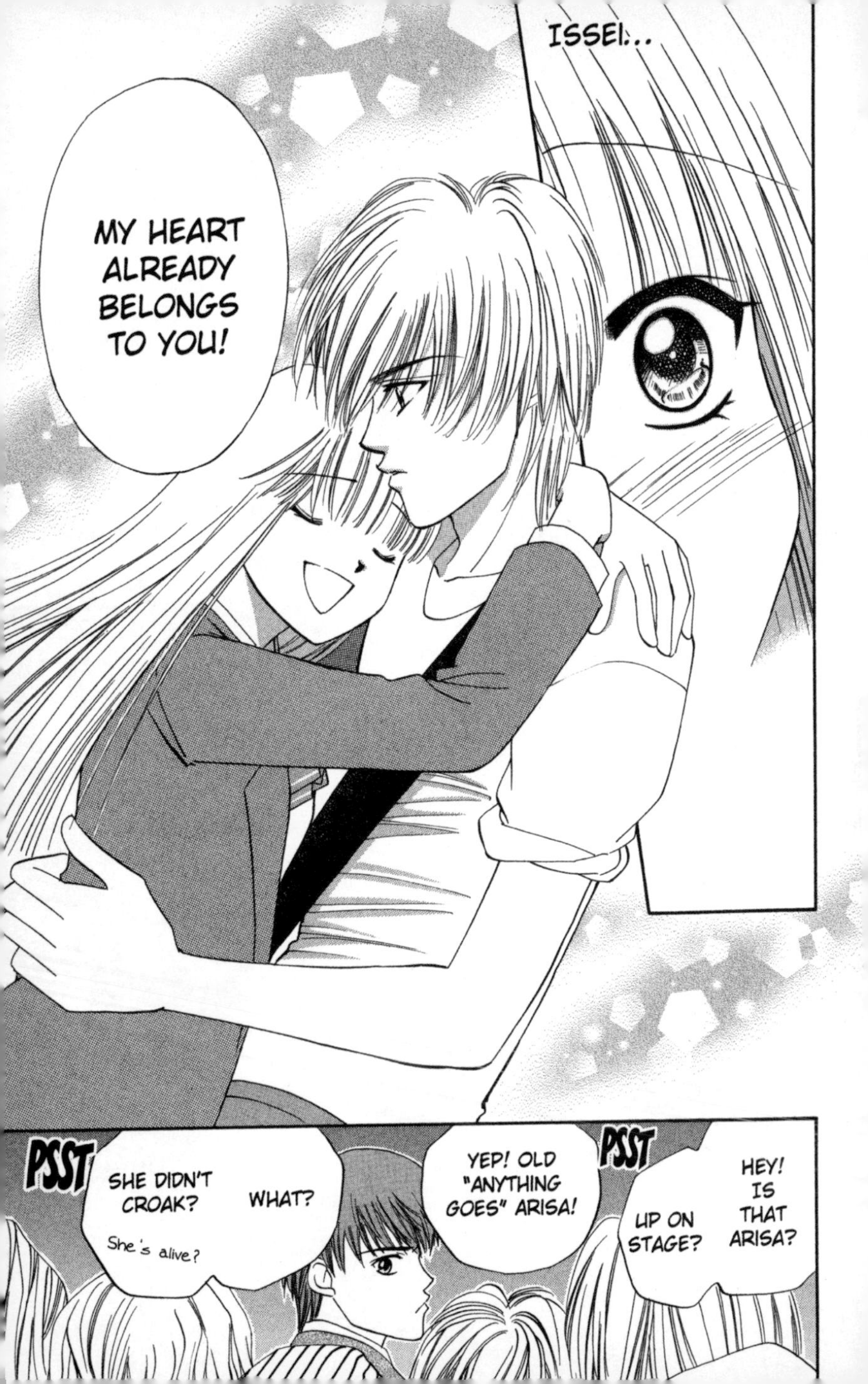
ISSEI...
MY HEART ALREADY BELONGS TO YOU!
PSST
HEY! IS THAT ARISA?
UP ON STAGE?
YEP! OLD "ANYTHING GOES" ARISA!
WHAT?
SHE DIDN'T CROAK?
She's alive?
PSST

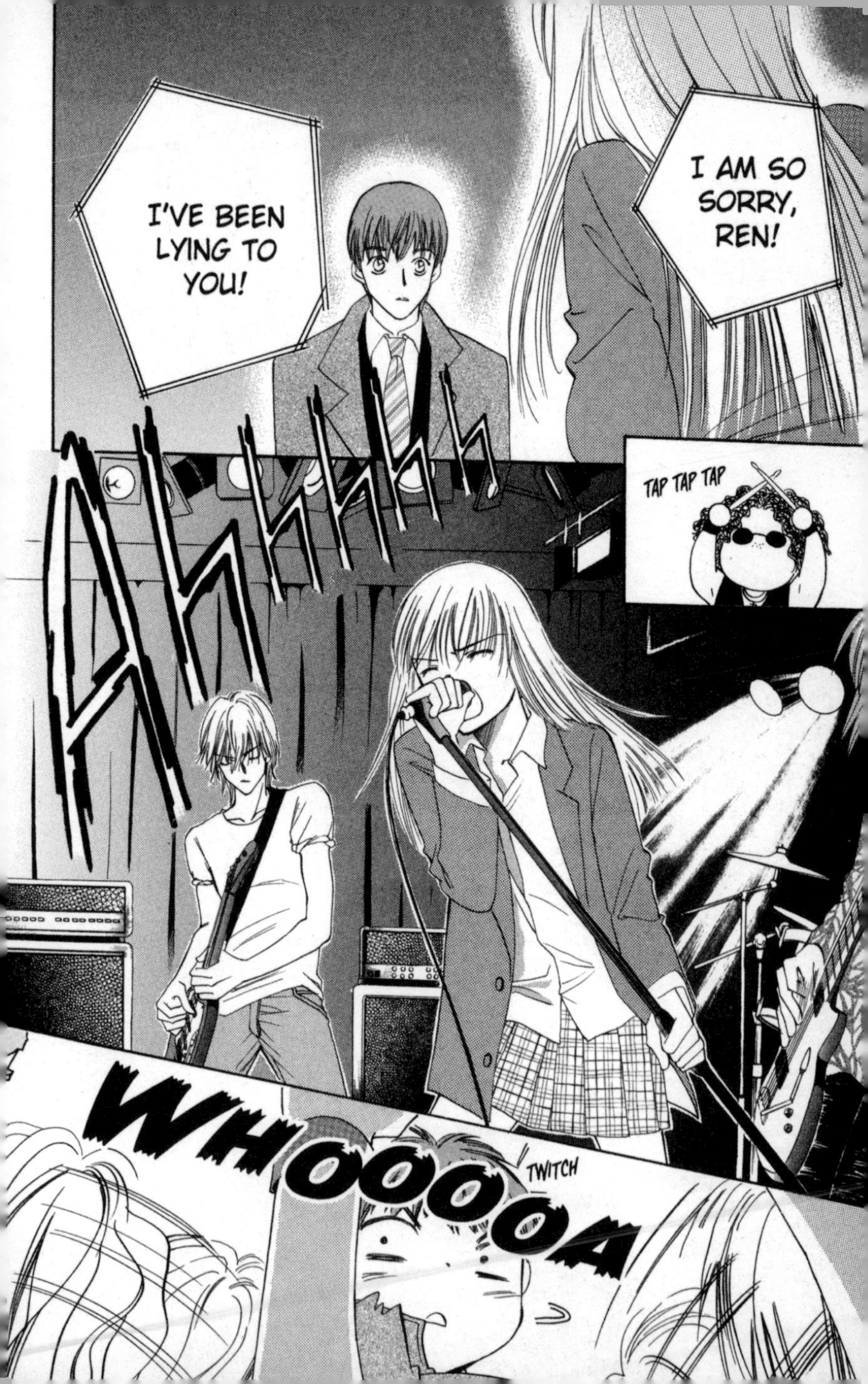
I AM SO SORRY, REN!
I'VE BEEN LYING TO YOU!
TAP TAP TAP
AHHHHHH
TWITCH
WHOOOOOA

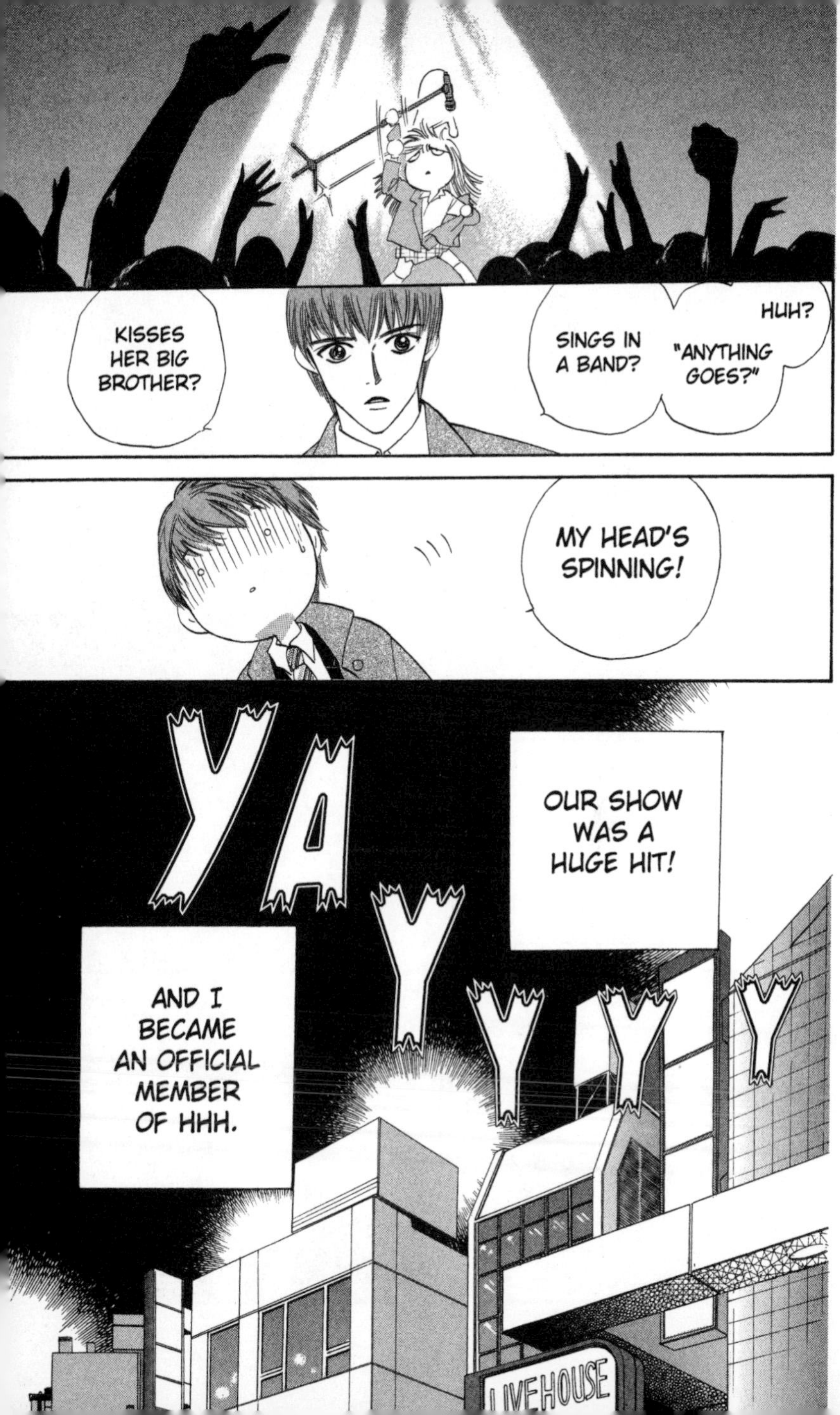
HUH?
"ANYTHING GOES?"
SINGS IN A BAND?
KISSES HER BIG BROTHER?
MY HEAD'S SPINNING!
YAYYYY
OUR SHOW WAS A HUGE HIT!
AND I BECAME AN OFFICIAL MEMBER OF HHH.
LIVE HOUSE

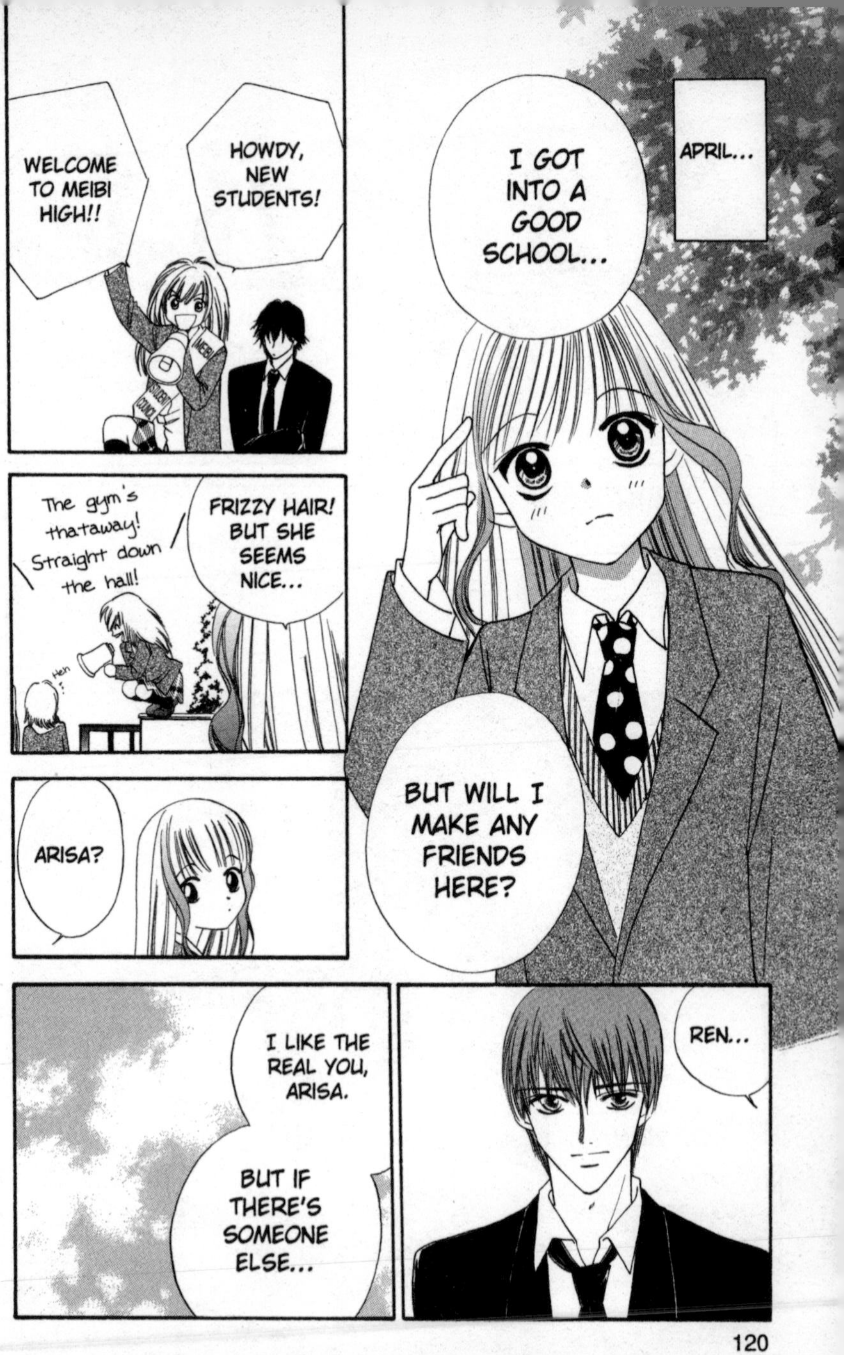
APRIL...
I GOT INTO A GOOD SCHOOL...
BUT WILL I MAKE ANY FRIENDS HERE?
HOWDY, NEW STUDENTS!
WELCOME TO MEIBI HIGH!!
FRIZZY HAIR! BUT SHE SEEMS NICE...
The gym's thataway! Straight down the hall!
ARISA?
REN...
I LIKE THE REAL YOU, ARISA.
BUT IF THERE'S SOMEONE ELSE...

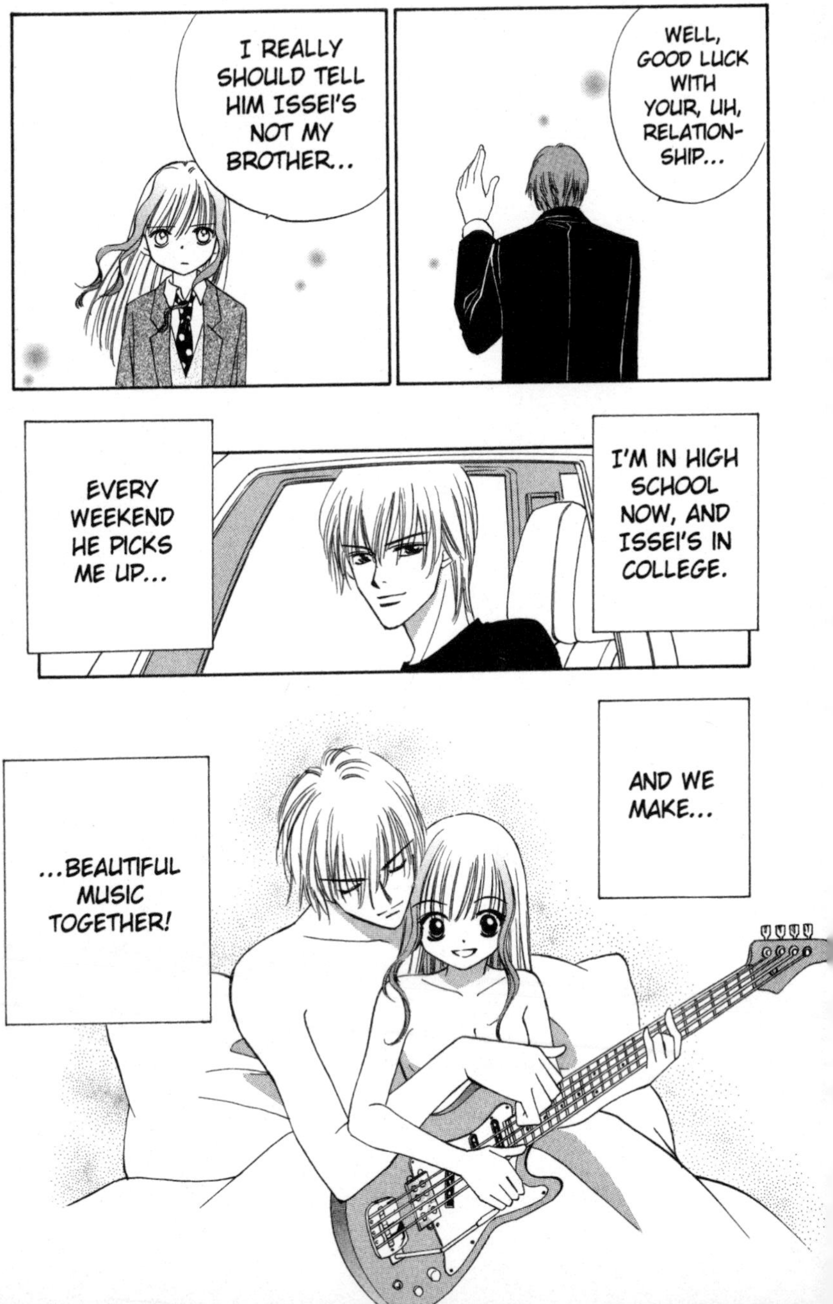
WELL, GOOD LUCK WITH YOUR, UH, RELATIONSHIP...
I REALLY SHOULD TELL HIM ISSEI'S NOT MY BROTHER...
I'M IN HIGH SCHOOL NOW, AND ISSEI'S IN COLLEGE.
EVERY WEEKEND HE PICKS ME UP...
AND WE MAKE...
...BEAUTIFUL MUSIC TOGETHER!

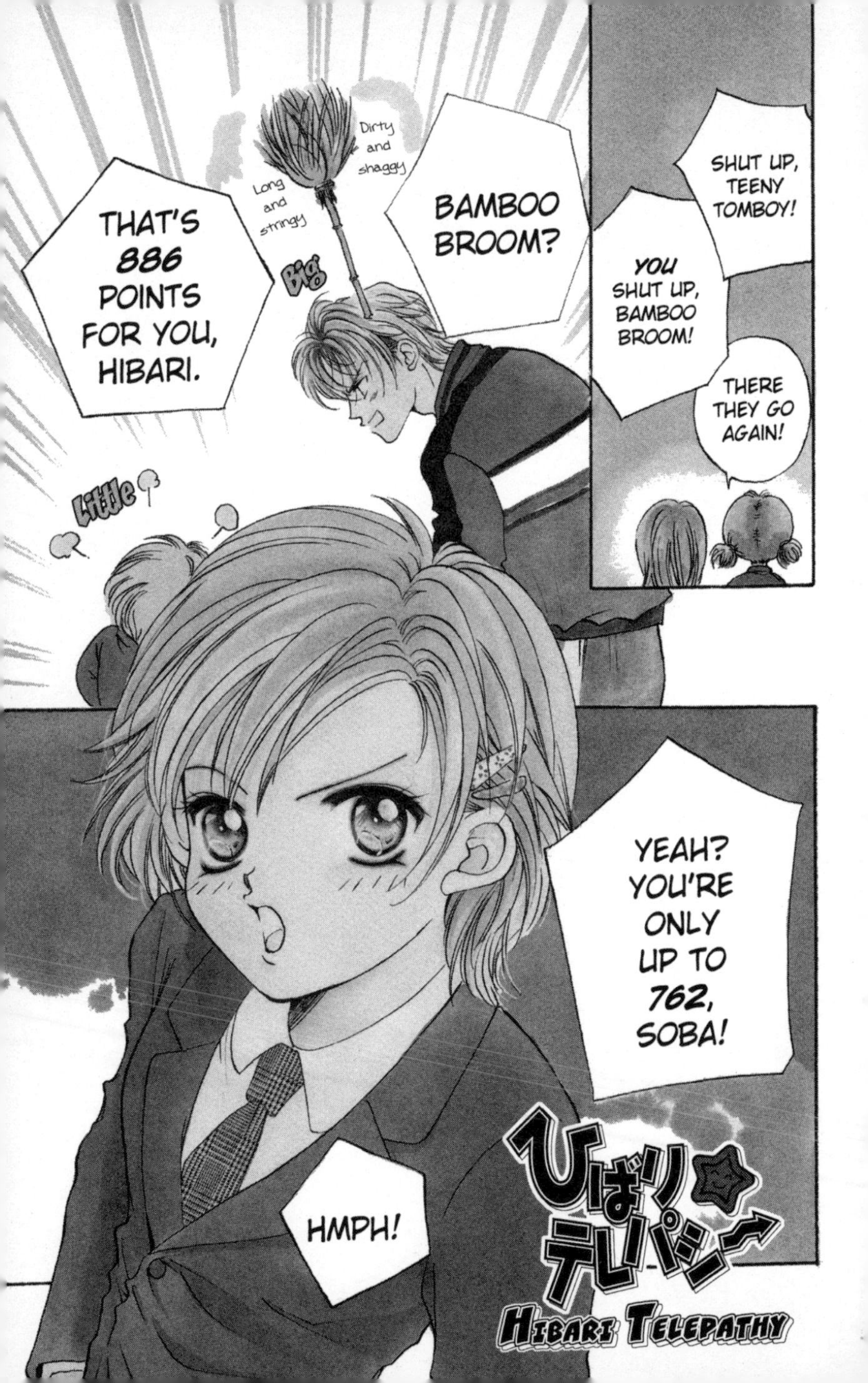
SHUT UP, TEENY TOMBOY!
YOU SHUT UP, BAMBOO BROOM!
THERE THEY GO AGAIN!
BAMBOO BROOM?
Dirty and shaggy
Long and stringy
Big
THAT'S 886 POINTS FOR YOU, HIBARI.
Little
YEAH? YOU'RE ONLY UP TO 762, SOBA!
HMPH!
ひばり☆テレパシー
HIBARI TELEPATHY

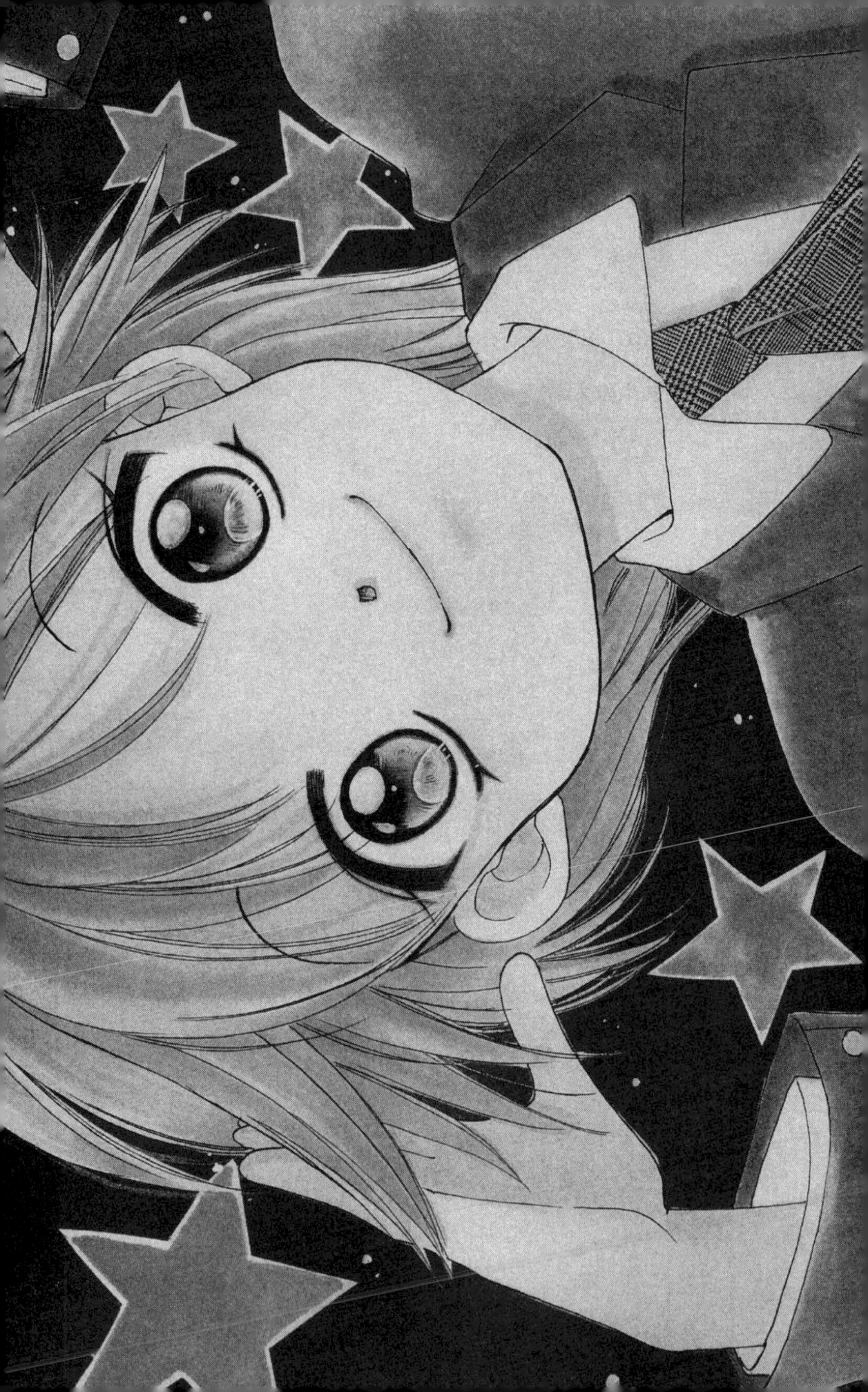

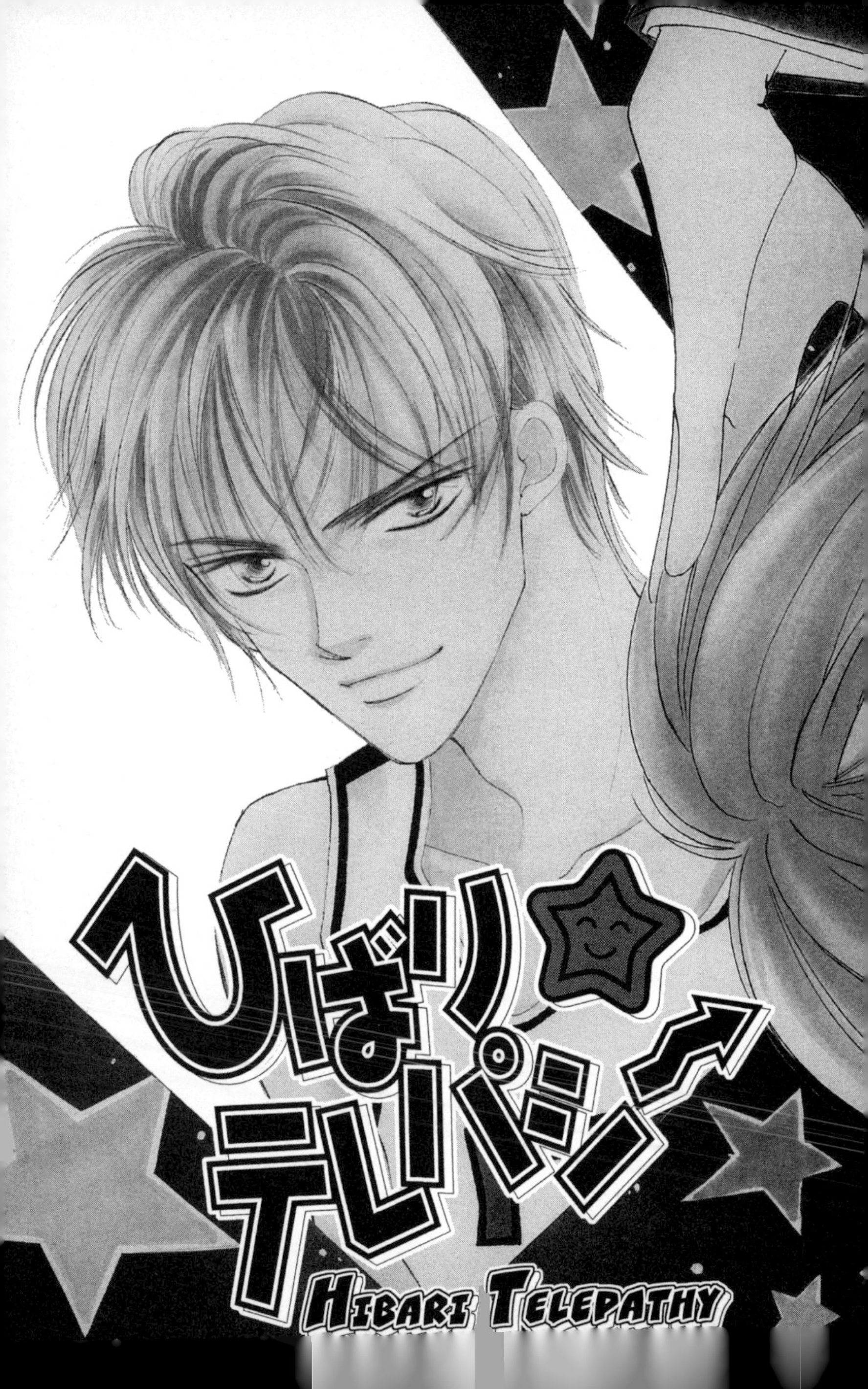
ひばりテレパシー
HIBARI TELEPATHY

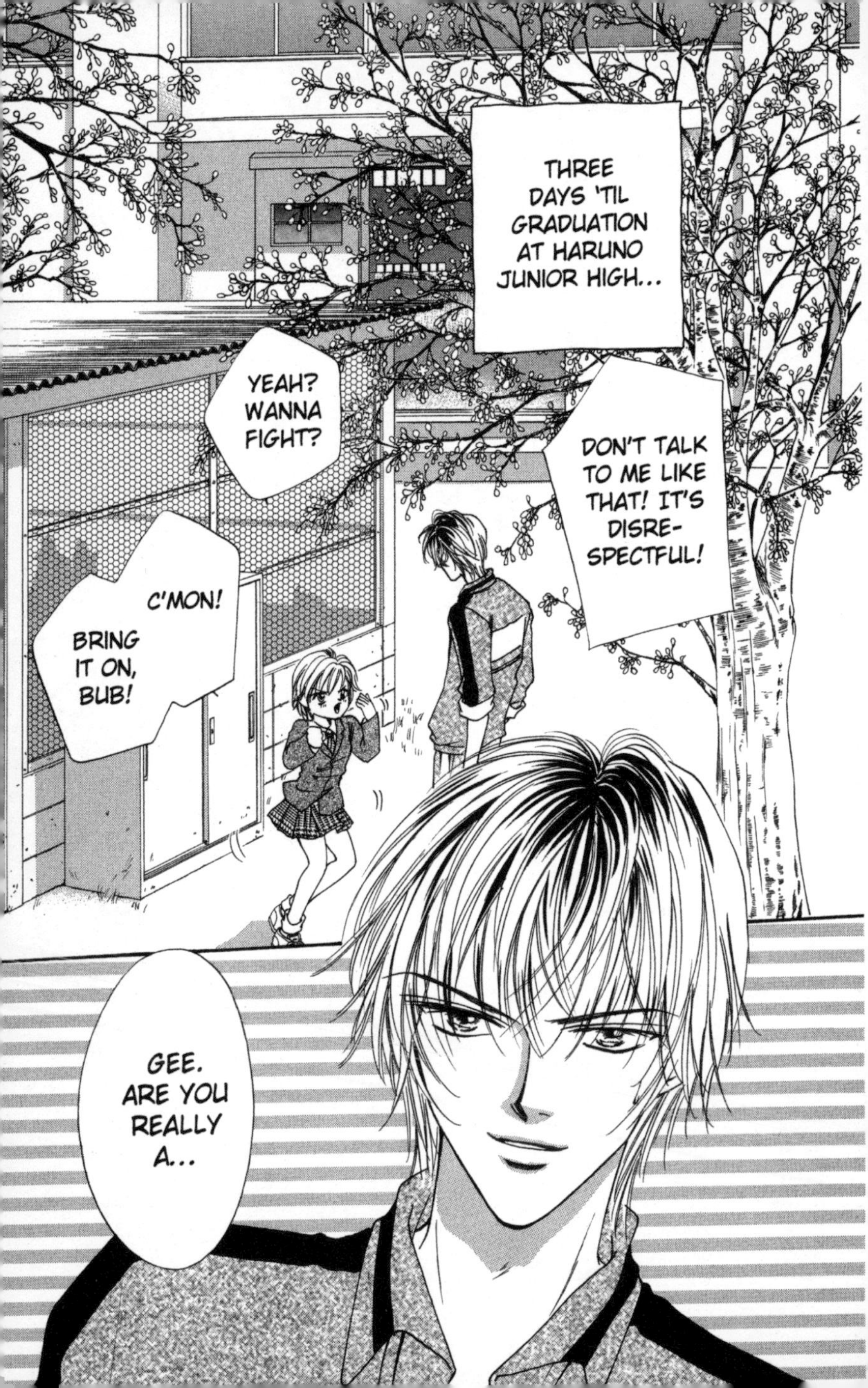
THREE DAYS 'TIL GRADUATION AT HARUNO JUNIOR HIGH...
DON'T TALK TO ME LIKE THAT! IT'S DISRE-SPECTFUL!
YEAH? WANNA FIGHT?
C'MON!
BRING IT ON, BUB!
GEE. ARE YOU REALLY A...

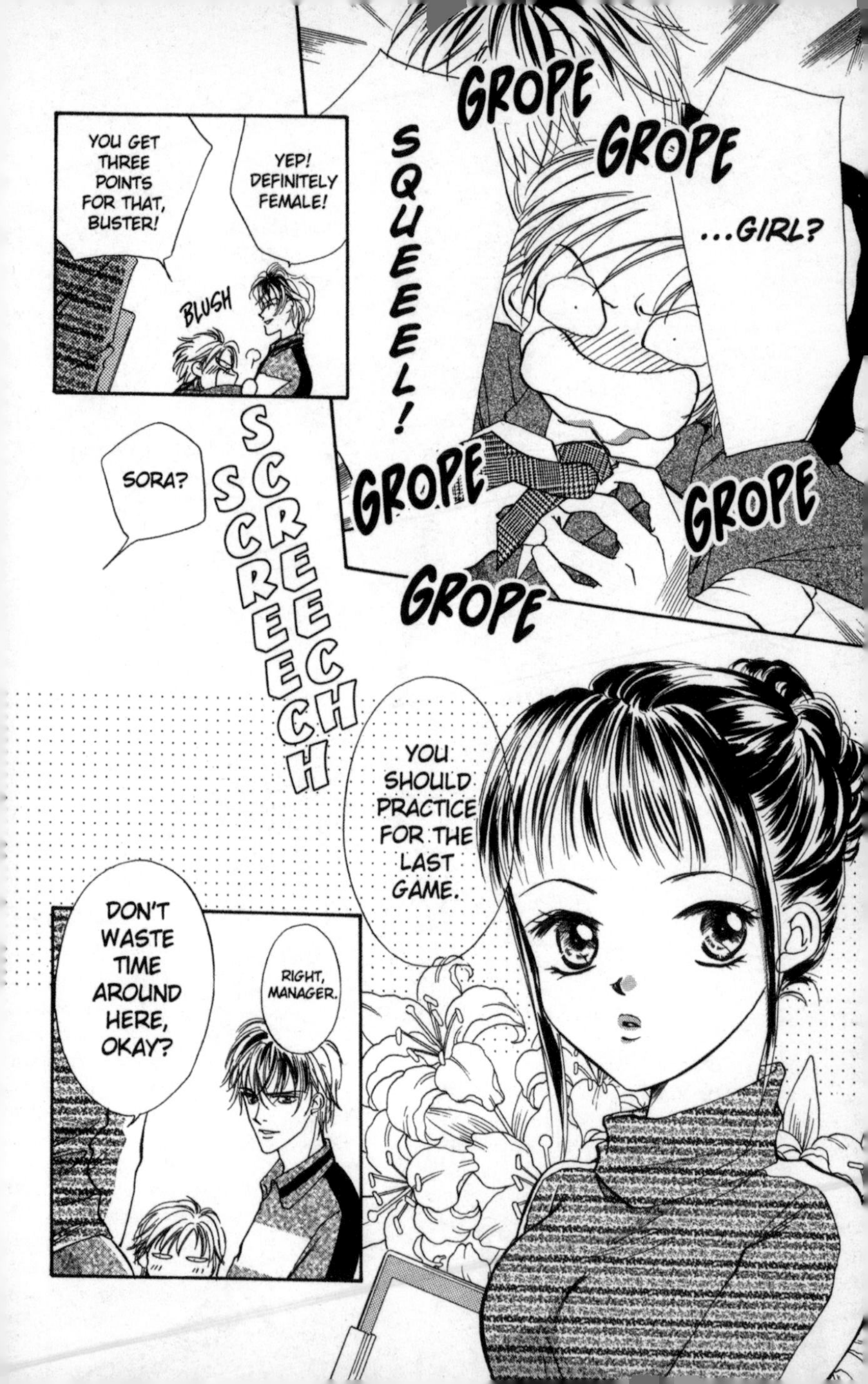
GROPE
GROPE
...GIRL?
SQUEEEEL!
GROPE
GROPE
GROPE
YEP! DEFINITELY FEMALE!
YOU GET THREE POINTS FOR THAT, BUSTER!
BLUSH
SORA?
SCREECH
SCREECH
YOU SHOULD PRACTICE FOR THE LAST GAME.
RIGHT, MANAGER.
DON'T WASTE TIME AROUND HERE, OKAY?

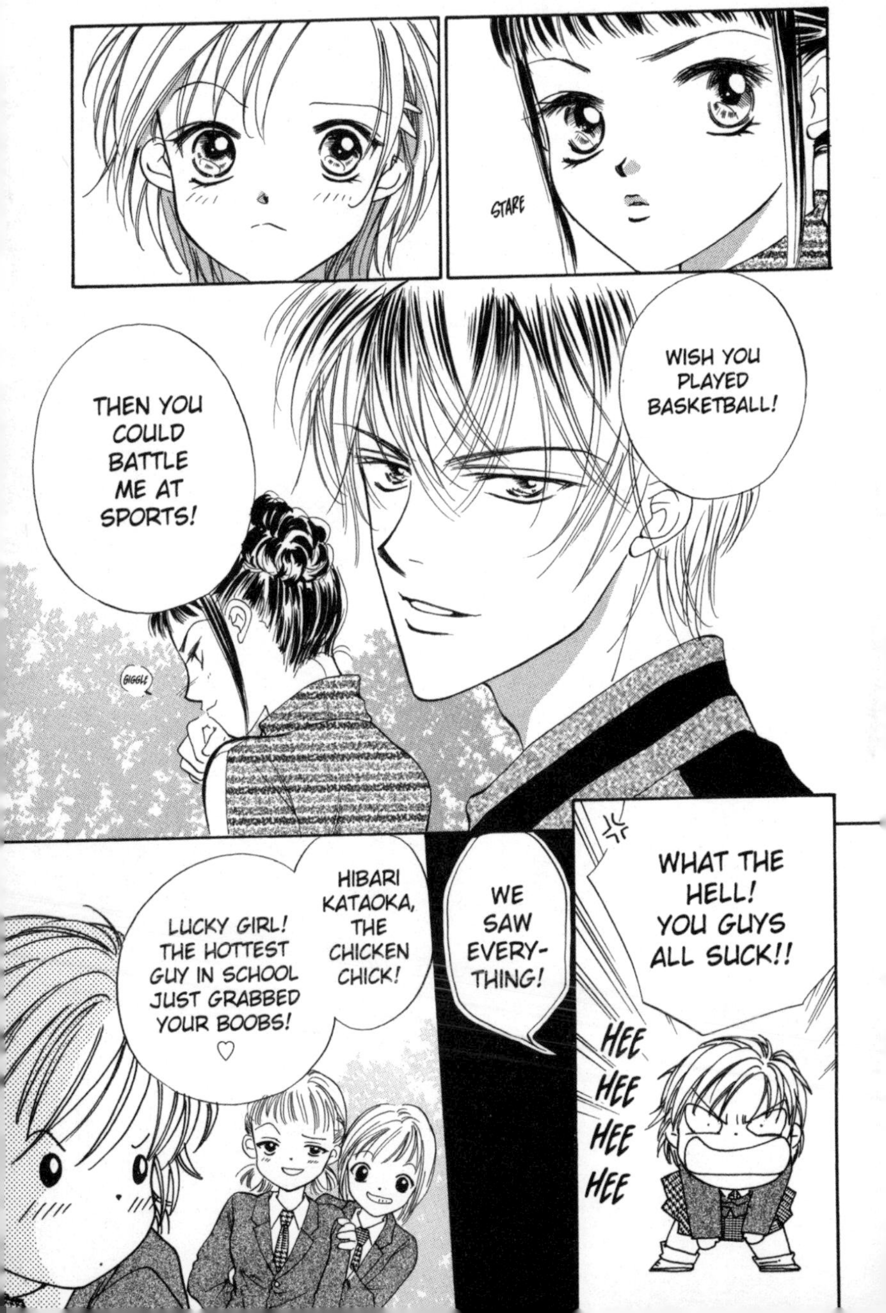
STARE
WISH YOU PLAYED BASKETBALL!
THEN YOU COULD BATTLE ME AT SPORTS!
GIGGLE
WHAT THE HELL! YOU GUYS ALL SUCK!!
HEE HEE HEE HEE
WE SAW EVERY-THING!
HIBARI KATAOKA, THE CHICKEN CHICK!
LUCKY GIRL! THE HOTTEST GUY IN SCHOOL JUST GRABBED YOUR BOOBS! ♡

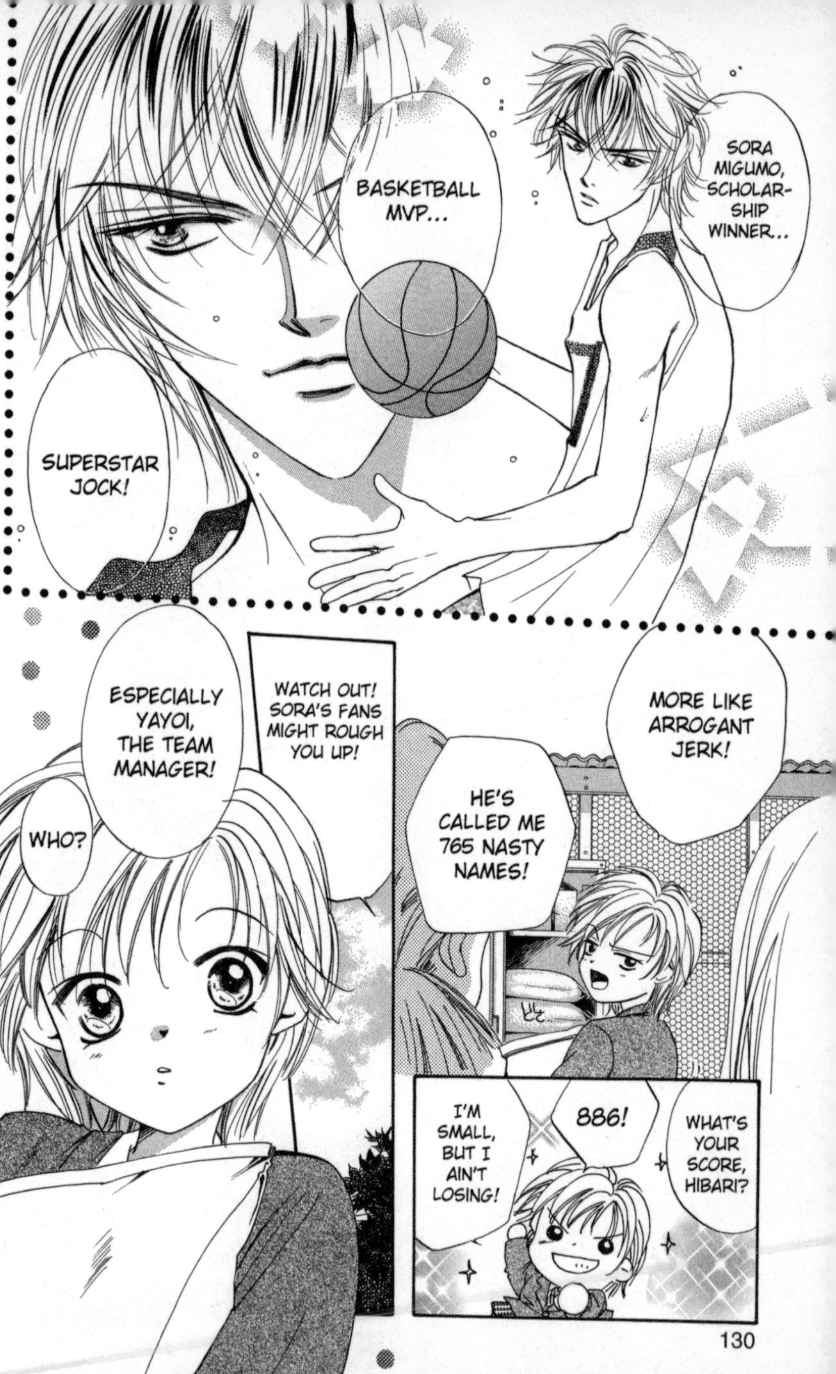
SORA MIGUMO, SCHOLAR-SHIP WINNER...
BASKETBALL MVP...
SUPERSTAR JOCK!
MORE LIKE ARROGANT JERK!
HE'S CALLED ME 765 NASTY NAMES!
WHAT'S YOUR SCORE, HIBARI?
886!
I'M SMALL, BUT I AIN'T LOSING!
WATCH OUT! SORA'S FANS MIGHT ROUGH YOU UP!
ESPECIALLY YAYOI, THE TEAM MANAGER!
WHO?

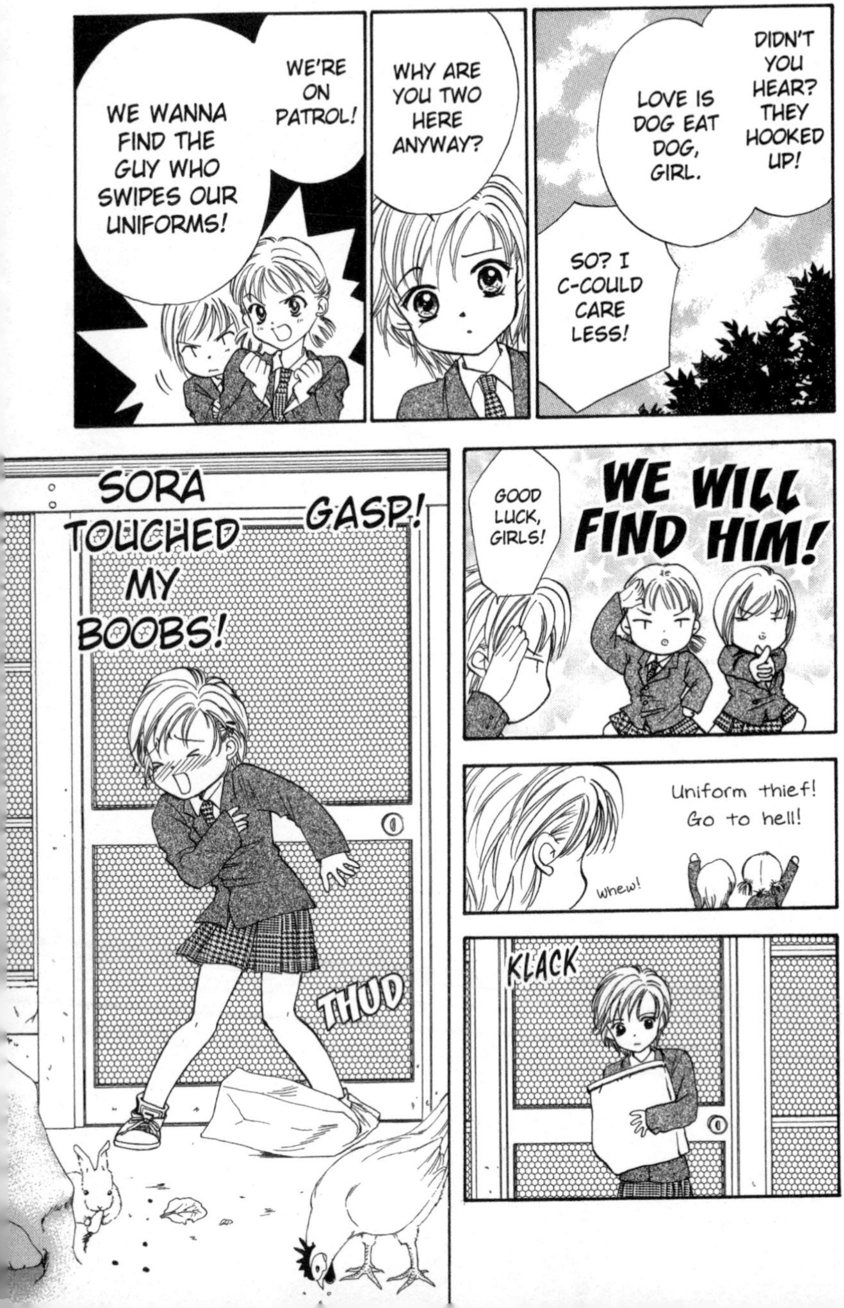
DIDN'T YOU HEAR? THEY HOOKED UP!
LOVE IS DOG EAT DOG, GIRL.
SO? I C-COULD CARE LESS!
WHY ARE YOU TWO HERE ANYWAY?
WE'RE ON PATROL!
WE WANNA FIND THE GUY WHO SWIPES OUR UNIFORMS!
WE WILL FIND HIM!
GOOD LUCK, GIRLS!
Uniform thief! Go to hell!
Whew!
KLACK
GASP!
SORA TOUCHED MY BOOBS!
THUD

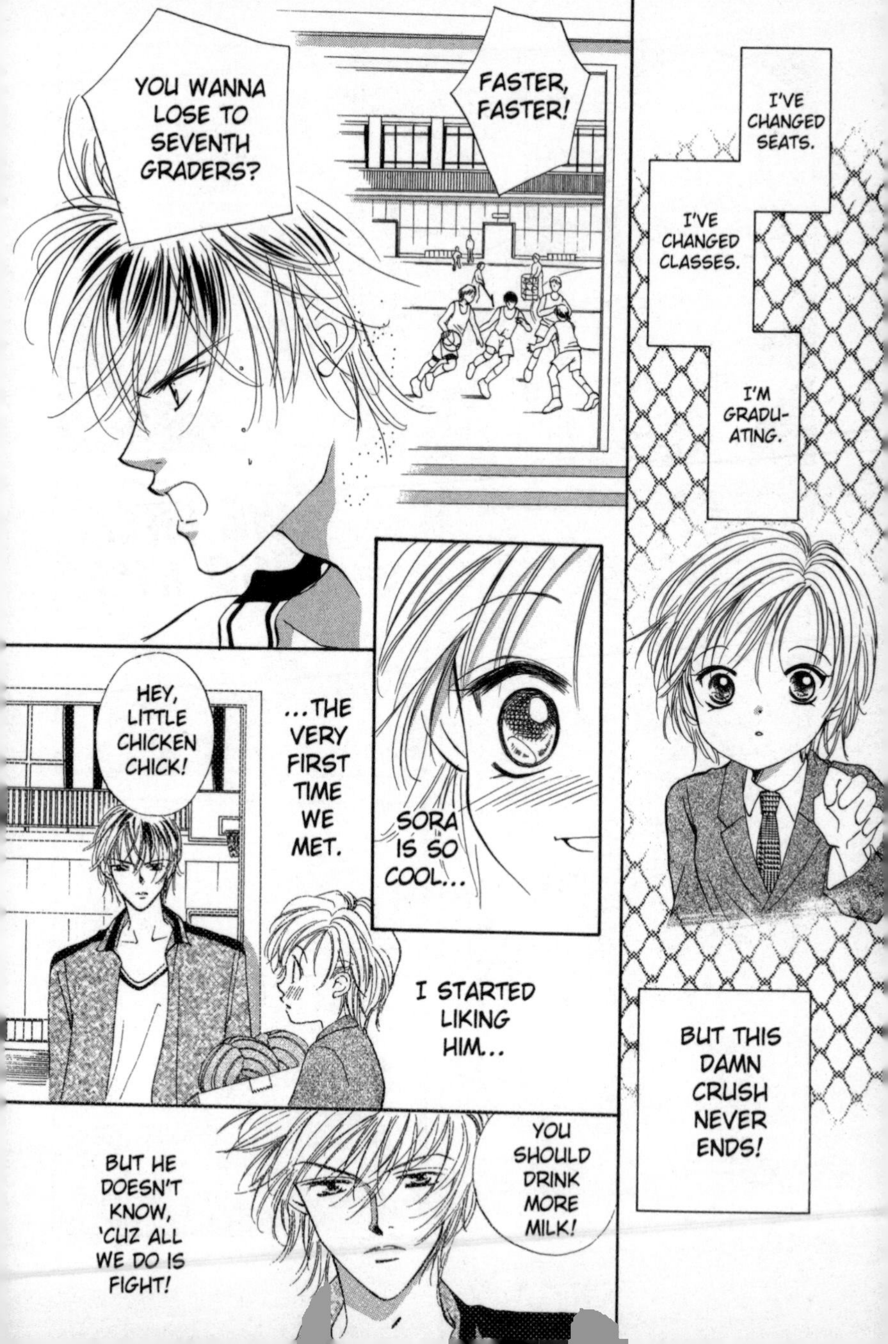
I'VE CHANGED SEATS.
I'VE CHANGED CLASSES.
I'M GRADUATING.
BUT THIS DAMN CRUSH NEVER ENDS!
FASTER, FASTER!
YOU WANNA LOSE TO SEVENTH GRADERS?
SORA IS SO COOL...
...THE VERY FIRST TIME WE MET.
HEY, LITTLE CHICKEN CHICK!
I STARTED LIKING HIM...
YOU SHOULD DRINK MORE MILK!
BUT HE DOESN'T KNOW, 'CUZ ALL WE DO IS FIGHT!

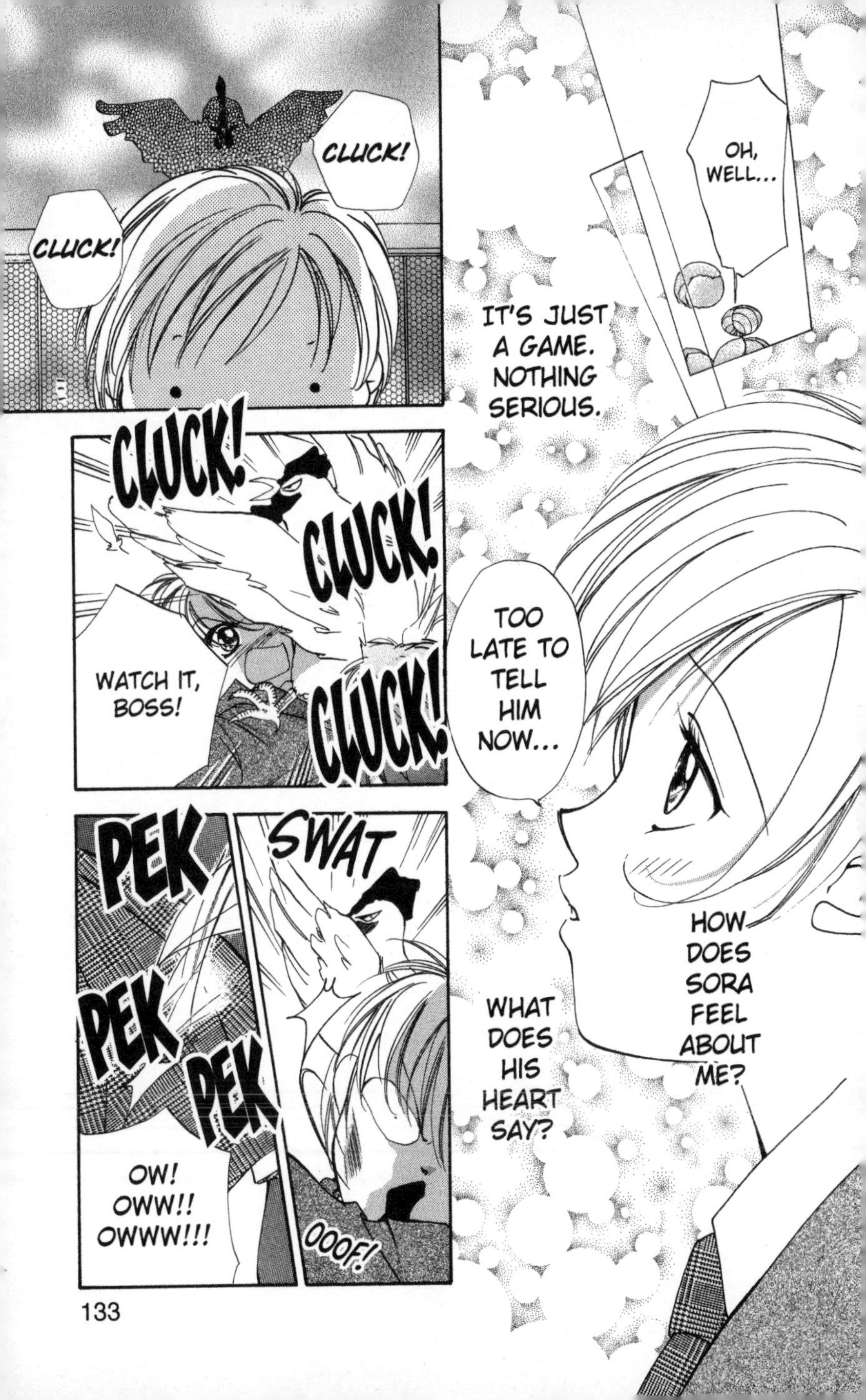
OH, WELL...
IT'S JUST A GAME. NOTHING SERIOUS.
TOO LATE TO TELL HIM NOW...
HOW DOES SORA FEEL ABOUT ME?
WHAT DOES HIS HEART SAY?
CLUCK!
CLUCK!
CLUCK!
CLUCK!
CLUCK!
WATCH IT, BOSS!
SWAT
OOOF!
PEK
PEK
PEK
OW! OWW!! OWWW!!!

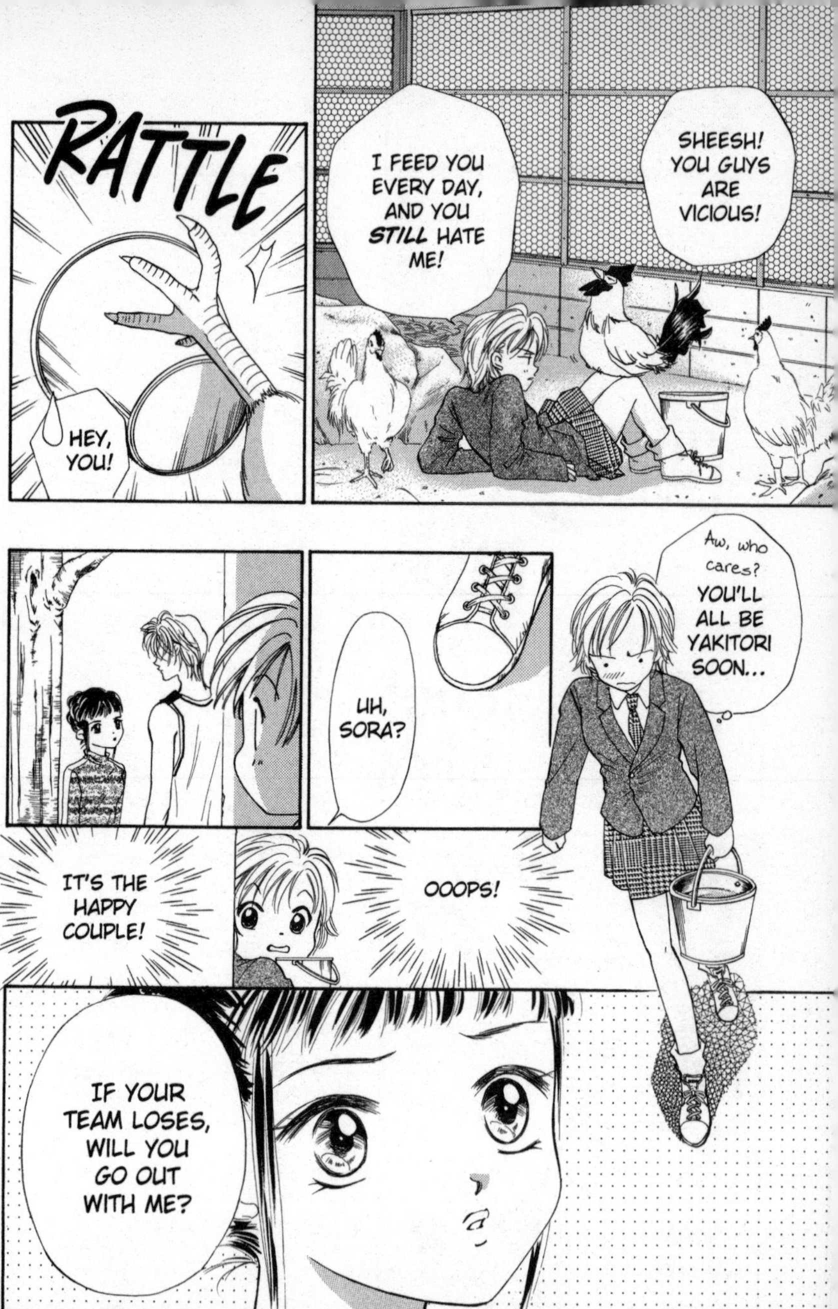
SHEESH! YOU GUYS ARE VICIOUS!
I FEED YOU EVERY DAY, AND YOU STILL HATE ME!
RATTLE
HEY, YOU!
Aw, who cares? YOU'LL ALL BE YAKITORI SOON...
UH, SORA?
OOOPS!
IT'S THE HAPPY COUPLE!
IF YOUR TEAM LOSES, WILL YOU GO OUT WITH ME?

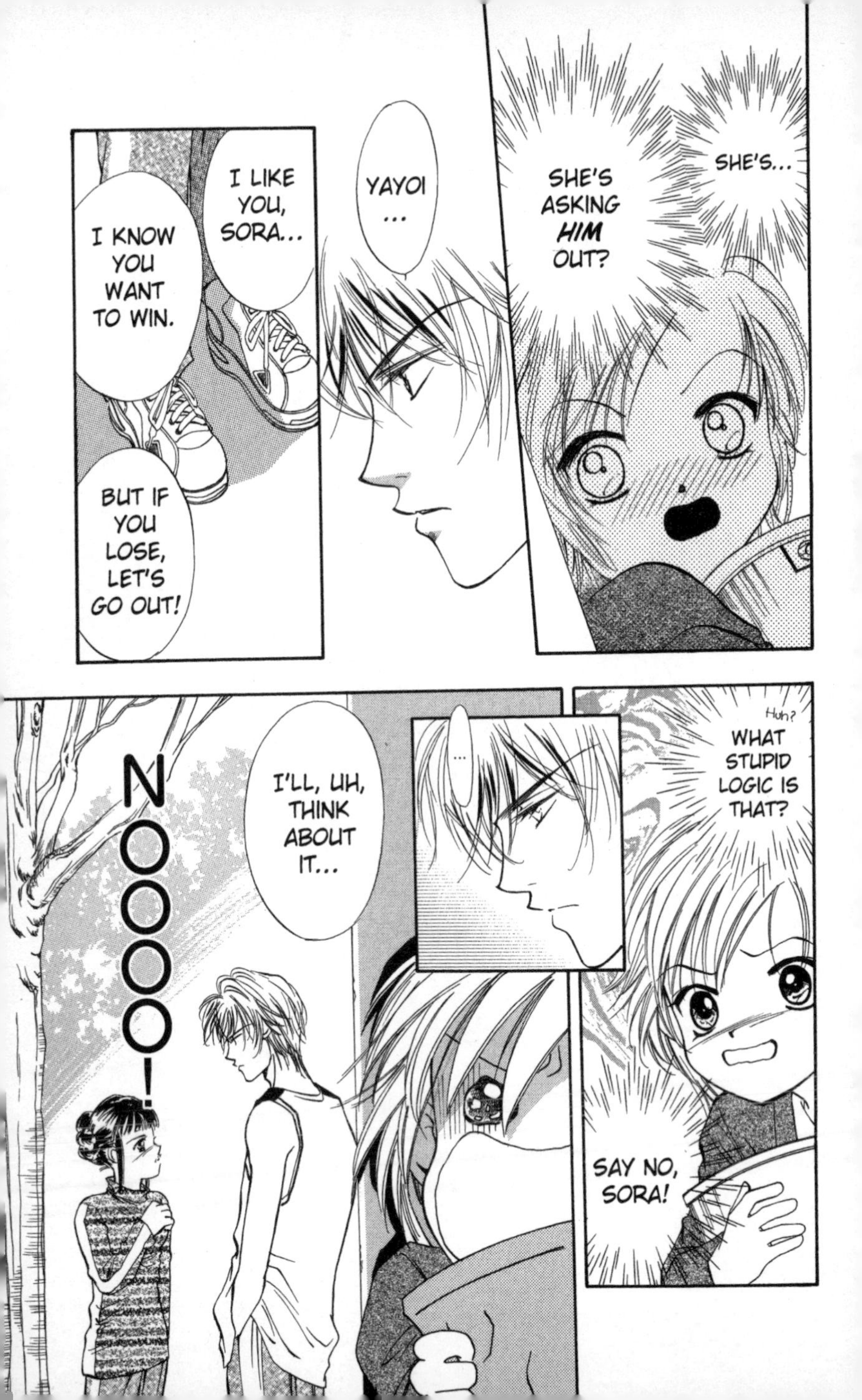
SHE'S...
SHE'S ASKING *HIM* OUT?
YAYOI ...
I LIKE YOU, SORA...
I KNOW YOU WANT TO WIN.
BUT IF YOU LOSE, LET'S GO OUT!
Huh?
WHAT STUPID LOGIC IS THAT?
SAY NO, SORA!
...
I'LL, UH, THINK ABOUT IT...
NOOOO!

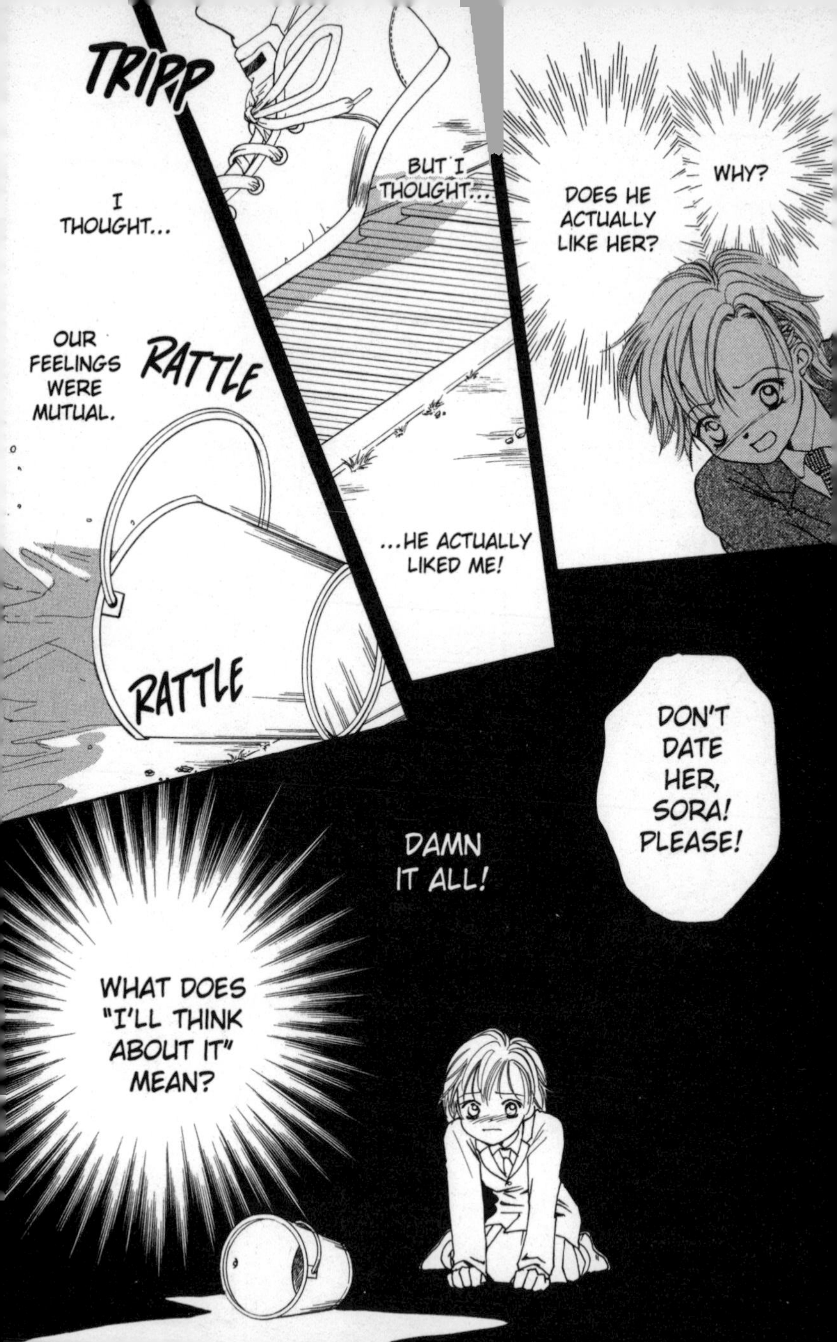
WHY?
DOES HE ACTUALLY LIKE HER?
TRIPP
BUT I THOUGHT...
...HE ACTUALLY LIKED ME!
I THOUGHT...
OUR FEELINGS WERE MUTUAL.
RATTLE
RATTLE
DON'T DATE HER, SORA! PLEASE!
DAMN IT ALL!
WHAT DOES "I'LL THINK ABOUT IT" MEAN?

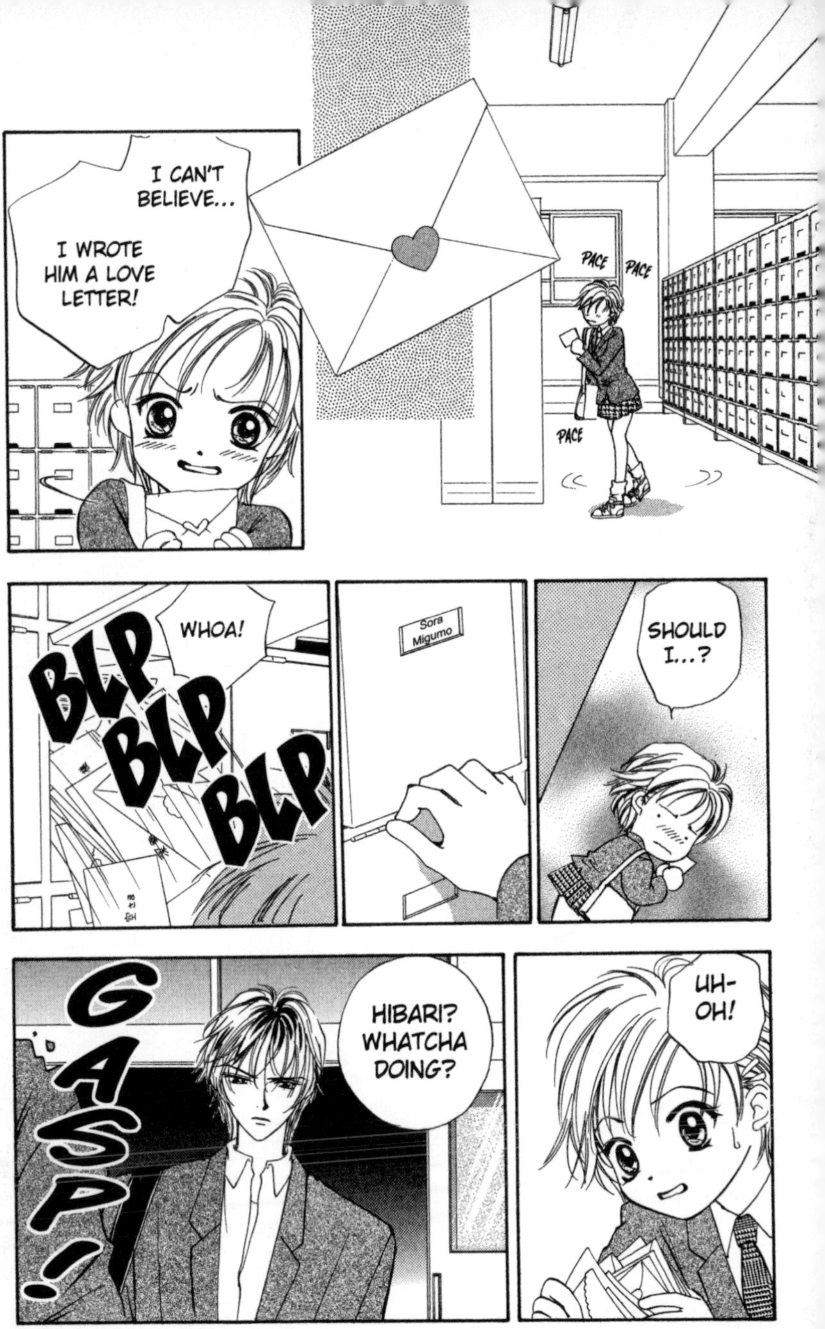
PACE
PACE
PACE
I CAN'T BELIEVE...
I WROTE HIM A LOVE LETTER!
SHOULD I...?
Sora Migumo
WHOA!
BLP BLP BLP
UH-OH!
HIBARI? WHATCHA DOING?
GASP!

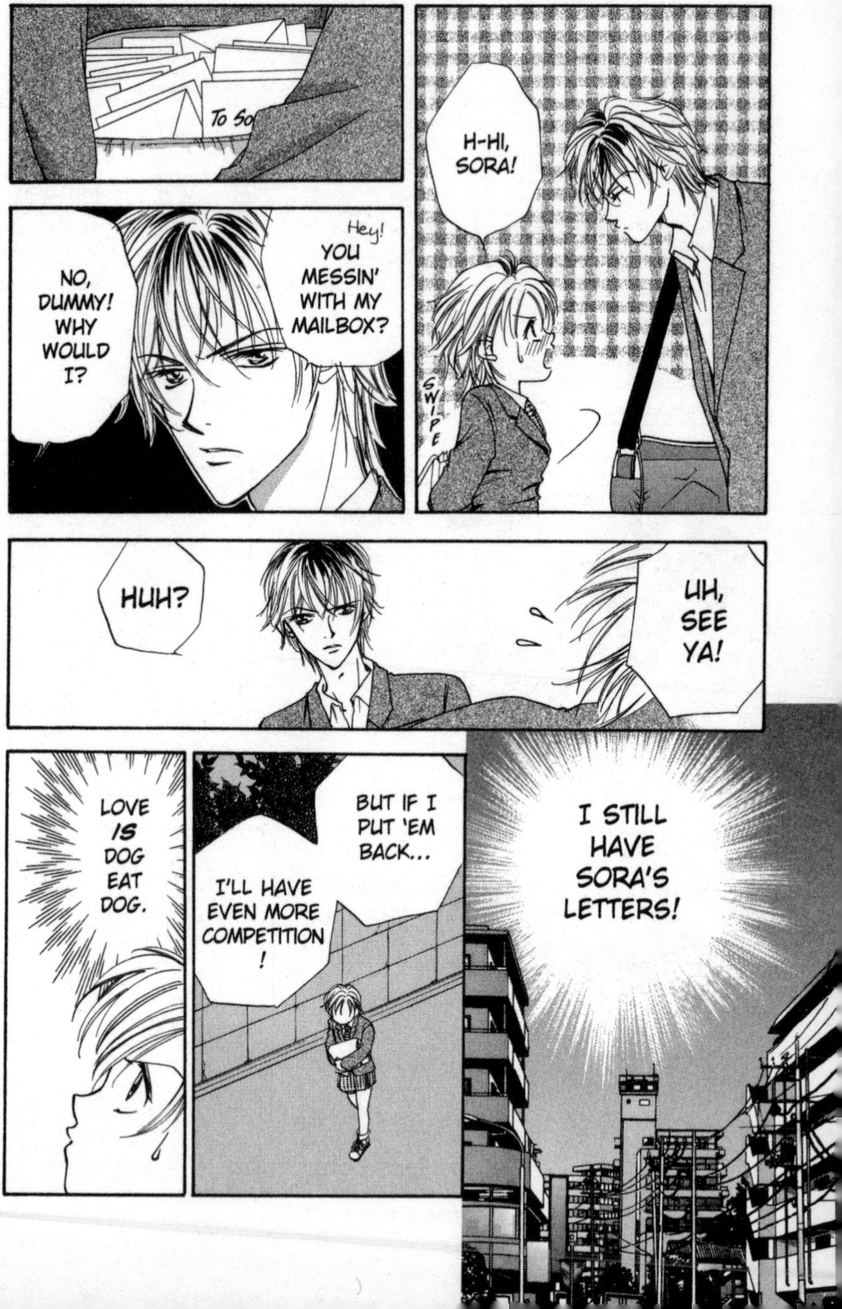
H-HI, SORA!
SWIPE
To So
Hey!
YOU MESSIN' WITH MY MAILBOX?
NO, DUMMY! WHY WOULD I?
UH, SEE YA!
HUH?
I STILL HAVE SORA'S LETTERS!
BUT IF I PUT 'EM BACK...
I'LL HAVE EVEN MORE COMPETITION!
LOVE *IS* DOG EAT DOG.

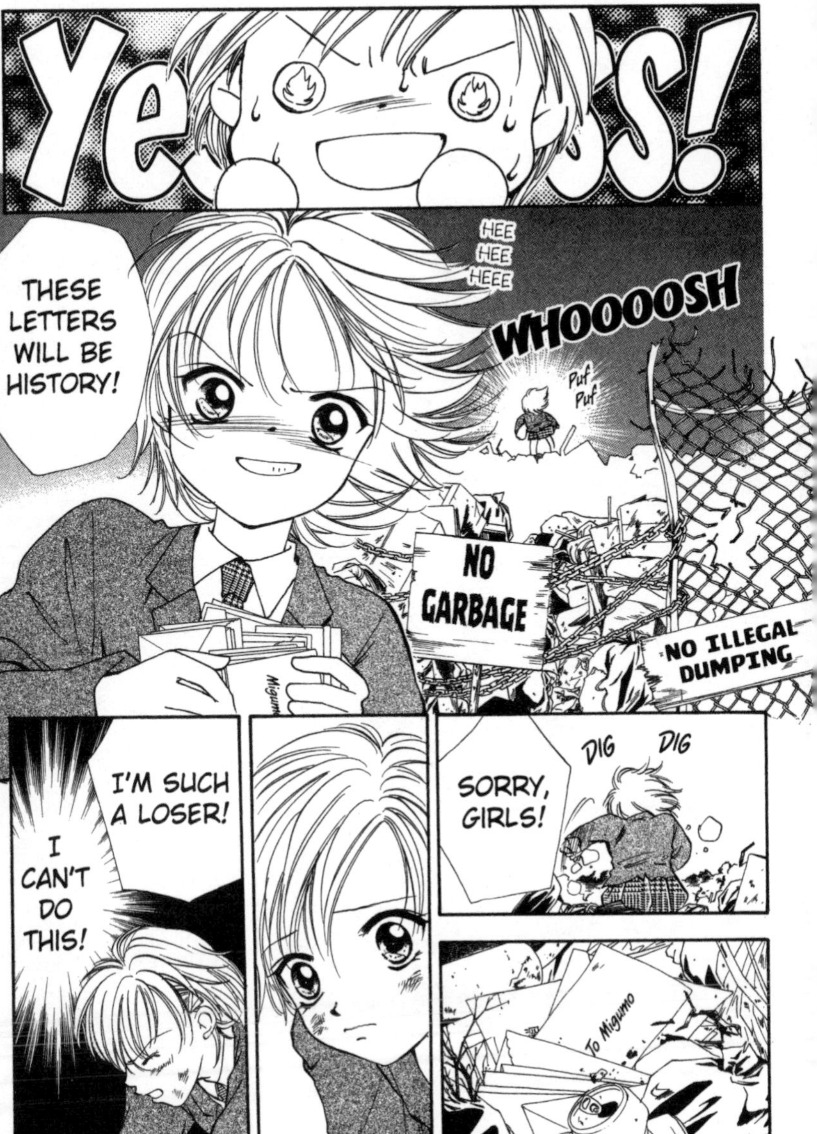
HEE HEE HEEE
WHOOOOOSH
Puf Puf
THESE LETTERS WILL BE HISTORY!
NO ILLEGAL DUMPING
NO GARBAGE
DIG DIG
SORRY, GIRLS!
To Migumo
I'M SUCH A LOSER!
I CAN'T DO THIS!

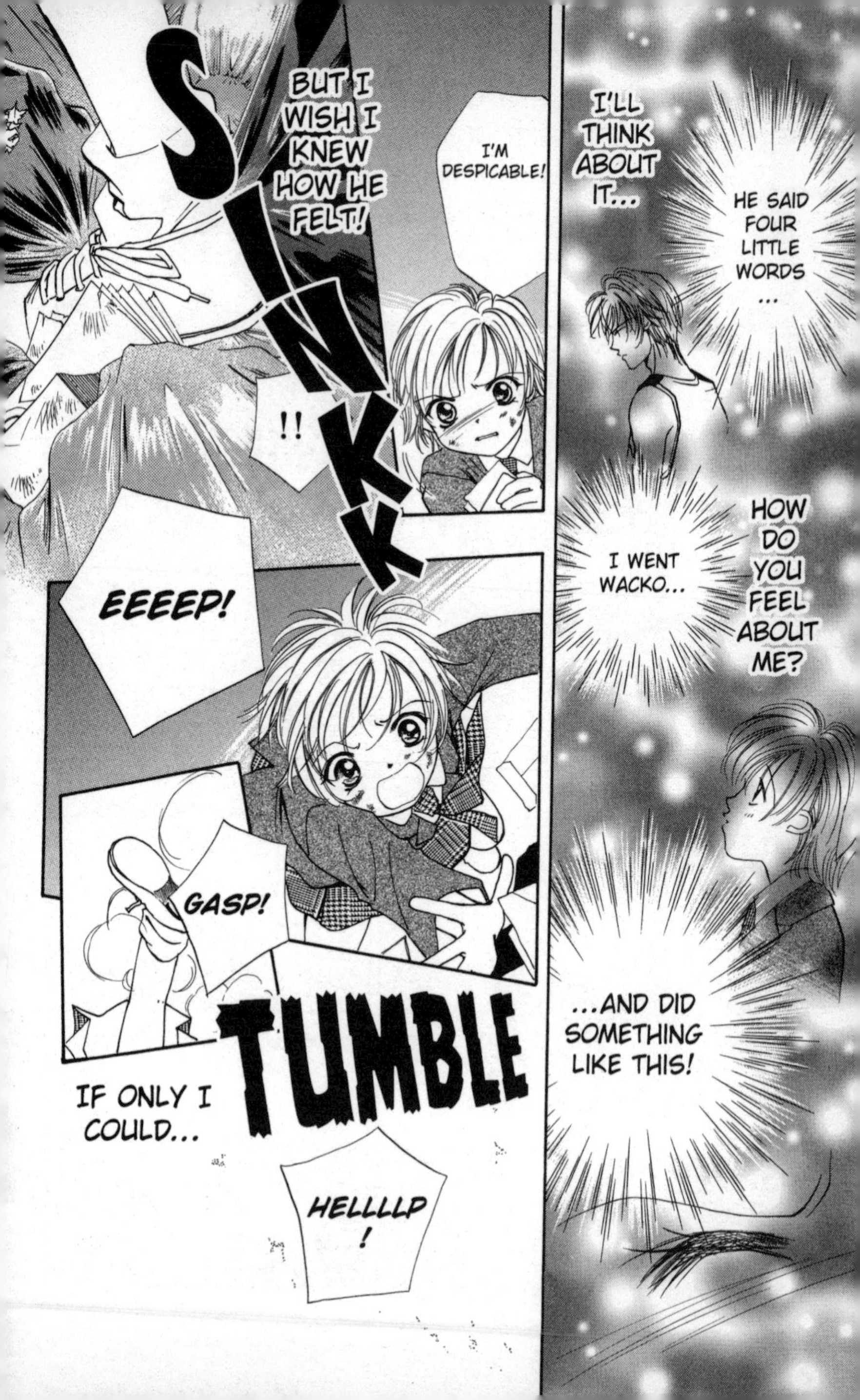
HE SAID FOUR LITTLE WORDS...
I'LL THINK ABOUT IT...
HOW DO YOU FEEL ABOUT ME?
I WENT WACKO...
...AND DID SOMETHING LIKE THIS!
I'M DESPICABLE!
BUT I WISH I KNEW HOW HE FELT!
SINKK
!!
EEEEP!
GASP!
TUMBLE
IF ONLY I COULD...
HELLLLP!

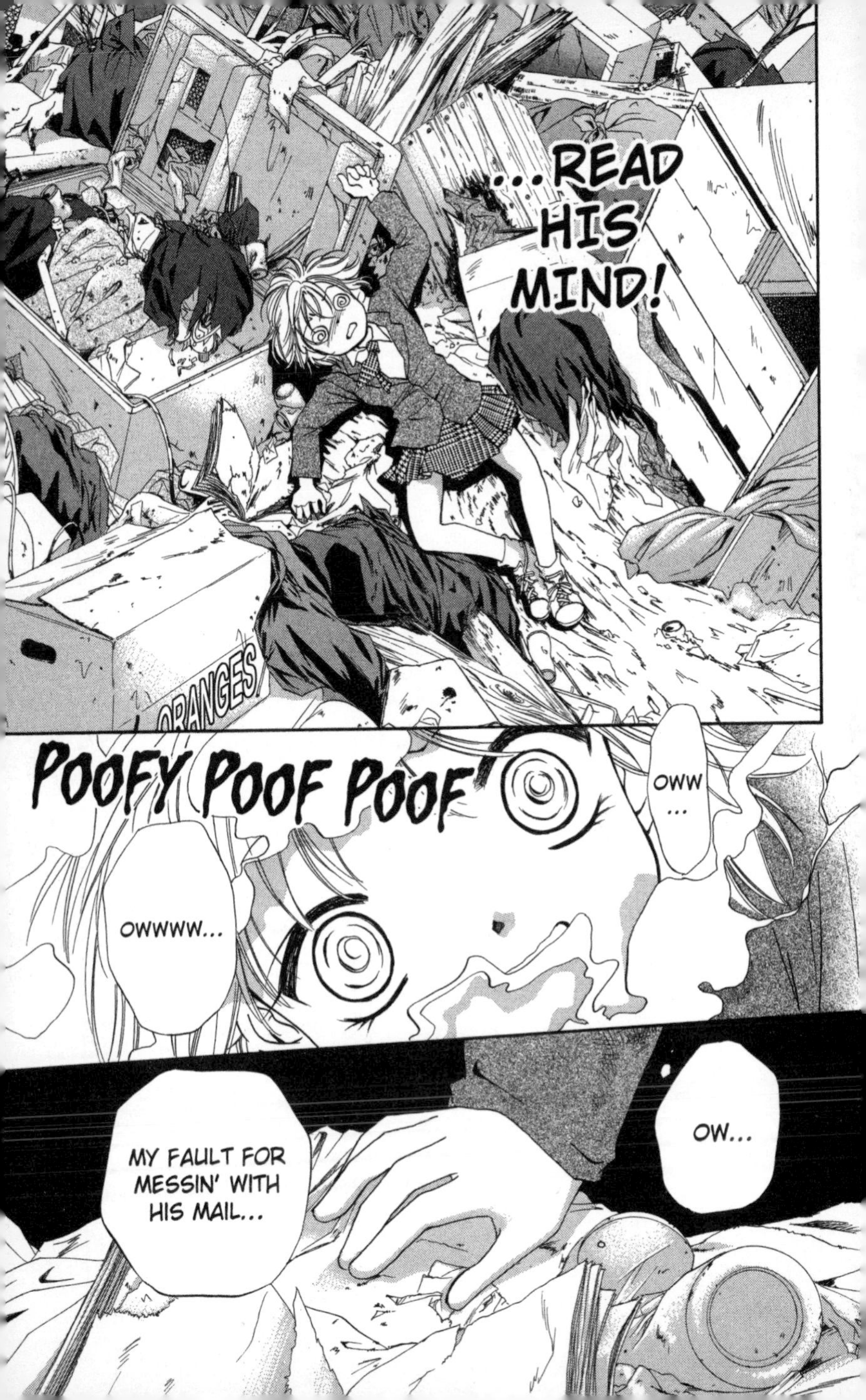

...READ HIS MIND!
OWW ...
POOFY POOF POOF
OWWWW...
OW...
MY FAULT FOR MESSIN' WITH HIS MAIL...
ORANGES

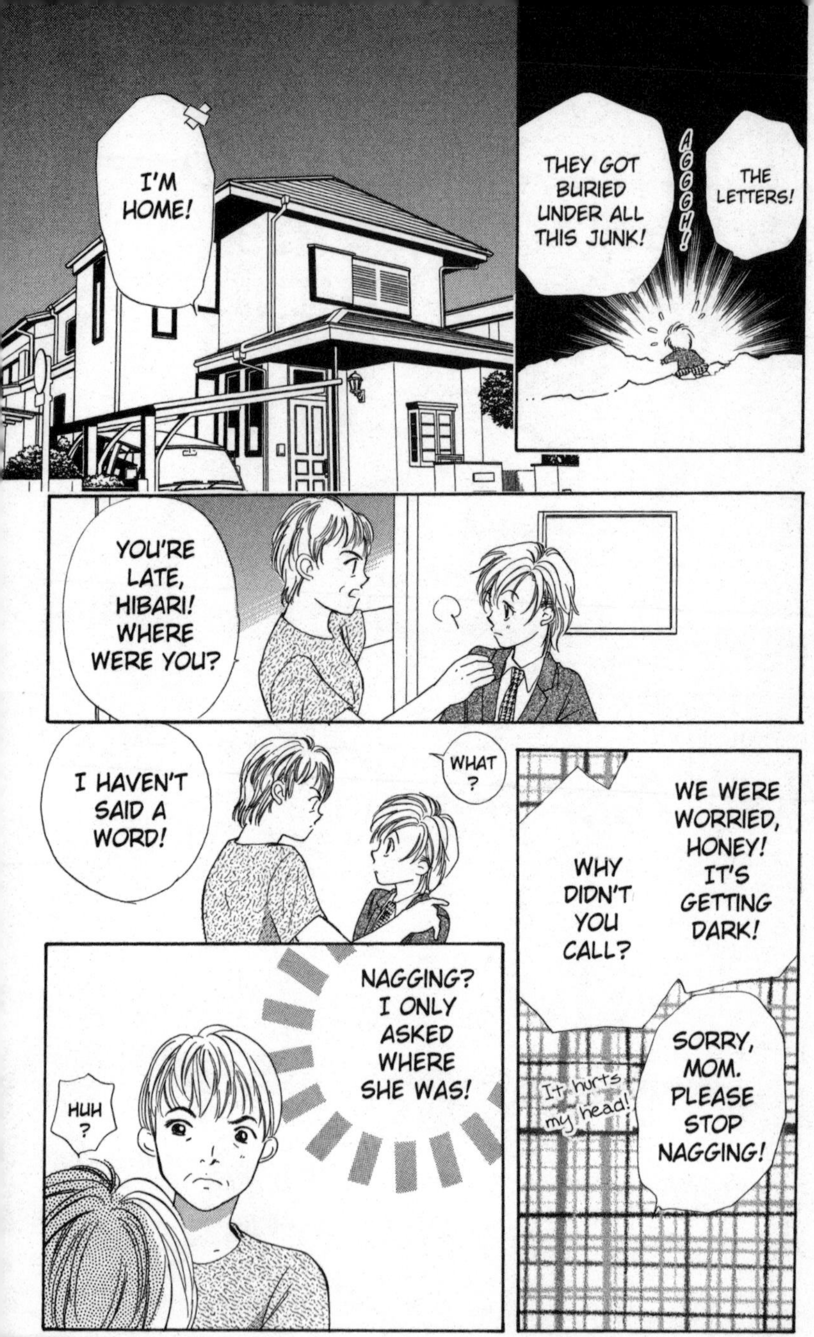
THE LETTERS!
AGGGH!
THEY GOT BURIED UNDER ALL THIS JUNK!
I'M HOME!
YOU'RE LATE, HIBARI! WHERE WERE YOU?
WE WERE WORRIED, HONEY! IT'S GETTING DARK!
WHY DIDN'T YOU CALL?
SORRY, MOM. PLEASE STOP NAGGING!
It hurts my head!
WHAT?
I HAVEN'T SAID A WORD!
NAGGING? I ONLY ASKED WHERE SHE WAS!
HUH?

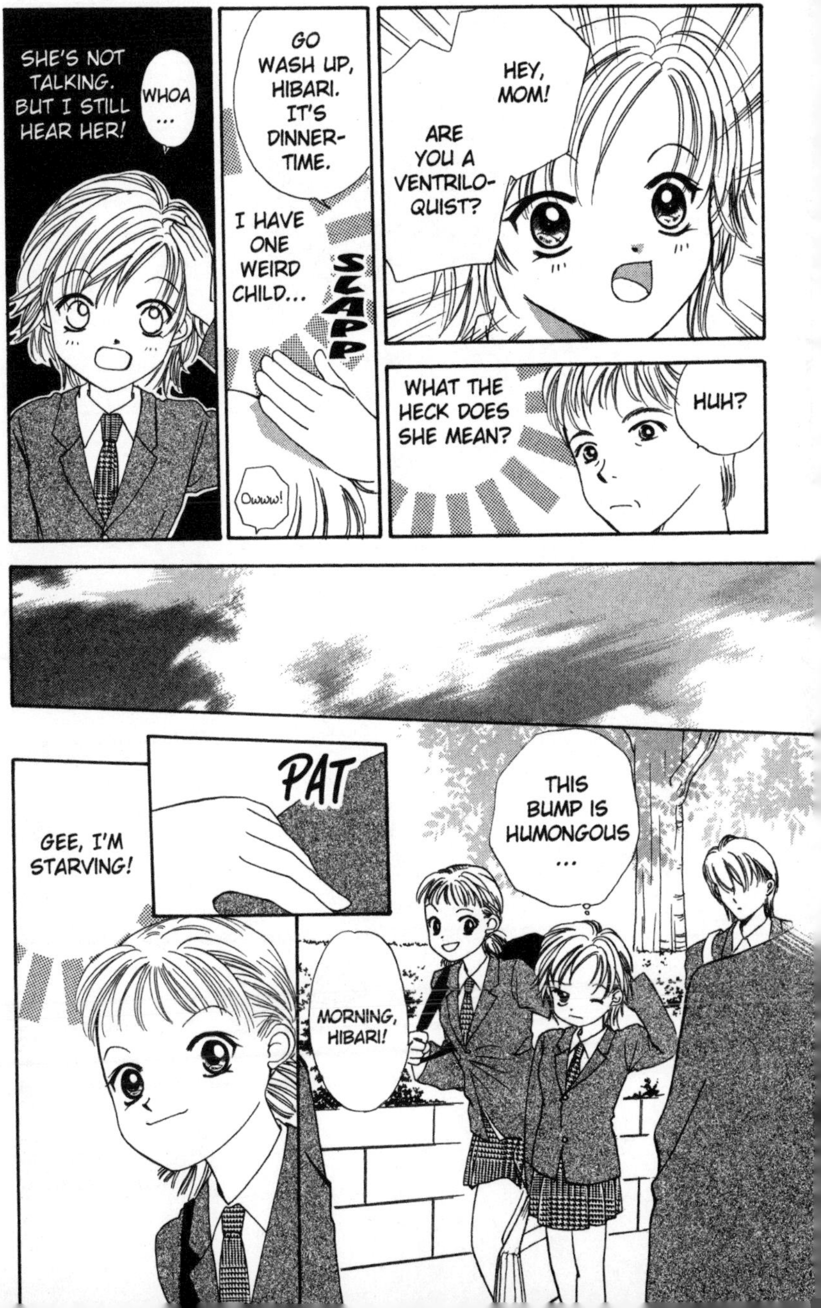
HEY, MOM!
ARE YOU A VENTRILOQUIST?
HUH?
WHAT THE HECK DOES SHE MEAN?
GO WASH UP, HIBARI. IT'S DINNER-TIME.
I HAVE ONE WEIRD CHILD...
SLAPP
Owww!
WHOA ...
SHE'S NOT TALKING. BUT I STILL HEAR HER!
THIS BUMP IS HUMONGOUS ...
MORNING, HIBARI!
PAT
GEE, I'M STARVING!

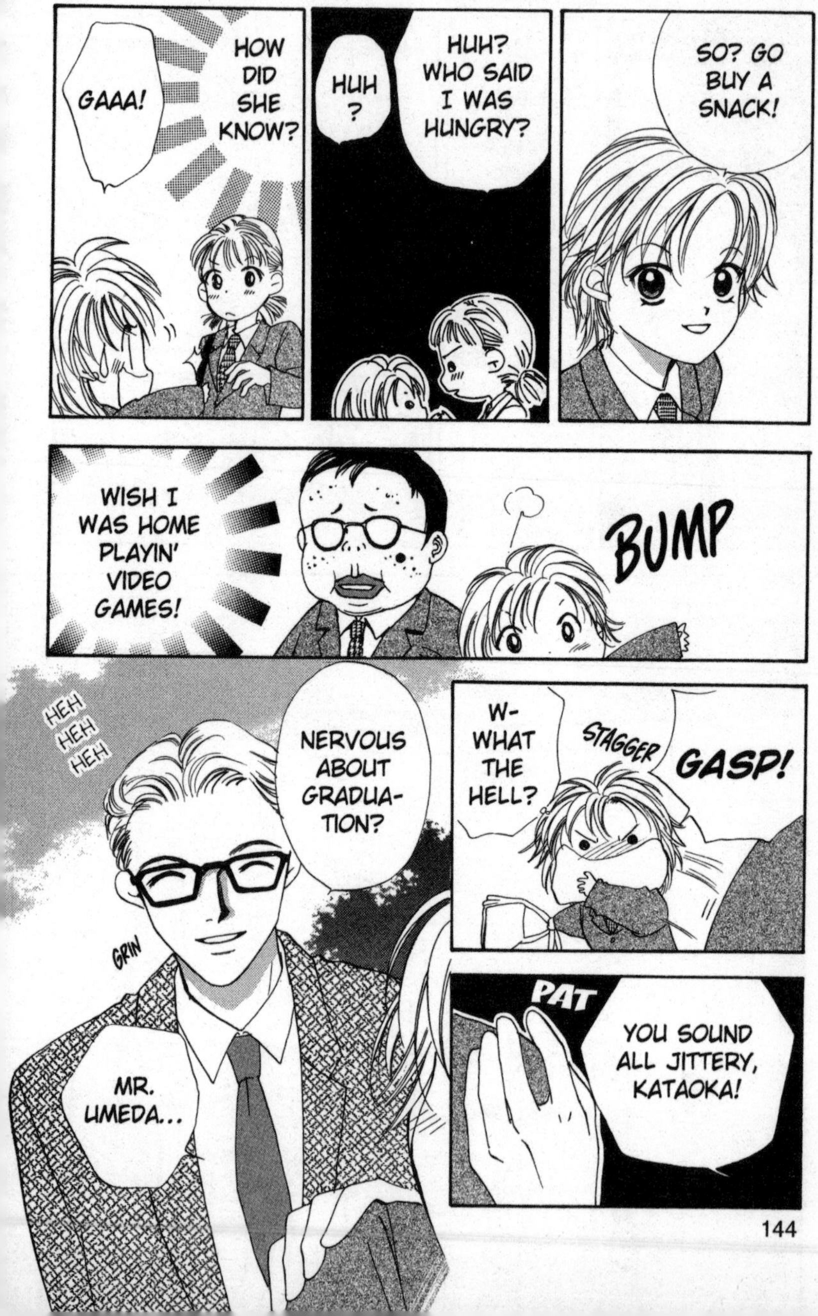
SO? GO BUY A SNACK!
HUH? WHO SAID I WAS HUNGRY?
HUH ?
HOW DID SHE KNOW?
GAAA!
BUMP
WISH I WAS HOME PLAYIN' VIDEO GAMES!
GASP!
STAGGER
W- WHAT THE HELL?
PAT
YOU SOUND ALL JITTERY, KATAOKA!
NERVOUS ABOUT GRADUA-TION?
HEH HEH HEH
GRIN
MR. UMEDA...

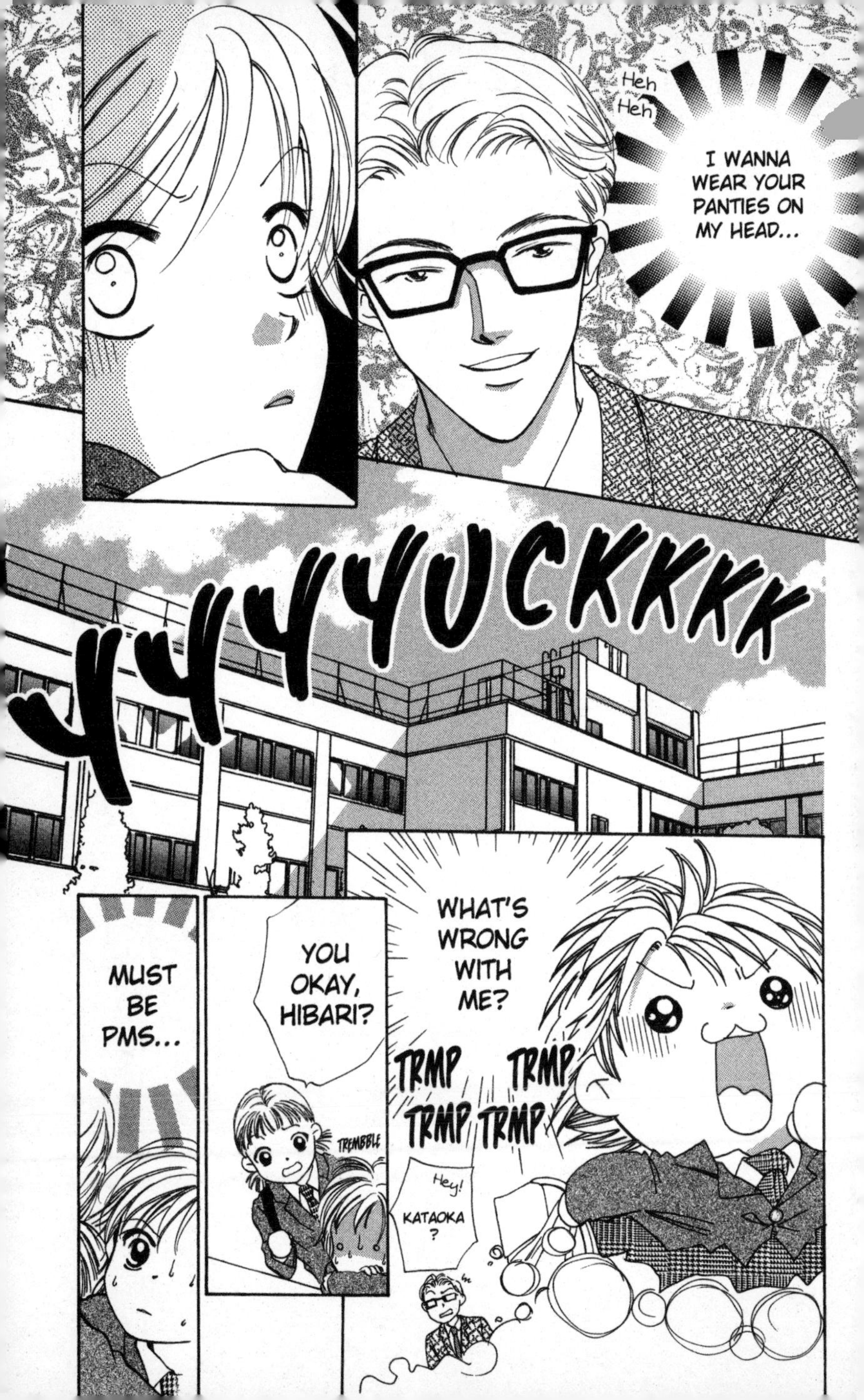
Heh Heh
I WANNA WEAR YOUR PANTIES ON MY HEAD...
YYYYYUCKKKKK
WHAT'S WRONG WITH ME?
TRMP TRMP
TRMP TRMP
Hey!
KATAOKA?
YOU OKAY, HIBARI?
TREMBLE
MUST BE PMS...

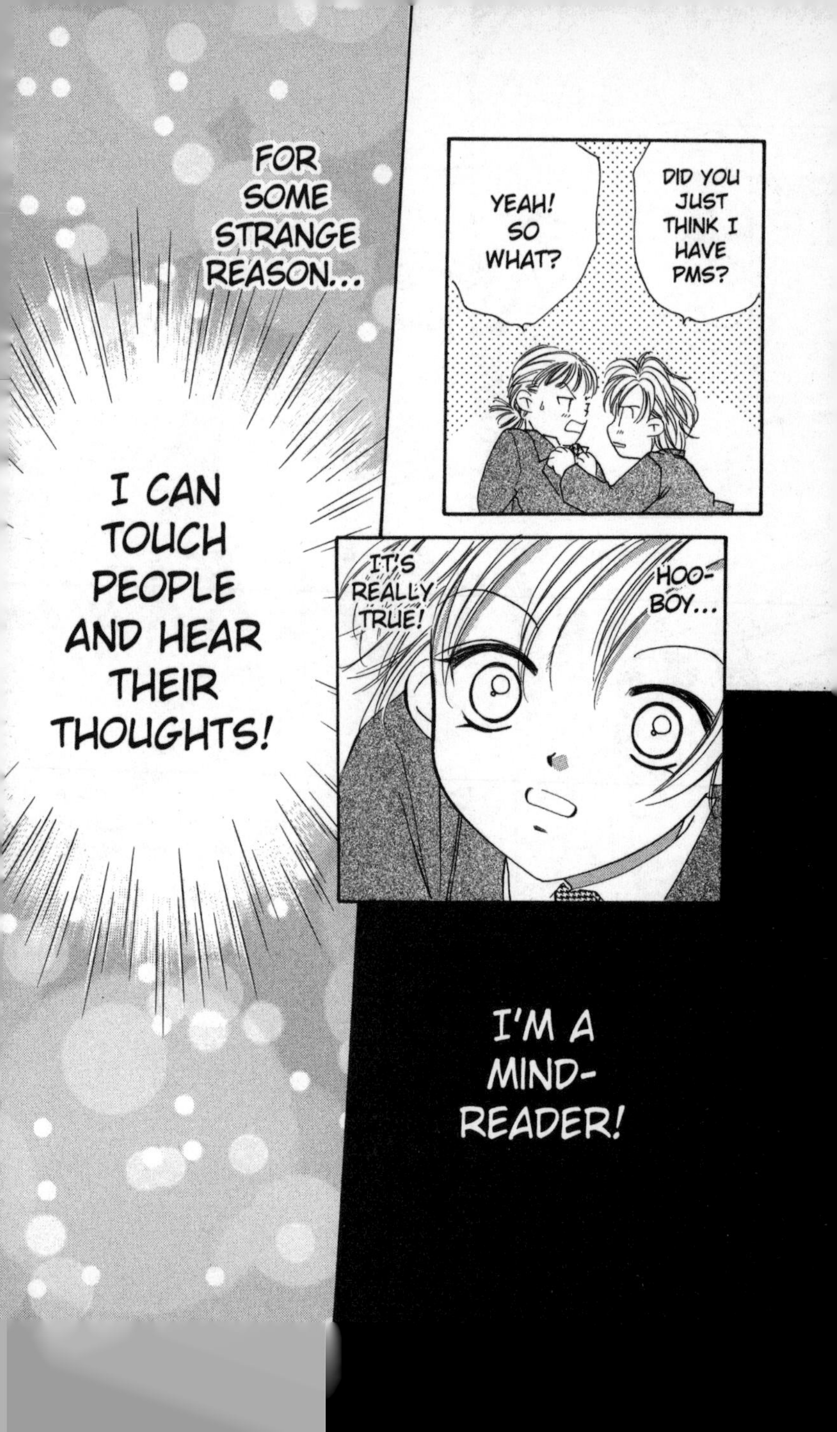
DID YOU JUST THINK I HAVE PMS?
YEAH! SO WHAT?
HOO-BOY...
IT'S REALLY TRUE!
I'M A MIND-READER!
FOR SOME STRANGE REASON...
I CAN TOUCH PEOPLE AND HEAR THEIR THOUGHTS!

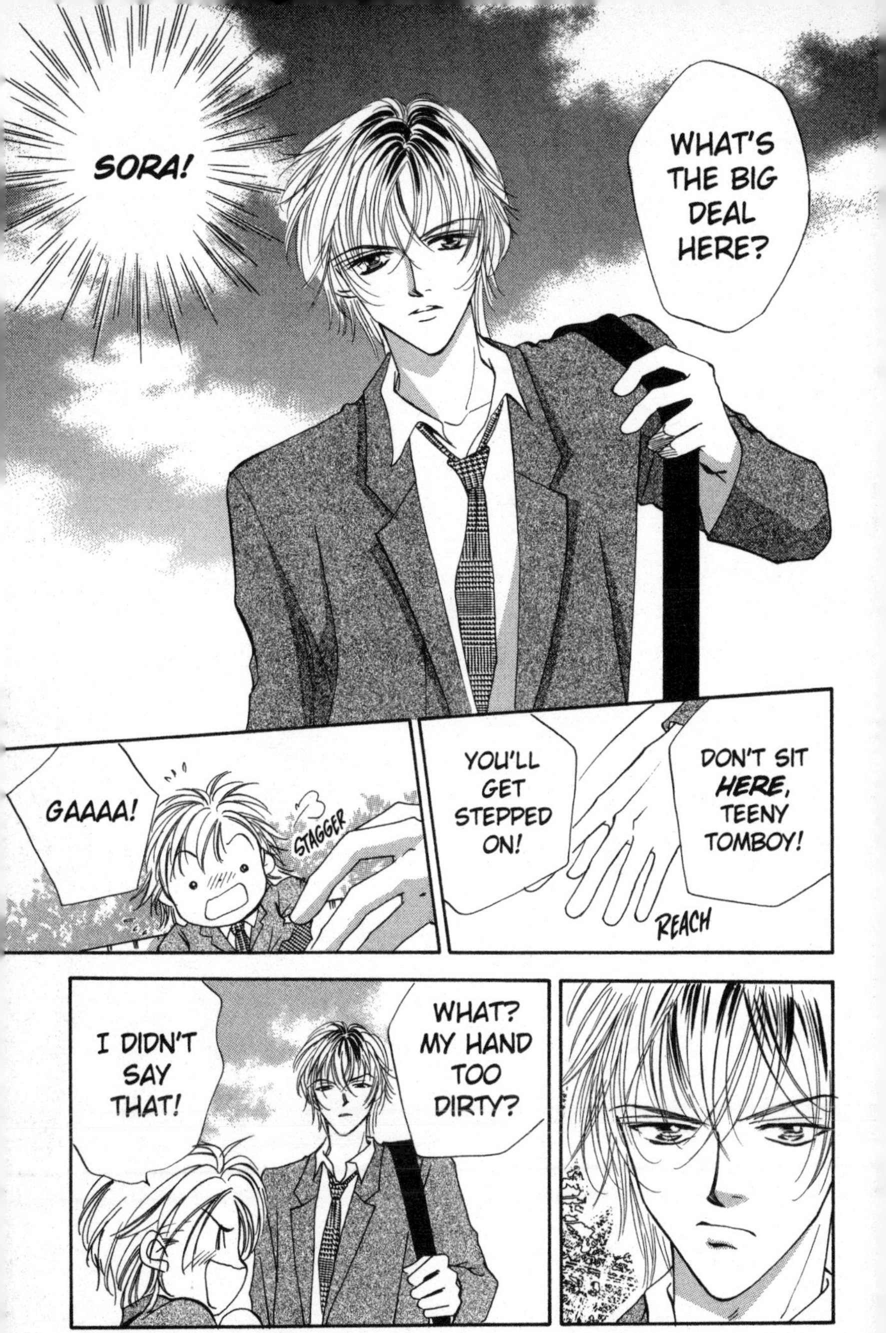
WHAT'S THE BIG DEAL HERE?
SORA!
DON'T SIT *HERE*, TEENY TOMBOY!
YOU'LL GET STEPPED ON!
REACH
GAAAA!
STAGGER
WHAT? MY HAND TOO DIRTY?
I DIDN'T SAY THAT!

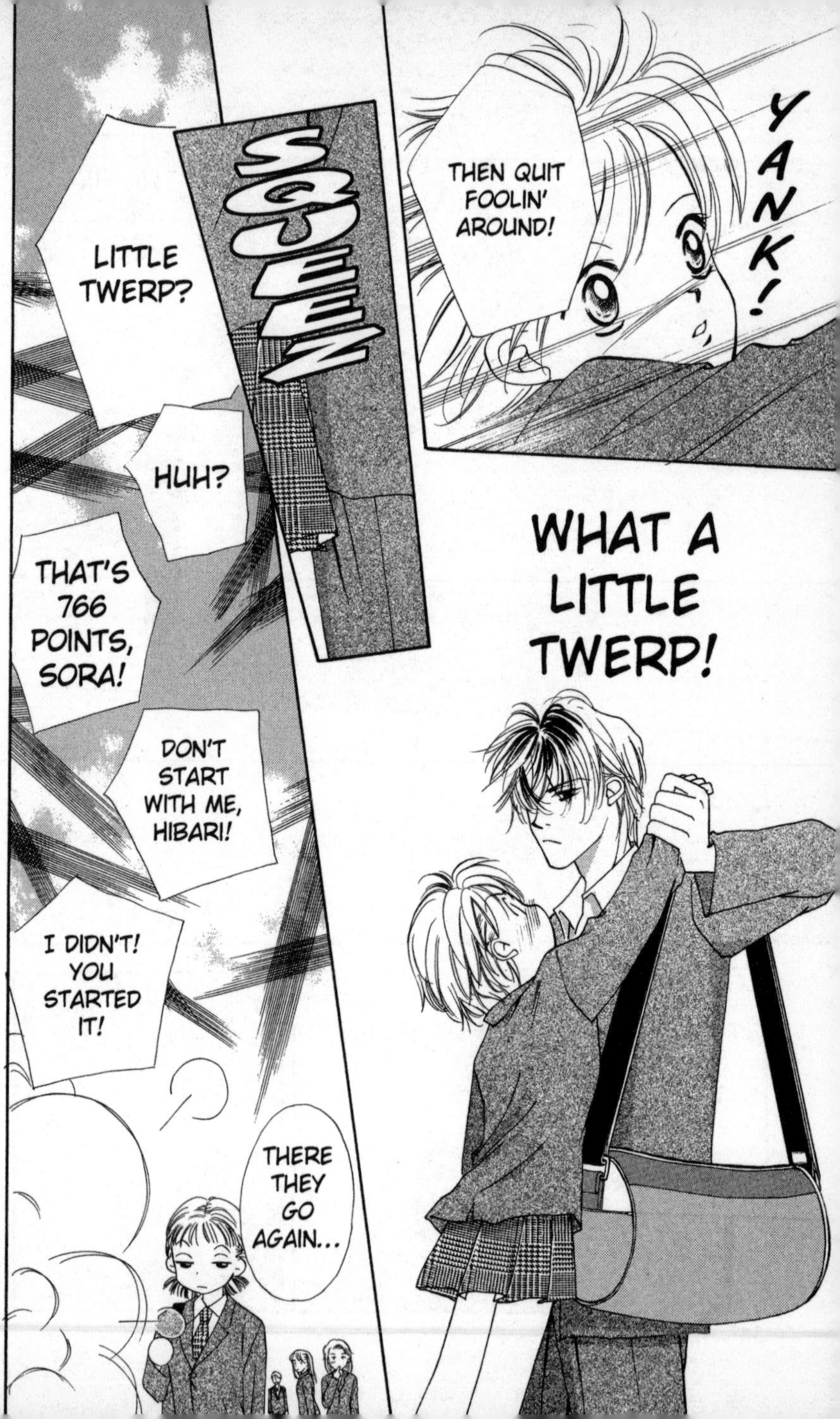
YANK!
THEN QUIT FOOLIN' AROUND!
WHAT A LITTLE TWERP!
SQUEEN
LITTLE TWERP?
HUH?
THAT'S 766 POINTS, SORA!
DON'T START WITH ME, HIBARI!
I DIDN'T! YOU STARTED IT!
THERE THEY GO AGAIN...

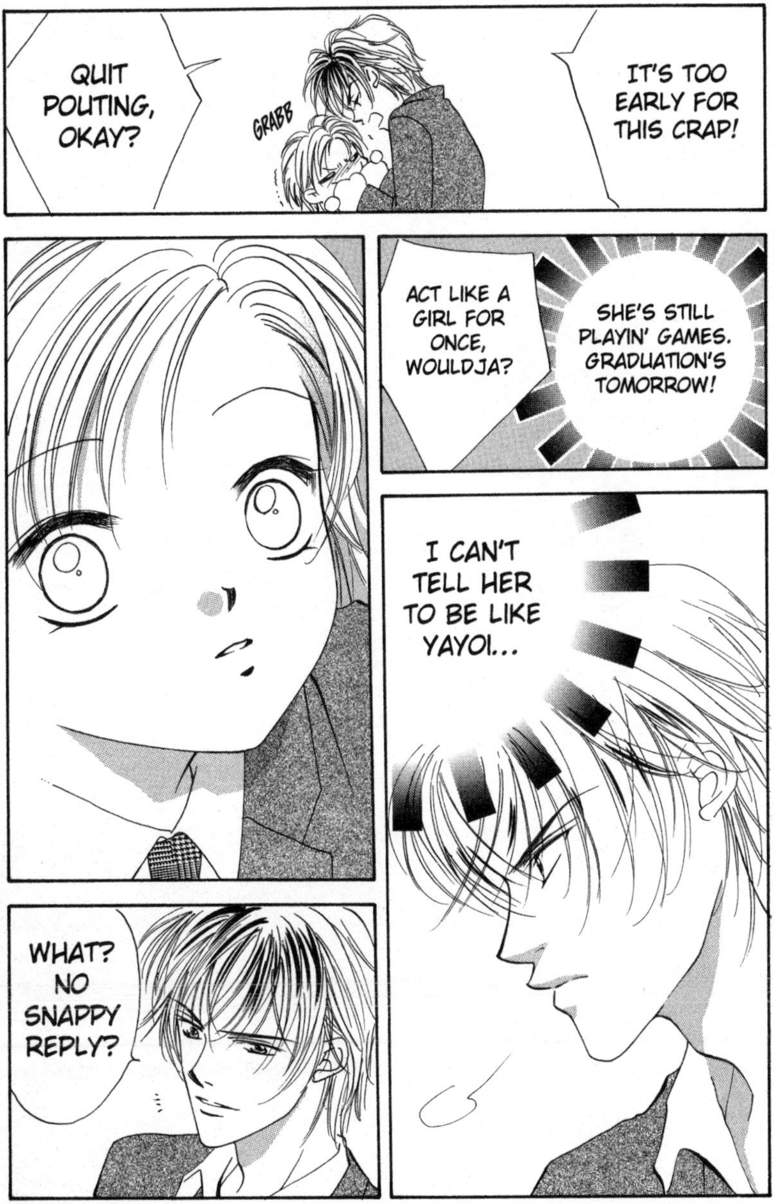
IT'S TOO EARLY FOR THIS CRAP!
GRABB
QUIT POUTING, OKAY?
SHE'S STILL PLAYIN' GAMES. GRADUATION'S TOMORROW!
ACT LIKE A GIRL FOR ONCE, WOULDJA?
I CAN'T TELL HER TO BE LIKE YAYOI...
WHAT? NO SNAPPY REPLY?

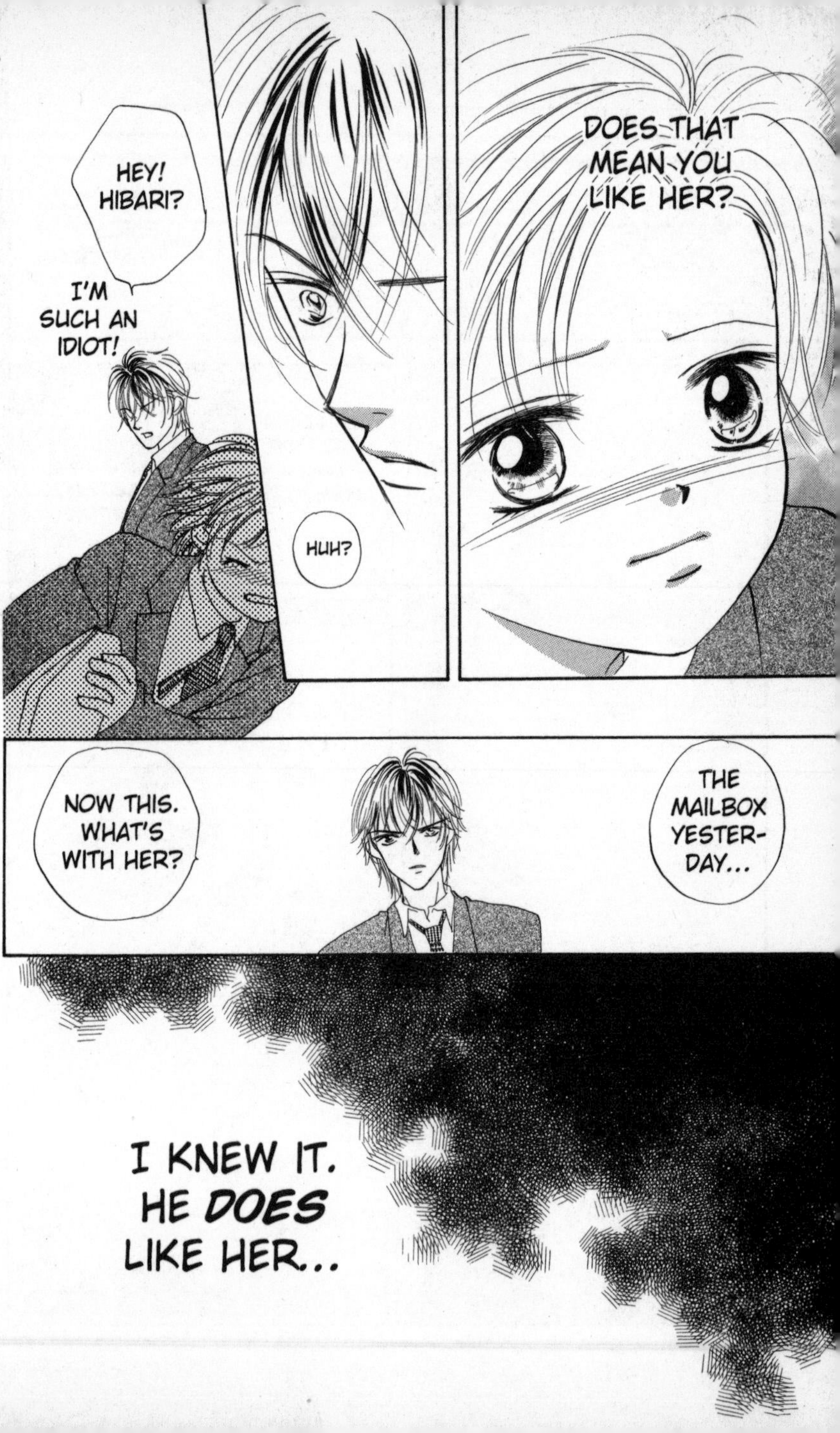
DOES THAT MEAN YOU LIKE HER?
HUH?
HEY! HIBARI?
I'M SUCH AN IDIOT!
THE MAILBOX YESTER-DAY...
NOW THIS. WHAT'S WITH HER?
I KNEW IT. HE *DOES* LIKE HER...

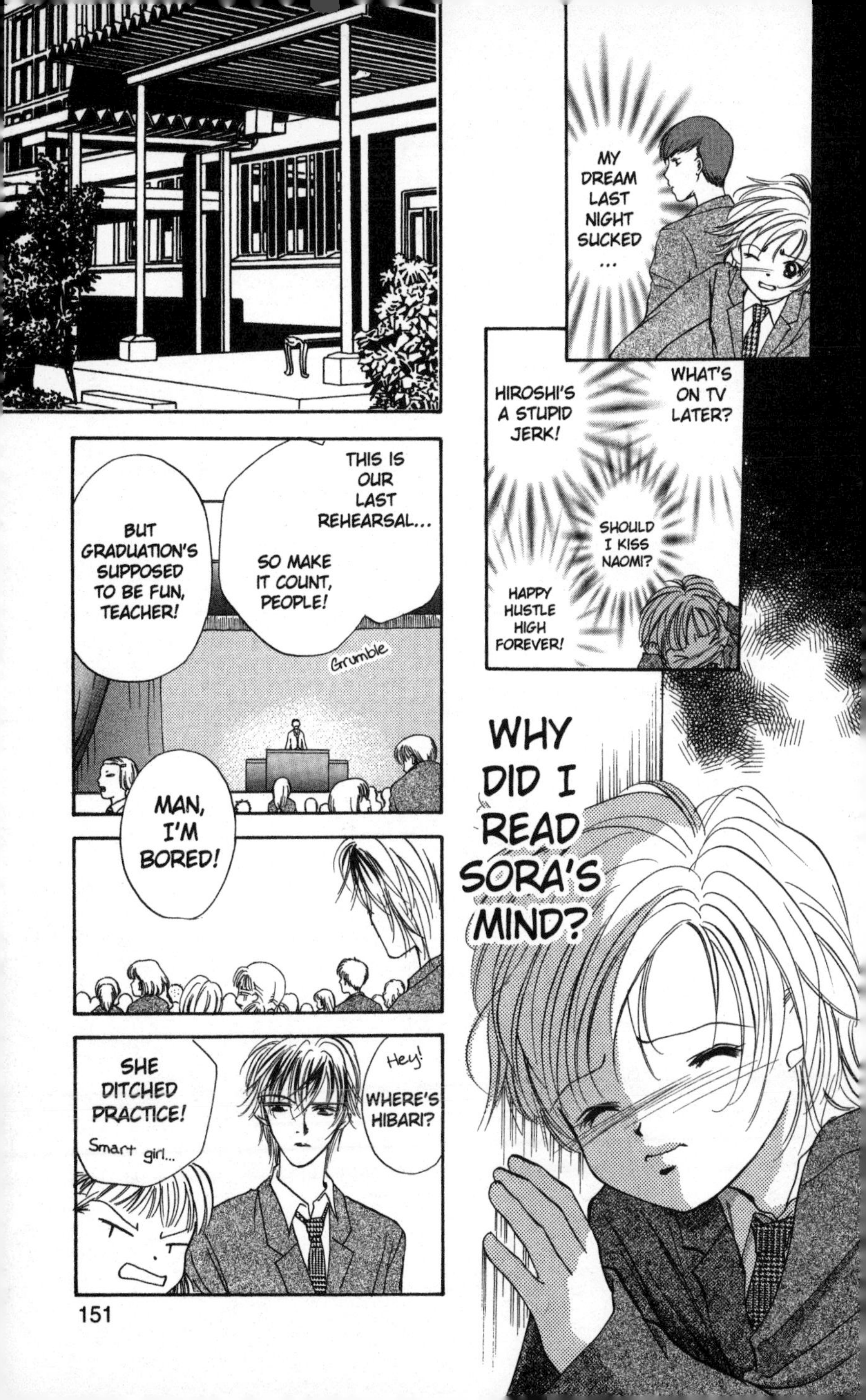
MY DREAM LAST NIGHT SUCKED...
WHAT'S ON TV LATER?
HIROSHI'S A STUPID JERK!
SHOULD I KISS NAOMI?
HAPPY HUSTLE HIGH FOREVER!
WHY DID I READ SORA'S MIND?
THIS IS OUR LAST REHEARSAL...
SO MAKE IT COUNT, PEOPLE!
BUT GRADUATION'S SUPPOSED TO BE FUN, TEACHER!
Grumble
MAN, I'M BORED!
Hey!
WHERE'S HIBARI?
SHE DITCHED PRACTICE!
Smart girl...

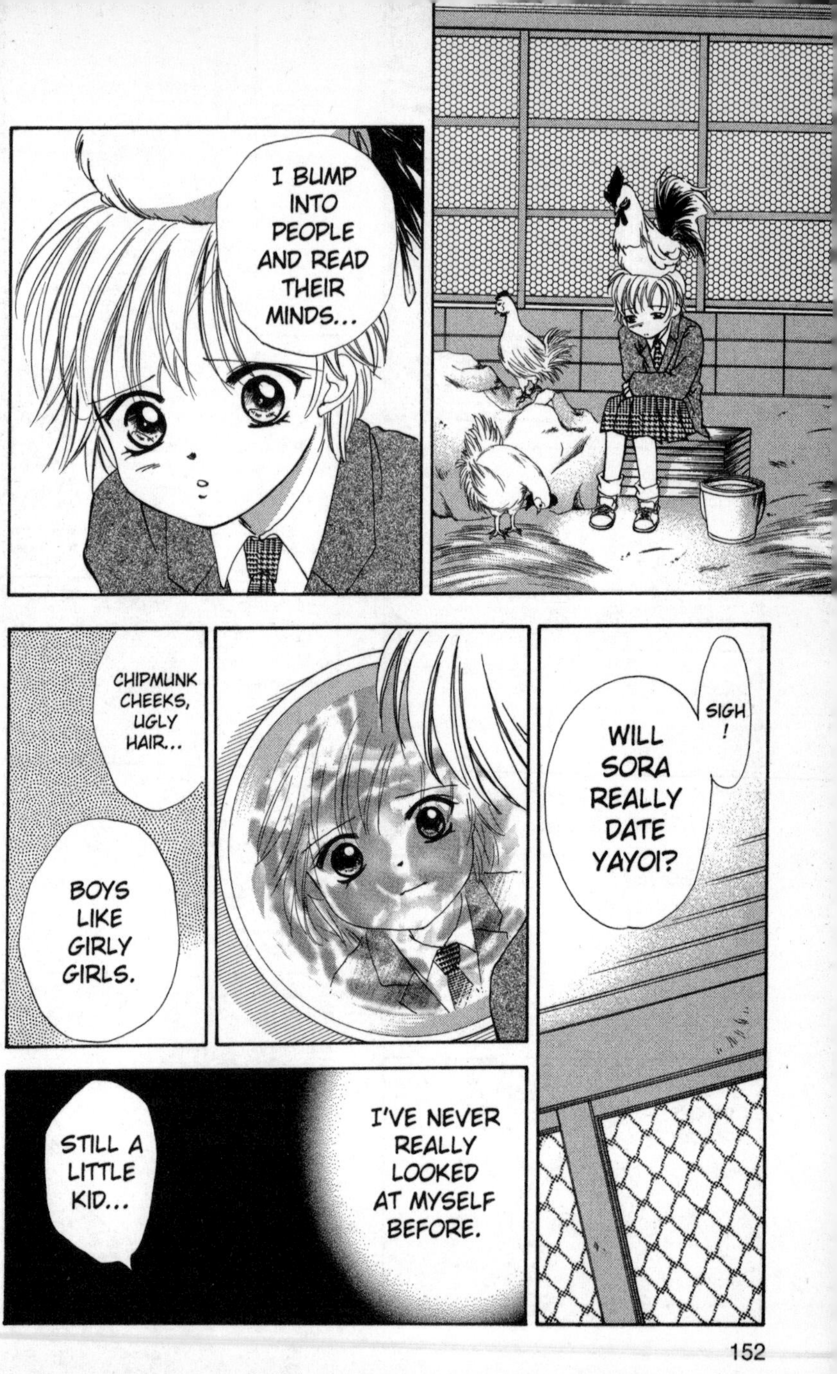

I BUMP INTO PEOPLE AND READ THEIR MINDS...
SIGH!
WILL SORA REALLY DATE YAYOI?
CHIPMUNK CHEEKS, UGLY HAIR...
BOYS LIKE GIRLY GIRLS.
I'VE NEVER REALLY LOOKED AT MYSELF BEFORE.
STILL A LITTLE KID...

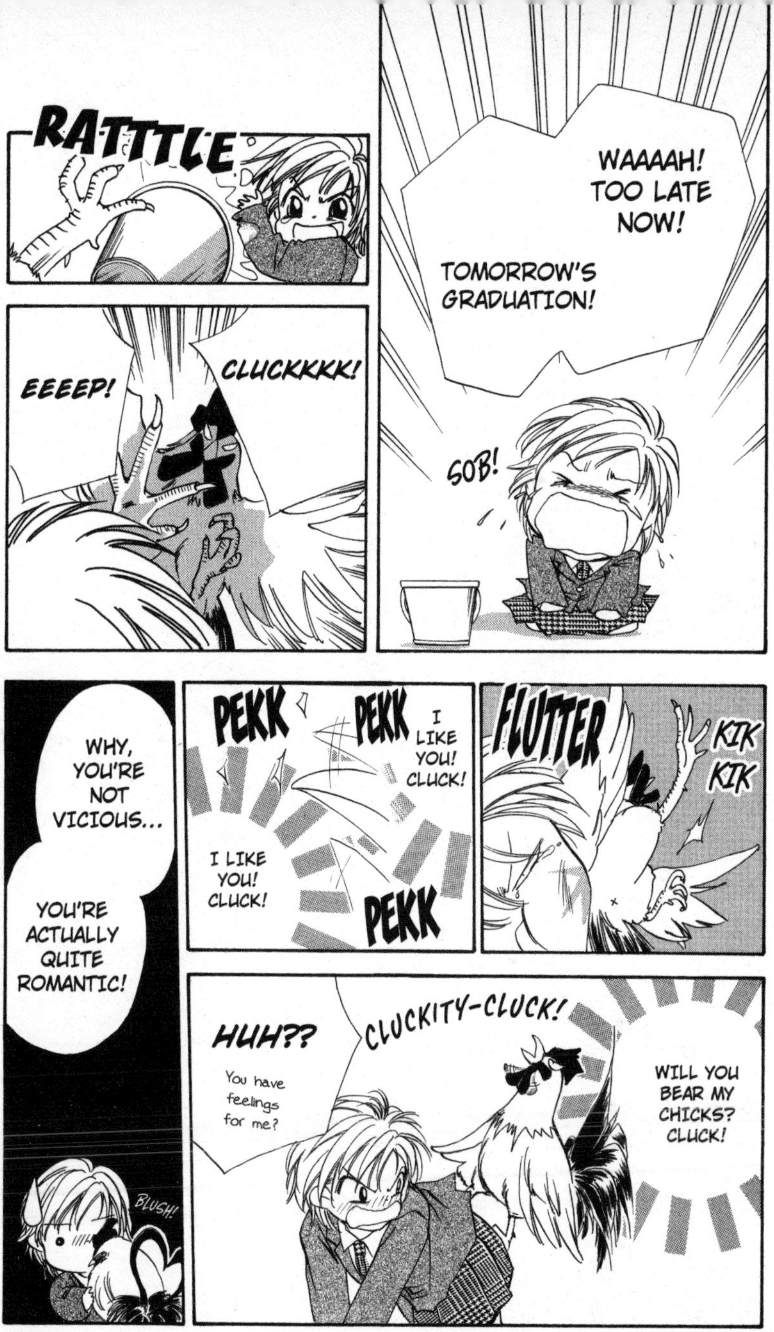
WAAAAH! TOO LATE NOW!
TOMORROW'S GRADUATION!
SOB!
RATTTLE
CLUCKKKK!
EEEEP!
KIK KIK
FLUTTER
I LIKE YOU! CLUCK!
PEKK PEKK
I LIKE YOU! CLUCK!
PEKK
WILL YOU BEAR MY CHICKS? CLUCK!
CLUCKITY-CLUCK!
HUH??
You have feelings for me?
WHY, YOU'RE NOT VICIOUS...
YOU'RE ACTUALLY QUITE ROMANTIC!
BLUSH!

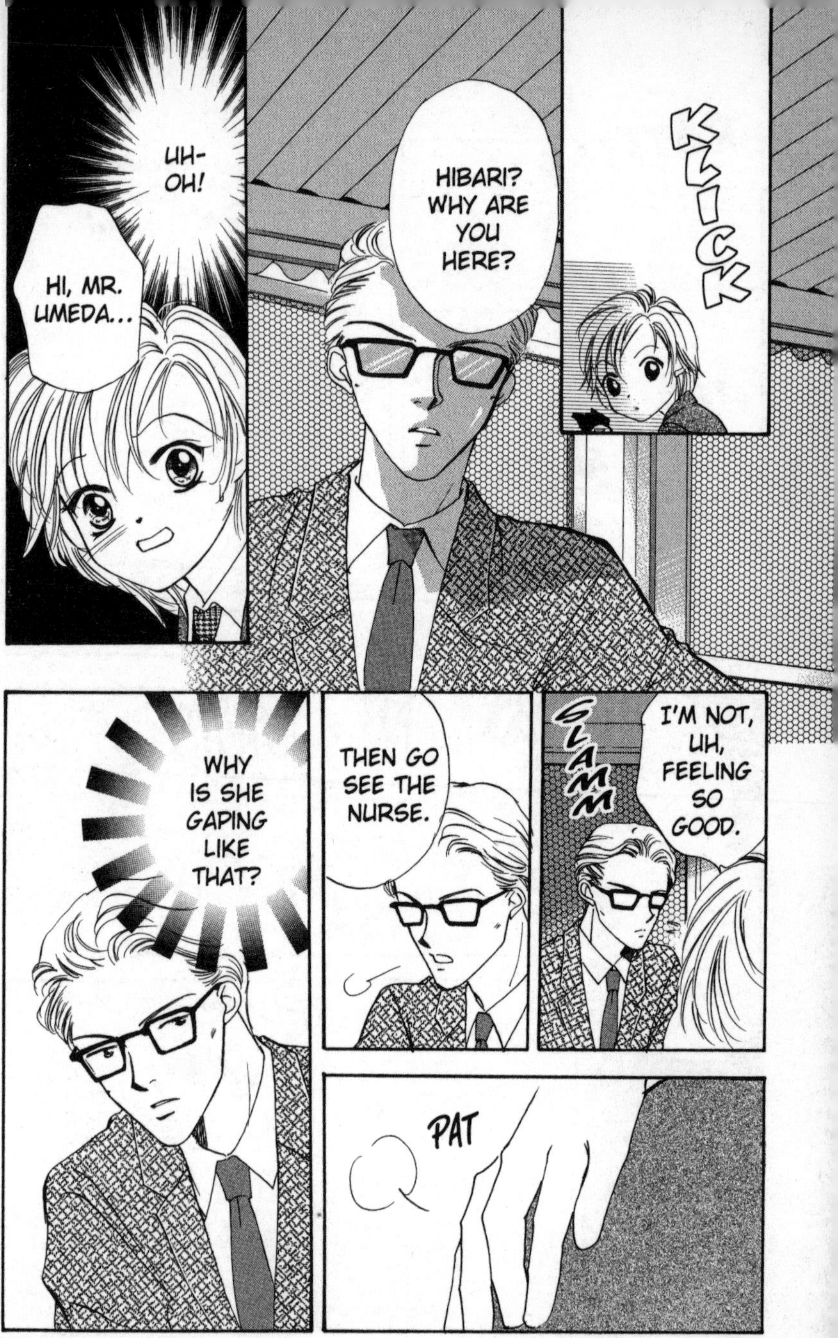
KLICK
HIBARI? WHY ARE YOU HERE?
UH-OH!
HI, MR. UMEDA...
SLAMM
I'M NOT, UH, FEELING SO GOOD.
THEN GO SEE THE NURSE.
PAT
WHY IS SHE GAPING LIKE THAT?

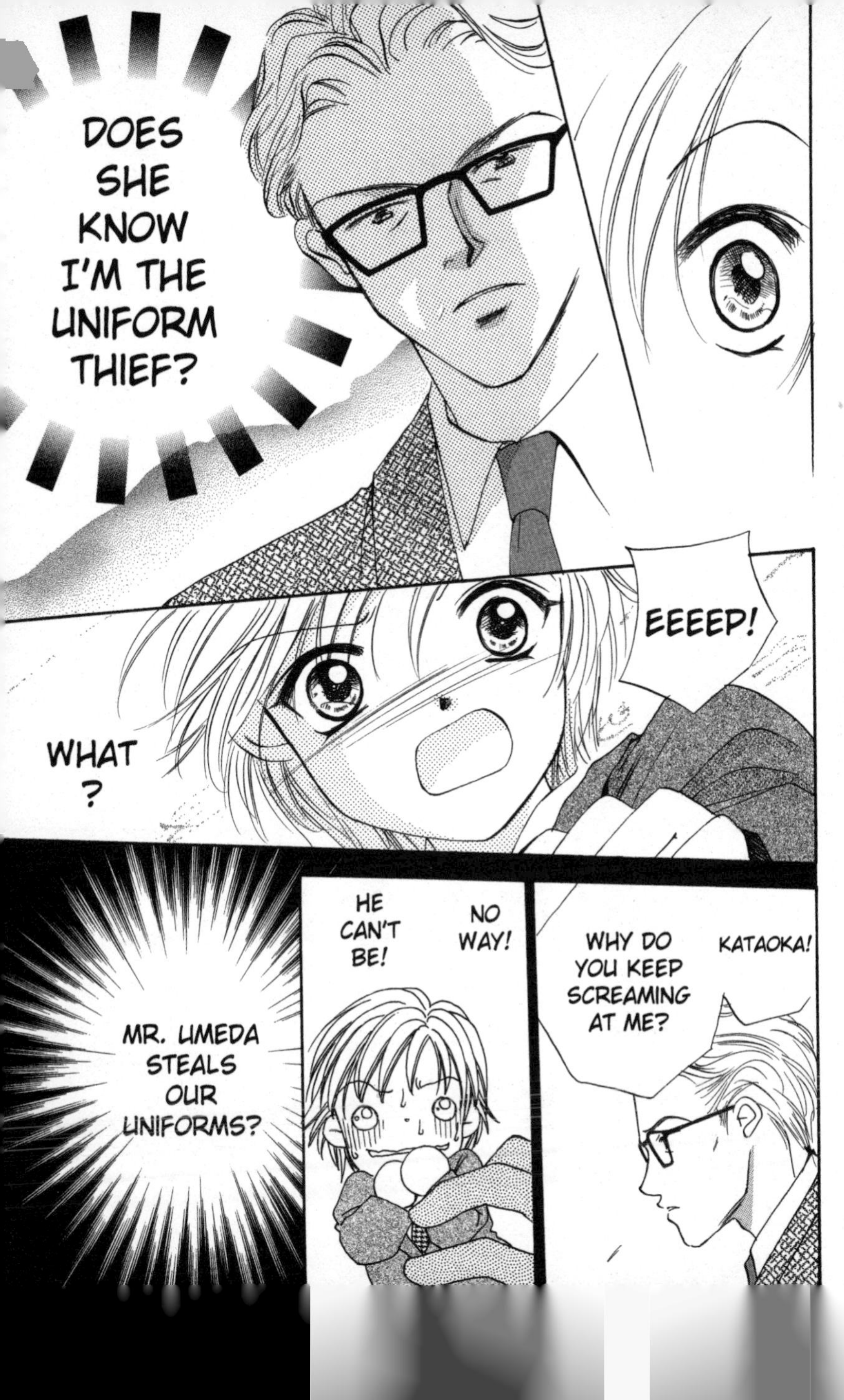
DOES SHE KNOW I'M THE UNIFORM THIEF?
EEEEP!
WHAT?
KATAOKA!
WHY DO YOU KEEP SCREAMING AT ME?
NO WAY!
HE CAN'T BE!
MR. UMEDA STEALS OUR UNIFORMS?

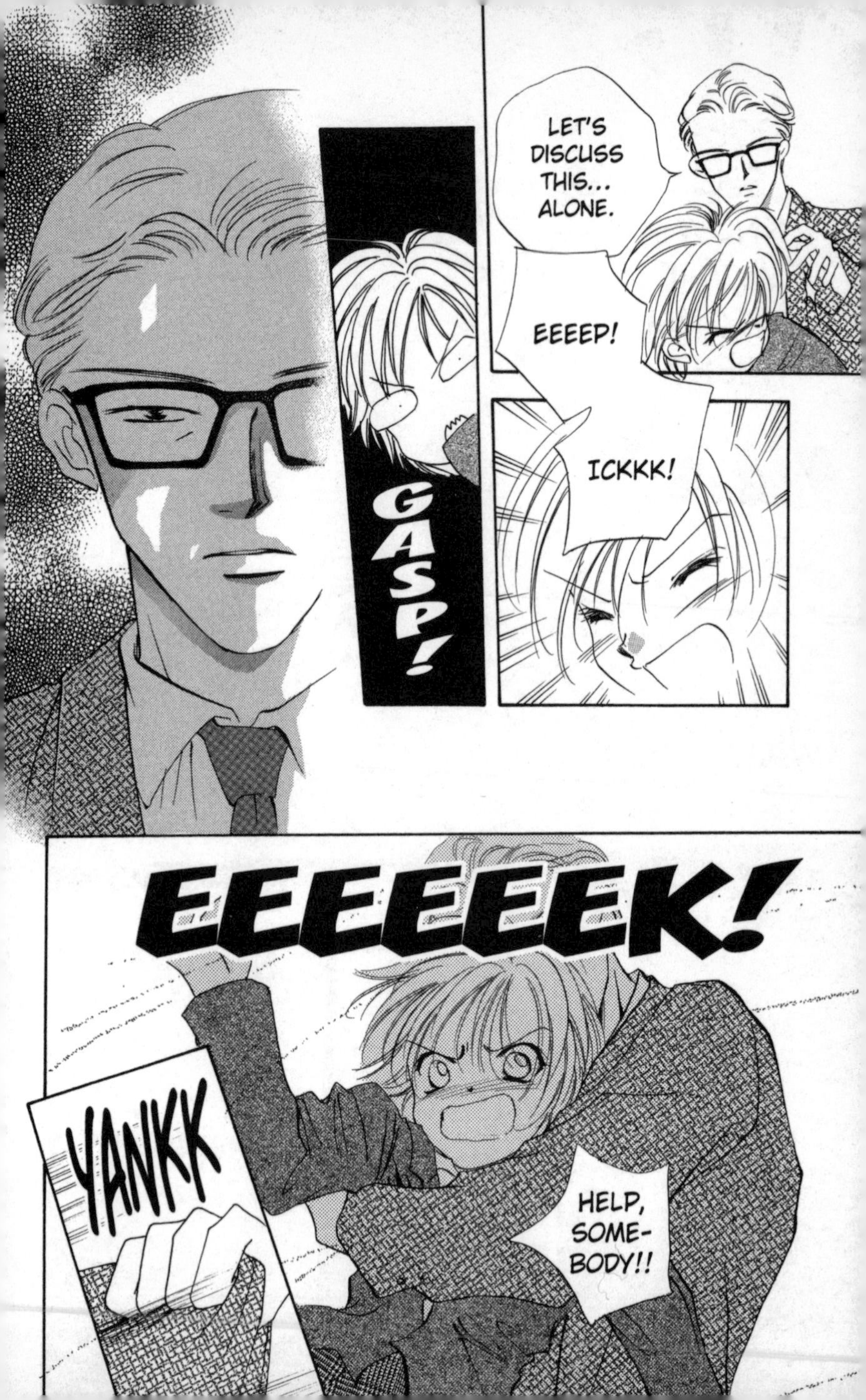
LET'S DISCUSS THIS... ALONE.
EEEEP!
ICKKK!
GASP!
EEEEEEK!
HELP, SOME-BODY!!
YANKK

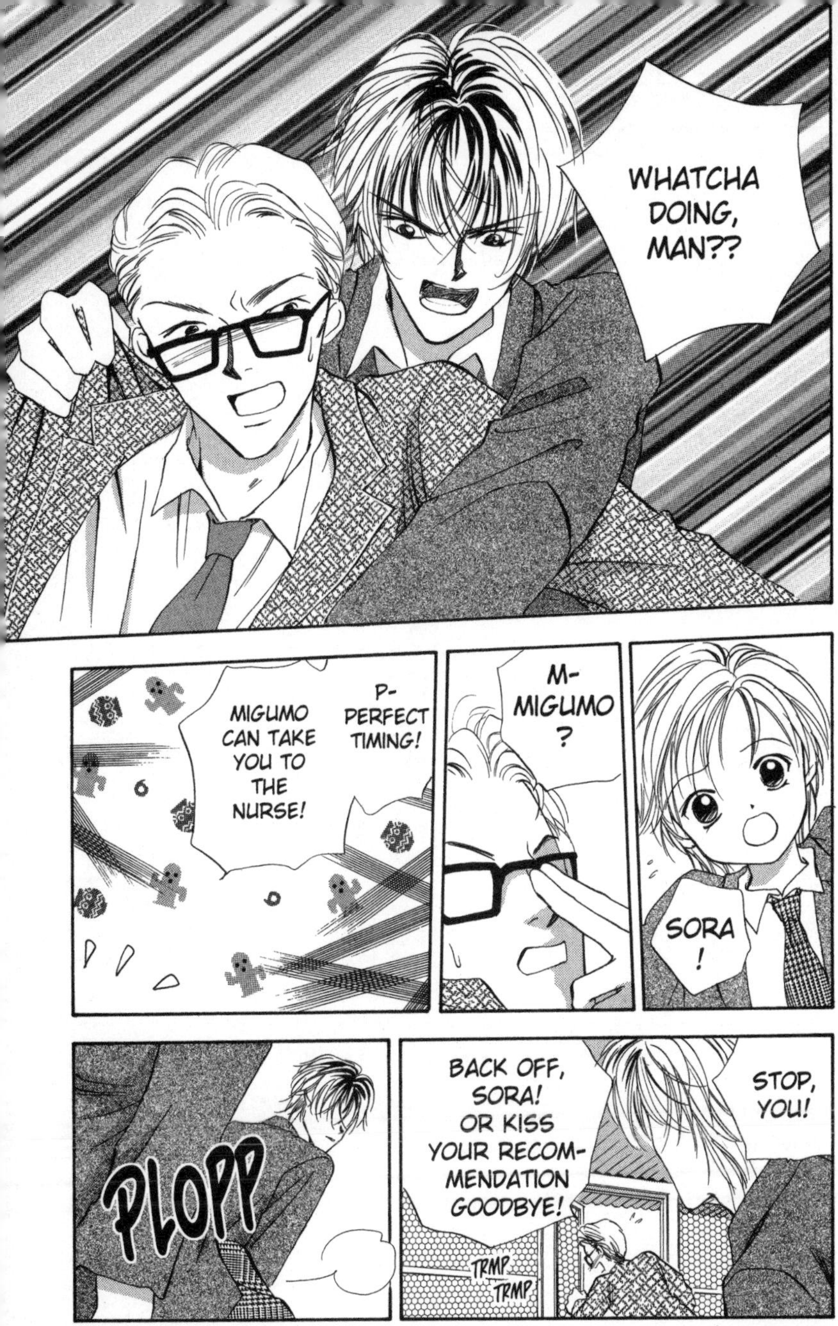
WHATCHA DOING, MAN??
SORA!
M-MIGUMO?
P-PERFECT TIMING!
MIGUMO CAN TAKE YOU TO THE NURSE!
STOP, YOU!
BACK OFF, SORA! OR KISS YOUR RECOM-MENDATION GOODBYE!
TRMP TRMP
PLOPP

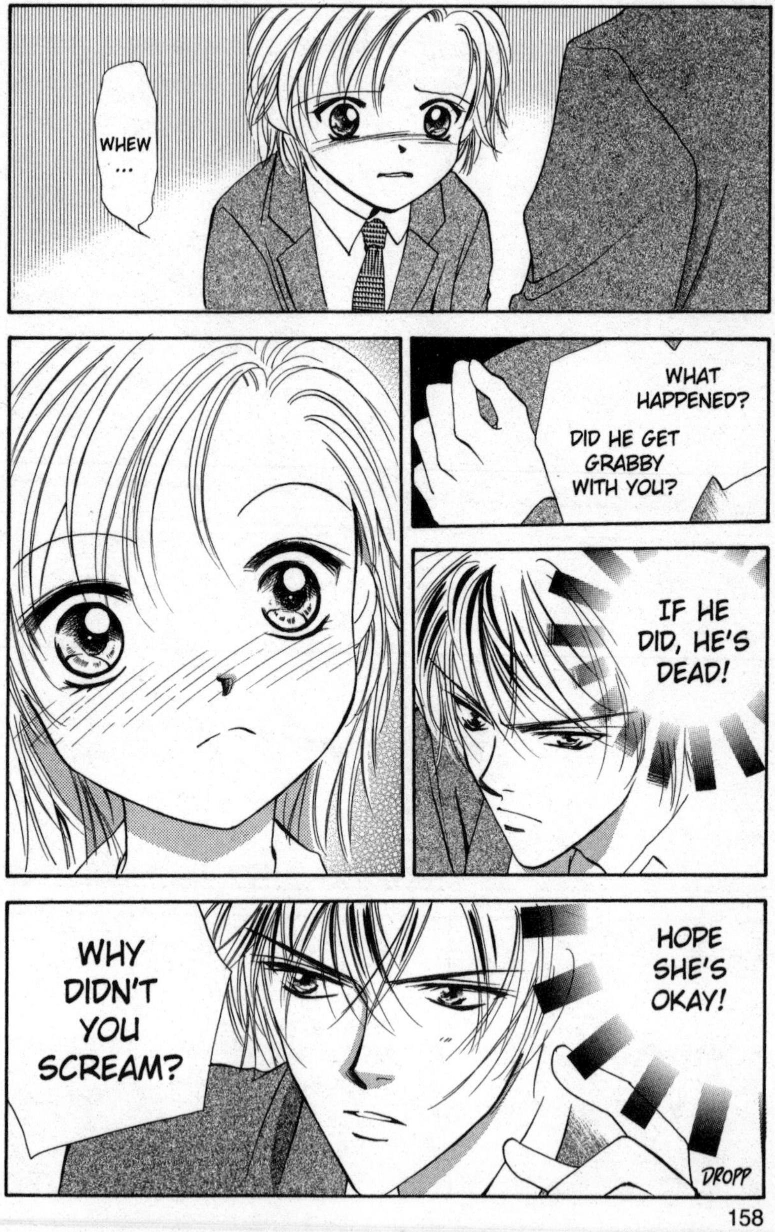
WHEW ...
WHAT HAPPENED?
DID HE GET GRABBY WITH YOU?
IF HE DID, HE'S DEAD!
HOPE SHE'S OKAY!
WHY DIDN'T YOU SCREAM?
DROPP

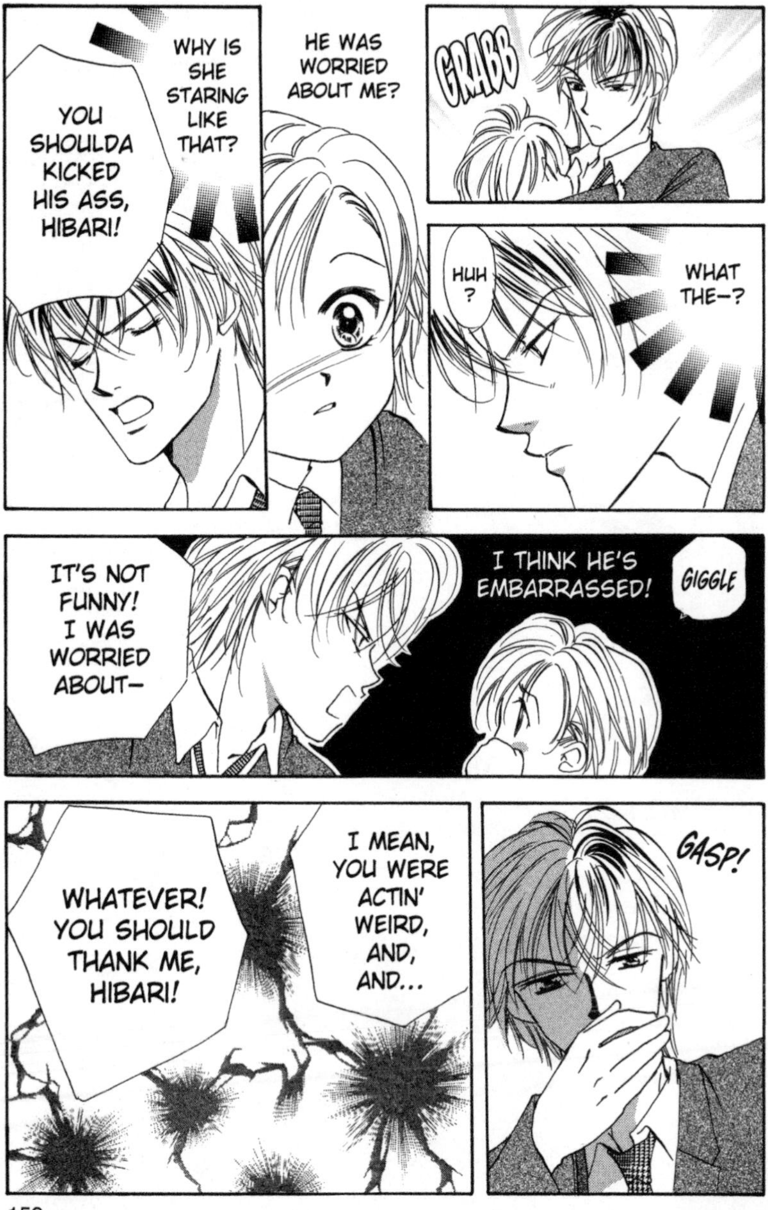
GRABB
HUH?
WHAT THE–?
HE WAS WORRIED ABOUT ME?
WHY IS SHE STARING LIKE THAT?
YOU SHOULDA KICKED HIS ASS, HIBARI!
GIGGLE
I THINK HE'S EMBARRASSED!
IT'S NOT FUNNY! I WAS WORRIED ABOUT–
GASP!
I MEAN, YOU WERE ACTIN' WEIRD, AND, AND...
WHATEVER! YOU SHOULD THANK ME, HIBARI!

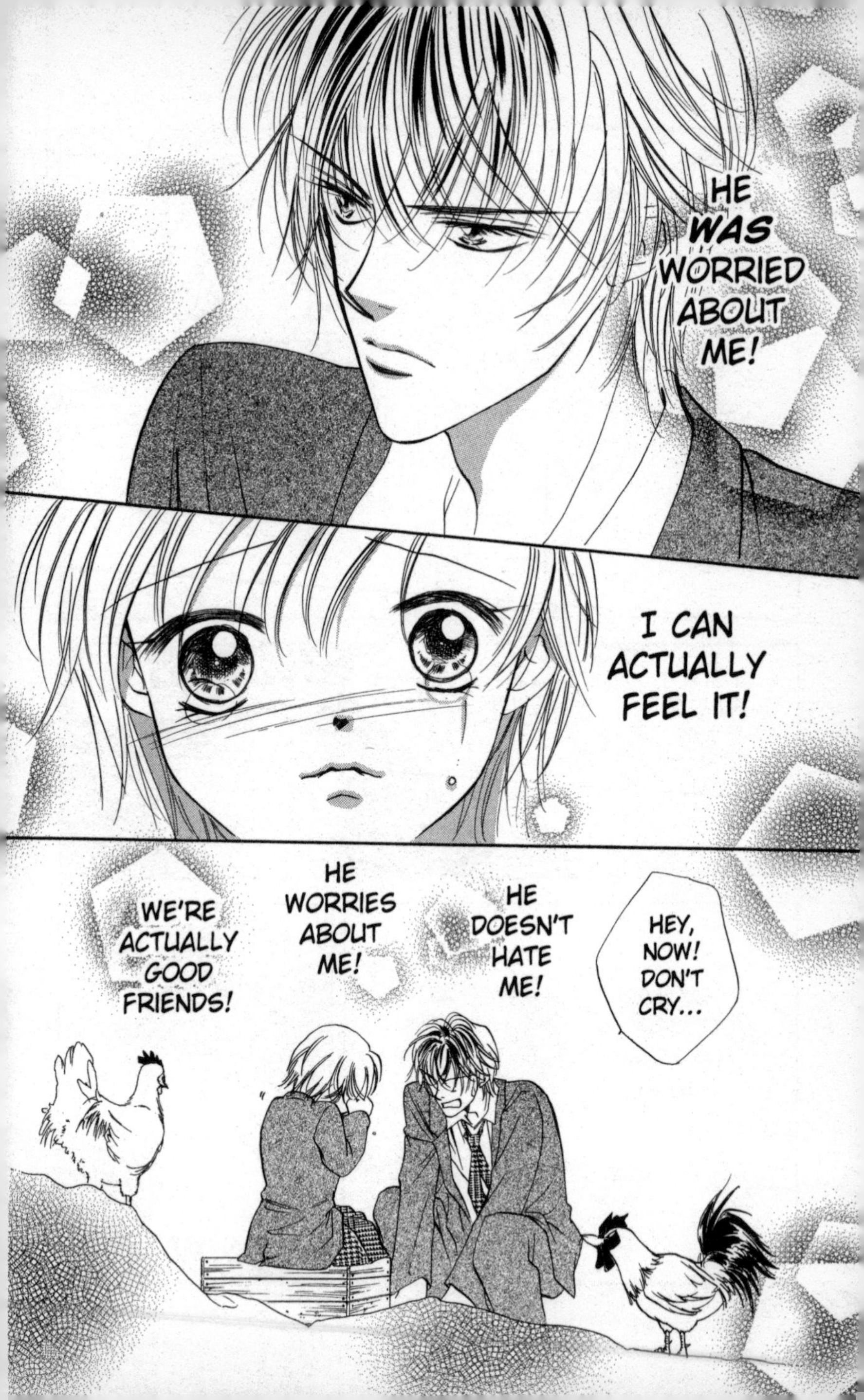
HE WAS WORRIED ABOUT ME!
I CAN ACTUALLY FEEL IT!
HEY, NOW! DON'T CRY...
HE DOESN'T HATE ME!
HE WORRIES ABOUT ME!
WE'RE ACTUALLY GOOD FRIENDS!

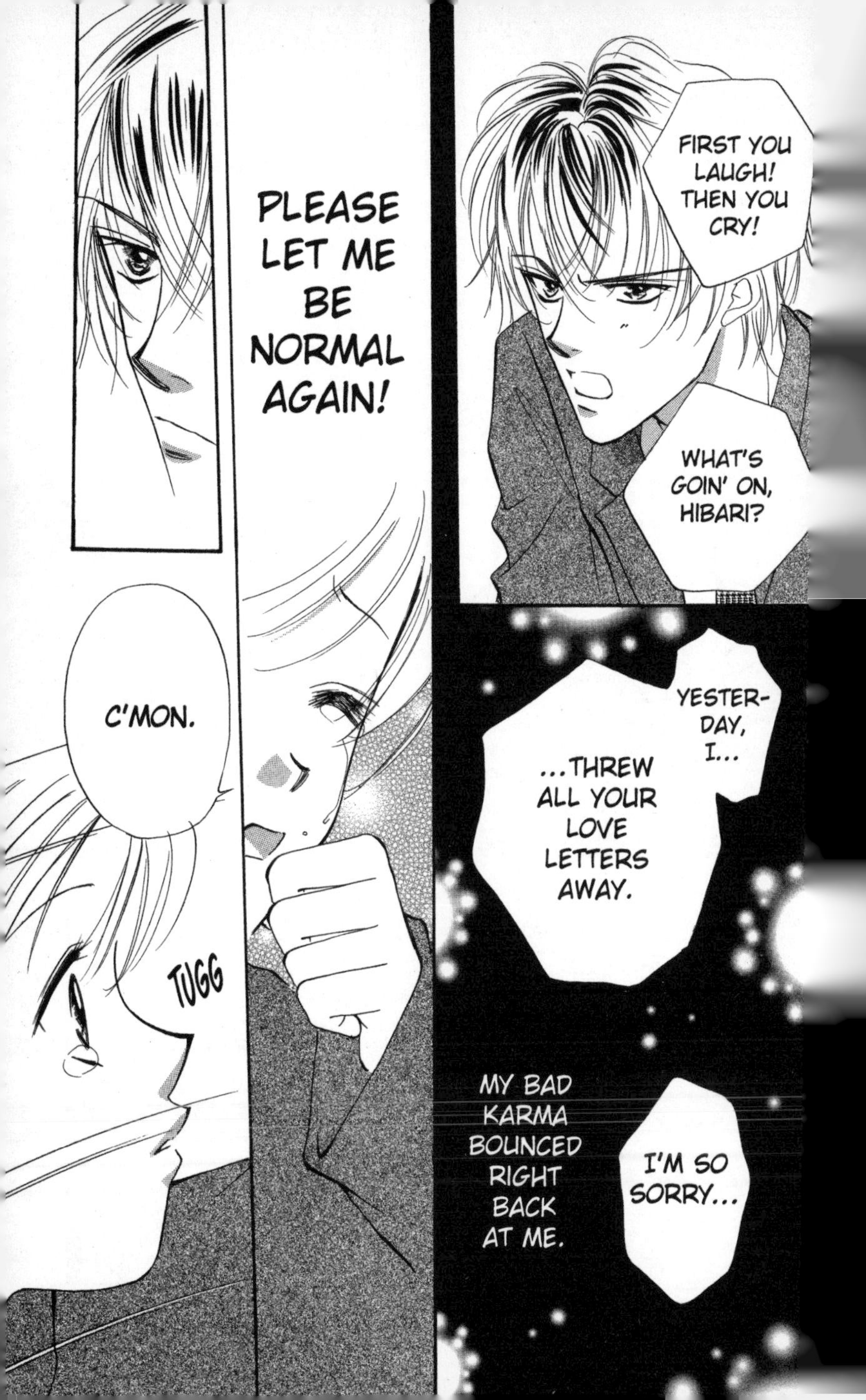
FIRST YOU LAUGH! THEN YOU CRY!
WHAT'S GOIN' ON, HIBARI?
YESTER-DAY, I...
...THREW ALL YOUR LOVE LETTERS AWAY.
I'M SO SORRY...
MY BAD KARMA BOUNCED RIGHT BACK AT ME.
PLEASE LET ME BE NORMAL AGAIN!
C'MON.
TUGG

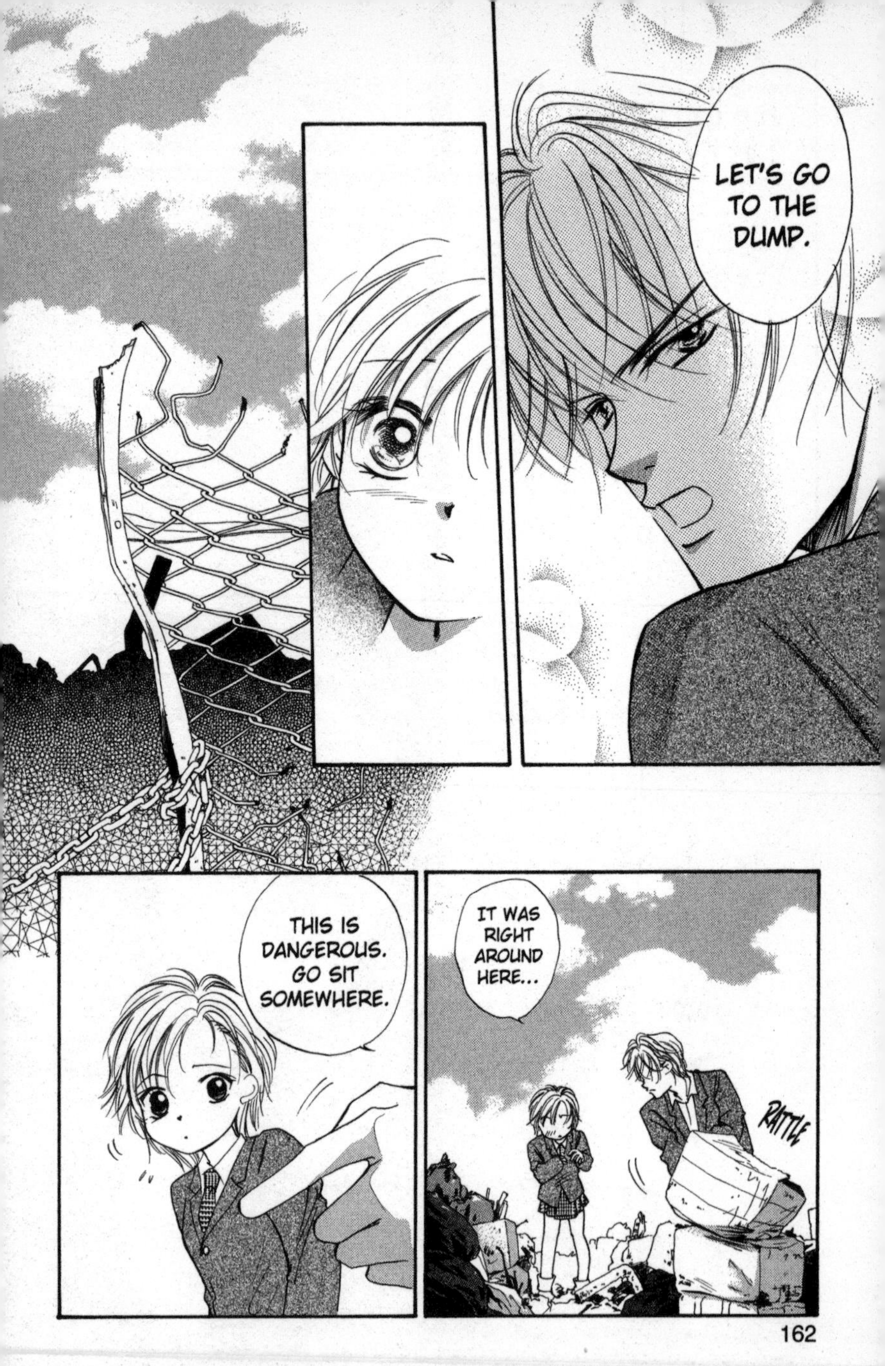
LET'S GO TO THE DUMP.
IT WAS RIGHT AROUND HERE...
RATTLE
THIS IS DANGEROUS. GO SIT SOMEWHERE.

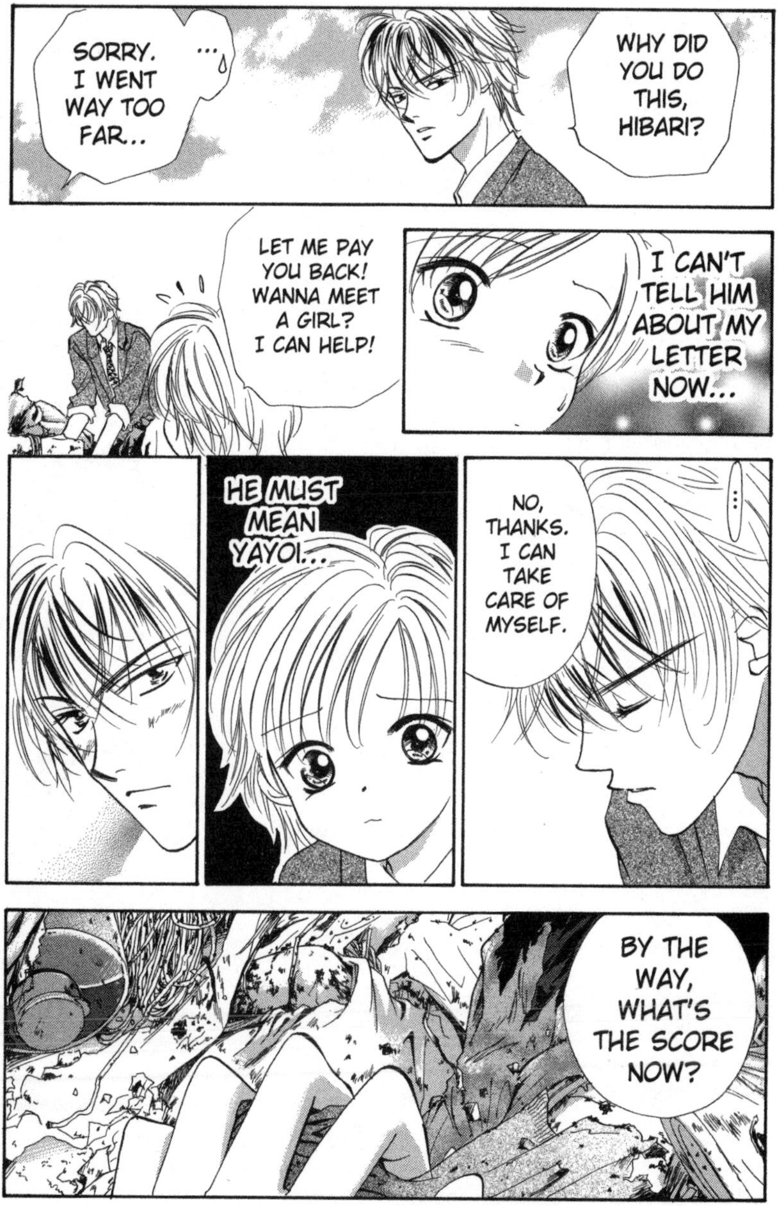
WHY DID YOU DO THIS, HIBARI?
...
SORRY. I WENT WAY TOO FAR...
I CAN'T TELL HIM ABOUT MY LETTER NOW...
LET ME PAY YOU BACK! WANNA MEET A GIRL? I CAN HELP!
...
NO, THANKS. I CAN TAKE CARE OF MYSELF.
HE MUST MEAN YAYOI...
BY THE WAY, WHAT'S THE SCORE NOW?

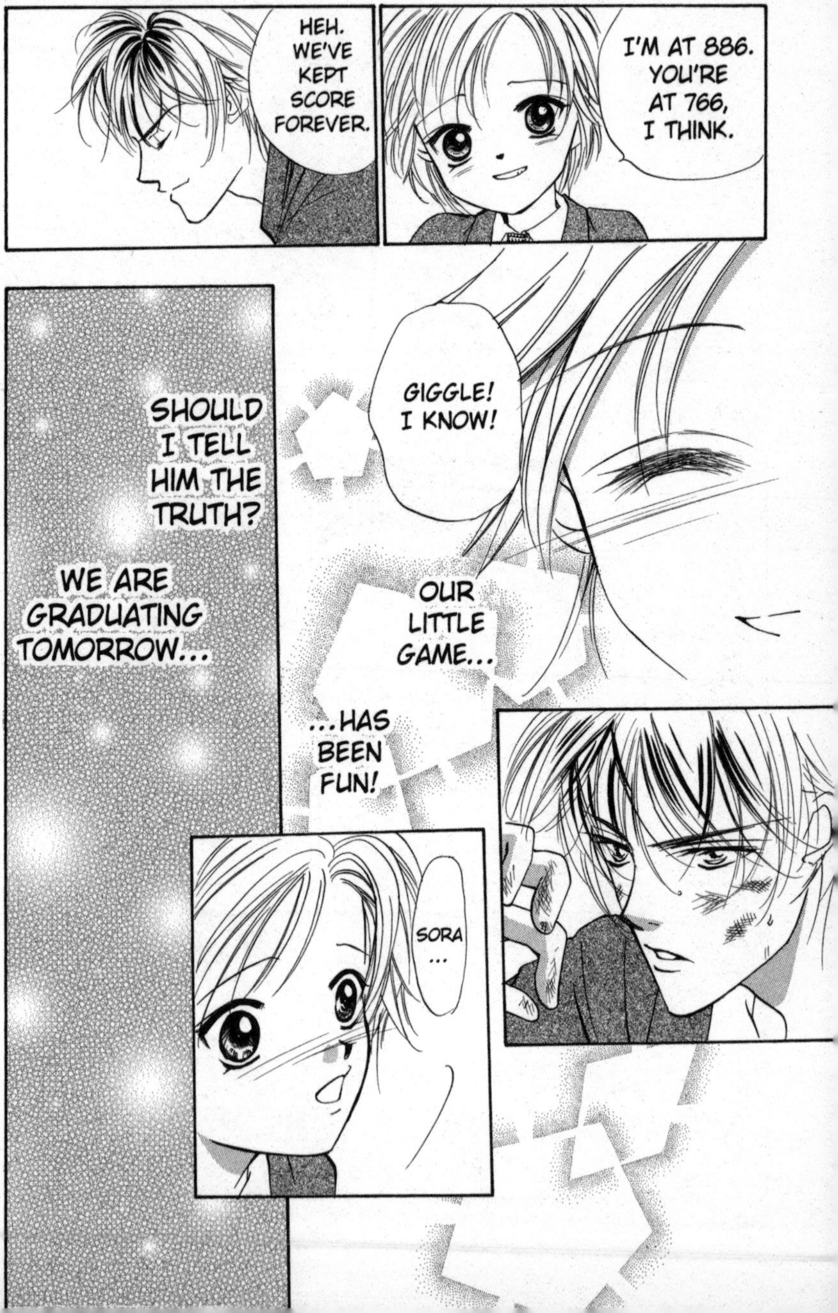
I'M AT 886. YOU'RE AT 766, I THINK.
HEH. WE'VE KEPT SCORE FOREVER.
GIGGLE! I KNOW!
OUR LITTLE GAME...
...HAS BEEN FUN!
SORA ...
SHOULD I TELL HIM THE TRUTH?
WE ARE GRADUATING TOMORROW...

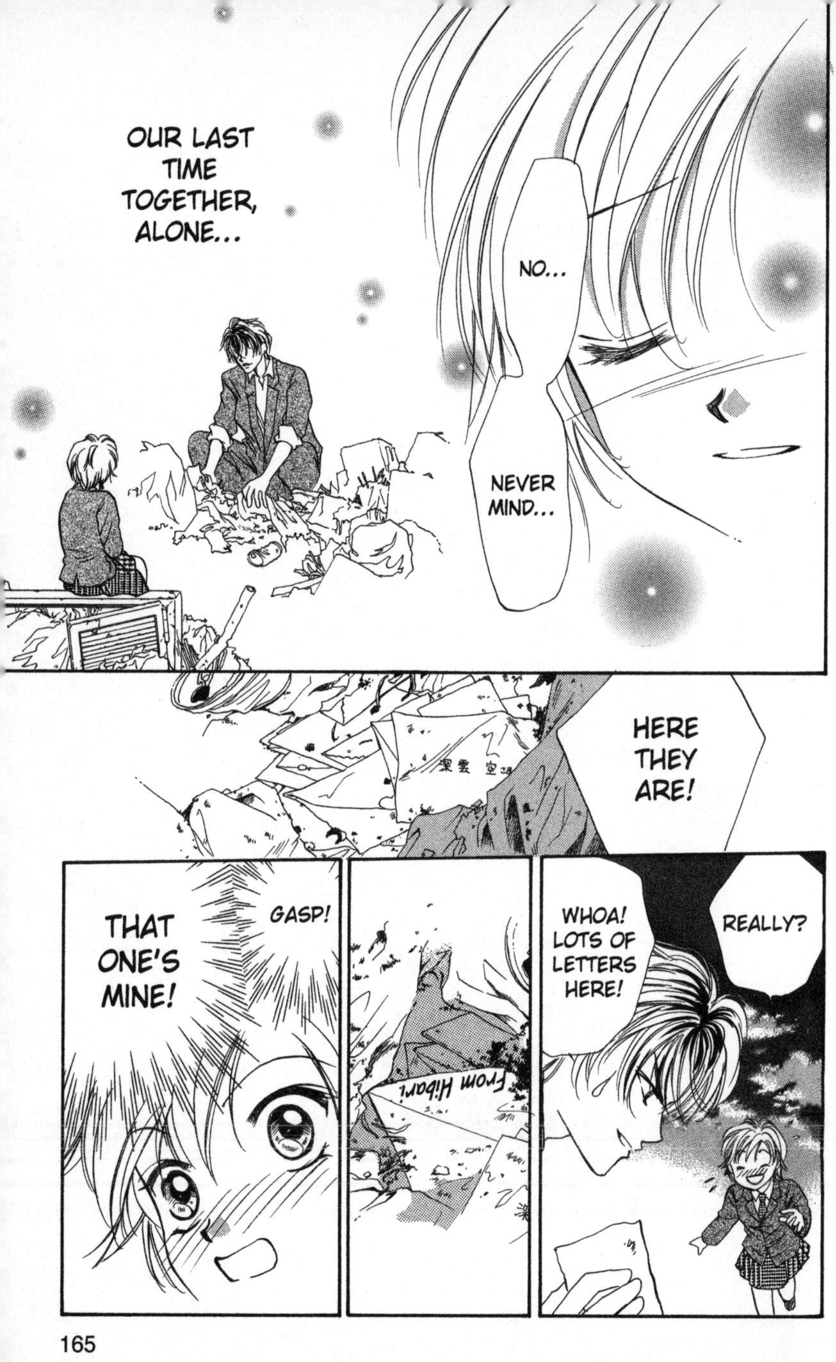
NO...
NEVER MIND...
OUR LAST TIME TOGETHER, ALONE...
HERE THEY ARE!
REALLY?
WHOA! LOTS OF LETTERS HERE!
From Hibari
GASP!
THAT ONE'S MINE!

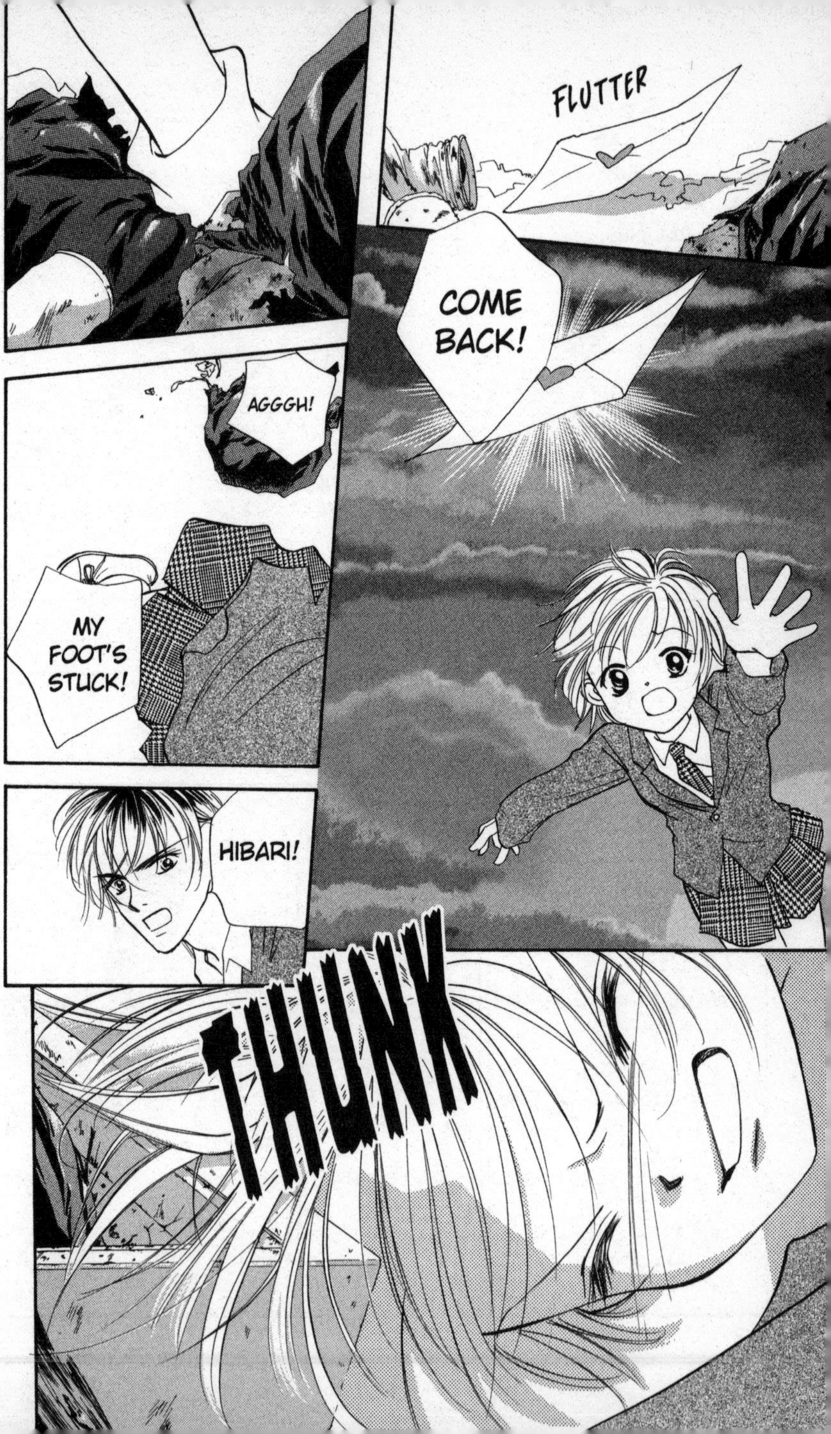
FLUTTER
COME BACK!
AGGGH!
MY FOOT'S STUCK!
HIBARI!
THUNK

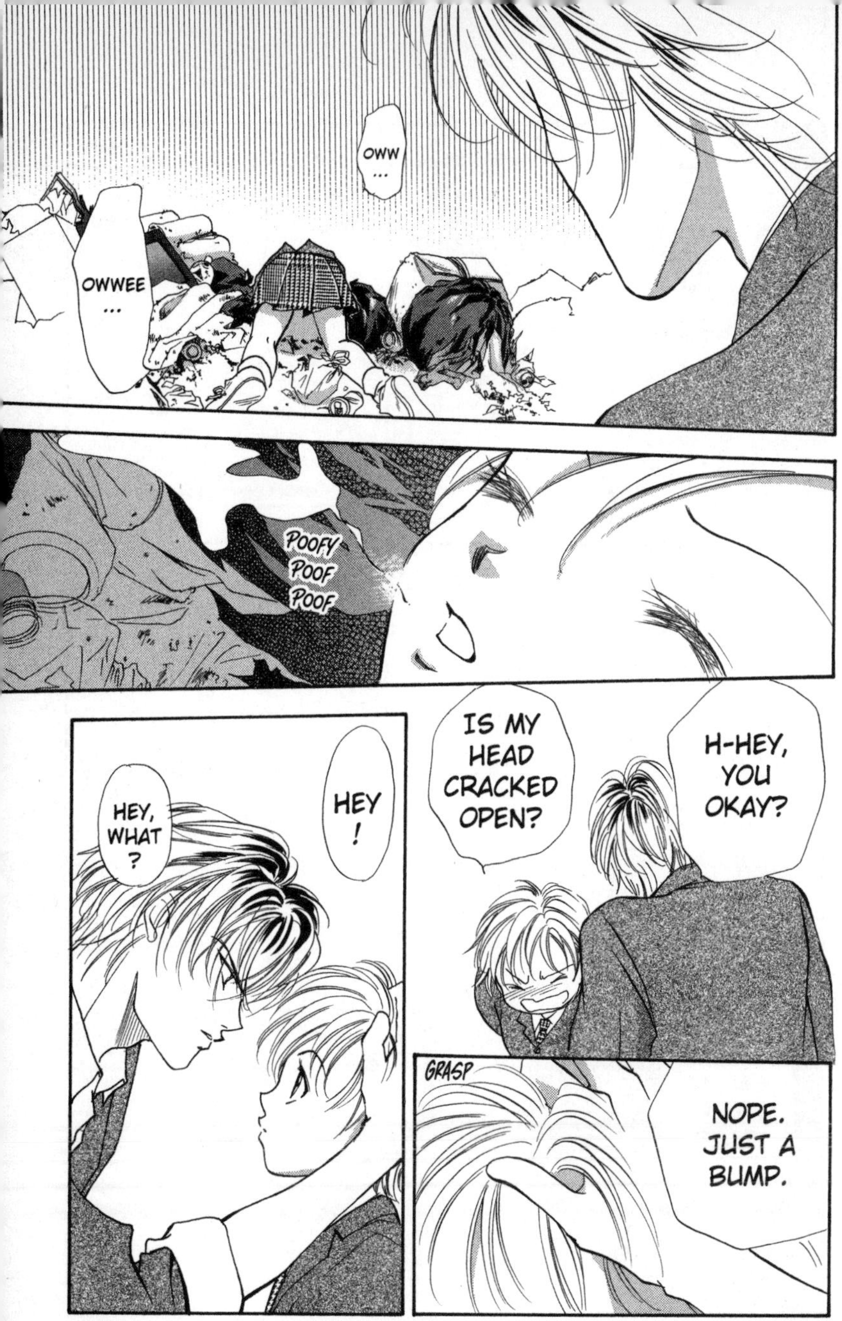
OWW ...
OWWEE ...
POOFY POOF POOF
H-HEY, YOU OKAY?
IS MY HEAD CRACKED OPEN?
GRASP
NOPE. JUST A BUMP.
HEY!
HEY, WHAT?

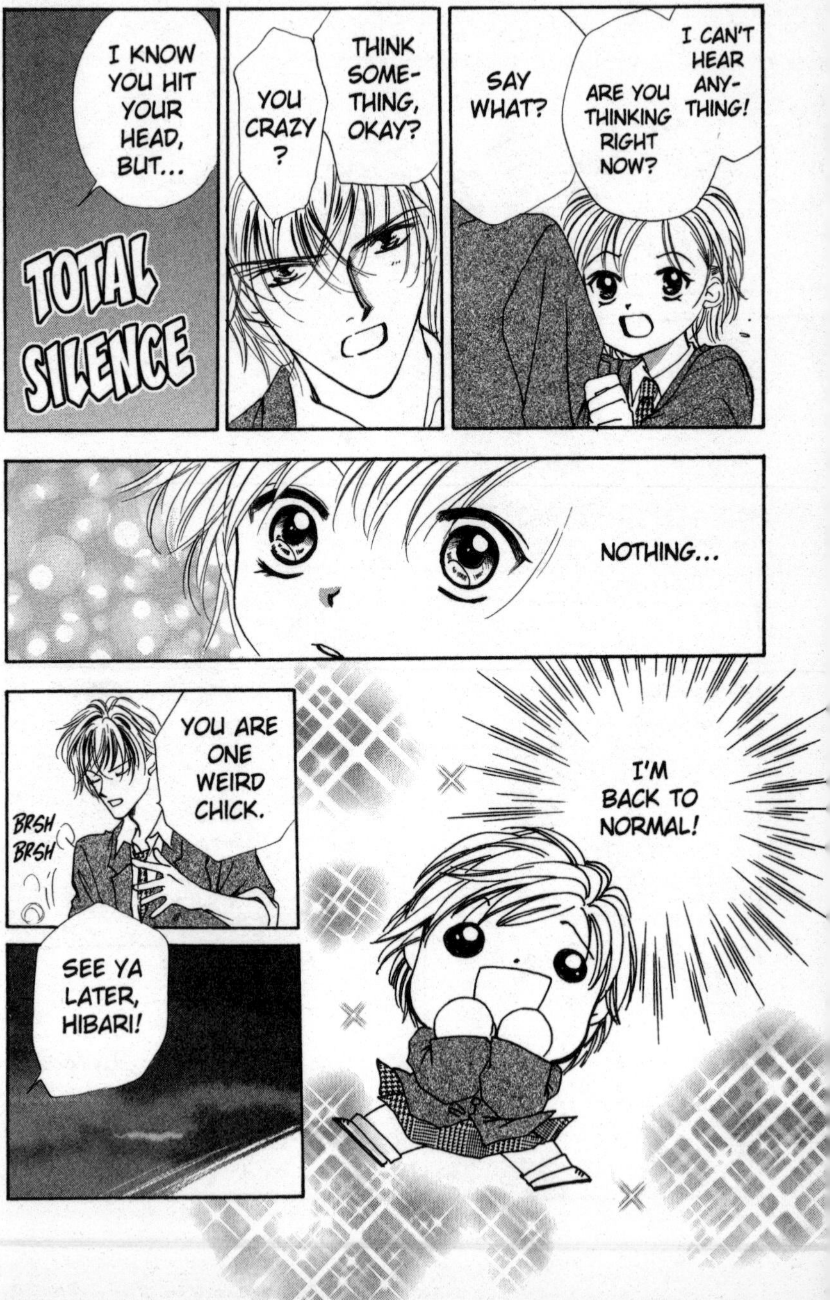
I CAN'T HEAR ANY-THING!
ARE YOU THINKING RIGHT NOW?
SAY WHAT?
THINK SOME-THING, OKAY?
YOU CRAZY?
I KNOW YOU HIT YOUR HEAD, BUT...
TOTAL SILENCE
NOTHING...
I'M BACK TO NORMAL!
YOU ARE ONE WEIRD CHICK.
BRSH BRSH
SEE YA LATER, HIBARI!

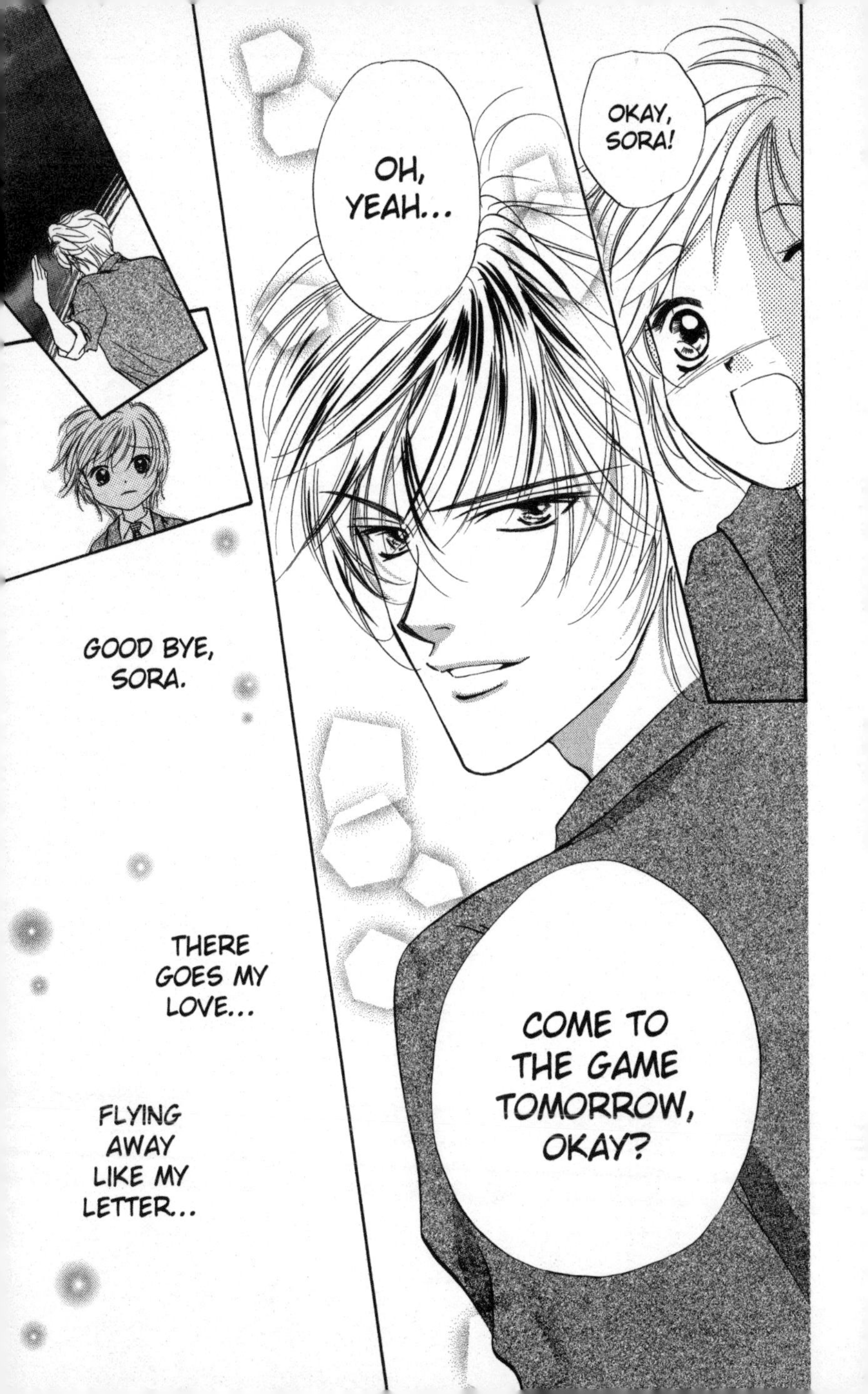
OKAY, SORA!
OH, YEAH...
COME TO THE GAME TOMORROW, OKAY?
GOOD BYE, SORA.
THERE GOES MY LOVE...
FLYING AWAY LIKE MY LETTER...

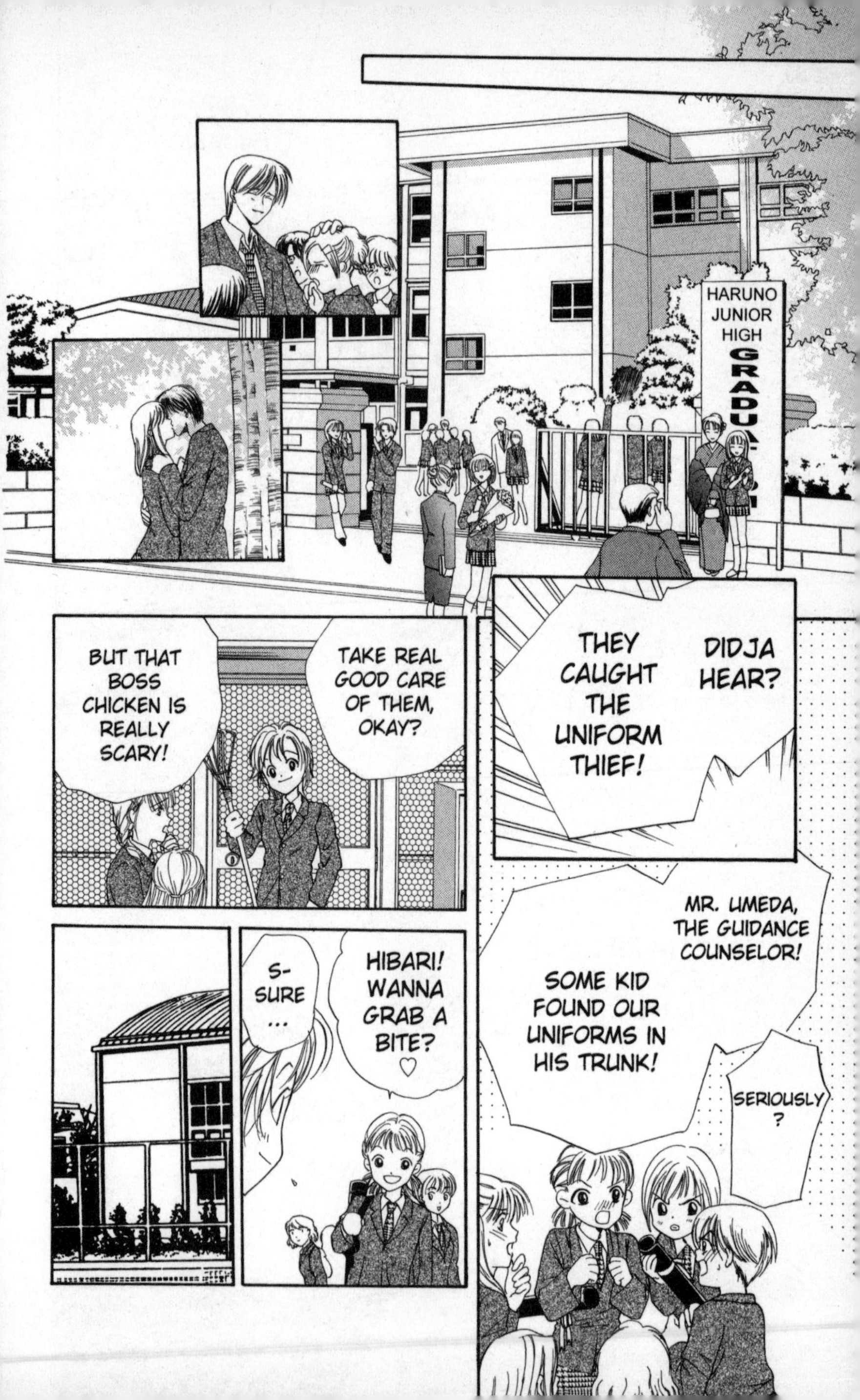
HARUNO JUNIOR HIGH
DIDJA HEAR?
THEY CAUGHT THE UNIFORM THIEF!
MR. UMEDA, THE GUIDANCE COUNSELOR!
SOME KID FOUND OUR UNIFORMS IN HIS TRUNK!
SERIOUSLY?
TAKE REAL GOOD CARE OF THEM, OKAY?
BUT THAT BOSS CHICKEN IS REALLY SCARY!
HIBARI! WANNA GRAB A BITE? ♡
S-SURE ...

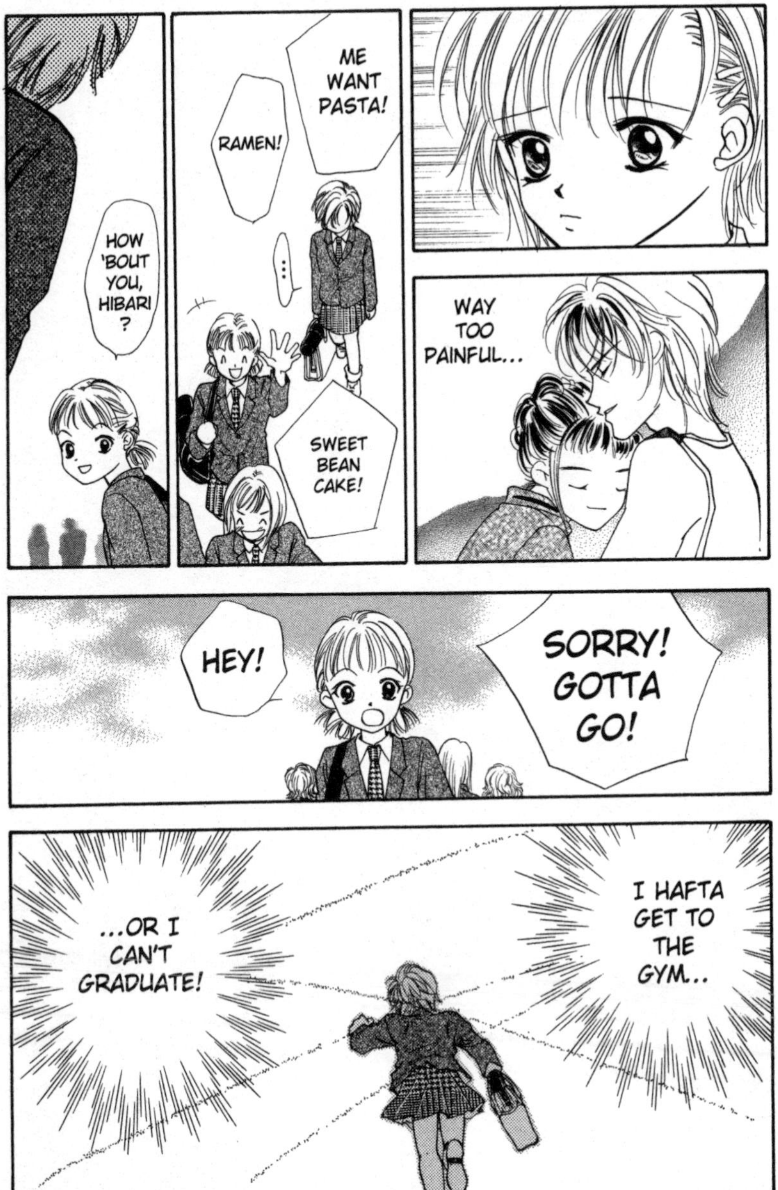
WAY TOO PAINFUL...
ME WANT PASTA!
RAMEN!
...
SWEET BEAN CAKE!
HOW 'BOUT YOU, HIBARI?
SORRY! GOTTA GO!
HEY!
I HAFTA GET TO THE GYM...
...OR I CAN'T GRADUATE!

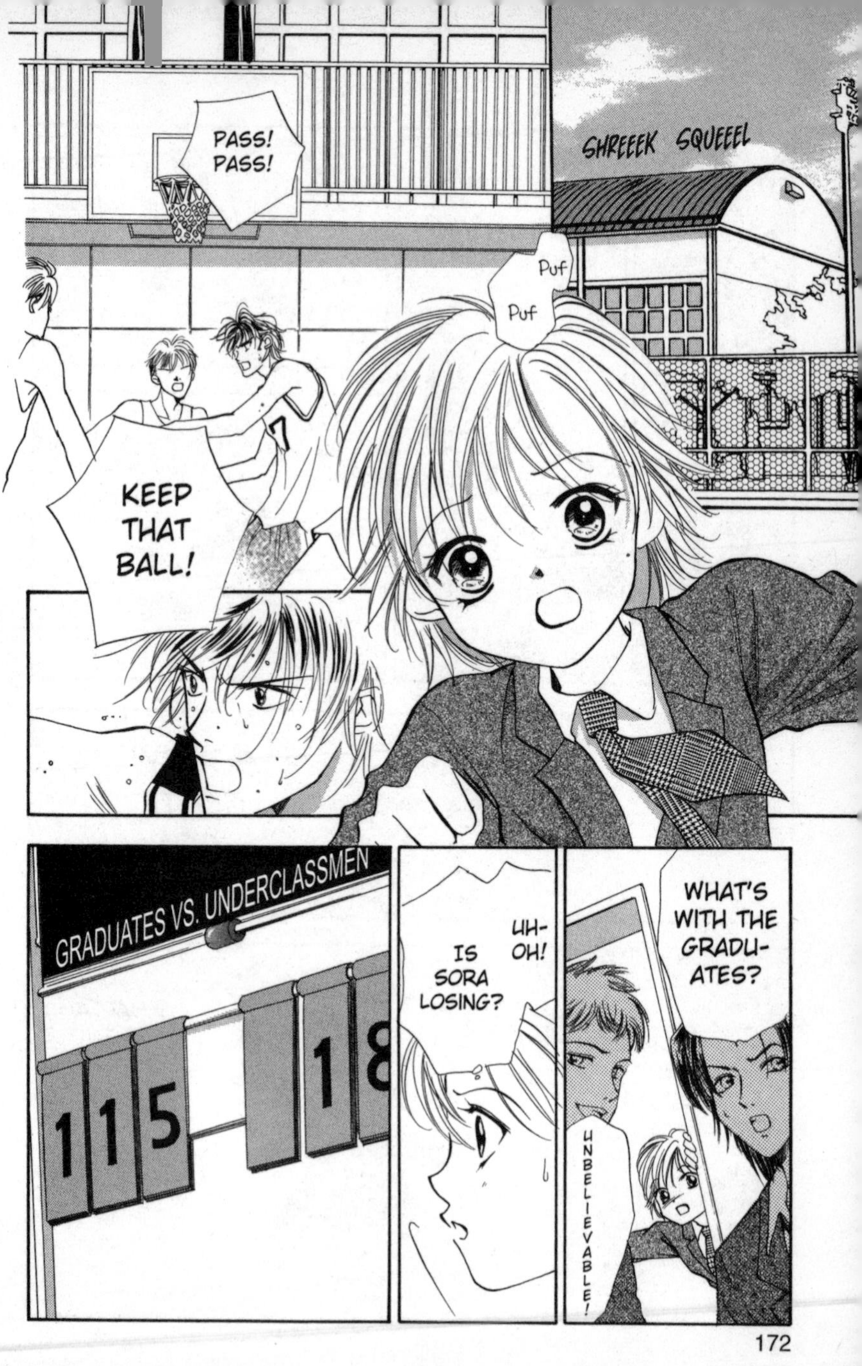
SHREEEK SQUEEEL
PASS! PASS!
Puf Puf
KEEP THAT BALL!
WHAT'S WITH THE GRADU-ATES?
UNBELIEVABLE!
UH-OH!
IS SORA LOSING?
GRADUATES VS. UNDERCLASSMEN
115
18

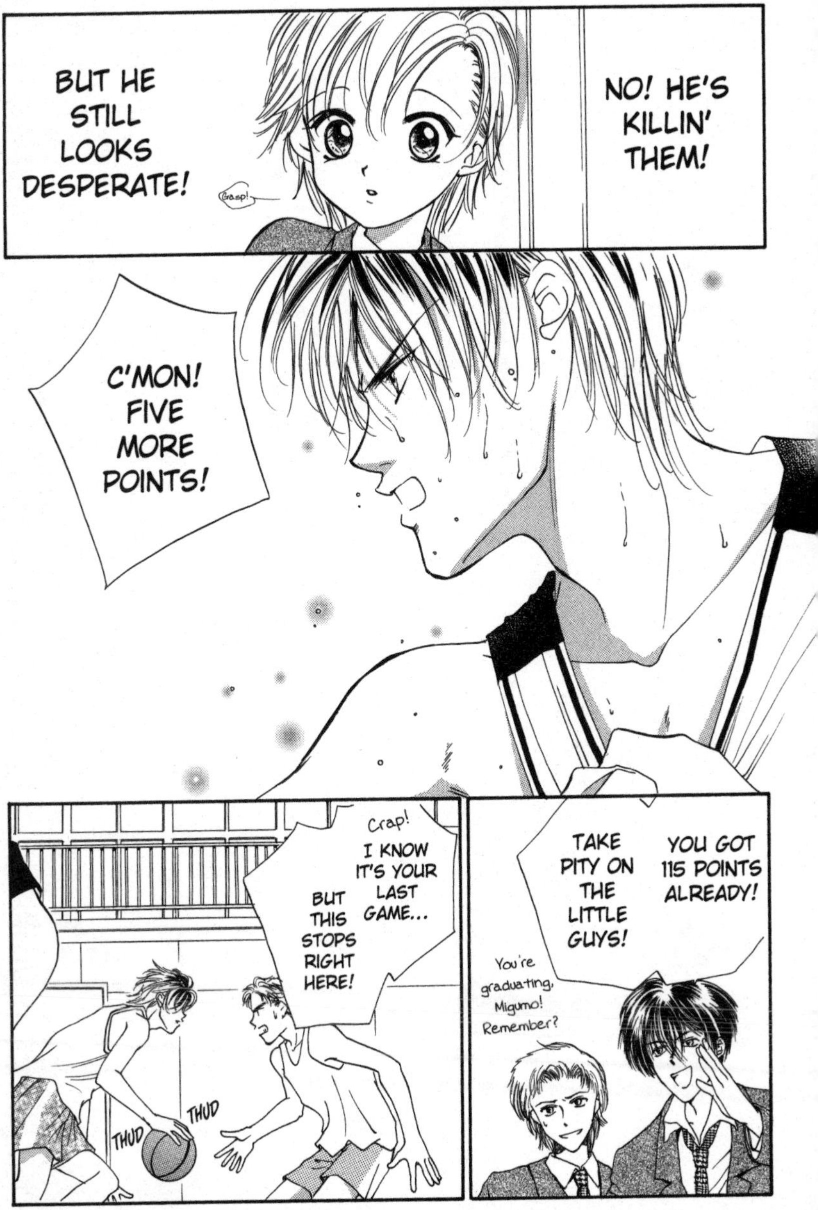
NO! HE'S KILLIN' THEM!
BUT HE STILL LOOKS DESPERATE!
Gasp!
C'MON! FIVE MORE POINTS!
YOU GOT 115 POINTS ALREADY!
TAKE PITY ON THE LITTLE GUYS!
You're graduating, Migumo! Remember?
Crap!
I KNOW IT'S YOUR LAST GAME...
BUT THIS STOPS RIGHT HERE!
THUD
THUD

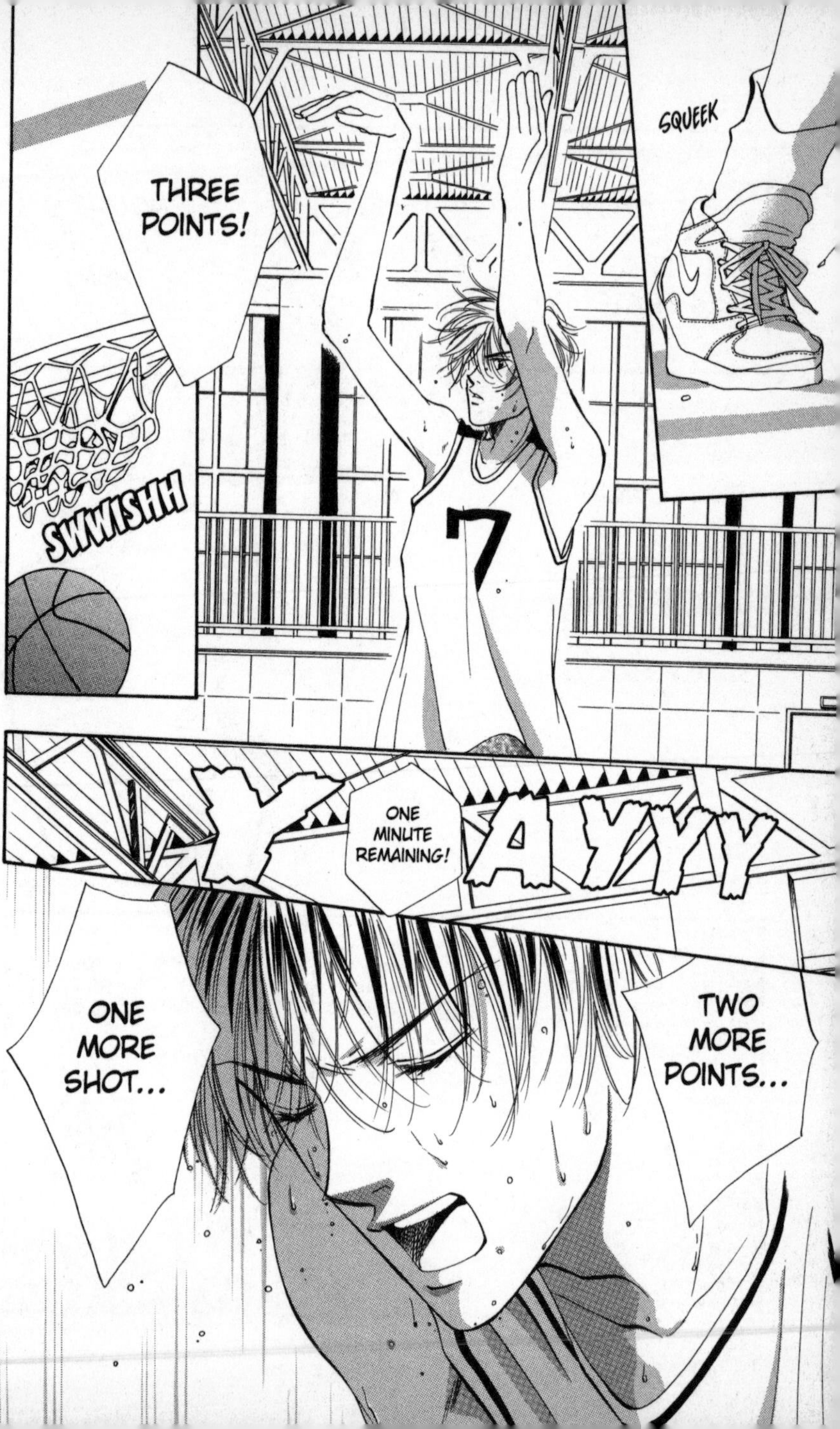
SQUEEK
THREE POINTS!
SWWISHH
YAYYY
ONE MINUTE REMAINING!
TWO MORE POINTS...
ONE MORE SHOT...

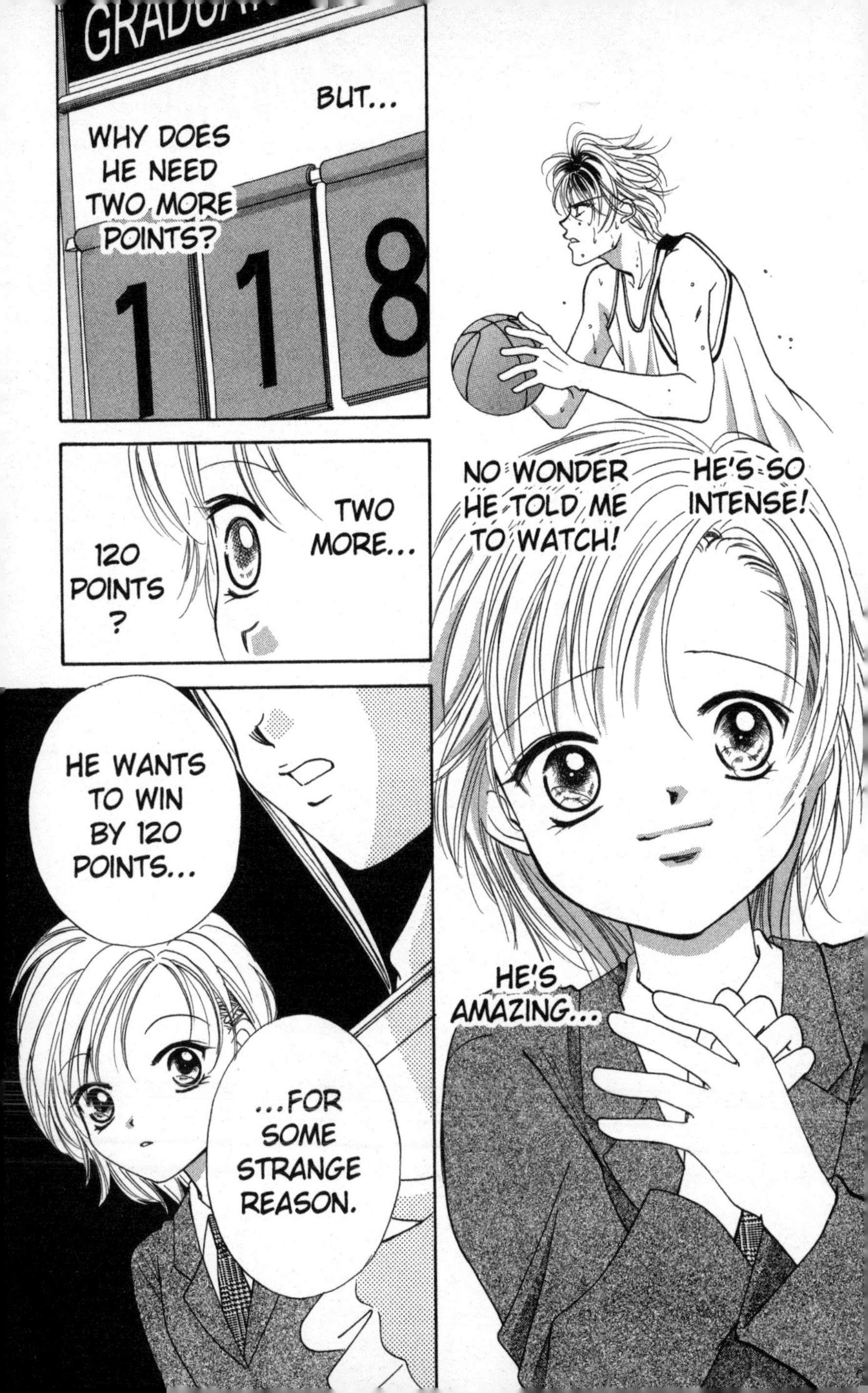
HE'S SO INTENSE!
NO WONDER HE TOLD ME TO WATCH!
HE'S AMAZING...
BUT...
WHY DOES HE NEED TWO MORE POINTS?
118
TWO MORE...
120 POINTS?
HE WANTS TO WIN BY 120 POINTS...
...FOR SOME STRANGE REASON.

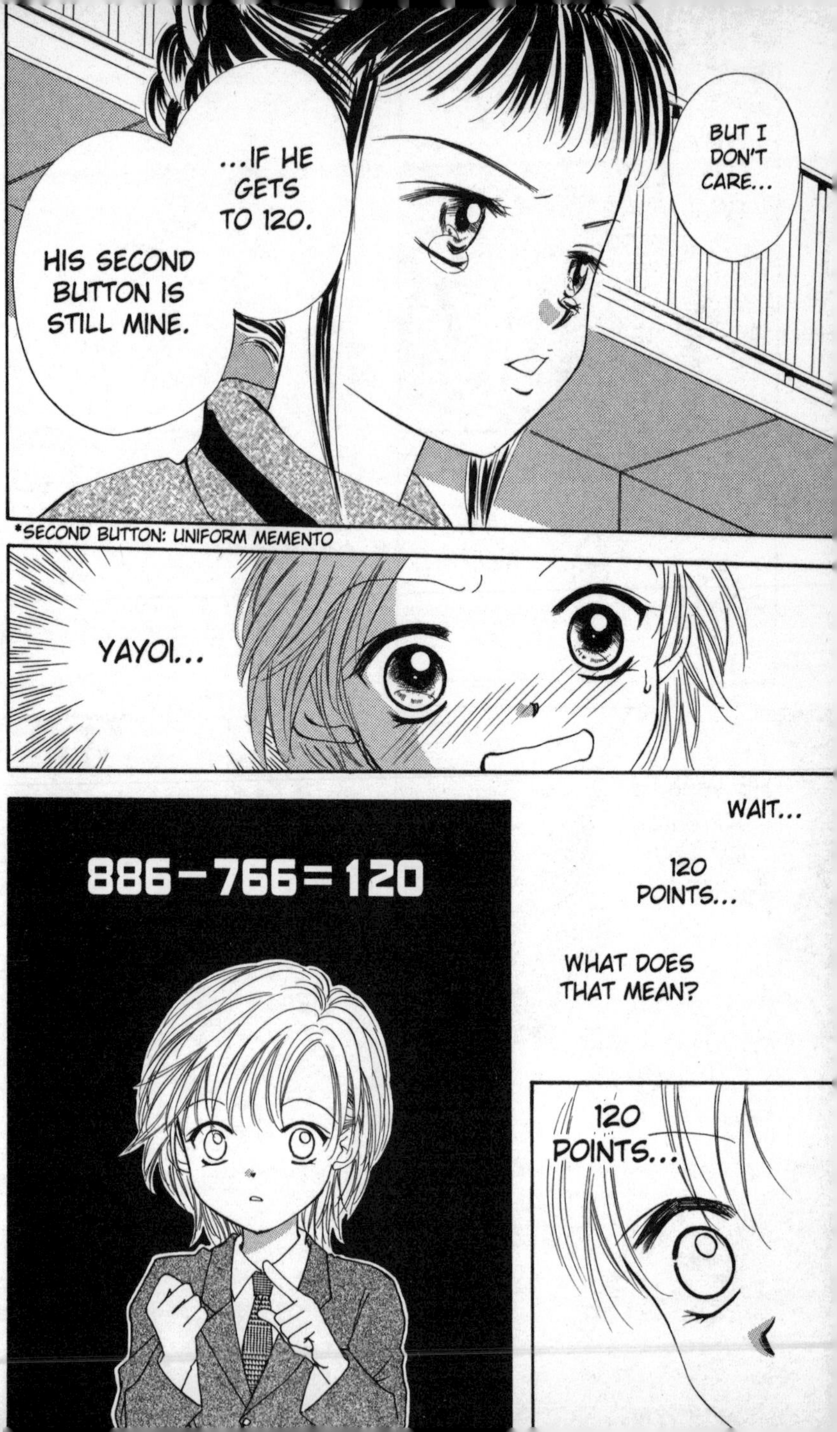
BUT I DON'T CARE...
...IF HE GETS TO 120.
HIS SECOND BUTTON IS STILL MINE.
*SECOND BUTTON: UNIFORM MEMENTO
YAYOI...
WAIT...
120 POINTS...
WHAT DOES THAT MEAN?
120 POINTS...
886-766=120

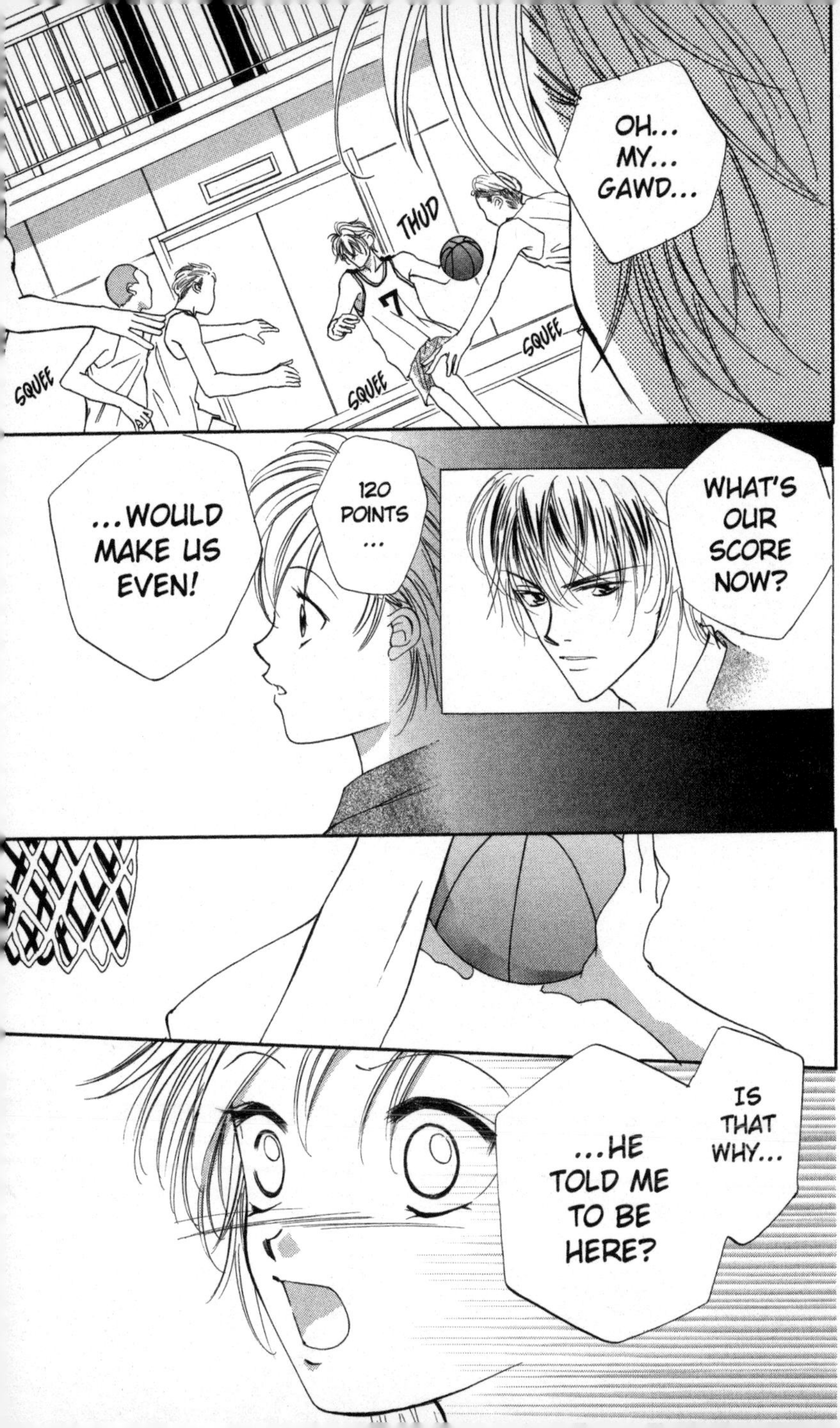
OH... MY... GAWD...
THUD
SQUEE
SQUEE
SQUEE
WHAT'S OUR SCORE NOW?
120 POINTS ...
...WOULD MAKE US EVEN!
IS THAT WHY...
...HE TOLD ME TO BE HERE?

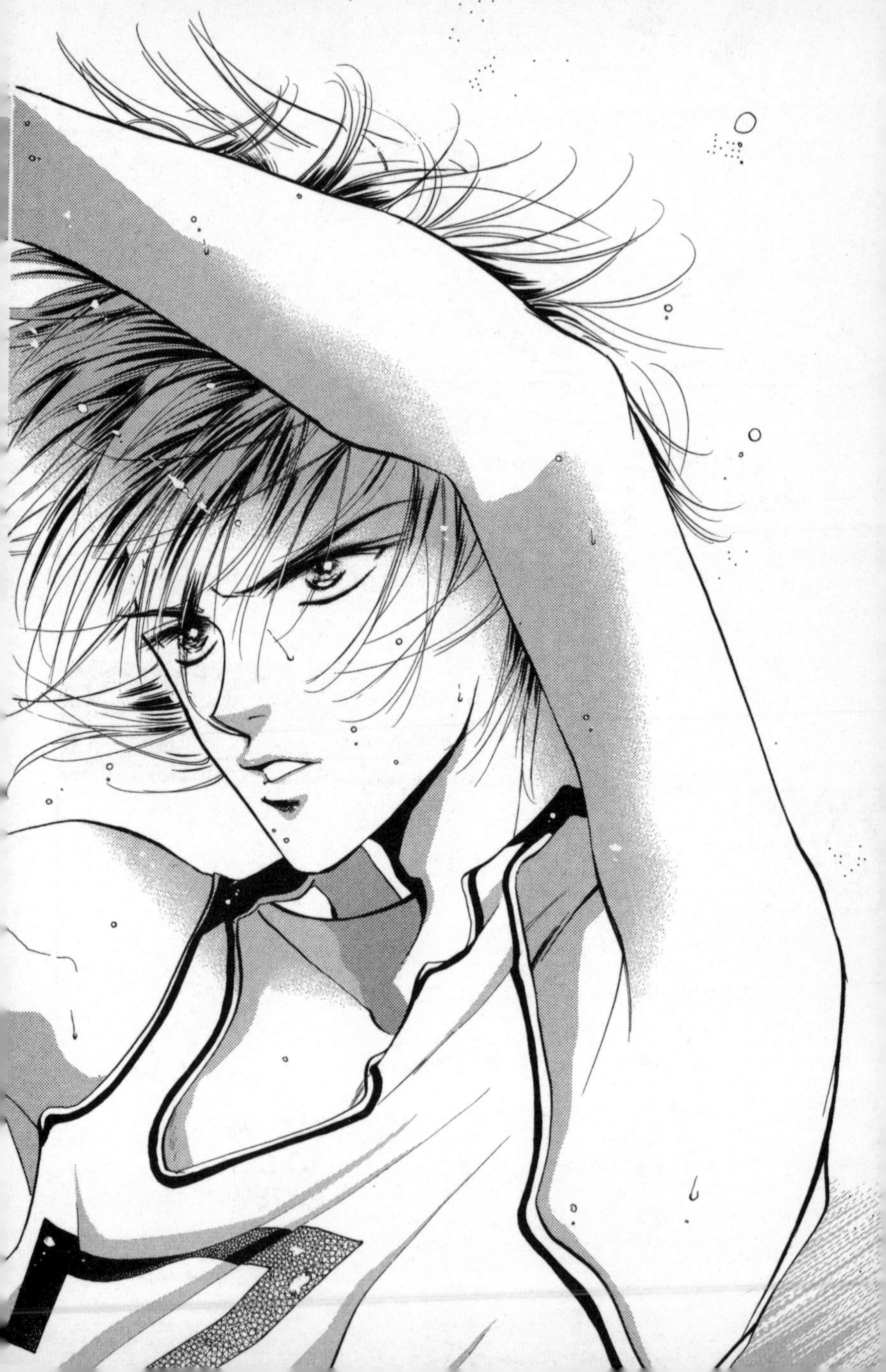

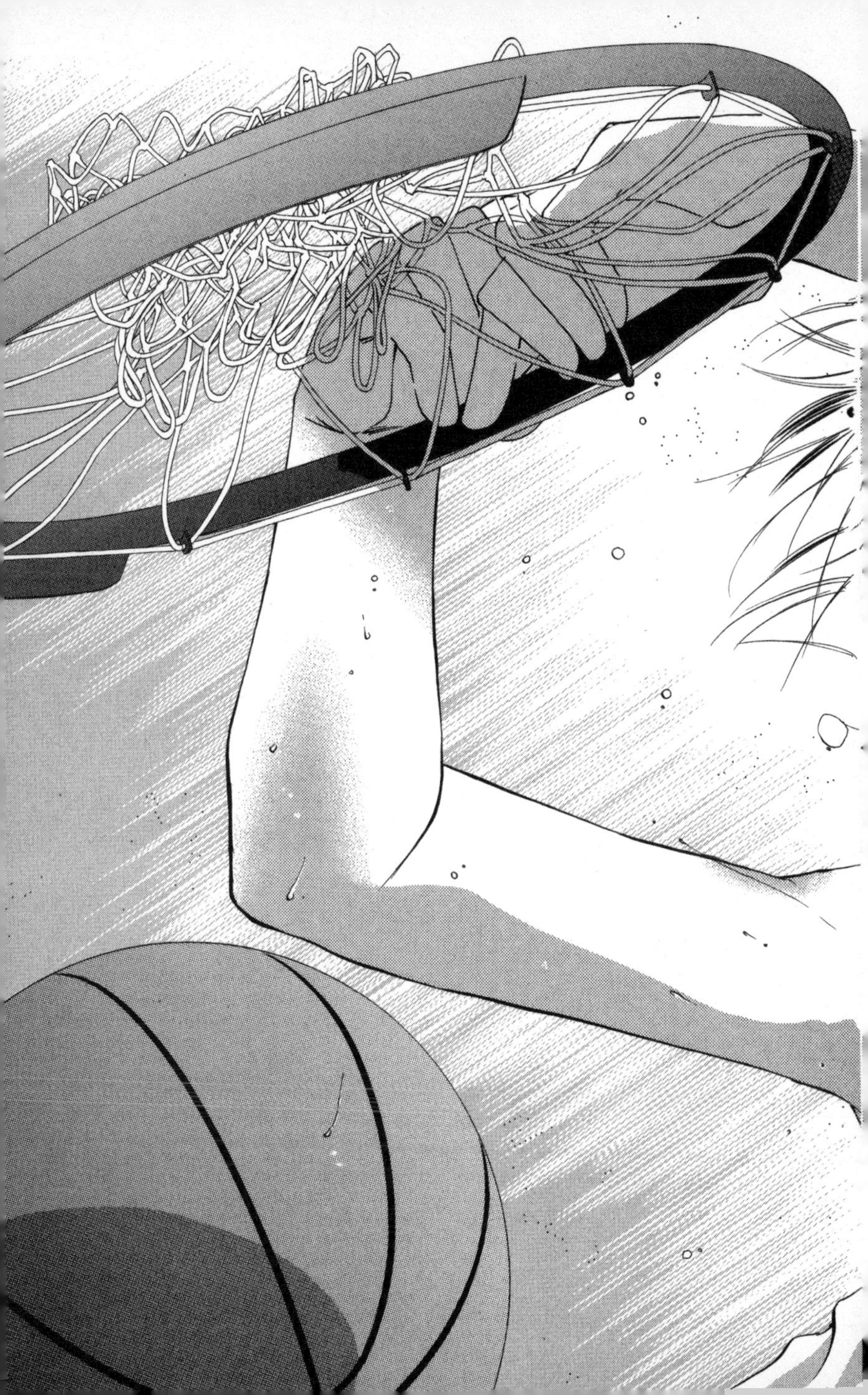

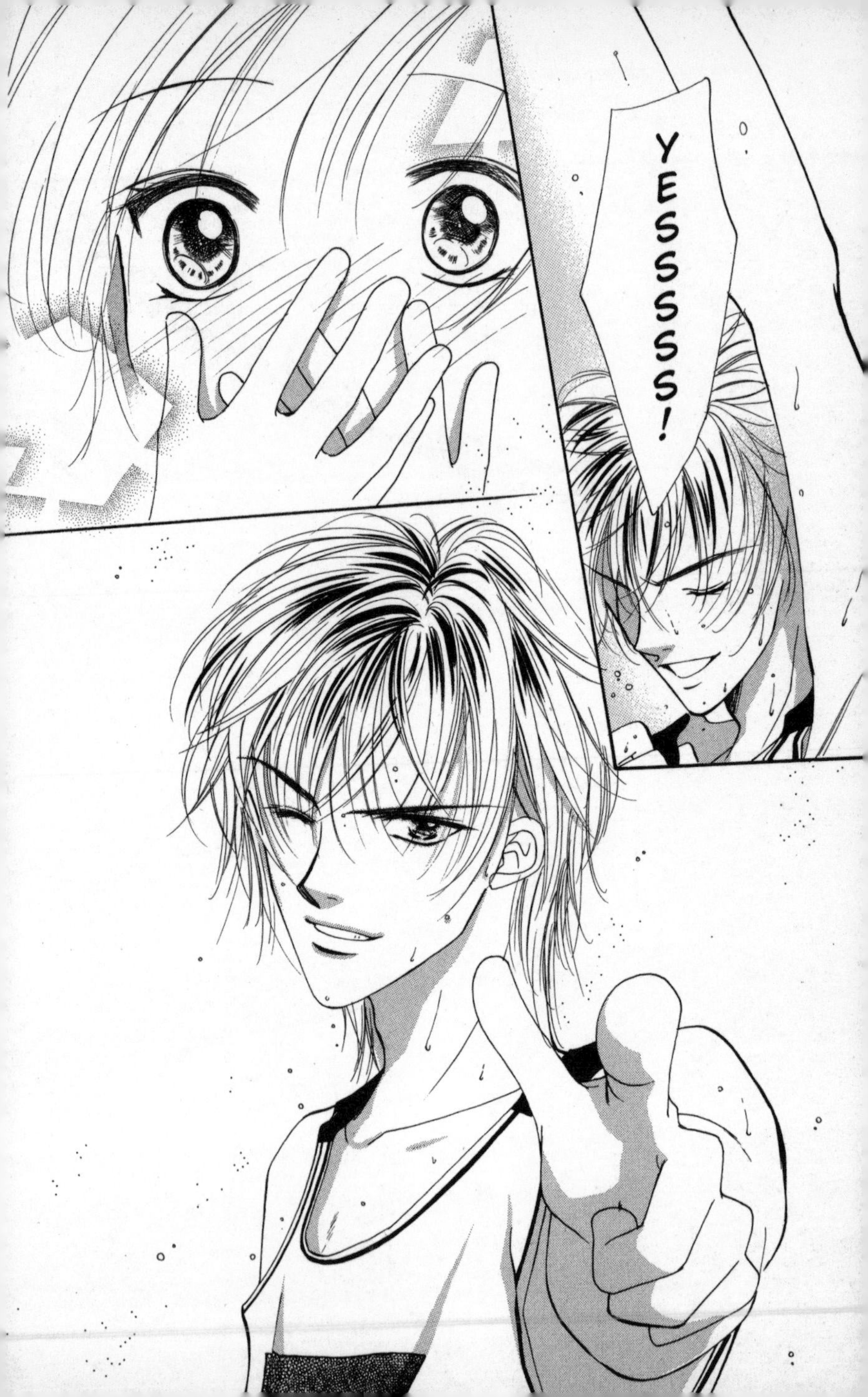
YESSSSS!

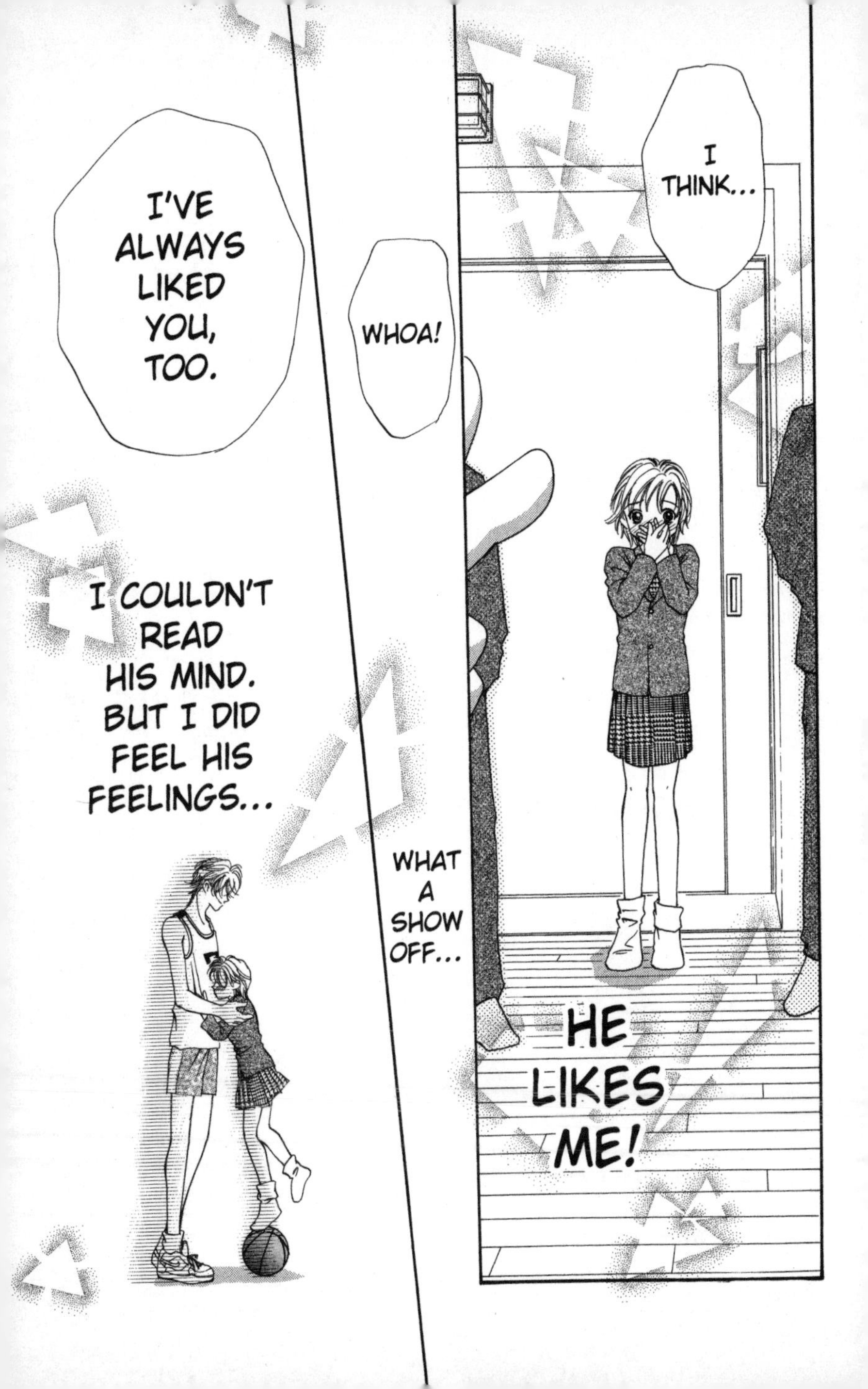
I THINK...
HE LIKES ME!
WHOA!
WHAT A SHOW OFF...
I'VE ALWAYS LIKED YOU, TOO.
I COULDN'T READ HIS MIND. BUT I DID FEEL HIS FEELINGS...

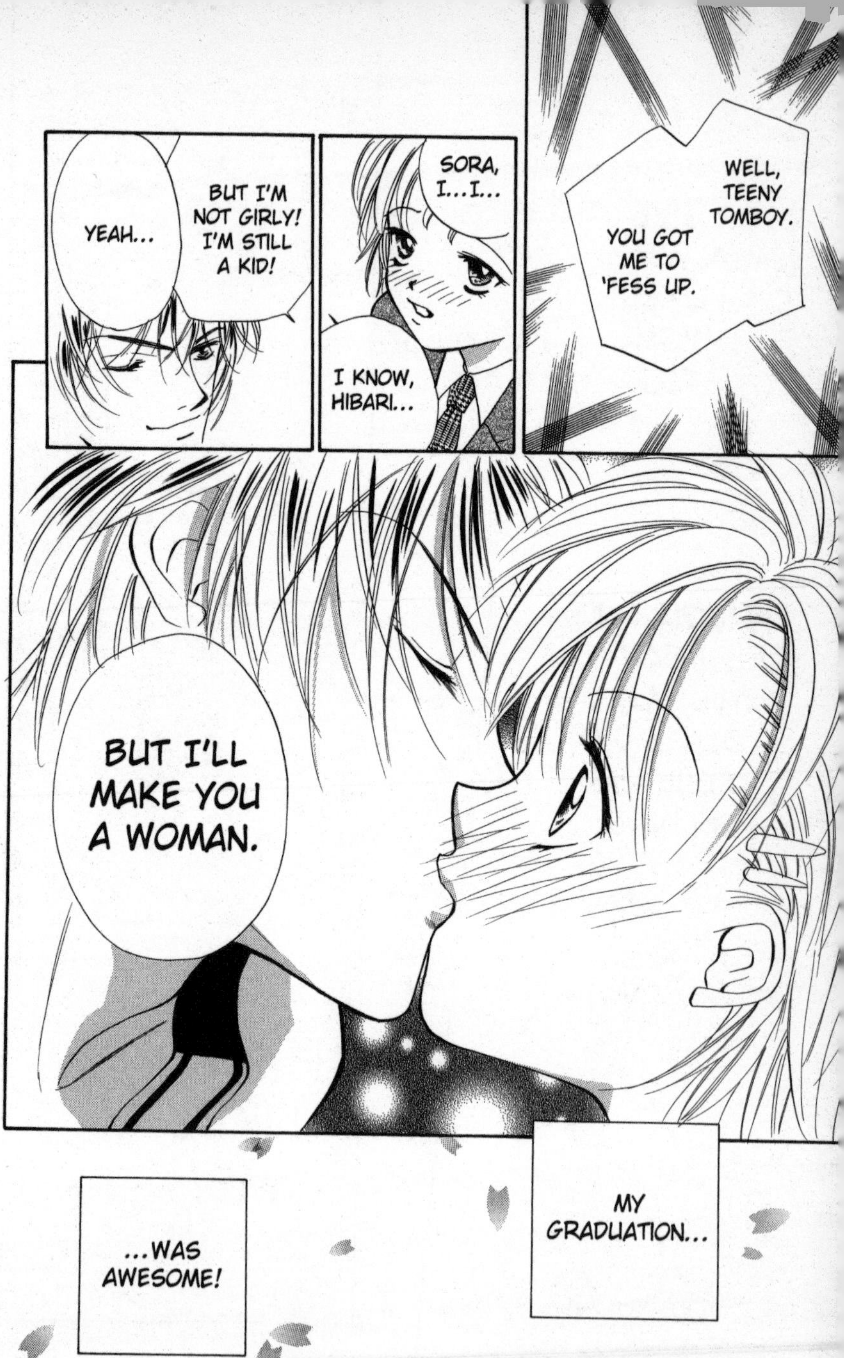
WELL, TEENY TOMBOY.
YOU GOT ME TO 'FESS UP.
SORA, I...I...
I KNOW, HIBARI...
BUT I'M NOT GIRLY! I'M STILL A KID!
YEAH...
BUT I'LL MAKE YOU A WOMAN.
MY GRADUATION...
...WAS AWESOME!

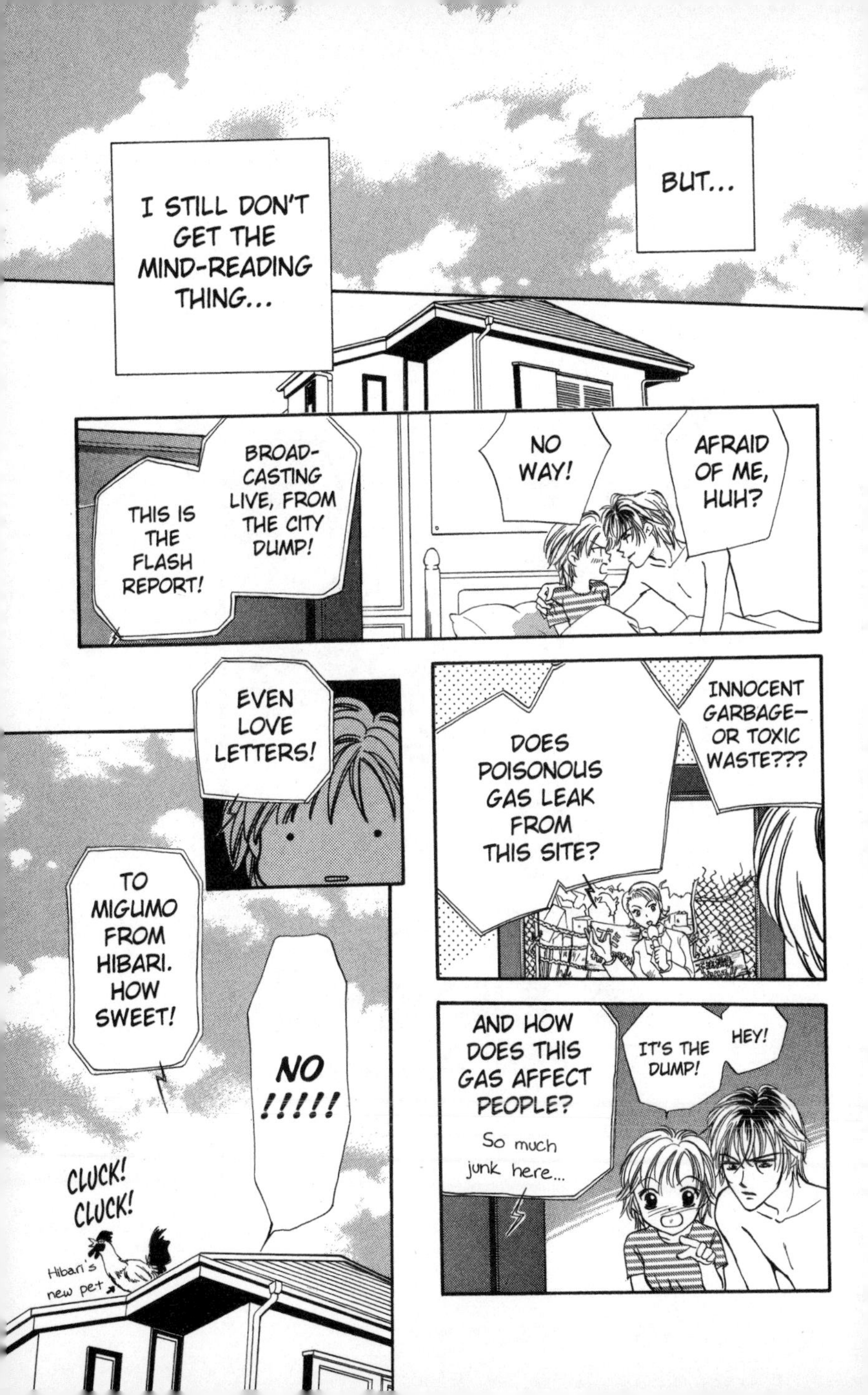
BUT...
I STILL DON'T GET THE MIND-READING THING...
AFRAID OF ME, HUH?
NO WAY!
BROAD-CASTING LIVE, FROM THE CITY DUMP!
THIS IS THE FLASH REPORT!
INNOCENT GARBAGE—OR TOXIC WASTE???
DOES POISONOUS GAS LEAK FROM THIS SITE?
HEY!
IT'S THE DUMP!
AND HOW DOES THIS GAS AFFECT PEOPLE?
So much junk here...
EVEN LOVE LETTERS!
TO MIGUMO FROM HIBARI. HOW SWEET!
NO!!!!!
CLUCK! CLUCK!
Hibari's new pet

Punch!
Rie Takada

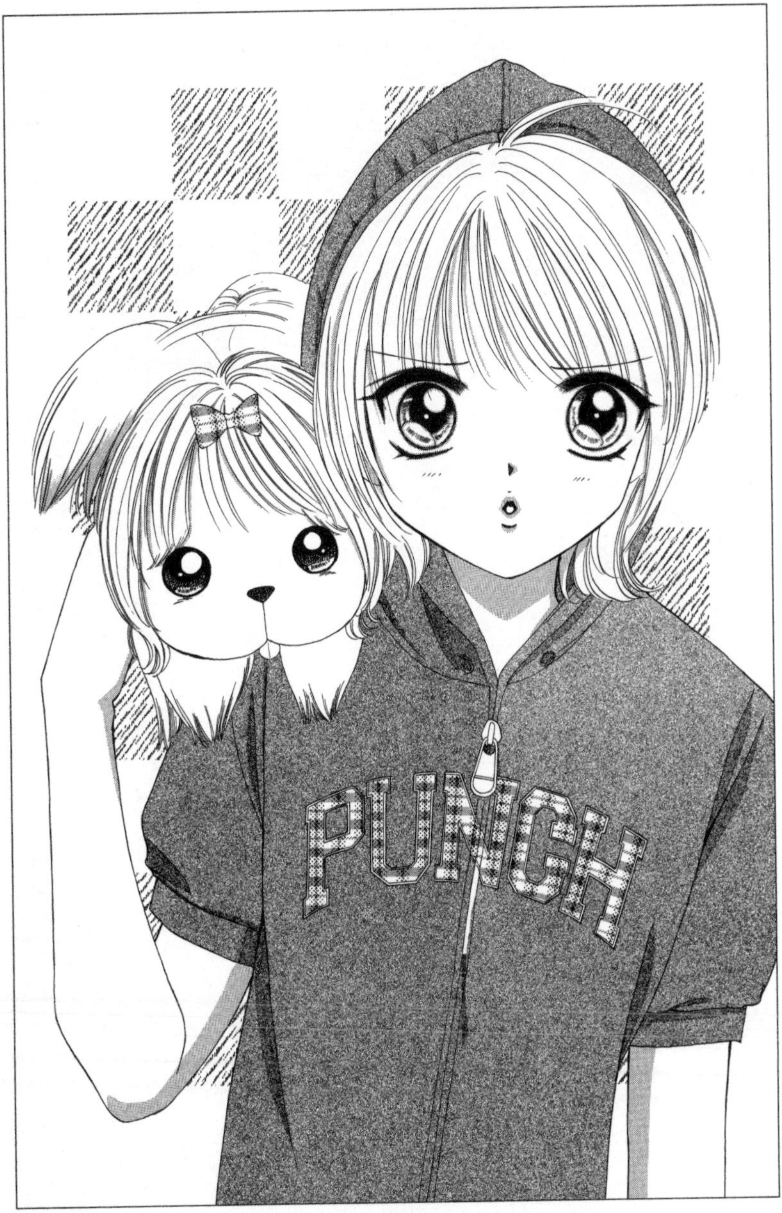
PUNCH

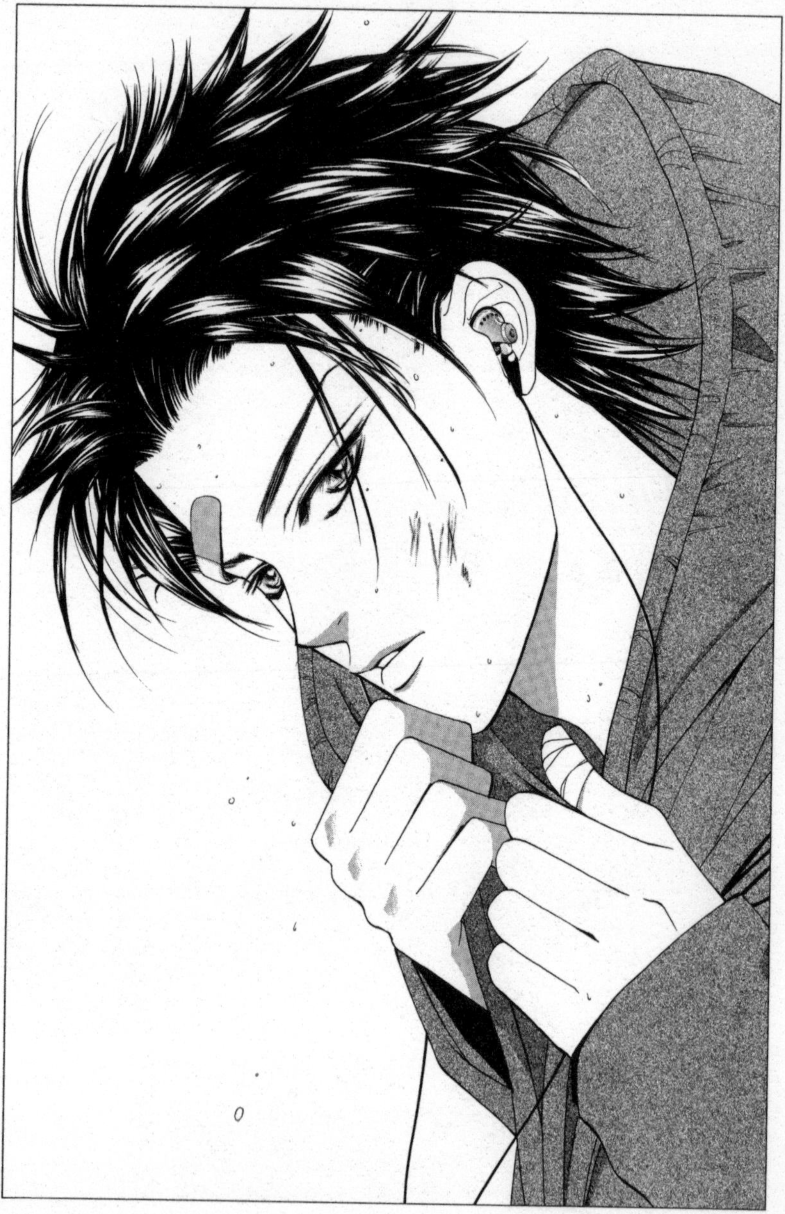

RIE TAKADA

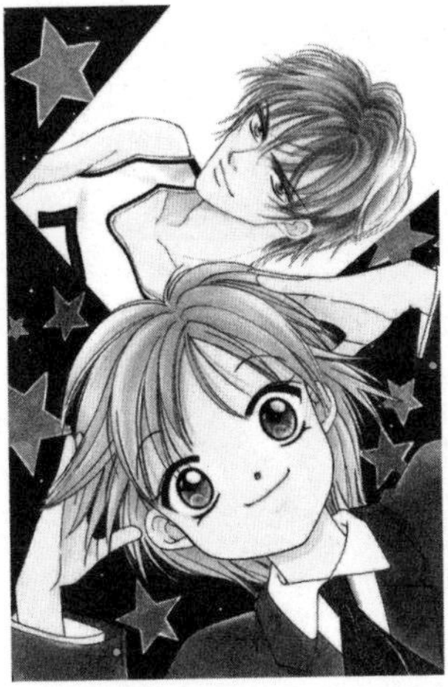

★Born August 10th in Hokkaido. Leo. Blood type O.
★Made her debut with *SP Girl* in 1990's *Shojo Comic* issue 17.
★Currently publishing in *Shojo Comic.*

I've met a lot of people while working on this comic. I even made a promise with a beautiful ring doctor friend of mine to fight in the ring...(laugh). The day I fight under the ring name Pansy Takada will come... maybe (ha ha ha).

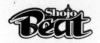

PUNCH!
VOL. 3
The Shojo Beat Manga Edition

STORY & ART BY
RIE TAKADA

English Adaptation/Janet Gilbert
Translation/Joe Yamazaki
Touch-up Art & Lettering/Primary Graphix
Design/Izumi Hirayama
Editor/Urian Brown

Managing Editor/Megan Bates
Editorial Director/Elizabeth Kawasaki
VP & Editor in Chief/Yumi Hoashi
Sr. Director of Acquisitions/Rika Inouye
Sr. VP of Marketing/Liza Coppola
Exec. VP of Sales & Marketing/John Easum
Publisher/Hyoe Narita

Printed in Canada

Published by VIZ Media, LLC
P.O. Box 77010
San Francisco, CA 94107

Shojo Beat Manga Edition
10 9 8 7 6 5 4 3 2 1
First printing, March 2007

store.viz.com

PARENTAL ADVISORY
PUNCH! is rated T+ for Older Teen and is recommended for ages 16 and up. This volume contains strong language and sexual themes.

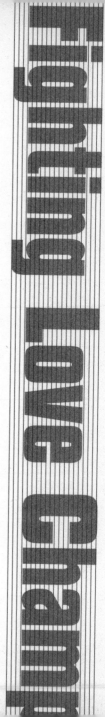

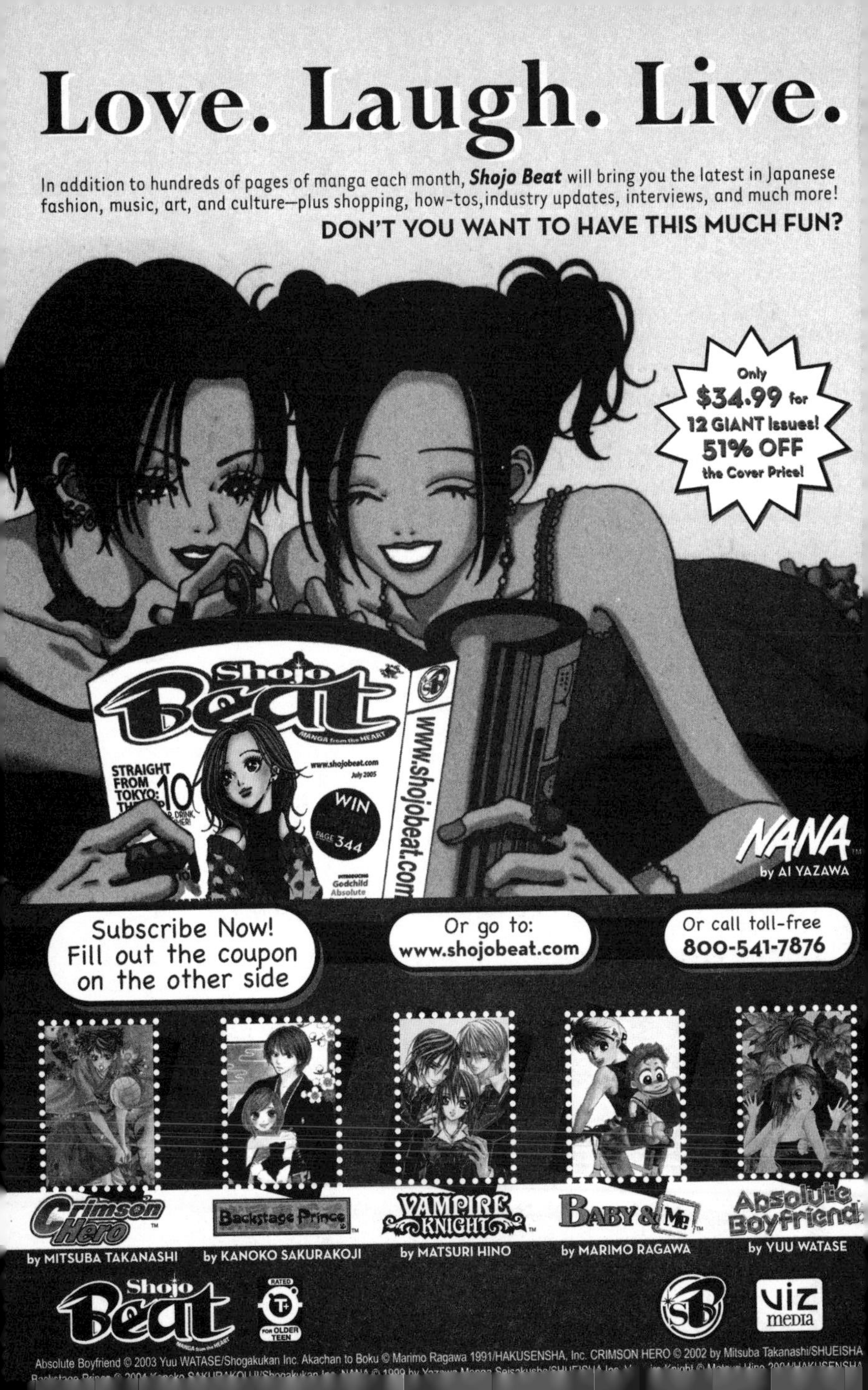
Love. Laugh. Live.
In addition to hundreds of pages of manga each month, Shojo Beat will bring you the latest in Japanese fashion, music, art, and culture—plus shopping, how-tos, industry updates, interviews, and much more!
DON'T YOU WANT TO HAVE THIS MUCH FUN?
Only $34.99 for 12 GIANT Issues! 51% OFF the Cover Price!
Shojo Beat
MANGA from the HEART
www.shojobeat.com
July 2005
STRAIGHT FROM TOKYO:
WIN
PAGE 344
Godchild
Absolute
www.shojobeat.com
NANA™
by AI YAZAWA
Subscribe Now! Fill out the coupon on the other side
Or go to: www.shojobeat.com
Or call toll-free 800-541-7876
Crimson Hero™
by MITSUBA TAKANASHI
Backstage Prince™
by KANOKO SAKURAKOJI
VAMPIRE KNIGHT™
by MATSURI HINO
BABY & Me™
by MARIMO RAGAWA
Absolute Boyfriend™
by YUU WATASE
Shojo Beat
RATED T+ FOR OLDER TEEN
viz media
Absolute Boyfriend © 2003 Yuu WATASE/Shogakukan Inc. Akachan to Boku © Marimo Ragawa 1991/HAKUSENSHA, Inc. CRIMSON HERO © 2002 by Mitsuba Takanashi/SHUEISHA